"This is sociology at its best. In this major study, Lareau provides the tools to make sense of the frenzied middle-class obsession with their offspring's extracurricular activities; the similarities between black and white professionals; and the paths on which poor and working-class kids are put by their circumstances. This book will help generations of students understand that organized soccer and pickup basketball have everything to do with the inequality of life chances."

— Michèle Lamont, author of *The Dignity of Working Men: Morality and the Boundaries of Race, Class, and Immigration*

"Drawing on intimate knowledge of kids and families studied at school and at home, Lareau examines the social changes that have turned childhood into an extended production process for many middle-class American families. Her depiction of this new world of childhood—and her comparison of the middle-class ideal of systematic cultivation to the more naturalistic approach to child development to which many working-class parents still adhere—maps a critically important dimension of American family life and raises challenging questions for parents and policy makers."

— Paul DiMaggio, Professor of Sociology, Princeton University

"With rich storytelling and insightful detail, Lareau takes us inside the family lives of poor, middle-class, and affluent Americans and reminds us that class matters. *Unequal Childhoods* thoughtfully demonstrates that class differences in cultural resources, played out in the daily routines of parenting, can have a powerful impact on children's chances for climbing the class ladder and achieving the American dream. This provocative and often disturbing book will shape debates on the U.S. class system for decades to come."

— Sharon Hays, author of *Flat Broke with Children*

"Drawing upon remarkably detailed case studies of parents and children going about their daily lives, Lareau argues that middle-class and working-class families operate with different logics of childrearing, which both reflect and contribute to the transmission of inequality. An important and provocative book."
     —Barrie Thorne, author of *Gender Play: Girls and Boys in School*

"Annette Lareau has written another classic. Her deep insights about the social stratification of family life and childrearing have profound implications for understanding inequality—and for understanding the daily struggles of everyone attempting to raise children in America. Lareau's findings have great force because they are thoroughly grounded in compelling ethnographic evidence."
     —Adam Gamoran, Professor of Sociology and Educational Policy Studies, University of Wisconsin-Madison

Unequal Childhoods

Unequal Childhoods

Class, Race, and Family Life

Annette Lareau

UNIVERSITY OF CALIFORNIA PRESS
Berkeley · Los Angeles · London

University of California Press
Berkeley and Los Angeles, California

University of California Press, Ltd.
London, England

Library of Congress Cataloging-in-Publication Data

Lareau, Annette.
   Unequal childhoods : class, race, and family life /
Annette Lareau.
      p.   cm.
   Includes bibliographical references and index.
   ISBN 0–520–23763–3 (cloth : alk. paper) — ISBN 0–
520–23950–4 (pbk. :
alk. paper)
      1. Children—Social conditions.   2. Family.   I. Title.

HQ767.9 .L37 2003
305.23 — dc21   2002154940

Manufactured in the United States of America
12   11   10   09   08   07   06   05   04   03
10   9   8   7   6   5   4   3   2   1

The paper used in this publication is both acid-free
and totally chlorine-free (TCF). It meets the minimum
requirements ofANSI/NISO Z39.48–1992 (R 1997)
(Permanence of Paper).⊚

*For Samuel, for the many ways
in which he enriches my life,
and in memory of George McClure,
who offered me, and many other young
scholars, criticism, care, and confidence*

Contents

Acknowledgments

I am very grateful to the children and their families who very graciously welcomed us into their lives, allowed us to follow them around, laughed at us and with us, and helped us understand them. Because of issues of confidentiality, I cannot name them. Nor do I feel I can adequately thank them. But without them this book would not exist. I am also indebted to the teachers and administrators at the schools we visited, especially the teachers who welcomed us into their classrooms. I also appreciate the numerous parents, coaches, dance teachers, and adults working with children who shared their experiences.

No one ever works alone in social science research. In this instance, since the project spanned a number of families as well as a number of years, I was blessed to have very talented assistance. I am deeply grateful to the field-workers, especially for how they gave themselves to the project in a wholehearted fashion. It was a lot to ask. The following research assistants did fieldwork with one or more of the twelve families: Mary Woods, Mimi Keller, Greg Seaton, Caitlin Howley, Robin Rogers-Dillon, Gillian Johns, Wendi Starr Brown, Mark Freeman, and Christine Paul. In addition, other research assistants helped carry out interviews: Karima Jefferies, Rashida Thomas, Kate Wilson, and at a late stage Mary Stricker, Janice Johnson, and Jennifer Murphy. Patricia Berhau played a special role with both her organizational talents and her formidable conceptual skills. She did everything: hired work-study students, talked on the phone with field-workers when I was out of town, and coded the data for all of the interviews. She also generously shared with me her interviews with some of the families for her dissertation and was a friendly, highly knowledgeable critic.

The Spencer Foundation generously funded this project. I am very thankful for the funding as well as the feedback and encouragement of the staff of the foundation. I am also grateful to the Alfred P. Sloan Foundation, particularly Kathleen Christiansen, for assisting with a writing grant at a crucial time. In addition, early on in the project, I received a National Science Foundation grant as well as support from Temple Grant-in-Aid, Southern Illinois University Grant-in-Aid, Temple Summer Research Fellowship, and the ASA/NSF small grant. Of course, the responsibility for any errors or omissions rests with me, not the sponsoring agencies.

At Temple University, I have benefited from the intellectual companionship of other members of the sociology department as well as key administrative support. Although the entire department has been helpful, David Elesh, Robert Kidder, Magali Sarfatti Larson, and Sherri Grasmuck each played a special role, as did Nikki Johnson, Sasha Sisser, and Maria Rosario. A number of people helped to "liberate" the data from tapes to transcripts. For their diligent work, I am obliged to Bernice Fischman, Amy Erdman, Abby Knerr, Irene Arnold, and Rebecca Raley. Also, Sue Tomlin, Paul Reed, Sarah Rose, and Valerie Johnson worked on the project at an early point.

Hugh Mehan deserves special thanks. He flew across the country to visit the project in the middle of the fieldwork and gave sage advice. Although he clearly thought I was crazy, he supported the project anyway. Aaron Cicourel gave me the original impetus for the work, and his work has provided a thoughtful model. The Center for Working Families, directed by Arlie Russell Hochschild and Barrie Thorne, gave me a vibrant intellectual home for a semester at the University of California, Berkeley, where I could try out my ideas. Anita Garey and Karen Hansen were especially helpful. Also during that period, Martin Sanchez Janowski was welcoming at the Center for Urban Ethnography.

The work also benefited from the feedback of a number of audiences when I presented findings at the University of California, Berkeley; the University of California, San Diego; the University of California, Davis; the Joint Center for Policy Research at Northwestern University; Princeton University; the University of Pennsylvania; University of Wisconsin, Madison; and, at an early point, the University of California, Los

Angeles. My graduate class at Temple University read the manuscript and gave me numerous helpful suggestions. Donald Eckert and his class were also very helpful.

A large number of people talked about the project or gave comments on written work as I stumbled my way through. They include Michael Burawoy, Michelle Byng, Gretchen Condran, Paul DiMaggio, Frank Furstenberg, Flo Gelo, Arlie Hochschild, Trish Houck, Jim Houck, Mike Hout, Robin Leidner, Sam Kaplan, John Ogbu, David Minkus, Aaron Pallas, Jeff Shultz, David Swartz, Janet Theophano, Barrie Thorne, Gale Uchiyama, and Cathy and Tom Vigran. My sociology of education reading group has been helpful in countless ways. At the University of California Press, I benefited from the reviews and, especially, the assistance of Naomi Schneider.

For detailed comments on earlier drafts of the book, I am indebted to Donald Eckert, Anita Garey, David Karen, Paul Kingston, Demie Kurz, Michele Lamont, Kristine Lewis, Vincent Louis, Mimi Keller, Salvatore Saporito, Wes Shumar, Amy Steinbugler, Lisa Smulyan, Cathy Vigran, Dan Weinles, and Julia Wrigley. Elliot Weininger deserves special thanks for listening to me talk through my argument and for clarifying the ideas of the late Pierre Bourdieu. M. Katherine Mooney not only straightened out my grammar; she also offered valuable substantive feedback and professional help on the art of writing. Erin McNamara Horvat and Karen Shirley helped me in countless ways to bring this project to closure, reading the manuscript multiple times and offering patient and thoughtful advice. Bonnie Jeanne Casey, Elizabeth Freeman Fox, Joan-Erin Lareau, Lucille Lareau, and Anna Vigran graciously checked the proofs for errors. My eighty-three-year old mother, Anne K. Lareau, assiduously read the entire book manuscript, finishing it just a day before she died unexpectedly. It was the last of a lifetime of gifts she gave to me.

Writing a book has been known to induce crankiness and self-absorption in the author. Perhaps it is for this reason that by tradition, in acknowledgments, children and spouses get the last word. In this realm of thanking family members, I have two favorites: One, said in jest, is something like, "Without the constant nagging of my wife this book would have been done earlier and would have been better, too," and the other, more serious one, is, "My husband deserves public acknowledgment for the gratitude he knows I feel." The humorous statement highlights for me the contradictory ways in which the effort needed to write a book is in mutual conflict with dynamics of family life. The demands of writing lead one to not be present at home, and the demands of family life can, at times, impede one's work. But family members also provide private sustenance; this support is critical.

I am grateful to my children by marriage, Dillon and Rachel Freeman, whom I met after the research was completed, for the ways in which they have added laughter and zest to my life. My biggest debt is to my husband, Samuel Freeman, for the many ways in which he supported me to help make this book come to pass even as we faced demands — and distractions — in our lives. In the clockwork of careers, wherein we are assessed according to our productivity, families are not really counted as a legitimate force. But to be speedy is not everything, or even, when all is said and done, much at all. To have the gifts of companionship, nurturance, and good humor in daily life, however, is quite a lot. I appreciate having them, and him, in my life.

CHAPTER I

Concerted Cultivation and the Accomplishment of Natural Growth

Laughing and yelling, a white fourth-grader named Garrett Tallinger splashes around in the swimming pool in the backyard of his four-bedroom home in the suburbs on a late spring afternoon. As on most evenings, after a quick dinner his father drives him to soccer practice. This is only one of Garrett's many activities. His brother has a baseball game at a different location. There are evenings when the boys' parents relax, sipping a glass of wine. Tonight is not one of them. As they rush to change out of their work clothes and get the children ready for practice, Mr. and Mrs. Tallinger are harried.

Only ten minutes away, a Black fourth-grader, Alexander Williams, is riding home from a school open house.[1] His mother is driving their beige, leather-upholstered Lexus. It is 9:00 P.M. on a Wednesday evening. Ms. Williams is tired from work and has a long Thursday ahead of her. She will get up at 4:45 A.M. to go out of town on business and will not return before 9:00 P.M. On Saturday morning, she will chauffeur Alexander to a private piano lesson at 8:15 A.M., which will be followed by a choir rehearsal and then a soccer game. As they ride in the dark, Alexander's mother, in a quiet voice, talks with her son, asking him questions and eliciting his opinions.

Discussions between parents and children are a hallmark of middle-class child rearing. Like many middle-class parents, Ms. Williams and her husband see themselves as "developing" Alexander to cultivate his talents in a concerted fashion. Organized activities, established and controlled by mothers and fathers, dominate the lives of middle-class children such as Garrett and Alexander. By making certain their children have these and other experiences, middle-class parents engage in a process of *concerted cultivation*. From this, a robust sense of entitlement takes root in the children. This sense of entitlement plays an especially important role in institutional settings, where middle-class children learn to question adults and address them as relative equals.

Only twenty minutes away, in blue-collar neighborhoods, and slightly farther away, in public housing projects, childhood looks different. Mr. Yanelli, a white working-class father, picks up his son Little Billy, a fourth-grader, from an after-school program. They come home and Mr. Yanelli drinks a beer while Little Billy first watches television, then rides his bike and plays in the street. Other nights, he and his Dad sit on the sidewalk outside their house and play cards. At about 5:30 P.M. Billy's mother gets home from her job as a house cleaner. She fixes dinner and the entire family sits down to eat together. Extended family are a prominent part of their lives. Ms. Yanelli touches base with her "entire family every day" by phone. Many nights Little Billy's uncle stops by, sometimes bringing Little Billy's youngest cousin. In the spring, Little Billy plays baseball on a local team. Unlike for Garrett and Alexander, who have at least four activities a week, for Little Billy, baseball is his only organized activity outside of school during the entire year. Down the road, a white working-class girl, Wendy Driver, also spends the evening with her girl cousins, as they watch a video and eat popcorn, crowded together on the living room floor.

Farther away, a Black fourth-grade boy, Harold McAllister, plays outside on a summer evening in the public housing project in which he lives. His two male cousins are there that night, as they often are. After an afternoon spent unsuccessfully searching for a ball so they could play basketball, the boys had resorted to watching sports on television. Now they head outdoors for a twilight water balloon fight. Harold tries to get his neighbor, Miss Latifa, wet. People sit in white plastic lawn chairs outside the row of apartments. Music and television sounds waft through the open windows and doors.

The adults in the lives of Billy, Wendy, and Harold want the best for them. Formidable economic constraints make it a major life task for these parents to put food on the table, arrange for housing, negotiate unsafe neighborhoods, take children to the doctor (often waiting for city buses that do not come), clean children's clothes, and get children to bed and have them ready for school the next morning. But unlike middle-class parents, these adults do not consider the concerted development of children, particularly through organized leisure activities, an essential aspect of good parenting. Unlike the Tallingers and Williamses, these mothers and fathers do not focus on concerted cultivation. For them, the crucial responsibilities of parenthood do not lie in eliciting their children's feelings, opinions, and thoughts. Rather, they see a clear boundary between adults and children. Parents tend to use directives: they tell their children what to do rather than persuading them with reasoning. Unlike their middle-class counterparts, who have a steady diet of adult organized activities, the working-class and poor children have more control over the character of their leisure activities. Most children are free to go out and play with friends and relatives who typically live close by. Their parents and guardians facilitate the *accomplishment of natural growth*.[2] Yet these children and their parents interact with central institutions in the society, such as schools, which firmly and decisively promote strategies of concerted cultivation in child rearing. For working-class and poor families, the cultural logic of child rearing at home is out of synch with the standards of institutions. As a result, while children whose parents adopt strategies of concerted cultivation appear to gain a sense of entitlement, children such as Billy Yanelli, Wendy Driver, and Harold McAllister appear to gain an emerging sense of distance, distrust, and constraint in their institutional experiences.

America may be the land of opportunity, but it is also a land of inequality. This book identifies the largely invisible but powerful ways that parents' social class impacts children's life experiences. It shows, using in-depth observations and interviews with middle-class (including members of the upper-middle-class), working-class, and poor families, that inequality permeates the fabric of the culture. In the chapters that lie ahead, I report the results of intensive observational research for a total of twelve families when their children were nine and ten years old. I argue that key elements of family life cohere to form a cultural logic of child rearing.[3] In other words, the differences among families seem to cluster together in meaningful patterns. In this historical moment, middle-class parents tend to adopt a cultural logic of child rearing that stresses the concerted cultivation of children. Working-class and poor parents, by contrast, tend to undertake the accomplishment of natural growth. In the accomplishment of natural growth, children experience long stretches of leisure time, child-initiated play, clear boundaries between adults and children, and daily interactions with kin. Working-class and poor children, despite tremendous economic strain, often have more "childlike" lives, with autonomy from adults and control over their extended leisure time. Although middle-class children miss out on kin relationships and leisure time, they appear to (at least potentially) gain important institutional advantages. From the experience of concerted cultivation, they acquire skills that could be valuable in the future when they enter the world of work. Middle-class white and Black children in my study did exhibit some key differences; yet the biggest gaps were not within social classes but, as I show, across them. It is these class differences and how they are enacted in family life and child rearing that shape the ways children view themselves in relation to the rest of the world.

CULTURAL REPERTOIRES

Professionals who work with children, such as teachers, doctors, and counselors, generally agree about how children should be raised. Of course, from time to time they may disagree on the ways standards should be enacted for an individual child or family. For example, teachers may disagree about whether or not parents should stop and correct a child who mispronounces a word while reading. Counselors may disagree over whether a mother is being too protective of her child. Still, there is little dispute among professionals on the broad principles for promoting educational development in children through proper parenting.[4] These standards include the importance of talking with children, developing their educational interests, and playing an active role in their schooling. Similarly, parenting guidelines typically stress the importance of reasoning with children and teaching them to solve problems through negotiation rather than with physical force. Because these guidelines are so generally accepted, and because they focus on a set of practices concerning how parents should raise children, they form a *dominant set of cultural repertoires* about how children should be raised. This widespread agreement among professionals about the broad principles for child rearing permeates our society. A small number of experts thus potentially shape the behavior of a large number of parents.

Professionals' advice regarding the best way to raise children has changed regularly over the last two centuries. From strong opinions about the merits of bottle feeding, being stern with children, and utilizing physical punishment (with dire warnings of problematic outcomes should parents indulge children), there have been shifts to equally strongly worded recommendations about the benefits of breast feeding, displaying emotional warmth toward children, and using reasoning and negotiation as mechanisms of parental control. Middle-class parents appear to shift their behaviors in a variety of spheres more rapidly and more thoroughly than do working-class or poor parents.[5] As professionals have shifted their recommendations from bottle feeding to breast feeding, from stern approaches to warmth and empathy, and from spanking to time-outs, it is middle-class parents who have responded most promptly.[6] Moreover, in recent decades, middle-class children in the United States have had to face the prospect of "declining fortunes."[7] Worried about how their children will get ahead, middle-class parents are increasingly determined to make sure that their children are not excluded from any opportunity that might eventually contribute to their advancement.

Middle-class parents who comply with current professional standards and engage in a pattern of concerted cultivation deliberately try to stimulate their children's development and foster their cognitive and social skills. The commitment among working-class and poor families to provide comfort, food, shelter, and other basic support requires ongoing effort, given economic challenges and the formidable demands of child rearing. But it stops short of the deliberate cultivation of children and their leisure activities that occurs in middle-class families. For working-class and poor families, sustaining children's natural growth is viewed as an accomplishment.[8]

What is the outcome of these different philosophies and approaches to child rearing? Quite simply, they appear to lead to the *transmission of differential advantages* to children. In this study, there was quite a bit more talking in middle-class homes than in working-class and poor homes, leading to the development of greater verbal agility, larger vocabularies, more comfort with authority figures, and more familiarity with abstract concepts. Importantly, children also developed skill differences in interacting with authority figures in institutions and at home. Middle-class children such as Garrett Tallinger and Alexander Williams learn, as young boys, to shake the hands of adults and look them in the eye. In studies of job interviews, investigators have found that potential employees have less than one minute to make a good impression. Researchers stress the importance of eye contact, firm handshakes, and displaying comfort with bosses during the interview. In poor families like Harold McAllister's, however, family members usually do not look each other in the eye when conversing. In addition, as Elijah Anderson points out, they live in neighborhoods where it can be dangerous to look people in the eye too long.[9] The types of social competence transmitted in the McAllister family are valuable, but they are potentially less valuable (in employment interviews, for example) than those learned by Garrett Tallinger and Alexander Williams.

The white and Black middle-class children in this study also exhibited an emergent version of the *sense of entitlement* characteristic of the middle-class. They acted as though they had a right to pursue their own individual preferences and to actively manage interactions in institutional settings. They appeared comfortable in these settings; they were open to sharing information and asking for attention. Although some children were more outgoing than others, it was common practice among middle-class children to shift interactions to suit *their* preferences. Alexander Williams knew how to get the doctor to listen to his concerns (about the bumps under his arm from his new deodorant). His mother explicitly trained and encouraged him to speak up with the doctor. Similarly, a Black middle-class girl, Stacey Marshall, was taught by her mother to expect the gymnastics teacher to accommodate her individual learning style. Thus, middle-class children were trained in "the rules of the game" that govern interactions with institutional representatives. They were not conversant in other important social skills, however, such as organizing their time for hours on end during weekends and summers, spending long periods of time away from adults, or hanging out with adults in a nonobtrusive, subordinate fashion. Middle-class children also learned (by imitation and by direct training) how to make the rules work in their favor. Here, the enormous stress on reasoning and negotiation in the home also has a potential advantage for future institutional negotiations. Additionally, those in authority responded positively to such interactions. Even in fourth grade, middle-class children appeared to be acting on their own behalf to gain advantages. They made special requests of teachers and doctors to adjust procedures to accommodate their desires.

The working-class and poor children, by contrast, showed an emerging *sense of constraint* in their interactions in institutional settings. They were less likely to try to customize interactions to suit their own preferences. Like their parents, the children accepted the actions of persons in authority (although at times they also covertly resisted them). Working-class and poor parents sometimes were not as aware of their children's school situation (as when their children were not doing homework). Other times, they dismissed the school rules as unreasonable. For example, Wendy Driver's mother told her to "punch" a boy who was pestering her in class; Billy Yanelli's parents were proud of him when he "beat up" another boy on the playground, even though Billy was then suspended from school. Parents also had trouble getting "the school" to respond to their concerns. When Ms. Yanelli complained that she "hates" the school, she gave her son a lesson in powerlessness and frustration in the face of an important institution. Middle-class children such as Stacey Marshall learned to make demands on professionals, and when they succeeded in making the rules work in their favor they augmented their "cultural capital" (i.e., skills individuals inherit that can then be translated into different forms of value as they move through various institutions) for the future.[10] When working-class and poor children confronted institutions, however, they generally were unable to make the rules work in their favor nor did they obtain capital for adulthood. Because of these patterns of legitimization, children raised according to the logic of concerted cultivation can gain advantages, in the form of an emerging sense of entitlement, while children raised according to the logic of natural growth tend to develop an emerging sense of constraint.[11]

SOCIAL STRATIFICATION AND INDIVIDUALISM

Public discourse in America typically presents the life accomplishments of a person as the result of her or his individual qualities. Songs like "I Did It My Way," memoirs, television shows, and magazine articles, celebrate the individual. Typically, individual outcomes are connected to individual effort and talent, such as being a "type A" personality, being a hard worker, or showing leadership. These cultural beliefs provide a framework for Americans' views of inequality.

Indeed, Americans are much more comfortable recognizing the power of individual initiative than recognizing the power of social class. Studies show that Americans generally believe that responsibility for their accomplishments rests on their individual efforts. Less than one-fifth see "race, gender, religion, or class as very important for 'getting ahead in life.'"[12] Compared to Europeans, individuals in the United States are much more likely to believe they can improve their standard of living. Put differently, Americans believe in the American dream: "The American dream that we were all raised on is a simple but powerful one—if you work hard and play by the rules, you should be given a chance to go as far as your God-given ability will take you."[13] This American ideology that each individual is responsible for his or her life outcomes is the expressed belief of the vast majority of Americans, rich and poor.

Yet there is no question that society is stratified. As I show in the next chapter, highly valued resources such as the possession of wealth; having an interesting, well-paying, and complex job; having a good education;

and owning a home, are not evenly distributed throughout the society. Moreover, these resources are transferred across generations: One of the best predictors of whether a child will one day graduate from college is whether his or her parents are college graduates. Of course, relations of this sort are not absolute: Perhaps two-thirds of the members of society ultimately reproduce their parents' level of educational attainment, while about one-third take a different path. Still, there is no question that we live in a society characterized by considerable gaps in resources or, put differently, by substantial *inequality*. As I explain in the next chapter, however, reasonable people have disagreed about how best to conceptualize such patterns. They also have disagreed about whether families in different economic positions "share distinct, life-defining experiences."[14] Many insist that there is not a clear, coherent, and sustained experiential pattern. In this book, I demonstrate the existence of a cultural logic of child rearing that tends to differ according to families' social class positions. I see these interweaving practices as coming together in a messy but still recognizable way. In contrast to many, I suggest that social class does have a powerful impact in shaping the daily rhythms of family life.

THE STUDY

It is a lot of work to get young children through the day, especially for their parents. When I embarked on this study, I was interested in understanding that labor process. In choosing to look at families, rather than just at children *or* parents, I hoped to capture some of the reciprocal effects of children and parents on each other. My approach also meant moving beyond the walls of the home to understand how parents and children negotiate with other adults in children's lives.

This book is based on intensive "naturalistic" observations of twelve families (six white, five Black, and one interracial) with children nine and ten years old. The twelve families are part of a larger study of eighty-eight children from the middle-class, working-class, and poor.[15] (For details of how the study was done, see Appendix A, Methodology.) I met most of these children when I visited their third-grade classrooms in an urban school, Lower Richmond, and a suburban school, Swan (both of which are described in the next chapter). With the help of white and Black research assistants, I carried out interviews first with the mothers and then with many of the fathers of these children. To better understand the expectations that professionals had of parents, I also interviewed the children's classroom teachers and other school personnel.

From this pool of children the research assistants and I selected twelve families for intensive observations.[16] We generally visited each family about twenty times in and around their home, usually in the space of one month. We followed children and parents as they went through their daily routines, as they took part in school activities, church services and events, organized play, kin visits, and medical appointments. Most visits lasted about three hours; sometimes, depending on the event (e.g., an out-of-town funeral, a special extended family event, or a long shopping trip), we stayed much longer. In most cases, we also arranged one overnight visit in each family's home. Often, especially after the families got used to us, we carried tape recorders.

When we introduced ourselves to each family, we said that, following a famous study, we wanted to be treated like "the family dog."[17] We wanted parents to step over and ignore us, but allow us to hang out with them. In reality, our presence had a more active character. Still, after some initial chatter, we often slipped into the background, letting the children and their parents set the pace. In the house, we sat on the floor with children and, as a rule, insisted on sitting in the backseat of cars when we rode along on family outings. Outside, we played ball with children or hung around while they played with their friends. Middle-class children, especially, spent quite a bit of time waiting for adults. We waited, too. As I explain in Appendix A, the rule of thumb was not to criticize and not to intervene unless a child was in imminent danger. We encouraged families not to worry about entertaining us, we told children to feel free to curse in front of us if they would do so normally, and we asked that other normal "guest" rules be dissolved.

Unquestionably, our presence changed the dynamics as we were sitting in living rooms watching television, riding along in the backseat of the car to a soccer game, watching children get into their pajamas, or sitting in church with them. Over time, however, we saw signs of adjustment (e.g., as families got used to us, yelling and cursing increased). Many families reported that, especially after the initial adjustment, their behavior changed only in modest ways, if at all.

The children found participating in the project enjoyable. They reported it made them feel "special." They were demonstrably happy to see the field-workers arrive and, at times, were reluctant to let them leave. Some parents also, at times, said they "had fun." Delight in the study was clearly stronger in the working-class and poor families, possibly because it was rare for these children to meet adults outside of their extended family, neighbors, and teachers. In middle-class families, children routinely interacted with nonfamilial adults outside of the home environment or school.

ENDURING DILEMMAS

In a seminar I attended recently, a Black anthropologist rebuffed another scholar's statement with the words, "Yes, but that is a white perspective." In this line of thought, membership in a particular racial or ethnic group crucially shapes a person's intellectual trajectory. Accordingly, there are those who believe that as a white woman, I should not have studied Black families. Conversely, they might object to having a Black research assistant visit a white middle-class family. They assert that it is more desirable, or even necessary, for gays to study gays or women to study women. Some worry that outsiders may get it wrong. Others assert that having white researchers in Black families is not a legitimate undertaking.

There are no easy answers to these contentious debates. In this study, the design grew out of the local context (see Appendix A for details). But more generally, I have a philosophical difference with the young woman in the seminar that evening. I question whether something called "a white perspective" exists.[18] To follow out the logic of her critique means that members of (dominant) racial and ethnic groups ought to refrain from studying social questions involving dominated groups. This does not strike me as the best approach for understanding complex social problems. (It also has the invidious effect of relegating every Black social scientist to studying Black Americans rather than whatever suits his or her fancy.) Moreover, the "groups" at hand are always diverse. What about members of the same ethnic group who are of a different gender: Are the walls blocking understanding equally high? In a series of ever-reflecting mirrors, does this tension mean that the only person you can truly "cross the divide" to study is yourself? This book takes the position that it is possible for outsiders of a group to study across boundaries. It reports findings from a study that used ethnographic methods to try to understand children in a wide variety of social locations: boys and girls, middle-class, working-class and poor families, and white and Black families. In addition, the research teams were racially and ethnically diverse (as well as diverse by social class background), which, as I show in Appendix A, influenced what we learned in our visits.

Some reviewers worried that given the contested character of race relations in the United States, the behavior patterns described in this book might reinforce negative stereotypes of certain groups. The results could be taken out of context and exploited by others, particularly political conservatives. Some early readers encouraged me *not to report* results that might be used to reinforce negative images of, for example, poor Black families. The fact that the manuscript includes portraits of poor white families as well as Black families did not completely assuage these concerns. A key problem is that most readers will be middle class or, as college students, on the road to becoming middle class, even if they had working-class or poor origins. As readers, they will have their own childhoods and their own lives as parents or future parents as a base for what they consider appropriate. This cultural and historical frame can become the basis for interpreting the discussion. Indeed, some (middle-class) readers of earlier drafts felt that a child's life that consists of watching television all day would be "boring" or "bad" for the child. This interpretation, though, is rooted in a particular vision of childhood — one involving development and concerted cultivation. The historical and cultural character of readers' beliefs often are thrown into relief only through sharp cross-cultural or historical comparisons.[19]

In sum, the fear is that some readers will project their own cultural beliefs on the material. This pattern of projection makes it difficult to "see" alternative conceptions of child rearing as legitimate. As a result, although I make an assiduous effort to report the complexity of family life, at times I spend more time pointing out drawbacks of middle-class child rearing than I do drawbacks of working-class and poor families' approach. Still, it is in fact possible that the results of this study could be distorted or used to promote political positions that I find repugnant. But squelching results due to fears about how they could be interpreted (particularly worries that the examples could reinforce "deficit" theories of social life) seems wrong. Thus, although urged to do so, I have not omitted data on this criterion.

ORGANIZATION OF THIS BOOK

The next chapter describes the schools that most of the children in the study attended and where we visited during the year. It also briefly discusses different approaches to understanding why inequality exists. The book then proceeds by devoting a chapter per family to highlight three ways in which social class makes a difference in children's lives and family life: the organization of daily life, language use, and interactions between families and institutions. In Part I, I show that middle-class children had a hectic schedule of organized activities by looking at the white middle-class family of Garrett Tallinger (Chapter 3). Although the Tallinger family was wealthier than many, the same patterns appeared over and over again in other middle-class families. By contrast, children such as Tyrec Taylor (a Black working-class boy) spent time playing outside with friends (Chapter 4). Even then, as the case of a white poor girl, Katie Brindle, shows, mothers engaged in enormous labor to get children through the day (Chapter 5). Unlike children in the Tallinger family, both Tyrec Taylor and Katie Brindle played in a sphere separate from that of adults.

In Part II, I show how these differences in the organization of daily life are also interwoven with language use, with an emphasis on reasoning in middle-class families and directives in the working-class and poor families. I illustrate this with the case of Alexander Williams (Chapter 6), a boy from a Black middle-class home, and Harold McAllister (Chapter 7), a Black boy living in poverty.[20]

Part III demonstrates how parents differ in the ways they monitor and intervene in their children's schooling. The case of Stacey Marshall, a Black middle-class girl whose mother constantly scrutinized and interceded in her life outside the home, is the subject of Chapter 8. Another example of this behavior, albeit one where the behavior is much less effective, is found in the case of Melanie Handlon, a white middle-class girl (Chapter 9) whose mother's frequent interventions, particularly around homework, created unhappiness and conflict. In contrast to their middle-class counterparts, working-class and poor parents depended on the leadership of professionals. At times, since the educators expected parents to follow strategies of concerted cultivation, the results could be difficult, as with Wendy Driver, who was not reading in fourth grade (Chapter 10). Other times, working-class parents found themselves powerless and frustrated, as standards of behavior they felt were appropriate (such as self-defense on the playground or hitting a child for purposes of discipline) were denigrated and, indeed, seen as possible signs of child abuse. The case of Billy Yanelli (Chapter 11) shows these tensions.

In the conclusion, Chapter 12, I revisit the general question of the influence of social class on daily life. I point to important ways that social class did not appear to matter in shaping daily life in such areas as neatness, order, and sense of humor. Overall, however, I identify important ways that class shapes the logic of child rearing in the home and the value these strategies are accorded as children move into the rest of the world. Appendix A provides an "insider" tale of the questions and dilemmas that emerged during the study.

In sum, I see it as a mistake to accept, carte blanche, the views of officials in dominant institutions (e.g., schools or social service agencies) regarding how children should be raised. Indeed, outside of institutional settings there are benefits and costs to both of these logics of child rearing. For example, concerted cultivation places intense labor demands on busy parents, exhausts children, and emphasizes the development of individualism, at times at the expense of the development of the notion of the family group. Middle-class children argue with their parents, complain about their parents' incompetence, and disparage parents' decisions. In other historical moments, a ten-year-old child who gave orders to a doctor would have been chastised for engaging in disrespectful and inappropriate behavior. Nor are the actions of children who display an emerging sense of entitlement intrinsically more valuable or desirable than those of children who display an emerging sense of constraint. In a society less dominated by individualism than the United States, with more of an emphasis on the group, the sense of constraint displayed by working-class and poor children might be interpreted as healthy and appropriate. But in this society, the strategies of the working-class and poor families are generally denigrated and seen as unhelpful or even harmful to children's life chances. The benefits that accrue to middle-class children can be significant, but they are often invisible to them and to others. In popular language, middle-class children can be said to have been "born on third base but believe they hit a triple." This book makes the invisible visible through a study of pleasures, opportunities, challenges, and conflicts in the daily lives of children and their families.

CHAPTER 2

Social Structure and Daily Life

The life of an individual cannot be adequately understood
without references to the institutions within which his
biography is enacted.

C. Wright Mills

The families described in this book created their lives within a specific
social context. They did not build the roads they rode on, hire the teachers who taught in the schools their children attended, decree which parks
would be well maintained, decide how rapidly the city would clear snow
from the streets, establish the values of the homes on their street, or
compose the racial, ethnic, or social class balance of their schools or
neighborhoods. Nor did they determine the availability of high-paying
jobs in the area, set the education and skills required to fill those jobs,
pace the growth of the national economy, or guide the position of the
United States in the world economy. Yet these elements impinged on the
lives of these families, albeit on some more directly than on others. One
way to conceive of this context is to say that individuals carry out their
lives within a *social structure*.

There are many definitions of social structure, but they generally stress
regular patterns of interaction, often in forms of social organization. The
key building blocks are groups (or, in one common definition, "collections of people who interact on the basis of shared expectations regarding one another's behavior").[1] Individuals have a variety of socially
defined positions, or statuses, within the group(s) to which they belong.
The actions of individuals are guided by norms (rules or guidelines for
specific situations). Over time, some of these rule systems — encoded in
bureaucracies, legal proceedings, and bureaucratic regulations — coalesce
into institutions.[2] Marriage, the family, the army, corporations, political

parties, and racial segregation are all examples of institutions. In *The Sociological Imagination,* Mills stresses the importance of institutions: "Much of human life consists of playing . . . roles within specific institutions. To understand the biography of an individual, we must understand the significance and meaning of the roles he has played and does play; to understand these roles we must understand the institutions of which they are a part."[3] Individuals' chances of interacting with any given kind of institution are not random: Families from elite backgrounds tend to participate in institutions serving the elite, and families in poverty tend to be involved with institutions serving the poor. Some institutional settings — zoos, parades, certain stores, and, sometimes, public transportation — are "great equalizers," drawing families of all kinds. This kind of mingling of rich and poor is relatively unusual, however.

In short, children grow up within a broad, highly stratified social system. In this chapter, I sketch key aspects of this social structural context for the children and families who participated in the study. I focus on the two target schools, Lower Richmond in the city and Swan in the suburbs, describing each institution and its surrounding community. I also discuss some of the ways social scientists and others explain the persistence of inequality in our society.

LOWER RICHMOND SCHOOL
AND SURROUNDING COMMUNITY

Lower Richmond School serves children from kindergarten through fifth grade. Located on a narrow street in a large northeastern city, the school looks forbidding: it is three stories tall and is surrounded by a high, gray chain-link fence. The building is old, with a dirty beige exterior and few windows. There are patches of paint splotched on the walls here and there to cover up the graffiti that appears regularly. To the side and back of the school are an asphalt playground and a small basketball court; in front, there are trees and a patch of grass, but the children may not play in this area during school hours. Kindergartners have a separate playground, also all asphalt, but the walls surrounding the play area display cheerful murals painted by the children. Just inside the entrance to the school, a security guard sits at a desk. Overall, Lower Richmond is "a very nice place," according to one teacher. She noted that, unlike other facilities in the district, where beer bottles and broken glass litter the school yard, "It's safe [here]. It's a pretty place when you walk in. There's some grass and trees, and there's a parking lot and the building is clean."

The residential neighborhoods surrounding Lower Richmond are racially segregated. Many of the students come by bus from a poor Black housing project about ten minutes away. The school itself is located in a mainly white working-class residential neighborhood dominated by small, inexpensive homes. (See Table C2, Appendix C for descriptive social and demographic data.) There are also apartment complexes, including some that rent to low-income families who qualify for government assistance ("Section 8"). These complexes are racially integrated. Lower Richmond enrolls about one-half Black students and one-half white students. Less than 5 percent of the students are Asian or Hispanic. Most of the educational staff members, including the principal, are white; but there are Black educators too, including the third-grade teacher whose classroom I observed, the school counselor, the reading resource teacher, and the music teacher. Most of the support staff members, such as the secretary, security guard, janitor, and bus driver, are African American. A majority of the student body qualifies for free lunches.

Only a few blocks from the school is a small shopping district with gas stations, a pizza shop, an ice cream shop (open only in warmer months), a 7–11 convenience store, and a hardware store. Unlike in some urban neighborhoods, in this area, commercial and residential rental properties are fully occupied; abandoned buildings are not a problem here. It is a solid, working-class neighborhood, with narrow streets, older two-story red brick buildings in good repair, and enough business customers and employees that parking is scarce. There are sufficient trees and flowers growing here and there to break the monotony of the concrete pavement and buildings and to mark changes in the seasons. Buildings are densely packed. Large stores are uncommon: Supermarkets are few and far between, and discount stores, such as Target and Wal-Mart, are not part of the neighborhood. Residents must drive to the suburbs to gain access to cheaply priced goods.

Traffic in the area around Lower Richmond is hectic. City buses roar up and down the street a few times per hour, and cars speed through intersections. Horn blasts are frequent. The high density of housing and the lack of garages bring neighbors into more contact with one another than might occur otherwise. Many auto-related activities, from washing or repairing cars to digging them free of snow, take place in the street. As in most urban centers nationwide, crime is a concern here, particularly graffiti, burglary, and petty theft. Armed robberies (on the street or in local stores) are relatively uncommon, but they happen often enough to undermine residents' sense of safety and security.

Lower Richmond School has been well regarded by parents, children, and educators for many years. Ms. Bernstein, a fourth-grade teacher, calls Lower Richmond a "cream puff" compared to other city schools. Institutionally, Lower Richmond provides students with a variety of valuable resources: There are a computer laboratory and a computer teacher, as well as specialty teachers for art, music, and gym. The school has a library and a science program specially funded to provide an emphasis on technology. School-sponsored extracurricular activities include a choir and a band; both perform at school, district, and local community events.[4] Lower Richmond also puts on a popular spring fair.

Still, the school has its share of problems, ranging from a shortage of teaching supplies, such as paper and art materials, to a shortage of teachers, to an unwieldy administrative structure that can shortchange students' education. Although teaching in city schools is widely viewed as more challenging than teaching in suburban schools, salaries (as well as expenditures per pupil) are less than in the suburbs. Qualified teachers are not always available. Some students at Lower Richmond experience this teacher shortage at a very personal level: one third-grade class, for example, had a series of different substitutes for their entire school year. District rules do not require classroom rosters to be finalized until several weeks into the school year. As late as mid-October, a child may be reassigned to a new teacher (the district sometimes reconstitutes classrooms in order to meet staffing and budgetary concerns). Other aspects of the district-imposed bureaucracy create difficulties as well. As a teacher explained, a seemingly simple request could require a cumbersome, time-consuming response:

The grandmother called and said that [an after-school program] needed information. And I'm not allowed to give out any written information on a student unless you have the written consent of the parents and something on letterhead [from the requesting organization]. And then the counselor and the principal has to sign it.[5]

Parents (and educators) often are bewildered and frustrated by district guidelines in academic matters, too. A referral to full-time special education, for example, requires two pre-referrals (each involving efforts to improve the situation without recourse to full-time intervention) before a child can be formally considered for special education. Since each stage takes at least 60 days, and the school year is only 180 days, an entire academic year can elapse without a decision having been made. As I show later in the book, this kind of bureaucratic infrastructure sometimes results in children "slipping through the cracks" as major learning problems go untreated.

During the years of the study, local political figures openly criticized the district for doing a poor job educating children. At Lower Richmond, one of the district's more accomplished schools, about one-half of each class reads below grade level and about one-third of the fourth-grade cohort is at least two years below grade level. The district is under pressure to raise test scores, but the budget is very limited, and shortfalls occur annually. Unlike in the suburbs, inner-city schools do not have wealthy parent associations capable of supplementing individual site budgets. At Lower Richmond, few parents participate in the Parent-Teacher Association; meetings often have only three or four attendees (usually the officers). Social relations among the teachers are another potential cause for concern. Real tensions underlie a generally cordial atmosphere. Some of the Black teachers feel that white teachers treat certain Black children unfairly, as a Black third-grade teacher charged angrily:

There are some faculty members — some of the children aren't treated equally. Some Black children with certain reputations did certain things and . . . [got] kicked out to another school. Some white children would do serious things and they would get detention, call parents, or suspensions.

Although white administrators and teachers generally did not agree, other Black educators at the school echoed these concerns.

Relations among the children at Lower Richmond also are strained sometimes. Serious threats to safety are unusual.[6] But physical fights between children are common on the playground throughout the week. Teachers estimate that at least one-half of the children have serious life problems, often involving a parent who is absent or incapacitated. The school counselor works regularly with Child Protective Services to address the needs of students she feels are being neglected (e.g., those who come to school in winter without coats) or abused. In a single classroom, it is common to have several children who have "serious issues." In Mr. Tier's fourth grade, among the white students, there is Lisa, whose mother left her and who now "lives with her father, who likes to drink to excess"; Thomas, whose mother disappeared one day and, although she eventually returned, still has no contact with her son; and Shaun, whose father "does cocaine, . . . is paranoid, and was arrested twice this year." Among the Black students in the class, there is Tanisha, who lacks even the most basic school supplies (such as a school bag) teachers prefer students to have. Another student, Toya, is disruptive. She "gets in fights all the time . . . but her mother . . . [instead of reprimanding her daughter, spends her time] explaining to me why it's not Toya's problem." Julius is from a home where "there is a whole history of drug abuse and violence." Teachers at Lower Richmond note that in addition to being emotionally upsetting, their students' life problems are academically disruptive. Uniformly, the teachers want their students to arrive at school each day "well groomed" and "prepared to learn." They also want parents to be involved in their children's education, to "sign homework, help with projects" and "be positive," in the words of one fourth-grade teacher.

These expectations are met by some. There are both Black and white children whose parents are steadily employed, as well as those whose parents are energetically striving to move up in the world. In Mr. Tier's class, there are three such Black children—Isaiah, whose mother is absent but whose father is devoted to him; Morrell, whose mother has "gone back to college to become an elementary school teacher," and Danielle, whose mother works at "Joe's Steaks." There are comparable white children, including those with parents Mr. Tier describes as "upwardly mobile types."

In sum, Lower Richmond is a school with many positive aspects, particularly in comparison to other schools in the district. Still, it shares with other urban schools core limitations, such as teacher shortages, lower teacher salaries, limited supplies, and a cumbersome bureaucracy. Parents are not a major force in the school, either financially or politically. Students are drawn from racially segregated neighborhoods where historical patterns of land use and market forces limit the availability of large stores. Homes are small and built close to one another, traffic is hectic, and crime is a common concern. Thus, when compared to a suburban school like Swan (described below), Lower Richmond ranks a very distant second on many criteria.

SWAN SCHOOL AND SURROUNDING COMMUNITY

Like Lower Richmond, Swan School serves children from kindergarten through fifth grade. It is located in one of the townships in the suburbs that ring the large northeastern city in which Lower Richmond School is located. Swan, like many other suburban schools, is a sprawling facility. It consists exclusively of one-story buildings that are spread out over the school grounds. The buildings have windows lining one entire wall of each classroom. Although all the windows open, in the fall and spring the classrooms can be sweltering (there is no air conditioning). Outside is an expanse of grass on a gently sloping hill, large enough for multiple games to occur at the same time. Unlike at Lower Richmond, the school playground has an elaborate swing set and bars, with a red-hued mulch of shredded wood under the bars to protect children if they fall. There is no fence around Swan; the entire facility looks open and inviting.

The school is located in a quiet residential neighborhood of one-story, single-family, middle-class homes. Each is fronted by a large swath of green grass. The houses sell for twice the amount of houses in the Lower Richmond area (See Table C2 for detailed data).[7] Land seems plentiful and lots are larger than in the city; parking near the school is ample, except on nights when there is a scheduled event and parents swarm to the school. The school grounds and the surrounding neighborhoods are extensively landscaped. There are so many trees, flowering shrubs, and flowers that when the seasons shift, the presence of nature is almost overwhelming. In fall, burnt-orange-colored leaves carpet the ground; in spring, a sea of yellow daffodils appears, while overhead, white and pink dogwoods pop into bloom.

There are no stores within walking distance of Swan or the surrounding neighborhood. The local shopping district lies along a major road; the stores are huge and set back from the street, behind large parking lots. Shoppers may choose among many different retailers, including several discount stores. The selection of products is wider and more attractively priced than in the city. Because the stores are so large, families frequently drive between stores located only a few blocks from one another. Children also need to be driven to their various activities and usually need a ride in order to visit friends (some, however, are permitted to ride their bikes to friends' houses). Despite the reliance on cars in this suburb, traffic congestion usually is not a problem, and drivers tend to drive more sedately than is common in the city. The roads are in strikingly better condition than those in Lower Richmond's vicinity. There are fewer potholes on suburban streets and snow removal is prompt, often within twenty-four hours of a snowstorm. Thus, in January, when the parking lot at Lower Richmond School was dangerously icy for several days running, the lot at Swan School was completely clear of snow and ice.

During interviews, some adults mentioned how "dangerous" they considered the city and noted that they avoided it. Despite parents' anxiety about crime and their concern for the safety of their children, it is common for family members to leave valuable objects such as bikes, baseball mitts, or bats lying in their yards unattended. Burglary and petty theft occur rarely in the neighborhoods near Swan, and armed robberies on residential streets are almost unheard of. Generally, there is less concern about crime than in urban areas.

The neighborhoods surrounding Swan School are predominantly white, but Black families are present as well and Black students constitute almost 10 percent of the school population (with less than 5 percent Asian and Hispanic students). A "multicultural" theme predominates, with quilts, posters, assemblies, and curricula devoted to the topic. Despite this close attention to multiculturalism, the emphasis on diversity is largely symbolic since, unlike at Lower Richmond, here nearly all students, educators, administrators, and service personnel are white.

Parents and district administrators are strongly positive in how they view the school and the district. At back-to-school night, the assistant superintendent stressed the "special feeling" apparent at Swan and underscored the district's interest in hearing from parents. He provided his telephone number and encouraged audience members to call. Teachers at Swan have access to more supplies than do their counterparts at Lower Richmond; there is a photocopier for their use and ample paper and art materials. Referrals to special education are less common and less bureaucratic. Parents must formally agree (by signing a permission form) to have their children tested for learning problems, but the paperwork generally takes weeks, not months, to be processed. At Swan, most children in the fourth grade, including the low achievers, perform at grade level; in reading, many of the students are two or three years above grade level. Although both Lower Richmond and Swan offer computer training, art, music, choir, and gym, the character of the coursework, supplies, and instruction at Swan is more elaborate. For example, at Lower Richmond, the students enjoyed making art projects out of Popsicle sticks. At Swan, the children used square pieces of white cloth and dark black ink to make banners with Japanese characters on them. The choir at Lower Richmond is open to whomever attends practices; the children perform at local nursing homes. The choir at Swan is "select"; children must audition for their positions. With the help of an extensive fund-raising effort, the choir traveled by bus to the Midwest to perform in a competition, and, as a result of arrangements made by the music teacher, the children also visited a recording studio during the school year. Finally, parent participation is far greater at Swan than at Lower Richmond. The two schools are comparably sized, but the Swan PTA meetings attract ten times more participants than those at Lower Richmond, and the suburban organization raises (and spends) significantly larger sums. For example, the Swan PTA spent around $3,000 annually to provide

supplemental school assemblies. They sponsored "artists in residence" as
well as puppet shows, plays, and other professional performances. They
also helped out with the annual school fair, which is a much more elaborate event than Lower Richmond's.

Still, parents and educators at Swan complained of problems, albeit
different ones from those that plagued Lower Richmond. Economic security generally is not an issue. Most children come from families where
both parents are employed outside the home, often as professionals, such
as lawyers, social workers, accountants, managers, teachers, and insurance executives. Many mothers work full time outside the home. Some
teachers at the school worry that the children do not receive sufficient
attention at home because their parents are "too busy." Ms. Nettles,
noting that during the first few weeks of the school year ten of her
twenty-six students did not do their homework, comments:

I have been here seven years, and it has been getting worse. There are changes in
family life; more two parents working and single-parent families. Parents come
home and for obvious reasons they don't want to deal with it [homework] to
make sure it happens.

Parents also often have an exaggerated sense of their children's accomplishments. For instance, they describe their children as "being bored"
with schoolwork when, from the teacher's perspective, these children
have not mastered the material. In addition, parents can be quick to criticize teachers. As this third-grade teacher reports, the mother of a high-
achieving student was outraged to learn that her daughter's grade had
been read aloud:

She came in one day [to complain] because I had read Chloe's grade [aloud] as an
eighty-six and Chloe was humiliated — because Chloe does not get eighty-sixes.

The teacher feels that the mother does not have an accurate view of her
daughter's performance:

Chloe is very, very bright and in the addition and subtraction pretest she got a fifty-
eight. Her mother was telling me how bored she was. "Chloe has done this and
knows it so well." I showed her the fifty-eight. Well, she was absolutely shocked.

Parents watch teachers closely and do not hesitate to intervene on their
children's behalf. As one third-grade teacher reported, "Mothers are influenced by the PTA. [The principal] himself has said that he thinks the PTA
is trouble. You know, it's a close-knit little group." Parents' robust sense
of entitlement is evident to the teachers, as this Swan teacher makes clear:

These parents, so many of them, are so self-centered, not all of them, but some, and it's being transmitted to their children. And it's almost like, "You owe me something. Now, what can you do for me?" . . . or, "You owe an explanation for what you're doing." You almost feel at times that you have to defend yourself in some cases.

Clashes between parents and teachers occur now and again. The choir teacher, for example, felt parents who chatted in the back of the room during choir performances were being rude. She included on the inside of the program a list of recommended behaviors for parents who attended the daytime performance, but after parents complained, the principal removed the guidelines. It is not unusual for parents whose children do not initially qualify for the gifted program (at Swan the cutoff is an IQ of 125) to have them tested privately; if the children then score high enough for entry, the parents will insist they be enrolled. To reduce problems, the principal (who parents feel is sometimes too supportive of teachers) engages in preemptive strikes, such as sending letters home to ask parents to respect educators' professional judgments in assigning children to specific classrooms for the next school year:

The principal did state in a letter to the parents that, you know, all factors are taken into consideration but to please respect his judgment and the teachers' as to placement for next year. Because it can get out of hand, the requests. It really can.

The level of involvement among Swan parents is strikingly higher than at Lower Richmond, but parents who are active at the school complain that it is a constant struggle to recruit enough volunteers for events such as "Donuts with Dad," the annual third-grade luncheon with mothers, the luncheon put on for teachers by the parents' group, and the all-school spring fair.[8]

Thus, daily life is not always smooth at Swan School. Parents complain about teachers; teachers complain about parents. Recruiting parent volunteers to staff the many school functions is arduous. Still, overall, this school enjoys many social structural resources not available at Lower Richmond. Salaries are higher, there is no teacher shortage, classroom supplies are ample, and the teachers can make photocopies of educational materials. Although the resources are already more than those available at Lower Richmond, they are further amplified by the robust contributions of the PTA. This organization raises thousands of dollars, enabling the school to offer a professional-quality arts and music program.

In sum, between the two target schools, there are important differences in key structural resources, including physical facilities, educational supplies, teacher salaries, and supplemental financing and volunteer efforts contributed by parents.[9] If social class did not matter, these differences would be randomly distributed. They are not. Across the country, communities where the average social class position of parents is higher have vastly more favorable public school systems.[10]

ESTABLISHED PROFESSIONAL PRACTICES AND INSTITUTIONAL STANDARDS

While there were differences between the schools, there were also similarities. Elementary schools in America have many shared elements, including for example, the organization of the school day. Educators at Lower Richmond and Swan Schools also appeared to share similar visions of what constitutes appropriate and desirable childhood experiences. They agreed, in broad terms, on the proper role of families in promoting children's educational development. These premises were not simply expressions of the educators' personal beliefs. Instead they echoed a body of cultural practices that have gained widespread acceptance among professionals.[11]

The teachers in this study generally supported practices of concerted cultivation, with an emphasis on the development of the child through organized activities, development of vocabulary through reasoning and reading, and active parent involvement in schooling and other institutions outside of the home. Educators selectively praised children during the school day, expressed their approval and disapproval of parents in informal conversations with the research assistants and me during our classroom observations, and conformed to established school and district practices that encoded particular approaches to child rearing. Teachers also followed concerted cultivation in raising their own children. As I show next, within the confines of a limited sample, there is a striking level of agreement between educators at Lower Richmond and Swan schools.

THE VALUE OF CULTIVATING THE CHILD

Educators were quite supportive of parents' efforts to cultivate their children's talents and skills through out-of-school activities. In interviews, teachers at both schools reported viewing children's organized activities as helpful:

They all need some physical activity. I think the activities are good, because physical activity can stimulate the mind. The music lessons help with the concentration. I think that it is good to have outside activities.

There is an awful lot going on in the world. The wider variety you expose them to—you never know if you have a future playwright in the group or not. It is just something that they can enjoy and participate in, even if it is not their occupation. They just need to be aware and to talk about the different talents and occupations.

In their interactions with children, teachers also express approval, as in this fourth-grade classroom:

[The Monday following Thanksgiving, Ms. Nettles asked the children to describe what they did for Thanksgiving.] Garrett Tallinger volunteered, "My soccer team won a tournament." Ms. Nettles says, "Your soccer team won a tournament this weekend?" Garrett nods. Ms. Nettles says, "You must be very proud."

At both schools, children's out-of-school activities routinely spill into classroom life. In Ms. Nettles' classroom, students are required to keep a journal in class. Children's activities are a common theme, as field notes from October 11 show:

Five of the five boys talked about soccer games. One said that "after the game I am mad because we lose." Two of the four girls talked about playing soccer.

At Lower Richmond, Wendy Driver proudly describes her dance recital to her third-grade teacher, Ms. Green, as the children are getting ready to line up for recess. She also brought in her trophy to show Ms. Green and her classmates. Adults give organized events such as tournaments and dance recitals more weight than informal play by children, such as playing ball in the yard or watching television. When children volunteer to teachers that they watched particular television shows or that they played an informal game with cousins the previous day, teachers did not express the same level of interest or approval that they do when the children reveal their involvement in an organized activity.

Teachers also promote the concerted cultivation of their own children through a busy schedule of organized activities. Lower Richmond teacher Ms. Stanton had a daughter enrolled in a fourth-grade suburban school relatively close to Swan School. Her daughter's program of activities is similar to that of the other middle-class children in this study: art lessons, dance lessons, music lessons, Sunday school, youth church choir, and horseback riding were regular weekly events. Another third-grade teacher reported that she has all of her children enrolled in Catholic instruction (CCD), Scouts, Little League, piano lessons, and swim team.

Through their actions at home, teachers demonstrate their commitment
to the logic of child rearing of concerted cultivation.

Still, teachers complain about children being overscheduled and about
concerted cultivation diminishing children's school experience through
exhaustion or absence. As a teacher at Swan complained:

Soccer will take precedence over homework, regularly . . . Sometimes they would
go on weekend trips. They would play soccer, would be up late, and they would
be tired. I like sports, but when it interferes with what the children need to do for
their academics, I think it needs to be looked at again.

You can't fight City Hall. It's their child and they have a right to do it. Tommy
Daniels was on three one-week vacations with his family this year. Then she [his
mother] is concerned about his progress in math! Hey, keep him in school.

Teachers also support parents' efforts to develop their children's
vocabulary. They all encourage parents to read to children, take children
to the library, buy children books, and make sure that the children read
at home. Ms. Bernstein, a fourth-grade teacher at Lower Richmond, gave
her students a homework assignment of at least ten minutes of reading
each night. When Ms. Stanton, who also teaches fourth grade, made a
list of Christmas gifts that parents might give their children, she included
books. At Swan, Ms. Nettles has a bulletin board where she lists the
books that her students have read recently outside of class.

Teachers said relatively little to parents directly about the value of reasoning with children (as opposed to giving them directives). Still, there
were numerous indications that educators at both Lower Richmond and
Swan strongly prefer verbal interactions oriented to reasoning over directives. In their classroom interactions, these educators, like their counterparts nationwide, often use reasoning with the children, particularly in
lessons. As teachers answer questions with questions[12] they seek to
develop children's reasoning capacities in routine interactions. In addition, educators are generally (although not uniformly) supportive of parents' use of "time outs" as a form of discipline.

INTERVENTIONS IN INSTITUTIONS

Teachers want parent involvement in schooling, especially parental
supervision of homework. At Swan School, children must have their parents sign their homework book daily. Teachers interpret a failure to show
up for a parent-teacher conference as a sign that parents do not value
schooling — even though at Lower Richmond the conferences were

scheduled on relatively short notice and without parents' input regarding their assigned time slot. In emphasizing parental intervention in education, these educators mirror practices common in the profession.[13] Still, educators are selective in the kind of parent involvement they prefer, as this Lower Richmond fourth-grade teacher indicates:

An unsupportive parent is one who is antagonistic with the teacher. I've had situations like that. And it makes the job virtually impossible. If you have a problem with the child, the parent is not supportive of you or the school's position. And [then] the child is at odds with you and they fight you tooth and nail and they basically say, "I don't have to listen to you; [I] don't have to do what you say."

A third-grade teacher from Swan School uses strikingly similar terms in expressing her concern:

[Parents have] gotten this attitude now where they question so much. The children see and hear this. Then they come to your classroom with an attitude. Not many, but you can sure pick it up right away. Some of them are very surly . . . I think a lot of it comes from home.

Although educators want parents to offer them positive and deferential support, they also feel strongly that parents should respond to their requests for educational assistance. Ms. Bernstein is frustrated by how few parents actually read to their children:

The [parents] want them to do well in school. They all say that they want their kids to do their homework. They always say that, but they don't know how to accomplish it in many situations . . . They want to . . . They want to. But do they ever sit down and read to their child? But they mean well.

Educators at both schools believe parents should take a leadership role in solving their children's educational problems. They complain about parents who do not take children's problems "seriously" enough to initiate contact with educators. In short, educators want contradictory behaviors from parents: deference and support, but also assertive leadership when children had educational problems.

Moreover, by law, educators are required to intervene if a family violates state standards for child rearing. Some child-rearing practices that were commonplace throughout society in earlier historical periods (e.g., vigorously beating children) are now condemned. Regardless of their personal opinion, educators are bound by the law to turn a child over to authorities if, for example, she shows up at school with red welts on her body from being disciplined. As I show in subsequent chapters, this legal requirement put working-class and poor families in the study at risk for intervention by school officials in a way that middle-class families were not.

In sum, there is a paradox in the institutions that children and their families encounter. On the one hand, there are profound differences in the quality of services provided by institutions. On the other hand, institutions accept and promote the same standards regarding cultural repertoires. Thus, teachers placed a shared emphasis on the cultivation of children's talents through organized activities, the importance of parental development of children's vocabulary, and the importance of responsive and positive parental participation in schooling. As we shall see, these standards privileged the cultural practices of middle-class families over those of their working-class and poor counterparts. This pattern made it more comfortable, and easier at times, for middle-class children and their parents to achieve their wishes.

INEQUALITY

The differences in the quality of school life in Lower Richmond and Swan schools are part of a more general pattern of inequality in the broader society. A relatively small number of people, and institutions such as schools, in the population have considerably more assets than others. For example, across families, key resources are unequally distributed. Parents' income and wealth, educational accomplishments, and quality of work life all vary dramatically. If inequality were not a powerful force in the United States, then these coveted resources would be distributed in a much more equitable fashion.

In terms of income and wealth, the richest 10 percent of families in our society own almost 80 percent of all real estate (other than family homes), more than 90 percent of all securities (stocks and bonds) and about 60 percent of all the money in bank accounts. [14] One widely used indicator of inequality in income is the child poverty rate, a rate that is heavily dependent on social policy. (There are many more poor children in the United States than in most Western European countries.)[15] In the United States, one-fifth of all children live below the poverty level, and the figure is approximately twice as high for Black children.[16] The distribution of income and wealth became even more heavily concentrated in the hands of a few during the last decades of the twentieth century.[17] Still, during the study period, one-seventh of Black Americans were making over fifty thousand dollars annually.[18]

Educational accomplishments are also lopsided. In the United States, just under one-quarter of all adults have completed a bachelor's degree; the figure is a bit higher for individuals in their twenties. More than 10 percent of high school students drop out.[19] Even among younger people, for whom college education is becoming increasingly common, a clear majority (from two-thirds to three-quarters) do not graduate.[20] Although some studies show that, after taking into account parents' social position, Black youth are *more* likely to pursue higher education than whites, overall levels of educational attainment are far lower for Black children.[21] Substantial stratification also exists within higher education, ranging from community colleges to elite universities. The more elite the school, the more richly graduates are rewarded.[22]

Moreover, there has been a profound shift in the U.S. and world economies, with a decline in "good jobs" with high wages, pensions, health benefits, and stability, and a rise in "bad jobs" with relatively low wages, no benefits, little opportunity for career promotion, and lack of stability.[23] In the lives of most people, these separate threads — their educational attainment, what kind of job they get, and how much money they earn — are all tightly interwoven. Together, these factors constitute parents' social position or social structural location.

Many studies have demonstrated that parents' social structural location has profound implications for their children's life chances. Before kindergarten, for example, children of highly educated parents are much more likely to exhibit "educational readiness" skills, such as knowing their letters, identifying colors, counting up to twenty, and being able to write their first names.[24] Schooling helps, and during the school year the gap in children's performance narrows quite a bit (but widens again during the summer). Children of highly educated mothers continue to outperform children of less educated mothers throughout their school careers. By the time young people take the SAT examinations for admission to college, the gap is dramatic, averaging 150 points (relative to an average score of 500 points) between children of parents who are high school dropouts and those with parents who have a graduate degree.[25] There are also differences in other aspects of children's school performance according to their parents' social structural location. [26] Many studies demonstrate the crucial role of educational success in determining occupational success. Parents' social class position predicts children's school success and thus their ultimate life chances.[27]

UNDERSTANDING INEQUALITY

Many people in the United States hold the view that the society is, in fundamental ways, *open*. They believe that individuals carve out their life paths by drawing on their personal stores of hard work, effort, and talent. All children are seen as having approximately equal life chances. Or, if children's life chances appear to differ, this is seen as due to differences in raw talent, initiative, aspirations, and effort. This perspective directly rebuffs the thesis that the social structural location of the family systematically shapes children's life experiences and life outcomes. Rather, the outcomes individuals achieve over the course of their lifetime are seen as their own responsibility.

A second perspective, held by some social scientists, recognizes the existence of important forms of social inequality. Differences in parents' educational levels, occupational experiences, income, and other factors are all duly noted. Yet these social scientists, such as Paul Kingston, in his book *The Classless Society*, argue that inequalities of this sort are best understood as a series of disparate patterns. In other words, these scholars adopt a *gradational* approach . They see it as helpful to focus on differences within the society as a matter of degree. Put strongly, sharply defined categories of social class are useless in understanding "life-defining experiences" within the family. In addition, Kingston and others do not believe that these gradational differences cohere across spheres. Instead, they see haphazard patterns, results here and there, but no clear, definitive, overarching pattern. [28] Kingston is joined in this approach by those who stress the lack of "class consciousness" or "class identification" on the part of those who are similarly situated within the economic domain. Taking a historical perspective, these authors assert that "the communal aspects of class, class subcultures and milieu, have long since disappeared."[29] These social scientists are simply not persuaded that there are recognizable, categorical differences by social class.

One problem with these claims, however, is that the studies on which they draw have been fragmented and overly specialized, asking precise but small questions. In assessing the common linkages, researchers have drawn on multiple studies that they put together in an ill-fitting, jigsaw-puzzle form of explanation. What is needed is research that is less narrow. Specifically, studies are required that investigate wide swaths of social life in order to determine how social class makes a substantial difference in children's lives *and* also acknowledge those areas of life that may be largely immune to class influence. In short, we need a more holis-

TABLE I. TYPOLOGY OF DIFFERENCES
IN CHILD REARING

	Child-Rearing Approach	
	Concerted Cultivation	*Accomplishment of Natural Growth*
Key Elements	Parent actively fosters and assesses child's talents, opinions, and skills	Parent cares for child and allows child to grow
Organization of Daily Life	Multiple child leisure activities orchestrated by adults	"Hanging out," particularly with kin, by child
Language Use	Reasoning/directives Child contestation of adult statements Extended negotiations between parents and child	Directives Rare questioning or challenging of adults by child General acceptance by child of directives
Interventions in Institutions	Criticisms and interventions on behalf of child Training of child to take on this role	Dependence on institutions Sense of powerlessness and frustration Conflict between child-rearing practices at home and at school
Consequences	Emerging sense of entitlement on the part of the child	Emerging sense of constraint on the part of the child

tic picture that accurately reflects both the permeability and impermeability of the home-to-class forces. And, such research needs to be conceptually guided but nonetheless open to the possibility of erring in its expectations.

In this study, the research assistants and I followed a small number of families around in an intensive fashion to get a sense of the rhythms of their everyday lives. On the basis of the data collected, I develop the claim that common economic position in the society, defined in terms of social class membership, is closely tied to differences in the cultural logic of child-rearing. Following a well-established Western European tradition, I provide a categorical analysis, grouping families into the social

categories of middle class, working class, and poor. [30] (See Table C1,
Appendix C for details on how these categories were defined in this
study.) I see this approach as more valuable than the gradational analysis
often adopted by American scholars.[31] In addition, I demonstrate that
class differences in family life cut across a number of different and distinct spheres, which are usually not analyzed together by social scientists.

In particular, I delineate a pattern of concerted cultivation in middle-
class families and a pattern of the accomplishment of natural growth in
working-class and poor families. Table 1 provides an overview of the
main points of the book. It indicates that concerted cultivation entails an
emphasis on children's structured activities, language development and
reasoning in the home, and active intervention in schooling. By contrast,
the accomplishment of natural growth describes a form of child rearing in
which children "hang out" and play, often with relatives, are given clear
directives from parents with limited negotiation, and are granted more
autonomy to manage their own affairs in institutions outside of the home.
These patterns help us unpack the mechanisms through which social class
conveys an advantage in daily life. In addressing these important issues, I
have been guided heavily by the work of the late Pierre Bourdieu (see
Appendix B for a brief exposition of his theoretical ideas).[32]

Despite these differences in social structural experiences, some important aspects of children's lives are *not* differentiated by class, including
watching favorite television shows, having meals at fast food restaurants
such as McDonald's, taking an interest in specific dolls and action figures, and eagerly anticipating Halloween and important family holidays.
As I show in subsequent chapters, all parents (regardless of social class)
face the task of getting children up, dressed, fed, and transported to
school, and getting them medical attention when sick. Thus, some experiences are threaded through the lives of all families. Nevertheless, social
class differences influence the very pace and rhythm of daily life. The
next chapter, which examines the life of Garrett Tallinger, shows how
middle-class parents' efforts to develop their children's talents through
organized leisure activities can create a frenetic family life.

PART I

Organization of Daily Life

SOCIAL CLASS DIFFERENCES IN CHILDREN'S life experiences can be seen in the details of life. In our study, the pace of life was different for middle-class families compared to working-class and poor families. In the middle class, life was hectic. Parents were racing from activity to activity. In families with more than one child, parents often juggled conflicts between children's activities. In these families, economic resources for food, clothing, shelter, transportation, children's activities, and other routine expenses were in ample supply. Of course, some parents often *felt* short of money. At times they were not able to enjoy the vacations that they would have liked. But, as I show, families routinely spent hundreds and even thousands of dollars per year promoting children's activities.

Because there were so many children's activities, and because they were accorded so much importance, children's activities determined the schedule for the entire family. Siblings tagged along, sometimes willingly and sometimes not. Adults' leisure time was absorbed by children's activities. Children also spent much of their time in the company of adults or being directed by adults. They also had informal free time, but generally it was sandwiched between structured activities. In the organization of daily life, children's interests and activities were treated as matters of consequence.

In working-class and poor families, the organization of daily life differed from that of middle-class families. Here, there was economic strain not felt by many middle-class families. Particularly in poor families, it took enormous labor to get family members through the day, as mothers scrimped to make food last until they were able to buy more, waited for buses that didn't come, carried children's laundry out to public washers, got young children up, fed, dressed, and ready for school and oversaw children's daily lives. Children were aware of the economic strain. Money matters were frequently discussed.

Although money was in short supply, children's lives were more relaxed and, more importantly, the pace of life was slower. Children played with other children outside of the house. They frequently played with their cousins. Some children had organized activities, but they were far fewer than in middle-class families. Other times, children wanted to be in organized activities, but economic constraints, compounded by lack of transportation, made participation prohibitive. When children sought to display their budding talents and pursue activities more informally around the house, adults often treated children's interests as inconsequential. In addition, since they were not riding around in cars with parents going to organized activities or being directed by adults in structured activities, children in working-class and poor families had more autonomy from adults. Working-class and poor children had long stretches of free time during which they watched television and played with relatives and friends in the neighborhood, creating ways to occupy themselves. In these activities, there was more of a separation between adults' worlds and children's worlds.

In sum, there were social class differences in the number of organized activities, pace of family life, economic strain of family life, time spent in informal play, interest on the part of adults in children's activities, domination by children's activities of adult lives, and the amount of autonomy children had from adults. To be sure, other things also mattered in addition to social class. Gender differences were particularly striking. Girls and boys enjoyed different types of activities. Girls had more sedentary lives compared to boys. They also played closer to home. Race also played a role, particularly as racial segregation of residential neighborhoods divided children into racially segregated informal play groups (although race did not influence the number of activities children had).

Part I takes us through the lives of three families to illuminate these issues. First, it provides a close look at one middle-class family to show the life of Garrett Tallinger, a white middle-class boy. (Although I selected a white middle-class boy for this chapter, at some level, the decision was arbitrary. Any of the other middle-class children we observed, including the Black middle-class boy and the Black middle-class girl, could have this place in the book.) Then, I seek to show that there are important differences between the lives of middle-class children and working-class and poor children. I also discuss differences between working-class and poor families, as well as highlight differences in the experiences of boys and girls. In particular, I compare the life of Garrett with two other children: a Black working-class boy, Tyrec Taylor, and a white girl from a poor family, Katie Brindle. Although each chapter provides some basic information about each child, each chapter also seeks to highlight particular dimensions in social class differences. In particular, Chapter 4 portrays a less hectic life that emphasizes the importance of informal play with fewer organized activities (Tyrec Taylor), and Chapter 5 discusses economic strain and the treatment of children's activities as inconsequential (Katie Brindle). Both Chapters 4 and 5 highlight the autonomy of children from adults. While these chapters seek to offer an in-depth portrait of selected families, the tables in Appendix C offer an overview of the schedule of organized activities for the twelve families we visited as well as a summary for the eighty-eight children with whose families we conducted interviews.

CHAPTER 3

The Hectic Pace of Concerted Cultivation: Garrett Tallinger

(One Wednesday in May, Don Tallinger arrives home from work. It's about 10:00 P.M.) Don wanders over to [the] phone and stands in front of the calendar, looking to see what is written in on it. When he discovers that the next evening is blank except for "Mary" [the field-worker], Don emulates the way weight lifters celebrate a victory as he [silently] lifts both arms above his chest with fists clenched. (He has a slight smile as he does this.)

Mr. Tallinger's elation over an evening with no prior commitments is testimony to his family's hectic pace. His reaction highlights the degree to which the concerted cultivation of children controls adults' leisure time. Both Don Tallinger and his wife, Louise, work full time in professional jobs with travel requirements. Their three children, Garrett (a fourth-grader), Spencer (a second-grader), and Sam (a preschooler), are enrolled in a variety of activities. On any given weeknight or weekend day, one, two, or sometimes all three of the boys have events, often at different times and in different parts of town. Organized sports are a top priority for the family. The Tallingers' Christmas card, which shows the three boys standing in their front yard on a crisp-looking fall day, captures the central role accorded to organized sports. Garrett, Spencer, and Sam are dressed in their soccer uniforms — shiny blue-and-white shorts and shirts — and each boy has one foot poised on his own soccer ball. All are smiling broadly.

This chapter focuses on the organization of daily life in the middle-class Tallinger family. This family's busy schedule is not unique; it is one we found repeated, with variations, in many middle-class homes.[1] The Tallingers and others like them are committed to child-rearing strategies that favor the individual development of each child, sometimes at the expense of family time and group needs. By encouraging involvement in activities outside the home, middle-class parents position their children to receive more than an education in how to play soccer, baseball, or piano. These young sports enthusiasts and budding musicians acquire skills and dispositions that help them navigate the institutional world. They learn to think of themselves as special and as entitled to receive certain kinds of services from adults. They also acquire a valuable set of white-collar work skills, including how to set priorities, manage an itinerary, shake hands with strangers, and work on a team. They do so at a cost, however.

Compared to their working-class and poor counterparts, the middle-class children we observed are more competitive with and hostile toward their siblings, and they have much weaker ties with extended family members. Ironically, the greater the number of activities children are involved in, the fewer opportunities they have for face-to-face interaction with members of their own family. In the Tallinger household, except for times when they share meals (this occurs only once every few days), parents and children are rarely all together in the same room. Since both Mr. and Ms. Tallinger work, getting the children to their many and separate activities requires divvying up transportation responsibilities. Rather than go to a practice or game as a family, the Tallingers are more likely to each take a car and shepherd one (or two) of the children to a given event. During activities, children spend most of the time away from their parents. They are across the soccer field or in the middle of the basketball court; and in the Tallinger boys' cases, age differences further divide the siblings. They never play together on the same team.

The Tallinger home is a forty-year-old, white, two-story house with four bedrooms and three bathrooms. The house is located on a cul-de-sac in a quiet suburb near a major northeastern city. The surrounding homes are well kept; many sell for a quarter of a million dollars. The house has a large picture window facing the street and overlooking an expansive green lawn. There is a large tree in the middle of the front yard; a swing made of a thick white rope dangles from an upper limb. Near the asphalt driveway that leads to the garage stand two tall poles that support a basketball hoop and backboard emblazoned with the official NBA logo. A seven-foot-long, fine-mesh black net is stretched immediately behind the backboard and poles to keep errant balls from tumbling into the neighbors' bushes. A wooden gate provides access to the large, fenced backyard and swimming pool. All in all, it's a classic home in the suburbs.

Inside, there are hardwood floors, wallpapered rooms, and an assortment of pets (a dog, Farley; a turtle, Ivan; and assorted fish). A baby grand piano shares the living room with color-coordinated furniture (including antique tables and a wingback chair) positioned on thick rugs. Most action, however, takes place in the kitchen, the den (where the television is located), or the large screened-in porch that overlooks the backyard and pool. Housecleaners come regularly, but the Tallinger children help out by making their beds, feeding the pets, and putting the family's newspapers, cans, and bottles out for the recycling pickup each week. Mr. Tallinger oversees the outdoors; he periodically calls a man who comes and mows the lawn. He also manages the chemicals for the pool as well as the gas grill. When his wife is away for work, he takes care of the children by himself, making him a more active father in parenting than many.

Mr. Tallinger and Ms. Tallinger enjoy sports, especially golf, which they play at the elite private country club where they are members. Both are forty, and they have been married twelve years. They are "retreads," as Ms. Tallinger puts it; when they met, each had been previously married and divorced (neither had had children). Ms. Tallinger is trim and fit, with fashionably cut, short blond hair. She has a calm, unruffled air about her.

She often is stylishly dressed, as [she is] one afternoon returning from work in a black-and-white herringbone light wool skirt, which falls mid-knee, and fuchsia wool cropped jacket. She wears white hose and black two-inch heels.

Mr. Tallinger is a tall (just over six feet), broad-shouldered man with thinning reddish-blond hair who favors expensive suits for work and golf shirts and long khaki shorts on weekends. He likes to make dry, witty comments, delivered with a slightly ironic twist. For example, when asked, "How are you?" he often responds, with only the slightest hint of a smile, "Peachy-keen."

Both Tallingers hold bachelor's degrees from the same Ivy League college, where both were involved in sports. Each is a consultant (Mr. Tallinger works in fund-raising, Ms. Tallinger in personnel). They earn a combined annual income of $175,000; until near the end of the study, both worked for the same firm. The Tallingers have sufficiently flexible hours to take time off for their children's school events, but they often work on evenings and weekends. At the time of the study, both also were required to travel. Mr. Tallinger spends an average of three days on the road per week and often does not arrive home from work until 9:30 P.M. Ms. Tallinger tries to avoid overnights. As a result, four or five days a month she gets up very early (4:30 A.M.) and takes a plane out of state, returning home after dinner. Their child-care arrangements include an all-day program about five minutes from home for the youngest boy and an after-school program for the two older boys.

The Tallingers' three sons range in age from ten (Garrett) to seven (Spencer) to four (Sam). Sam is a blond-haired, sturdy-looking pre-schooler. His laugh is a high-pitched giggle. Spencer, a second-grader, is outgoing and talkative. Fourth-grader Garrett, a tall, thin, serious boy with blond hair, is the "target child" of the study. Here's how Mr. Tallinger describes his oldest son:

He's shy and quiet, not very outgoing when you first meet him. But he's got a fierce desire to please, so he's very compliant. But he is also still very competitive. He likes to win, but he's still easy to manage.

Unlike Spencer, who keeps up an almost nonstop stream of conversation, Garrett is a selective speaker. He will toss a ball around silently or watch television without commenting on commercials or programs. Sometimes, though, especially when he is away from his parents, he is livelier. He makes up little diversionary games. For example, one night around 8:00 P.M., while waiting in line at Taco Bell after a baseball game, Garrett makes faces at himself in the mirror. He also holds his breath several times, for as long as possible. His face turns bright red, but no one in the family comments.

Observations and interviews show Garrett to be both a good student and a good athlete. During a parent-teacher conference, Garrett's teacher described him as "right where he should be." In interpersonal interactions, he seems poised and sophisticated. When meeting an adult, he shakes hands, looks the person in the eye, and generally seems at ease. As an athlete, he is proficient, as this field note, taken during soccer practice with the elite Intercounty team, reveals:

The young boys are now divided into two teams and they begin to scrimmage. Garrett is a stickler at his defensive position and does not let anyone pass him. His playing style is coolly aggressive. He doesn't seem to menace and overpower the other players, but instead projects an image of top control.

Garrett, like his parents, enjoys sports. His bedroom dresser is jammed with trophies, especially from soccer. He also has many soccer patches from team exchanges. At school, Garrett is popular and is widely seen as the best athlete in his class. During recess, he and other boys (with the rare girl) will take a soccer ball and, rushing to the grassy area, kick it around until recess ends.

Garrett's friends are white, as are most of the people he interacts with, whether he is at home, at school, or on the playing field. The family's baby-sitters are white teenagers; the man who comes to mow the lawn is white as well. Among the children in the two fourth-grade classes at Garrett's school, there are three Blacks and one Asian; about 90 percent of the school's total enrollment is white. Garrett's piano teacher is white, and so are all the members of the piano recital crowd. His swim team is all white. In fact, the field-worker who accompanied the Tallingers to their country club (for swim practice) saw only white children, parents, and club staff out by the pool (except for one Black swim instructor). Garrett's all-white baseball team occasionally plays teams that include Black children.

ORGANIZATION OF DAILY LIFE: DEVELOPING GARRETT

In the Tallinger family, the older children's schedules set the pace of life for all family members. Mr. and Ms. Tallinger often have limited time between work and the start of an activity. They rush home, rifle through the mail, prepare snacks, change out of their work clothes, make sure the children are appropriately dressed and have the proper equipment for the upcoming activity, find their car keys, put the dog outside, load the children and equipment into the car, lock the door, and drive off. This pattern repeats itself, with slight variations, day after day. Garrett has the most activities. Thus, it is his schedule, in particular, that determines where the adults must be and when they must be there, sets the timing and type of meals for everyone, including Sam, and even shapes the family's vacation plans.

As Table 2, showing Garrett's activities, indicates, during the month of May, Garrett has baseball, Forest soccer (a private soccer club), Intercounty soccer (an all-star, elite team of boys drawn from various soccer clubs), swim team practice, piano lessons, and saxophone. Only the saxophone lessons take place at school; all the rest are extracurricular activities that Garrett's parents have enrolled him in, with his consent. The table doesn't include Spencer's activities; nor does it reflect the parents'

TABLE 2. GARRETT TALLINGER'S SCHEDULE OF ACTIVITIES[1]

Sunday	Monday	Tuesday	Wednesday	Thursday	Friday	Saturday
[No data collected]	[May 9: Study began]	Baseball	Piano Lesson	Soccer I[2]		Baseball pictures Fund-raiser
Soccer Piano Recital	May 16	Baseball	Soccer I			School fair (overnight)
Baseball Soccer Soccer I	May 23	Baseball Soccer	Swim Soccer Spring concert (Performed)		Out of state trip: soccer I (travel)	Out of state soccer
Out of state soccer	May 30 Out of state soccer (travel)	Swim team Soccer tryouts Soccer I game	Swim team Baseball	Swim Soccer I	Swim Baseball	Soccer I tournament (travel)
Soccer I Tournament Swim party Soccer	June 6 Swim team	Swim Baseball Soccer I Practice	Swim Baseball	Swim Soccer I Practice	Swim Summer Basketball	Baseball

1. Table contains only scheduled activities, not all activities he attended, and does not include activities of others in the family.

2. Soccer I = Intercounty soccer; Soccer = Forest soccer

commitments. During the week of May 23, when Garrett has his regular baseball, soccer, and swim team events, Mr. Tallinger is scheduled to umpire a game on Monday evening, and Spencer has a baseball game on Tuesday and a Cub Scout meeting on Thursday. On the weekend, the entire family drives four hours to an out-of-state soccer tournament. They are gone Friday, Saturday, and Sunday and return home Monday. On Tuesday, Garrett has swim team practice, soccer tryouts, and Intercounty soccer practice. On Wednesday, he has swim team practice (which he can ride his bike to) and a baseball game. On Thursday, when Garrett has practice for swim team and for Forest soccer, Spencer has a baseball game at 5:45 P.M. Then, on Saturday, Spencer has another base-ball game (at 9:15 A.M.) and Garrett has two soccer games, one at 10:15

A.M. and one at 3:00 P.M. Not all middle-class families, of course, are as sports-oriented — or as busy — as the Tallinger family. Still, many middle-class children in the study had a hectic schedule of activities. Middle-class children also had more activities than did working-class and poor children (see Table C4, Appendix C). There were some gender differences in activities; boys had more athletic activities than did girls (Tables C5 and C6, Appendix C).

Mr. and Ms. Tallinger each have out-of-town travel scheduled in May. During the week of May 9, Mr. Tallinger, who had been slated to be on the West Coast, returns early. He takes a flight at midnight on Wednesday, arrives home Thursday morning, sleeps for a few hours, and then heads off to the office. That night, he takes Garrett to his soccer practice. The week of May 23, Mr. Tallinger is away overnight on Tuesday and comes home just before 10:00 P.M. on Wednesday. The next day, May 26, Ms. Tallinger catches a 6:30 A.M. flight out of state but returns home by 8:00 P.M. The following Wednesday repeats this pattern of Mr. Tallinger arriving home very late on Tuesday night and Ms. Tallinger leaving for a trip out of state early the next morning.

The sheer number of activities increases the potential for overlapping events and last-minute conflicts. Thus, *all* events — including outings for Sam — have to be scheduled:

Louise returns from getting the mail. She stands in the doorway and exclaims, "And Sam, this is for you!" She opens up the envelope and Sam scurries over next to her. She hands Sam the card (an invitation to a birthday party), and he smiles as he looks at the dinosaur-like animal on the front of the invitation.

Four-year-old Sam is already aware of the importance of the family calendar. He knows that his older brothers' commitments may preempt this invitation:

[Louise] says, "I know we have to be somewhere on the eleventh. If we are home in the morning, you can go to this." . . . Louise walks over to the calendar and flips ahead to June. She looks at the calendar for a moment. Sam asks hopefully, with a trace of concern, "Can I go to it?" Louise says, "You're in luck; we're home in the morning."

In some ways, though, Sam has *more* autonomy than his older brothers; less of Sam's daily life is taken up with discrete, prescheduled activities. Neither Garrett nor Spencer typically has long stretches of time to organize or define for himself. Scheduled activities are so central to their lives that the boys use activities to keep track of days of the week (including evenings). Garrett and Spencer also designate time as before, during, or after a given activity (e.g., soccer, practice, swimming, and piano). Moreover, like other middle-class children we observed, the boys spend a significant amount of time simply *waiting* for the next event. Most of their activities — including school — require adult-provided transportation, and most of these activities begin and end on timetables set by adults. Sports, such as Garrett's baseball games, all occur in settings organized and planned by adults; the kind of "pick-up" games of softball or basketball with neighborhood children that we observed among working-class and poor children are rare to nonexistent in Garrett's life.

Of course, not every moment of every day is adult-determined. The Tallinger boys sometimes take the bus home after school, make themselves a snack, and watch television for about an hour until their parents get home, all without adult supervision. Garrett, Spencer, and Sam also play outdoors informally. Before and after scheduled events, the three often run around the yard playing baseball (with a tennis ball), or they ride their bikes. Sometimes, their parents join them for backyard ball games. The Tallinger children do not, however, go out and play all day, the way children from poor families typically do. There are not many children in the Tallingers' neighborhood, and no boys their ages. Sometimes, a friend bikes over to visit, but more often, a parent drives the children to "play dates."

The Tallingers enjoy wordplay as well as physical play. One night, before the parents sit down to dinner, the boys tell riddles to each other and to the field-worker.

Spencer smilingly begins to probe me with a battery of riddles. He begins by asking, "Mary, if a rooster lays an egg on a barn roof, which side will the egg fall off?" I smile and pause for a moment, then say with a tone of mock suspicion, "Well, let's see. I didn't think that roosters laid eggs."

Joking occurs at the dinner table, too. Spencer reminds his mother to sign the form for his field trip to the art museum. In a display of intellectual competitiveness, Garrett tests his brother's knowledge of Van Gogh. This inspires Mr. Tallinger to wordplay of his own:

Garrett then challenges Spencer, "Do you know what Van Gogh did?" Spencer says, "Yes, he cut off his ear and sent it to his friend." Don chortles quietly and says, "So you could say, he sent it ear mail!" Everyone laughs at the pun.

Ms. Tallinger also enjoys being playful with her sons, as the following example shows:

In his bedroom, [Garrett] stands close to her, eye to eye, goofing around, looking right into her eyes, and then lifting his hands so his palms are pressing up against her palms. She plays along, not pushing him. She does it three times and laughs.

This evolves into a game of stare-down:

[Garrett] says, "Stare at me. Stare-down? And see who blinks first?" She says, "Okay." They stand, palm to palm, staring intently. Louise blinks first and moves away; they both laugh. He says, "Want to do it again?" She does it again, and they both hold it for about fifteen seconds and then, once again, she looks away. He laughs quietly, but pleased; she laughs also.

Quiet moments occur, too. One early morning, for instance, while he is still sleepy, Garrett slides his arm around his father's waist and stands next to him in the doorway to his parents' bedroom. Mr. Tallinger, dressed in a blue-and-white bathrobe, puts his arm around his son's shoulders. The two remain peacefully entwined for a few moments.

Periods of informal play and quiet moments between family members generally take place at the margins, however. The centerpiece of the Tallinger children's lives is their organized activities. These activities reach into the core of family life. Piano, soccer, baseball, and basketball become conversational focal points, both with parents and with visiting adult friends and relatives. For children like Garrett, who are not talkative by nature, exchanges related to organized activities can be short. For example, after the first practice for Intercounty soccer, Mr. Tallinger and Garrett "discuss" the new season as they come home in the car:

DON: So, how's coach Money?

GARRETT: Good.

DON: Did he talk to you at all, or just drill you?

GARRETT: Drills.

DON: Did he say anything about positions?

GARRETT: No.

Aside from a question Mr. Tallinger asks about who the "ball hog" is, this exchange constitutes the sum total of father-son interaction during the fifteen-minute ride home.

Garrett is capable of warm, intimate exchanges with both of his parents, but this kind of dialogue occurs infrequently. More common are conversations like the one with Mr. Tallinger, described above, and the one with Ms. Tallinger, described below. Notice that although Garrett and his mother make a clear emotional connection as they talk, the subject of their conversation is drawn from an activity of Garrett's:

(Louise sits on the edge of Garrett's bed; her arms are on his chest. Spencer is sleeping in his brother's room that night, to free a bedroom for the visiting field-worker. The room is dark, except for the light coming from the hallway. Louise and Garrett are discussing songs from the spring concert in which Garrett had performed earlier that evening.)

MOM: Oh, you know what? I confused "From a Distance" [with] that song you sang tonight, "From Where I Stand." I got it confused with "From a Distance," which is a Bette Midler song.

GARRETT: What does it sound like?

MOM (starts singing): From a distance — (breaks off, laughs, starts to sing and stops; can't remember) — I don't remember. You know your mother!

SPENCER (teasing): From a distance, I don't remember the words.

MOM: It's a great song.

They chat some about which teachers did and did not take part in the concert, and then say good night.

CONCERTED CULTIVATION: LOVE'S LABORS MULTIPLIED

Children's activities create substantial work for their parents. Parents fill out enrollment forms, write checks, call to arrange car pools, wash uniforms, drive children to events, and make refreshments. In the Tallinger family, these tasks are regularly doubled, depending on which boy is doing what. Simply getting ready for an activity — collecting the equipment, organizing the children, loading the car — can be exhausting.

For adults, in addition to the labor of preparing, there is the labor of watching. During one chilly evening in May, Mr. Tallinger, who had flown back home on the midnight "red eye," worked in the morning, and taken a two-hour nap in the afternoon, leaves the soccer practice. He explains that he is going to a local convenience store to get a cup of coffee:

At 7:05 P.M. Don said that he was going to go get coffee. He asked Tom (another father) if he wanted any. Tom shook his head. Don asked me if I wanted any. I asked if it would be all right if I go with him (mostly because I was cold). Don said sure. On the way to the store Don said, "I don't really want coffee. I was just bored. I used to go to all his practices and all his games, but now that he does so much I don't go all the time. But this was the first practice."

Mr. Tallinger is eager for the practice to end:

When we get back the boys are taking a break. Don says, "Is it over? We can't be
that lucky."

The impact of children's activities takes its toll on parents' patience as
well as their time. For example, on a June afternoon at the beginning of
summer vacation, Mr. Tallinger comes home from work to take Garrett
to his soccer game. Garrett is not ready to go, and his lackadaisical
approach to getting ready irks his father:

Don says, "Get your soccer stuff—you're going to a soccer game!" Garrett
comes into the den with white short leggings on underneath a long green soccer
shirt; he's number 16. He sits on an armchair catty-corner from the television and
languidly watches the World Cup game. He slowly, abstractedly, pulls on shin
guards, then long socks. His eyes are riveted to the TV screen. Don comes in:
"Go get your other stuff." Garrett says he can't find his shorts. Don: "Did you
look in your drawer?" Garrett nods . . . . He gets up to look for his shorts, comes
back into the den a few minutes later. I ask, "Any luck yet?" Garrett shakes his
head. Don is rustling around elsewhere in the house. Don comes in, says to
Garrett, "Well, Garrett, aren't you wearing shoes?" (Don leaves and returns a
short time later): "Garrett, we HAVE to go! Move! We're late!" He says this
shortly, abruptly. He comes back in a minute and drops Garrett's shiny green
shorts on his lap without a word.

This pressured search for a pair of shiny green soccer shorts is a typical event in the Tallinger household. Also typical is the solution—a parent ultimately finds the missing object, while continuing to prod the child
to hurry. The fact that today's frenzied schedule will be matched or
exceeded by the next day's is also par:

DON (describing their day on Saturday): Tomorrow is really nuts. We have a
    soccer game, then a baseball game, then another soccer game.

The Tallingers' commitment to concerted cultivation creates additional
labor for them when, as happens every few days, activities conflict. For
example, Garrett is on several soccer teams—the "A" traveling team of
the private Forest soccer club, the Township soccer team, and the
Intercounty soccer team. On Sunday, May 22, Garrett and a friend on his
team wait in the car to be driven to the first practice for the Intercounty
soccer program. Mr. Tallinger and the friend's father (Bill) discuss a
looming conflict:

Don adds, "I see we have a conflict with soccer practice and tryouts." Bill says,
"The Intercounty seems more pressing since they haven't had much chance to

work together." Don says, "Yeah, but if you don't try out, you don't get on the team." Bill says, "That's true. I'll talk to [the tryout coach] about it." He pauses and then, turning to walk down the step, looks back and says, "Maybe (winking) we can get special dispensation." He laughs and Don smiles.

Sometimes, the Tallingers resolve potential scheduling conflicts by adjusting their own work schedules. That they do so reluctantly is clear from Mr. Tallinger's observation that "there's something arrogant about soccer. I mean, they just assume that you have the time, that you can get off work, to lug your kids to games. What if you worked at a job that paid an hourly wage?" Other times, Garrett must skip one activity to attend another. For example, the night of the school concert, he makes it to swim practice but not to a soccer game. On Father's Day, Garrett cannot play in the father-child special golf tournament at the country club because, as he explains, "I have two soccers and a baseball game" that day. Spencer does play in the tournament, however. Thus, even on Father's Day, the family goes in different directions.

The fact that in families like the Tallingers conflicts between activities are inevitable doesn't necessarily reduce the tension or frustration they produce. Last-minute changes, whether in the timing of children's events, or weather-related adjustments in school openings or closings, or hastily scheduled work meetings for either Mr. or Ms. Tallinger (or both), sometimes threaten to topple the whole architecture of the family's master schedule. For example, on Wednesday, May 18, Garrett is told at his Intercounty soccer practice that a game has been scheduled for the coming Sunday. Neither parent is home; a high-school boy is baby-sitting. Mr. Tallinger comes home from work at 9:30, and Ms. Tallinger arrives about ten minutes later and begins preparing to take the baby-sitter home. As they all stand in the kitchen, Mr. Tallinger tells his wife the news:

Don said to Louise, "He has a game on the twenty-second." He showed her the soccer calendar. Louise replied, "It wasn't scheduled." Don sounded upset. He said, "I know. It changed." Louise walked over to the kitchen calendar hanging on the wall next to the telephone. She said, "What time is it at?" Don, without looking at the paper, said, "Four." Louise said, "So he could make it." Don, sounding more frustrated than I have ever heard him, said to the baby-sitter, "He has two soccer games, a baseball game, and a graduation party on the same day." Louise said (looking at the location), "It's too far away."

Conflicts like these escalate the "invisible labor" parents undertake as they keep the children fed, the house organized, and the different deadlines of multiple schedules reconciled. As the number of women working outside the home continues to grow, so too does the already formidable pressure on parents, particularly mothers. Arlie Hochschild has termed the work of women in taking care of the home "the second shift." She and others also have shown that despite increases in the amount of time men contribute to household work and child care, they still concentrate their home efforts on outdoor work (e.g., mowing the lawn, painting, or repairing the house). Mr. Tallinger was a very involved father and often played ball with the children outside. However, as in many families, when she was present, Ms. Tallinger took a leadership role in cooking, clothing, and coordinating the children's lives. He helped her.

Women's work at home, on the other hand, continues to be inside and deadline oriented (e.g., making meals, getting children ready for child care or school, and putting children to bed). Although researchers have documented many aspects of "invisible labor" at home, existing studies do not examine the impact of children's activities on those who work "the second shift." Unlike mealtimes or bedtimes, organized activities for children usually have starting and stopping times that are rigidly enforced. Parents are expected to deliver and pick up their children punctually. Safety concerns drive most of these rules and parents try very hard to comply. Over and over again, in our observations, parents showed up within a minute or two of when the activity let out. Regularly meeting those often arbitrarily set deadlines can take an emotional as well as a physical toll.

Mr. and Ms. Tallinger manage the pace of family life differently. For example, one weekday afternoon, Mr. Tallinger drives hurriedly up the driveway at 5:40 P.M. He jumps from the car, searches for his keys, opens the front door, and, almost immediately, sternly tells the boys to do their homework. When Ms. Tallinger arrives home, around 6:00 P.M., she seems more relaxed than her husband. Even when she is clearly under pressure, with multiple questions from the children and looming deadlines, Ms. Tallinger is typically less tense than Mr. Tallinger when she is alone with the children.

Moreover, pressures related to family life are not borne equally by Mr. Tallinger and Ms. Tallinger. Although Mr. Tallinger participates actively in his children's lives, his job keeps him away from home two to three days per week. When she worked full time, Ms. Tallinger typically assumed more of a leadership role in monitoring, feeding, and helping the children with daily life tasks. Still, Mr. Tallinger was an unusually competent father and played an active role in child care when Ms. Tallinger traveled for work.

It is also Ms. Tallinger who makes the career adjustments when faced with family conflicts. Near the end of the study, Ms. Tallinger decided to quit her job. Looking for an opportunity closer to home, so that she could be around as an "anchor" for the children, she eventually took a job as a high-level manager for a local nonprofit organization, one with minimal travel requirements. She describes this action as a decision to "put my career on the shelf."

Still, in some areas of home labor, Mr. Tallinger contributes far more than what we observed among fathers in other middle-class homes. He regularly and competently gets the children off to school on mornings when his wife has an early meeting or is out of town. One morning when Ms. Tallinger leaves early, he stays behind to take the children to school and to attend "Donuts with Dad," an event sponsored by the parent-teachers organization. The boys are in the basement, playing. They have stuffed pillows under their shirts to make themselves look more like hockey goalies:

All of a sudden [Don] calls down from upstairs in a semi-mad voice, "Spencer — did you feed Ivan and Farley? Garrett did you feed the fish?" Spencer says, "I fed Ivan." Both move quickly to head up the stairs; they walk up with the fat pillows under their chests. As they start to move, [Don] calls down, "Feed Farley. And Garrett — feed the fish." I follow them upstairs. Garrett goes in the den to feed the fish.

After Garrett feeds the fish, he walks into the kitchen (with the fat pillow still under his shirt) and stands near the table. His father is shuffling papers; the all-news radio station is playing loudly. Mr. Tallinger (not commenting on the pillow) begins a series of reminders:

[Don] says, "You are going to take the bus?" Garrett says, "Yes." ". . . What time does the bus come? . . . Do you have a key?" Garrett nods but looks in his backpack. [Don] nods and then says, "Don't miss the bus."

During this interaction, Mr. Tallinger appears rushed and irritable as he tries to remember various tasks. Sam and Spencer whine and complain as they wait by the front door for their father to take them to school. Their father, passing through the hallway, stops to reprimand Sam. "Sam! Cut it out," he orders.

In the families we observed, fathers were neither as knowledgeable of nor as involved in child care as Mr. Tallinger. But even he did not seem to define children's home-related responsibilities as labor that was equally his. When both parents were present, most family labor fell to Ms. Tallinger. She was the one who found and ironed the boys' pants the day of the piano recital and who arranged the recital refreshments (strawberries and poppy seed muffins), who bought the children's teachers Christmas and end-of-year gifts, and who wrote the teachers notes to thank them for their efforts during the year. Significantly, this pattern of gendered labor met the expectations of both children and school personnel: Mothers, not fathers, were expected to sign permission slips and help children with routine life tasks.

A CULTIVATED CHILDHOOD: GARRETT'S VIEW

Garrett is not an especially demonstrative child, but it is clear that he enjoys his activities, particularly those related to sports, and thinks that without them, his life would be "boring." Unlike Tyrec Taylor, a working-class boy who is discussed in the next chapter, Garrett does not complain about having to go to practices or games. If he has to miss a game, he is visibly disappointed. During an interview, Garrett reports that he especially enjoys competitive games. About basketball, for example, he notes that he likes "defense . . . pushing guys around." Forest traveling soccer and Intercounty soccer, where the teams are skillful and there are "bigger fields, bigger goals," rank high with him. By contrast, gym class soccer "gets boring after awhile." When asked by the interviewer, Garrett admits that days when he has two soccer games and a baseball game or three other activities are "tiring," but he notes, "It's not too much." Reflecting, he amends, "Not for me. Maybe for my dad [because] he has to take me and he has to watch me in the heat . . . He has to take me back and forth."

Garrett anticipates unusual soccer events such as a trip to another state for a tournament, with enthusiasm. On the Wednesday night before the weekend trip, when he is in bed and under the covers and his mother is wishing him good night, Garrett says excitedly: "Two more days 'til we go!" Similarly, Garrett is excited when he gets his new Intercounty soccer uniform emblazoned with the word "SELECT." He begins investigating the new clothes as soon as he and his father get in the car at the end of practice.

Don and Garrett put on their seat belts. Garrett immediately opened the bag and looked at the stuff. He took a green nylon jacket that said SELECT out of the bag. Garrett said, "I think I'm going to wear this." Don said, "That's what it's for." Garrett seemed excited by the jacket. He then peered into the bag (a brown paper bag) and said there are two shirts, pants (which were actually bright green shorts) and two pairs of socks. Garrett listed aloud everything in the bag. He sounded excited.

Once home, he immediately shows the uniform to his mother and siblings. Such displays of pleasure and enthusiasm for his activities are genuine, but they are also selective. For example, although Garrett is put on the all-star team in baseball, he reports that "I wasn't [as] excited [as] I was when I found out I made Intercounty and the Forest traveling team." But, he also explains, "baseball's like my fourth sport," ranking behind his two soccer teams and basketball. The number of major events in Garrett's life seems to dull their individual importance. For example, the spring concert at school, in which he plays saxophone in a trio, generates little interest for Garrett. In the working-class families we observed, comparable school events were the subject of extensive discussion and anticipation. Similarly, events that working-class and poor children find exciting — like having pizza, a bakery cake, or a party with extended family relatives — do not appear to matter to Garrett.

Some days, Garrett is exhausted and moody:

Garrett was in a bad mood . . . He got dropped off by Brian's dad at 8:20 P.M. He went inside. He didn't say hello to anyone. He didn't say anything to me when I commented on how he got his hair chopped off. He seemed quiet, remote. He basically said nothing the whole night. Don came home at 9:30 P.M. Don came in and said [to the baby-sitter], "Hi Frankie. It's good to see you." Frankie stood up and he and Don shook hands. Don then said, "Hi, Garrett." Garrett did not answer. Don said, "Hi, Garrett." Garrett looked at Don and said, "Hi." Don asked, "How are you, Garrett?" Garrett replied, "Okay." Don turned and went into the kitchen.

We observed similar exhaustion among other middle-class children. Alexander Williams, a Black middle-class boy, looked worn out as he traveled from after-school care to Friday night choir; a Black middle-class girl, Stacey Marshall, fell asleep under the hair dryer on a Saturday afternoon. We did not see comparable signs of exhaustion in the working-class and poor children. If anything, adults commented on these youngsters' boundless energy.

A CULTIVATED CHILDHOOD: SPENCER'S AND SAM'S VIEWS

The organization of middle-class family life around individual children's activities shapes the experience of all family members, including siblings who are not themselves involved in a given activity. Both Spencer and Sam — but especially Sam — spend large portions of their leisure time traveling to and/or from the sites of Garrett's activities and watching these events (or simply waiting for them to end). Sam's afternoons are hostage to his brother's schedule. He comes home briefly from day care, has a snack, and then gets back in the car with a parent and goes to one of Garrett's activities. Once there, he usually wanders around, asks for snacks, sometimes plays with other children, asks for more snacks, and waits for the game or practice to end. Not surprisingly, his interest and patience usually run out long before the activity is over. It is common for Sam to have four or five episodes a week of crying, whining, and complaining (this behavior is especially likely when he is hungry or tired).

Sometimes, however, his unhappiness escalates to a level that causes him to "fall apart," as his mother puts it. He whines loudly and interrupts often, if he doesn't like what is happening and, on occasion, will kick, scream, and cry. For example, the night Garrett performs at his school's spring music concert, Sam lasts about one half hour and then begins to unravel. He tests his mother's patience by refusing to sit still; then, he brings his outstretched feet just inches shy of the back of a woman seated in the row ahead:

His mother grabs his upper arm (looking angry) and says, "Watch your feet — you almost hit her! Sit still!" He sits for a few seconds and then moves his feet again. Again she grabs his arm and whispers, "Sit!"

A pattern of "falling apart" seems to occur a few times each month. Mr. Tallinger takes a direct approach, telling Sam to "cut it out." Ms. Tallinger usually responds to Sam's outbursts with warmth and tolerance, and she encourages his brothers to be empathetic (with only limited success).

Sam, at four years old, has few activities other than going to day care. Spencer, on the other hand, has a schedule that includes piano, Cub Scouts, soccer, and baseball. Still, he too spends more time than he would like as a spectator. Spencer doesn't "fall apart" like Sam, but he does communicate his frustration. His father is aware, for example, that "he does get angry that we always have to go to Garrett's games." In fact, watching Garrett perform is an integral part of Spencer's life. At the school's Donuts for Dad event, Spencer leads his father over to show him a picture that he had drawn. Spencer explains that the picture, which shows children on a field and figures to the side, watching, represents him and his family. The picture is titled, "Watching Soccer." Mr.

Tallinger, affectionately running his hand over the top of his son's head, remarks, "We do that a lot."

The flip side of watching, of course, is performing. Here, too, Spencer must adjust to standards set by Garrett. Although he plays baseball and soccer, Spencer seems less interested — and talented — in sports than his older brother. From his parents' perspective, this is a problem. On several occasions, Mr. and Ms. Tallinger (separately) mention their concern over Spencer's relative lack of interest in sports.

DON: We struggle with Spencer 'cause he doesn't like sports. We decided he's average. Louise and I decided. But when they ask, 'What can we do?' I say go out and play catch. I usually don't think of going and collecting spiders or doing something that Spencer would like. He's interested in science. I usually don't think about that.

FIELD-WORKER: That's hard.

DON: Sports just come naturally to us.

FIELD-WORKER: Does Spencer try to compete with Garrett?

DON: He knows he couldn't compete with him. Garrett is so much better.

Spencer seems aware of and somewhat anxious about his parents' concern over his relative lack of engagement with sports, as the following field note suggests:

Don says to Spencer (as if he just thought of it) in a questioning (but enthusiastic) manner, "Spencer, do you want to be on the swim team?" Spencer, looking slightly anxious and biting his lip, replies, "No." Slight pause and then his dad says, "Okay," in an accepting tone (although there is slight hint of disappointment). Spencer walks [into the kitchen] to find his backpack and his dad is there next to him. Spencer says, "I would — but I don't know how to do the strokes." His dad says, "That's what they teach you; they teach you the strokes."

The entire interaction takes less than a minute, but it is a tense minute, or at least it seems so for Spencer.

SIBLING COMPETITION AND CONFLICT

Spencer's relative inferiority as an athlete colors his relationship with Garrett. Sometimes he goes out of his way to identify areas in which his older brother is *not* accomplished. For example, one afternoon as Garrett and a field-worker are shooting baskets in the driveway, Spencer offers this observation:

"Garrett isn't really that good at basketball. He isn't." Garrett quickly refutes Spencer saying, "Oh yeah? I'm better than you." Spencer seems to ignore him. He is undaunted by Garrett's comment. Spencer continues, "I mean, this isn't what he does well in. He's not the best player." Garrett seems a bit more irritated by Spencer's comments and says with calm defensiveness, "Oh yeah? That's why I had [x] rebounds in the game. More than anyone in gym class." Spencer matter-of-factly states, "I am saying this isn't the game you are the best in."

Spencer also periodically flaunts his status as part of the school's gifted program. Garrett, despite two attempts, missed the program's cutoff of an IQ of 125 (he scored 119). When Spencer qualified, Garrett reacted with great, tearful distress. For his part, Garrett sometimes seizes opportunities to highlight his superior skills. During a piano lesson, for instance, he deliberately launches into the piece Spencer is to perform at an upcoming piano recital, knowing that he plays the piece better than his brother, and knowing that Spencer can hear him as he plays:

GARRETT: I can play . . .

PIANO TEACHER: Don't. (Garrett keeps playing.) Don't play that. It bothers
     him that he can't play it as fast. (Garrett continues playing and is grinning.)
     You are ruining the piece for him. (Garrett still plays.) I don't want you to
     play it anymore. (Garrett stops.)

Despite this kind of competition, though, the tenor of Spencer and Garrett's relationship is often friendly. Garrett can be helpful:

Garrett has pulled out a workbook and is looking down at the math problems on it . . . . Spencer says, "Garrett, I don't understand how to do this." Garrett quietly says, "Here, let me see." It is an addition problem. Garrett says, "What's seventy-five plus ninety-nine?" Spencer rolls his eyes and says, "I don't know. I can't add it in my head!" He sounds mildly annoyed by Garrett's question, as if he is incredulous that Garrett even asked it. Garrett puts the paper down near the corner of the table so that Spencer can see it, and he slowly says, "Okay, what's nine and five?" Spencer says, "Nine and five . . . um, fourteen. I got that." Garrett writes down the numbers and says, "And you carry the one here," and points to the carried number. He continues, "Now what is one and seven and nine?" Spencer pauses for a moment and says, "Seventeen." Garrett writes down the number. Don strides through the kitchen as Garrett hands the paper back to Spencer. Don asks suspiciously, "What's going on here?" Garrett replies quietly, "I showed him how to do something."

Spencer cannot seem to forge a workable relationship with Sam, however. The two squabble frequently and sometimes viciously.

Spencer suddenly shrieks from the living room, "Stop it! Stop it! Get away from me!" Sam begins to wail. I hear a door slam heavily upstairs and then Louise tramps loudly down the stairs. She walks into the living room and demands, "What is going on here?" Spencer explains, "He keeps following me around!" Louise says, with rising irritation, "I don't care if he follows you." She says accusingly, "You followed Garrett around when you were his age! There's no excuse for you to act the way you are acting. There's no excuse."

Spats like this are common and are usually resolved by a third party. One parent or the other intervenes and redirects one or both of the boys.

The Tallinger children, like many of their middle-class peers, frankly state their preferences regarding siblings. References to "hating" a family member are common and elicit no special reaction, either from other children or adults. For example, one evening when Spencer and Sam are out in the front yard playing softball with their teenage baby-sitter Frankie (and a field-worker),

Spencer asks Sam who he hated the most. Sam said Garrett. Spencer told Sam to pretend he was hitting [with the bat] Garrett's head. Frankie said, "Sam, you told me that you hated Spencer the most." Spencer repeats, "Pretend it's Garrett's head."

The open displays of hostility between siblings that we observed in the middle-class families we visited had no real equivalent in the working-class and poor homes. Siblings in those families clearly annoyed one another, but we never heard the frank, even casual, references to hatred that were common in middle-class homes. Likewise, the middle-class pattern of noisy sibling conflicts resolved by adult intervention was not common in working-class and poor families. In the latter, sibling conflict was both less vociferous and less likely to occur in a setting in which an adult was present.

THE RELATIVE UNIMPORTANCE OF RELATIVES

The Tallinger family's social life is organized mainly around the children's activities and the parents' jobs, rather than around contact with extended family. Such attenuated kinship ties contrast dramatically with the patterns we observed in working-class and poor families, where extremely strong social ties with immediate and extended family members are common. In the working-class and poor families, parents speak daily with their brothers and sisters and their parents. Cousins play together several times a week. The Tallingers see Ms. Tallinger's mother, who lives a few minutes away, at least once a week, but visits with Mr. Tallinger's mother, who lives about an hour and a quarter's drive away, occur only on major holidays (Mr. Tallinger sees his mother more frequently — about once a month, when his work brings him into her area).

Neither Garrett nor Spencer is pressured to forgo an organized activity in order to spend time with relatives, even those they see only a few times a year. When conflicts arise, the children are allowed, as Ms. Tallinger explains, "to choose" where to spend their time. Thus, when the Tallingers host an outdoor college graduation party for Mr. Tallinger's only nephew, a party that includes all of Mr. Tallinger's family (i.e., his mother, sisters, nieces, and nephews), Garrett does not plan to attend.

Louise explains, "He is going to go to baseball for a half hour, and then he is going with the Heaths to his soccer game, and then they are going to drive him to his Intercounty soccer game.". . . Don, with a deep sigh of frustration, says, "We aren't going to any of the games." Field-worker: "How did you choose between baseball and soccer?" Don says, "Soccer is more of a priority. Isn't that right, Garrett?" Garrett, standing in the middle of the kitchen, nods in agreement.

For Garrett, playing soccer is "more of a priority" than spending time with relatives, but the Tallingers do care about kinship ties. Ms. Tallinger and her mother talk on the phone at least three times a week, Nana (Ms. Tallinger's mother) frequently attends the children's school events, and she has a key to the Tallingers' house. Mr. Tallinger, as noted, visits his mother regularly, and his extended family gets together for all major holidays. Garrett has a male cousin his age who lives only twenty minutes away. According to Ms. Tallinger, Garrett and this cousin have a "wonderful" time when they are together — but they meet only on major holidays. For the Tallingers, time spent with extended family is not unimportant; it's just less important than sports.

MONEY: EVER PRESENT AND NEVER MENTIONED

In addition to spending large amounts of family time on sports, the Tallingers spend large amounts of money. Garrett's activities are expensive. Soccer costs $15 per month, but there are additional, larger expenses periodically. The Forest soccer team's new warm-up suits, socks, and shirts cost the Tallingers $100. Piano runs $23 per weekly lesson per child. Tennis clinic is $50; winter basketball, $30. It costs the family money to drive to out-of-state tournaments and stay overnight. Fees for Garrett's summer camps have varied; some have cost $200 per week. When, at our request, Ms. Tallinger tallied the cost of registration, uniforms, equipment for activities, camp costs, and hotel costs for one year, she reported expenditures for Garrett alone as exceeding $4,000 per year, a figure that other middle-class families also report.[2]

These costs are not discussed within earshot of Garrett, Spencer, or Sam. In fact, money matters of any sort are rarely mentioned in the Tallinger home. For example, when signing the form for baseball pictures, Mr. Tallinger queries Garrett regarding his height, weight, position, and team number. He plans to order nine trading cards, but when Garrett says, "Last year we got twelve," Mr. Tallinger (without comment) adjusts the form and fills in a figure of $11, which is never mentioned.

Near the end of the study, the Tallingers develop serious financial difficulties. Cash flow problems at the firm they both worked for result in irregular paychecks for both parents. This, in turn, leads to delayed mortgage payments, as Ms. Tallinger reveals in an interview:

I mean, we had seven thousand dollars in penalties on our mortgage. For being late . . . And the reason we're late is because our company can't pay us.[3]

Their financial problems are of great concern to both parents; Mr. Tallinger acknowledges that he is literally losing sleep. Still, no mention is made to the children. Ms. Tallinger, recalling the anxiety she felt as a child when her absent father's support checks did not arrive or arrived late, tries to spare her sons similar concerns. She does, though, let the children know that certain kinds of vacations, such as going to Disney World, are expensive and that all family vacations require saving in advance. But possible limits on money are never referred to when the family debates going out for fast food, when it is time to sign up for a sports team, when a dentist appointment is scheduled, or when arrangements are made to attend an out-of-state soccer tournament. By *not* mentioning money, the Tallingers and other middle-class parents convey a subtle sense of entitlement to their children. Garrett and his peers are never denied participation in an activity because of its cost. As I discuss in later chapters, in both white and Black working-class and poor homes the opposite is true. Financial matters are discussed openly and nearly constantly, and children are well aware of what their parents can or cannot afford to spend money on.

To be sure, middle-class children like the Tallinger boys are not oblivious to economic differences. Ms. Tallinger knows that her sons admire the larger, more affluent homes of some of the boys on Garrett's soccer team:

We don't pretend anything. When they go to other little boys' homes, [they are] very different than ours. (laughter) And they like that house a lot. They like the Jennings' house. They can see it's a bigger house. They have big-screen TVs. I mean, they notice that people live differently than they do. But they also go to other people's homes and see that there's a difference in the other direction.

Garrett has an additional reason for being attuned to relative deprivation. Most of his friends from soccer go to private school, and Garrett had, as well, for one year. Since the Tallingers could not afford to send three children to private school, however, they moved Garrett to the local public school. At the end of the study, when we asked Garrett during an interview what one change he would make in his family, if he could, he replied, "Have more money so I could go to my old school."

Thus, despite living in a $250,000 home with a swimming pool, having parents who earn more than $175,000 per year, and being regularly enrolled in activities that cost the family thousands of dollars, Garrett is bothered by what he perceives as insufficient wealth. From *his* perspective, his parents' financial reach is limited because it does not encompass something he very much wants — a return to private school. He takes for granted the fact that his parents can afford the cost of clothing, groceries, fast food, cars, medical appointments, and assorted activities for their children. In fact, when offered a free toothbrush by the dentist, he declines. For Garrett, expenditures like these are simply part of his life; they are (unexamined) *entitlements*. He can't — and doesn't — even imagine that for working-class and poor children, these same taken-for-granted items and opportunities are viewed as (unavailable) *privileges*.

LEARNING SKILLS FOR LIFE

Middle-class children may take for granted their "right" to be involved in various activities. Their parents, though, are conscious of the advantages such participation brings to their children. Both Mr. and Ms. Tallinger strongly believe that sports teach children crucial life lessons, such as knowing "when to practice and when to perform," as Ms. Tallinger puts it during an interview. Mr. Tallinger, noting that it's "good to be competitive," adds

You could apply all the clichés you can think of. But when you're the hero, you get all the satisfaction out of that; and when you're the goat, you find out who your friends are in a hurry . . . . I've found very few other activities where you can experience that as directly.

Young athletes get a head start on maturity:

I think it makes you mentally tough. So that when things are not going your way you have the ability to kind of buckle down or dig down deeper, whatever it is, and try harder and not look for excuses.

They also learn to be team players:

So you learn to play as part of a team . . . His soccer coach is fantastic, preaching to them. If our team scores a goal, it's the whole team that scores the goal, and if we get scored upon, it's the whole team that let the goal in, not one guy. And they all seem to be sucking that up and abiding by that attitude.

Finally, nine- and ten-year-old children who play on organized sports teams develop the ability to perform in public, in front of adults, including strangers.[4] As children regularly see themselves and other members of the team do well and do poorly, performance-based assessment gradually becomes routine. Also, exposure to public scrutiny is itself graduated. During practices, spectators tend to be mainly mothers who alternate between chatting with one another and watching the field; comments from the sidelines are low key. During games, however, parents' demeanors change. There is much more overt emphasis on the importance of children performing well. Cheering is mixed with explicit advice — and criticism — as this excerpt from a tape recording at an Intercounty soccer game shows (the speakers include Mr. Tallinger and the fathers of two other players):

— Garrett, hold the ball!

— That's it, Tom!

— Garrett! Look behind you!

— Garrett, come on! Get back.

— Hold up, Garrett!

— Yeah, that's it, that's it, take a run Garrett, take a run!

— Watch your feet, watch your feet!

— Paul, if you need a rest, ask for it!

— Way to go, Jim!

Organized sports, like the soccer teams Garrett is part of, with their mandatory tryouts and public games, can help prepare participants for performance-based assessment at school, as well. For example, auditions are required in order to qualify for the "select choir" at the middle-class neighborhood school the Tallinger children attend. Similarly, the "rules of the game" children learn on the playing field can be applied to school-work. Mr. Tallinger recalls, in an interview, making this point to Garrett:

Last week or the week before, he came down with semi-weepy eyes [saying] that homework was too difficult. So we said, "You know, it's like a soccer game. What do you do if you're playing in a soccer game? Do you start crying and say you can't do it? No, you know this is going to be a hard one, so you just try harder." So he went back upstairs and did his homework.

Although it is less obvious to both parents and children, skills acquired in organized activities will continue to be useful when, as teenagers or young adults, these youngsters take their first jobs. In their organizational style, many of the activities in which middle-class children routinely participate replicate key aspects of the workplace. Children like Garrett, who meet and learn to work effectively with a new set of adults for every activity they enroll in, are acquiring a basic job skill — the ability to work smoothly with acquaintances.[5] Most working-class and poor children, in contrast, have no opportunities for similar pre-employment training. Most of the adults they encounter outside of school are immediate family members or extended family members. Some working-class and poor children interact periodically with adult neighbors, but encounters with adult acquaintances in organized settings are very rare.

The kind of team-participation skills Mr. Tallinger notes that Garrett is gaining are directly applicable to a wide range of work environments, from fast-food service to high-tech design projects. Again, it is middle-class, not working-class or poor, children who consistently gain access to these lessons in formal teamwork. Similarly, involvement in multiple organized activities is common among middle-class children. Thus, they frequently need to choose one activity over another.[6] Knowing how to prioritize is a workplace skill that employers actively seek in prospective employees.

Other real-world advantages also bear noting. Unlike the working-class and poor children we observed, Garrett and his peers have broad horizons and are exposed to typically adult experiences, such as being issued photo identification cards. The cards require the holder's signature, and this increases the boys' excitement and sense of power:

Garrett is the fourth boy to sign. The man [in charge of the photo IDs] calls him up, "Garrett!" and then demonstrates with his finger and says, "Sign here, where it says 'player's signature.'" Other boys are crowded around watching. One boy is saying, "Sign Donald" (Garrett's full name is Donald Garrett Tallinger, after his father), but Garrett ignores him. He signs "Garrett Tallinger."

The Intercounty soccer team travels to out-of-state tournaments; players stay in hotels and eat in restaurants; during the games, they compete against children they have never met before. Garrett's friends and acquaintances are similarly mobile. The school's select chorus performs in the Midwest, the middle school's arts group goes to Europe, and classmates fly on commercial airlines to attend specialized summer camps. Overall, ten-year-old Garrett and his middle-class peers travel more frequently and cover more distance than do most working-class and poor adults.

The experiences and skills that Garrett and others gain from their participation in activities are reinforced by their parents' child-rearing strategies at home. Garrett's parents have taught him and his brothers to shake hands with adult men when they are being introduced. They explicitly coach Sam to "look him in the eye" as he shakes a man's hand. The Tallingers themselves usually make eye contact with their sons when they are speaking to them, and they expect reciprocal behavior from each of the boys. They also reinforce notions of responsibility to others. When Garrett toys with the idea of quitting saxophone, Ms. Tallinger urges him to weigh that desire against his obligations to the rest of the members of his band. Garrett decides not to quit.

Mr. and Ms. Tallinger also teach by example — both read. They regularly read the newspaper (which is often spread out over the kitchen table) and Ms. Tallinger, in particular, often has a novel in progress. Both parents use reasoning as their key mechanism of social control.[7] They frequently answer questions with more questions and whenever possible guide the children through situations rather than issue directives.

Like the organizational aspects of children's activities, these home-based practices contribute to the development of skills that have a particularly smooth fit with the behaviors and expectations of occupations and other social institutions. Thus, in their everyday experiences, middle-class children not only acquire a variety of important life skills, but they also have repeated opportunities to practice those skills. Their working-class and poor counterparts, on the other hand, typically neither participate in organized activities nor grow up in homes where the preferred approach to child rearing meshes seamlessly with the practices and values of society's dominant institutions.

THE FRENETIC FAMILY

In the nineteenth century, families gathered around the hearth. Today, the center of the middle-class home is the calendar — the middle-class homes we visited typically had a large, white paper monthly calendar, hung on the wall above or next to the kitchen telephone. Scheduled, paid, and organized activities for children are noted (sometimes in a colored pen) in the two-inch-square open spaces beneath each day of the month. Month after month, children are busy participating in sports, music, scouts, and play groups. And, before and after going to work, their parents are busy getting them to and from these activities. At times, middle-class houses seem to be little more than holding places for the occupants during the brief periods when they are between activities.

The pattern we observed among middle-class families like the Tallingers of involving children in many organized activities and adjusting family life to accommodate those activities does not fit neatly into existing sociological approaches. Social scientists interested in determining the dominant factors shaping children's lives are often preoccupied with a hunt for single determinants — they hope to be able to point to, for example, the overriding importance of income *or* education. We looked diligently for key causal elements, but across the twelve families we observed closely, what we found was a pattern of practices or strategies attached in various ways to class cultures. Among the middle class, the hectic schedule of children's activities is not directly attributable to any single dimension of their lives, such as family income, parents' educational levels or occupational conditions, neighborhood type, family size or gender composition, or parents' leisure preferences. And, at least in the Tallingers' case, the family's emphasis on organized activities was not an effort on the parents' part to reproduce their own childhood experiences. Mr. Tallinger's mother was a single parent from the time he was four. As a boy, he played outside for long periods, often in "pick-up" games with other boys in the neighborhood. Ms. Tallinger, too, grew up in a single-parent family. As a child, she had long stretches of unstructured time, which did not give way to organized activities until she was older.

Moreover, neither the benefits nor the costs of the strategies I term *concerted cultivation* seem to be fully understood by parents. For example, the close fit between skills children learn in soccer games or at piano recitals and those they will eventually need in white-collar professional or technical positions goes unnoted. Similarly, that middle-class children have trouble adjusting to unstructured time and that they often find it difficult to forge deep, positive bonds with siblings are largely unrecognized costs of concerted cultivation. So too are the ways that one child's schedule dominates family time, particularly at the expense of the schedules of younger siblings. Of course, sometimes parents grumble over the hectic schedules. Parents also note that they did not place similar demands on their own parents. But middle-class parents take for granted their obligation to develop their children's talents through means including organized activities.

Perhaps there is little understanding of the ways in which the middle-class approach to child rearing intertwines with the dominant ideology of our society, making the idea that a middle-class childhood might not be the optimal approach literally unthinkable. But, as the next chapters explain, the approach to child rearing favored by working-class parents *does* have real advantages for children.

CHAPTER 4

A Child's Pace:
Tyrec Taylor

He would come running in because either he just remembered
he had [football] practice or . . . one of us went and found him
or sent word for him to come home. And [his friends] would all
come with him, running in. Then it was just hard for him to
stop playing with them, to say, well, I have to go to practice
now . . . I would have to say, "Come on, Tyrec, we're gonna be
late!" And he'd be saying, "OK, I'm coming," but he'd still be
out chatting. (Interview with Ms. Taylor)

For nine-year-old Tyrec Taylor, organized activities were an interruption.
In contrast to Garrett Tallinger, Tyrec centered his life on informal play
with a group of boys from his Black, working-class neighborhood. Aside
from going to school and to summer day camp, Tyrec took part in only
two organized activities: he went to Sunday school periodically throughout the year and to Vacation Bible School in the summer. In fourth grade,
he pleaded with his mother for permission to play on a community football team that he learned about through a friend. Eventually, Ms. Taylor
relented and agreed that he could join the team. Once committed, she
was determined to meet both the time and money demands posed by
Tyrec's activity. But, as the quote above suggests, Ms. Taylor found the
experience taxing and she "pray[ed] that we don't have to do it again."

In focusing on the organization of daily life in Tyrec Taylor's working-
class family, this chapter highlights some aspects of the child-rearing
strategy I have termed *the accomplishment of natural growth*. The limited economic resources available to working-class and poor families
make getting children fed, clothed, sheltered and transported time-consuming, arduous labor. Parents tend to direct their efforts toward keeping children safe, enforcing discipline, and, when they deem it necessary,

regulating their behavior in specific areas. Within these boundaries, working-class and poor children are allowed to grow and to thrive. They are given the flexibility to choose activities and playmates and to decide how active or inactive to be as they engage in these activities. Thus, whereas middle-class children often are treated as a project to be developed, working-class and poor children are given boundaries for their behavior and then allowed to grow.

The greater emphasis on kinship in working-class and poor families means that children spend much more time interacting with family members and providing important goods and services to kin than do their middle-class counterparts. Despite occasional quarrels, siblings offer each other more companionship and support than seemed common in the middle-class families we observed. The cultural logic of the accomplishment of natural growth grants children an autonomous world, apart from adults, in which they are free to try out new experiences and develop important social competencies. Tyrec and other working-class and poor children learn how to be members of informal peer groups. They learn how to manage their own time. They learn how to strategize. Children, especially boys, learn how to negotiate open conflict during play, including how to defend themselves physically. Boys are also given more latitude to play farther away from home than are girls.

These social competencies are as real as those acquired by middle-class children. The two sets of competencies are not the same, however; and they are not equally valued in the institutional worlds with which *all* children must come in contact (e.g., schools, health-care facilities, stores, workplaces). Unlike Garrett Tallinger, Tyrec Taylor and his peers do not have opportunities to start developing the kinds of skills that reap the greatest benefits in institutional settings. For example, children from working-class and poor families typically do not learn how to choose among conflicting organizational commitments, read trip itineraries, sign identification cards, travel out of state or work on an adult-led team with formal, established rules. Nor do they have the same experience as Garrett and his friends of thinking of themselves as entitled to receive customized attention from adults in institutional settings. In fact, working-class and poor children are regularly instructed to defer to adults.[1]

Along with these significant class differences between middle-class children, on the one hand, and working-class and poor children, on the other, there are some important differences between the lives of children in working-class families and those in poor families. Compared to poor children, working-class children have greater stability; their lives are less contingent, especially in terms of the availability of food, transportation, money for treats, and other economic resources. There are also differences by race and by gender. Although working-class and poor children pursue the same or similar activities and organized their daily lives in much the same way, they generally do so in racially segregated groups. This pattern held even among children who lived only a few blocks from one another and who went to the same school and were in the same class. And, as other studies have shown, we found gender a very powerful force in shaping the organization of daily life. Despite some active moments, girls are more sedentary, play closer to home, and have their physical bodies more actively scrutinized and shaped by others than do boys. Nevertheless, the greatest gulf we observed is one that has not been fully recognized in the existing literature: a class-rooted difference in the organization of daily life whereby middle and upper-middle-class children pursue a hectic schedule of adult-organized activities while working-class and poor children follow a more open-ended agenda that is not as heavily controlled by adults. Some important aspects of this difference can be seen in the way in which Tyrec Taylor's involvement in football reverberates through his family members' lives.

THE TAYLOR FAMILY

Tyrec Taylor; his mother, Celeste; thirteen-year-old sister, Anisha; and eighteen-year-old stepbrother, Malcolm, live in a rented four-bedroom house located near major bus lines in a small, stable, working-class Black neighborhood. Houses in the area sell for about $50,000. The neighborhood is "pretty quiet" according to Ms. Taylor, but she adds that "crime is everywhere, so I still have to be careful." All of the residents on the streets immediately surrounding the Taylors' house are African American, but a larger white neighborhood is within easy walking distance. When Tyrec and his friends have money for treats, they head for the white neighborhood to buy ice cream or drinks. Thus, for Tyrec, when compared to Black housing project residents, whites are a far more visible part of his life.

The Taylors' house has three stories, with narrow, steep stairs. All the bedrooms are on the upper floors; there is one bathroom, which has darkly colored, exotic-looking fans opened out and hung on the walls, next to gold butterflies. On the first floor, there is a living room, a dining area, and a kitchen. The kitchen is large with metal cabinets, florescent lights, and a low table for food preparation. The living room, which is always tidy, has a multicolored shag rug on the floor, a dark blue velour couch with printed flowers wound across it, a large television angled in a corner of the room, and a bookshelf that holds a wooden giraffe, a clock, and framed pictures of the children when they were babies. In the middle of the table sits a round glass bowl filled with decorative pebbles that hold up several large, bright pink cloth flowers. The entire effect is of a carefully decorated home. Ms. Taylor, however, complains that the house is decrepit and, indeed, there are signs that it needs repair: there are rips in the screen door and rough, unfinished wood showing on the doors inside the house.

Tyrec's parents live apart. Together fifteen years, and married for nine, they separated four years ago. Tyrec Senior lives in an apartment in the central city, about fifteen minutes away from his wife and children's house. Ms. Taylor does not like the area where he lives; she calls it a "ghetto." While virtually all Black, Mr. Taylor's working-class neighborhood has many thriving stores, small gardens, inhabited old houses, and families. Generally, the area is seen as more desirable than numerous poor Black neighborhoods in the city. Tyrec Senior, a thin, wiry man with a serious, intense air, talks to the children on the telephone most days of the week and usually sees them once a week. He once had a substance abuse problem; he is proud of the fact that it is no longer an issue. He dropped out of school when he was young, and reading seems difficult for him. He has opinions on many issues, including the state of the world, which he offers freely to anyone who will listen. When the children protest that they cannot do something, he insists that they can. He also weighs in on decisions related to the children; for example, citing safety issues, he objected to Tyrec playing football (his opinion was overridden). He is currently unemployed; in the past, he has worked in social services, including in counseling for drug-related issues.

Ms. Taylor is a high school graduate; she works as a secretary. She is responsible for managing the company's fleet of cars, and she answers the phone when the regular operator takes her lunch break. She is a woman of medium height with springy, corkscrew curls that cascade around her face. She smiles often and often seems harried. Although she is only slightly overweight, she worries about her figure. When I remark that she is wearing a "cute outfit," she responds, "Oh, thanks, but I'm too fat. I can't fit into anything cute." The field-worker described Ms. Taylor this way:

At about 6:45 Celeste walks in. She is a slightly overweight woman with . . . a cute face. She smiles often. Later, in the dining room, where we sit at the dining room table, she often looks into a wall mirror hung near the table as she is talking (occasionally touching her hair). There are remnants of red lipstick on her lips, her nails are painted (bright) red, and she wears large earrings hidden by her hair and a thick silver bracelet. She comes in with a whoosh; she seems harried but glad to be home.

When her car is running, Ms. Taylor drives to work; when it is not (which is often), she takes the bus. Her job does include health insurance, but the annual salary for her position (approximately $20,000) is hard to stretch far enough to cover all the family's needs. Paying the monthly rent of $650, going out for fast food (often weekly), and having dinner in a restaurant such as "Sizzler" (once a month) leaves little for expenses such as fixing the car. The family usually takes a one-week vacation at the beach, but Ms. Taylor plans for this in advance and does overtime to cover the costs (which she does not normally do). In the Taylor family, there are frequent conversations about money. The children's lives are constrained by the shortage of funds. Mr. Taylor buys clothes for Tyrec and his sister, Anisha (in the last year, for example, he bought four pairs of sneakers, at $70 each, for them), but he does not pay child support. Although Tyrec would like many video games, his mother says, "I can't afford them." He only gets them as "big gifts" for a birthday, usually from a grandmother. On the other hand, Ms. Taylor is willing to absorb the $50 football registration fee and the cost of spikes and a protective cup and strap for Tyrec. She feels that on balance "it didn't cost a lot of money" for her son to be involved in this organized activity. She is struck, instead, by the fact that "it cost more of your time than anything."

Tyrec's sister, Anisha, is thirteen. While Ms. Taylor is away at work, Anisha frequently "mothers" her younger brother, for example, by reminding Tyrec to pick up his dishes. She enjoys socializing, and during the summer especially, she looks forward to spending at least part of each day hanging out with friends who live in the neighborhood. Eighteen-year-old Malcolm is in the process of graduating from high school and is also working full time. He is not certain of what he will do next; he might take some community college classes in the fall.

Tyrec is almost ten; he is a small, thin, sprite of a boy. He looks like his father. He is a solid student at Lower Richmond elementary school, getting mostly Bs and Cs and completing his homework regularly. He is compliant at school, but on his own turf, he can be very assertive with peers. As one field-worker noted:

Tyrec's peers are really important to him. He's much funnier, cooler (no whining) around his friends [than he is at home, when his mother is present]. With his peers he gets to have intimate conversations, games, forays around the neighborhood, [and] a context in which to develop a sense of autonomy.

Even in front of adults, including his mother, Tyrec is assertive sometimes. For example, in Burger King one Sunday afternoon, he puts his white Frisbee and his large drink (which he has not finished) on an empty table. An old white man in threadbare clothes comes in and heads directly for Tyrec's table. When Tyrec calls out, "HEY! That's mine," the man changes his course, veering away from the table. Ms. Taylor giggles; Anisha and I laugh as well.

Ms. Taylor has an assortment of rules to guide her children's behavior in and out of the home. Many of her expectations she articulates explicitly. She places a premium on respect for adults. All adults, whether they are related to Tyrec or not, receive automatic respect and deference from the children. They append a "Miss" to virtually all adult female names, for example, Miss Jo, with no prompting from their mother or any other adult, (something we observed other poor and working-class Black children do as well).[2] Ms. Taylor does not allow cursing. She expects Tyrec to come home when she sends for him. She sets boundaries on how far he may go from home, as well as what kinds of things he may do (e.g., walk to the public pool to swim, ride his bike, play ball in the street, since cars are infrequent) and things he may not do (e.g., go across town, come home hours later than expected, drink, use drugs). He must do his homework before he is allowed to go out and play. It is relatively common for Tyrec to go on short binges of misbehavior — repeatedly coming in late, for example. One evening he was banished from Vacation Bible School for his poor conduct. At home, when things are not going his way, he routinely demonstrates his feelings by looking annoyed, whining, or crying. Most of Ms. Taylor's disciplining consists of withdrawing privileges and restricting the children (Tyrec especially) to the house. At times, she turns a blind eye to Tyrec's violation of her rules (as when he was out in the street playing with friends when he was supposed to be home, on restriction). She remarks that she thinks Tyrec's periodic misbehavior is due to the fact that he has not had a beating recently. In her view, that kind of punishment can be helpful.

Ms. Taylor complains that Tyrec is often "hyper." But her affection for her son is visible and often demonstrated. Indeed, both parents regularly offer their son physical affection, rubbing his head or giving him a hug. For example, one evening Tyrec is watching a video (*The Game of Death*, with Bruce Lee), fast-forwarding the tape to the fight scenes.

At about 11:15, [Mr. Taylor] returns. Tyrec gets up, goes into kitchen where parents are. Mr. Taylor grabs his son and hugs him from behind, rocks him back and forth for about thirty seconds, says: "Are you watching that foolishness?" Tyrec: "It's not foolishness!" Mr. Taylor: "Yes, it is. You gettin' indoctrinated in there."

We observed this kind of aggressive edge to displays of affection between Black and white working-class fathers and sons.

Tyrec's parents, in another effort to save their marriage,[3] recently have started to "date." Although each separately wants the marriage to work, when they are together, they clash frequently. Routine aspects of family life are often hotly contested. One Sunday, after a Vacation Bible School program, the two square off briefly:

Ms. Taylor says, "Tyrec, ask Dad if he is going to take us out for lunch at McDonald's after the closing program." Mr. Taylor says (quietly, but angrily, looking her in the eye), "Don't set me up." Ms. Taylor stares at him (standing, looking down) and he repeats, "Don't set me up by telling them that." She doesn't say anything but walks off to the kitchen.

Mr. Taylor takes the family to Burger King, which is near his apartment. This choice prompts dissension, particularly from Ms. Taylor. She would have preferred going to eat in Millville, a shopping center located in a predominantly white area but frequented by a variety of racial groups:

[Ms. Taylor] says, "He had to come in the ghetto . . . [They have] dried up French fries . . . " [Mr. Taylor] says, "I don't like to go there. I am comfortable here; I like it here." [Ms. Taylor] again (speaking to the field-worker, who had driven in a separate car), "We wanted to go to Millville, but he wanted to come here."

This kind of verbal sparring and open conflict characterizes Mr. and Ms. Taylor's relationship. Although sometimes there are friendly exchanges as well as comfortable silences, laughter is rare and tension is common.

ORGANIZATION OF DAILY LIFE: FREE-FLOWING TIME

Working-class and poor families organize their time differently from middle-class families. Children's organized activities do not set the pace of life. Unlike the Tallingers, who consider a weekend quiet if they have only one or two events to go to, the Taylors are busy if they have one major event scheduled. Planned events of any kind are unusual for the Taylors, and the calendar is not the heart of the household. Children's out-of-school time is relatively unstructured and, unlike for Garrett Tallinger, separate from adults' worlds. When Tyrec and Anisha were young, Ms. Taylor's grandmother would come to the house and watch them until Ms. Taylor got home from work. Now they are allowed to stay at home together without an adult. They generally are free to set their own schedules and choose their own activities.

Sometimes, Tyrec simply hangs out at home. One July afternoon, for example, after he returns from day camp, he, his friend Clayton, and I pass the time lying around companionably on the living room floor.

Tyrec is on the floor on his back, watching cartoons (I am lying near Tyrec) . . . Clayton is on the couch, sprawled out; he is trying to convince Tyrec to go swimming [in the public pool, a few blocks away]. As he talks, Clayton is arching his fingers forward and back in sequence. He looks languid. They are talking in low voices. Clayton can't hear what Tyrec is saying. He slowly slides off the couch so that now he lies on his back on the floor in the small space between the couch and the coffee table. All three of us are lying on the floor with parts of our bodies jutting under the coffee table. (It all seems perfectly normal; no one makes jokes about it. We are just there.)

The amount of time allotted to any given activity varies. Television and video games are a major source of entertainment, but outdoor play can trump either of these. No advanced planning, no telephone calls, no consultations between mothers, no drop-offs or pickups — no particular effort at all — is required to launch an activity. For instance, one afternoon, Anisha and Tyrec walk out their front door to the curb of the small, narrow street their house faces. Anisha begins playing a game with a ball; she soon has company:

(Two boys from the neighborhood walk up.) Anisha is throwing the small ball against the side of the row house. Tyrec joins in the game with her. As they throw the ball against the wall, they say things they must do with the ball. It went something like this: Johnny Crow wanted to know. . . . (bounces ball against the wall), touch your knee (bounce), touch your toe (bounce), touch the ground (bounce), under the knee (bounce), turn around (bounce). Anisha and Tyrec played about four rounds.

Unexpected events produce hilarity:

At one point Anisha accidentally threw the ball and it bounced off of Tyrec's head. All the kids laughed; then Tyrec, who had the ball, went chasing after

Anisha. It was a close, fun moment — lots of laughter, eye contact, giggling, chasing.

Soon a different game evolves. Tyrec is on restriction. He is supposed to remain inside the house all day. So, when he thinks he has caught a glimpse of his mom returning home from work, he dashes inside. He reappears as soon as he realizes that it was a false alarm. The neighborhood children begin an informal game of baiting him:

The kids keep teasing Tyrec that his mom's coming — which sends him scurrying just inside the door, peering out of the screen door. This game is enacted about six times. Tyrec also chases Anisha around the street, trying to get the ball from her. A few times Anisha tells Tyrec that he'd better "get inside"; he ignores her. Then, at 6:50 [P.M.] Ken (a friend of Tyrec's) says, "There's your mom!" Tyrec scoots inside, then says, "Oh, man. You were serious this time."

Informal, impromptu outdoor play is common in Tyrec's neighborhood. A group of boys approximately his age, regularly numbering four or five but sometimes reaching as many as ten, play ball games together on the street, walk to the store to get treats, watch television at each other's homes, and generally hang out together.[4] One afternoon, the boys stand around on the street next to a parked car. Heads close together, Tyrec and his friends pursue interesting conversations:

The first topic is about weird finger tricks. Shawn tells a story about a girl who could bend her middle finger back to the back of her hand, then lock her pinky finger behind the middle finger . . . Somehow the conversation turns to health and babies. Ken tells the boys that "what you eat, what you feed them, is how they turn out. So, you want your babies healthy, you should feed them healthy." Tyrec: "I'll feed mine pizza." (laughter) Ken: "Nah, I'll feed mine healthy stuff like fruit . . . Shawn: "Carrots?" Ken says loudly, "No, FRUIT." Ken continues, "Even when your wife is pregnant, you got to feed her healthy." . . . Then they move on to talk about how health is related to sports . . . Next, they talk about how someone's sister is dating someone else . . . Soon after this exchange, Ken decides that he's going to the store. Shawn says he'll come. Shawn asks Tyrec if he is coming, too. Tyrec says that he needs to ask his mom first. He goes in; I follow.

Gender also played an important role in shaping Tyrec's activities with his friends. Compared to the girls in the study, he was more physically active and was given more latitude in the distance he could travel from home as well as how late he could be out with his friends. In addition, many of their activities had traditional masculine elements, showing speed, prowess, athletic ability, physical strength and courage. Sometimes they tested each other to see how hard and how far they could throw things and took turns trying to break something. Pretending to fight, chasing and threatening to fight, and actually fighting were common activities.

(Tyrec and Anisha have been eating blue ice-pops and watching television; when they finish their treats, they go outside.) There's a little boy, maybe six or seven, who immediately starts threatening Tyrec [saying], "I'm going to hit you! I'm going to beat you up!" Tyrec races around him, daring him to fight. Tyrec: "You first, man!" The boy prances around him, baiting Tyrec until he gets up the courage to hit Tyrec on the arm. Tyrec reacts, chasing him around in circles. The little boy laughs, enjoying the game. Tyrec looks a little less thrilled, but pretty enthusiastic about defending himself.

An ice cream truck selling treats comes down the street, interrupting the action briefly. When the truck leaves, the play resumes:

Tyrec picks up a stick, threatens to throw it. The boy laughs, races around until Tyrec does throw it in his direction. Anisha takes a break from talking to another girl to say, "Tyrec! Don't throw that!" Tyrec ignores her. The little boy picks up the thrown stick and comes after Tyrec. They run in ever widening circles.

Anisha now calls out to Tyrec to tell their mama that she is down the street with her friend. Tyrec hears her, but he doesn't answer.

An older boy, twelve, sitting on a neighbor's car, jokes with the little boy: "If you throw that stick again, I'm going to throw you over that fence" (gesturing). The little boy spits on Tyrec, who chases him, a little angered (he scowls, no laughing here) by this, until he catches up with him.

They have run down the street, so they are now near Anisha and her girl-friend, who have made it to the end of the block.

Tyrec spits hugely on the boy — the boy's shirt I later notice has a big blue stain from Tyrec's ice-pop mouth. Anisha notices this and turns around to yell at Tyrec, who has run away from the boy to the opposite end of the block. She says, in between his arguments with her, "Tyrec! Why you spittin'? That's disgusting! I'm going to tell mama when she gets home, you hear?"

As these examples make clear, unlike middle-class children, who tend to play only with children exactly their own age (organized activities are usually age-specific), Tyrec frequently plays with children of various ages. He is also comfortable joining older groups:

Tyrec disappeared around the corner . . . I walked to the corner and took a peek around. There were about nine people sitting on the steps and on a bench which was on the [sidewalk] pavement. Three of them appeared to be teenagers or [even] older.

Overall, daily life for working-class and poor children is slower paced, less pressured, and less structured than for their middle- and upper-middle-class counterparts. Because adults spend less time monitoring children's activities, there is less emphasis on performance and more latitude for children to pursue their own choices. Children have a separate world from adults. Of course, there are limits to Tyrec and his friends' autonomy. Parents impose rules to safeguard their children; and the timing of some events, such as errand running and meal times, is determined by adults. Visits to relatives also tend to be set by parents. As with most working-class and poor children, for Tyrec, contacts with kin — from large, extended family events on weekends to informal drop-ins on weekdays — are part of the fabric of daily life. His great-grandmother, several aunts, cousins, and both grandmothers live close by (three of his cousins live "around the corner, in the next block"). Two other cousins his age frequently stay overnight at Tyrec's house. He often helps his great-grandmother with household chores on the weekend; when she needs him, Tyrec is required to assist his great-grandmother *before* he begins playing with his friends.

The daily lives of working-class and poor children are not, of course, idyllic. The children we observed were aware of their families' often precarious financial position and of the constraints that lack of money imposes. They heard and repeated among themselves talk about the cost of things, the lack of money, and the need for more money.

SIBLINGS: SOMEONE TO COUNT ON

Tyrec's sister and to a lesser extent his older brother are an important part of his life. Although Anisha can be bossy at times, she and Tyrec are close companions. They help each other out, providing mutual support when, for example, their mother is in a bad mood. They spend time together both inside the house and outside. They often watch television together or play video games together. Sometimes they laugh out loud as they sit together in the living room watching television. Other times, they squabble:

Tyrec settles on the floor . . . [to] continue to watch "Cosby." Anisha comes back right at the end of the show, plunking down on the couch on the other end from me. Anisha says, "Tyrec, get this bowl off here. It's going to fall. Take it to the kitchen." Tyrec resists; he complains, I think, and doesn't get around to taking it. He starts to goof around with the pillows, throwing them up in the air above his head as he lies on his back and catches them. He does this for about a minute and a half before Anisha says, "Tyrec, stop. Throw them to me." Tyrec throws first one then the other at Anisha, who catches them and puts them on the couch neatly, with a disgusted "I'm-the-older-sister-I'm-tired-of-mothering-you" look. She says, "You're retarded!" Then they settle into watching the second episode of "Cosby."

Despite Anisha's frequent chastisements of Tyrec, their relationship is far more cordial than the acrimonious sibling relationships we observed in middle-class homes, both Black and white.

I HAD A DREAM: TRYING OUT FORMAL PLAY

Middle-class mothers often take the lead in proposing activities for their children. In working-class and poor families, enrollment in an organized activity is not likely to occur unless children specifically request it. In Tyrec's case, a passion for football led him to beg his mother to allow him to sign up for a team. She denied his repeated requests during third grade, citing many factors, including Mr. Taylor's concern about the boy's safety. As she listened to Tyrec's pleas one evening during the summer before fourth grade began, however, Ms. Taylor was impressed by the vividness of her son's longing:

He wanted to play last year, but we wouldn't let him. We thought he was too young and he was very upset . . . And then I think he went to one of the practices with someone around here, one of his friends, and he wanted to sign up. He told me that he wanted to play football, and I said, "No, I don't think so." He said he wants to play so bad that he dreams about it. He saw himself running across the football field with a football in his hand.

She relented.

Soon, though, Tyrec began having second thoughts. Attending football practice meant that he had to cut short after-school playtime with his neighborhood friends. Faced with these competing demands, it was the organized activity that he wanted to drop:

After he started, after maybe the third time, he wanted to quit . . . He was having the problem of not being able to play with his friends because he had to leave them to go to practice. And I just didn't let him—because he worked me over so good to get him signed up that I refused to let him not continue now. [Despite] all the frustration that went along with going, still, it was something that he started, so we were going to go ahead and get through it, and pray that we don't have to do it again.

As a single parent who worked full time and didn't get home until 6 P.M., Ms. Taylor found it difficult to meet the array of demands presented by Tyrec's involvement in football. She rearranged mealtimes, and she spent time getting him ready, time transporting him, and time watching him play:

He had football practice four nights a week in the beginning because school hadn't started back yet. It started in August . . . I would start calling [home] maybe at 4:00 from work. [I'd tell him] "Get your things together." [But] he was never ready . . . So I would come home and grab him and hurry up and find something to eat. [Sometimes] in the summer . . . we could eat afterwards.

Tyrec's mother also spent time fund-raising. She took a leadership role in selling cheesecakes, at ten dollars apiece, to co-workers, relatives, and neighbors. She sold more than twenty.

Although the pace of practices slowed in early September, football was still a demanding commitment. Games were on Saturday mornings at 8:30 or 9:00 A.M. Tyrec and his mother needed to get up at 7:00 in order to get to there on time. Often they would go out to eat after the game and would not get home until 3:00 or even 5:00 P.M. Frequent changes in the schedule, with practices ending early, games being shifted around, and other last minute changes further drained Ms. Taylor's energy. Before the season was even halfway over, she was exhausted:

By that time I was really tired. I mean, it had become a lot. When school started it went from four nights to two so that was a break right there. But that by the time it got cold — I mean they gave us a half hour because it started at 6:30, so you just — you come home and you eat and you run right out. After practice, we did homework.

Despite the difficulty involved, Tyrec's mother continued to show up to watch him play. She felt that it was important to be there for him.

I had to give him support that I was behind him; that's why I went. And I didn't want him to feel like I didn't care . . . I missed a few. I didn't feel bad about it, either, because I went to more than I missed. I usually was there.

Ms. Taylor believed that her son's involvement in football had been positive. She noted that Tyrec "loved it," and she stressed the way the sport helped develop her son's masculinity, especially his athletic skills.

Tyrec is all boy. His motor skills . . . He's very coordinated like that, so he can do anything like that . . . very well. He knew that he could do it, and I think he wanted to prove it to himself that he could do it. I think he just liked it. He had all the kids around here playing football every day (laughter) . . . right out here on the street.

When asked what she liked about Tyrec's involvement in football, she said that she thought the experience had given her son "a little bit of independence, and it showed that he had some [independence]." When pressed to explain what she meant by independence, Tyrec's mother elaborated:

That he's brave enough to go and meet people and, you know — and be on a team and blend in with the team. I was glad that he could do that. I think I would have had a hard time as a child. I wasn't that good at blending in.

Unlike middle-class parents, however, Ms. Taylor didn't see Tyrec's football experience as crucial to his overall development. "I don't know how it's helped him," was her reply to the question "Are there any ways that you think it has helped him in other aspects of his life . . . Even in little ways?" Ms. Taylor's first and most decisive point was that she could not think of any way that it helped him. When asked, "Were there any spillover effects that you didn't expect — in some other areas of his life?" she generated this answer:

Well, just the responsibility part, knowing that this is what I have to do and this is what I'm gonna do. They give him a routine of his very own: I have to do this and then I have to do my homework and then I have to eat, you know. So I thought that was good.

When the season ended, so too did Tyrec's participation.[5] He did not play on the team as a fifth-grader. Although Ms. Taylor seemed genuinely pleased that her son had enjoyed being on the football team, she saw no reason for him to repeat the experience. She loved Tyrec, cared for him, and wanted him to be happy. Since simply stepping out the front door and joining his neighborhood friends for informal play obviously gave Tyrec much pleasure, his mother felt that was preferable to having him involved in an activity that required extensive involvement on her part. For her, as with other working-class and poor mothers, being a good mother did not include an obligation to cultivate her children's various interests, particularly if doing so would require radically rearranging her own life.

LEARNING SKILLS FOR LIFE

Tyrec plays over and over with a relatively stable group of boys. Because the group functions without adult monitoring, he learns how to construct and sustain friendships on his own and how to organize and negotiate. By contrast, Garrett's playmates change frequently, forming and dispersing with each new season and each new organized activity. The

only constant is the presence of adults in each setting, ensuring that the
players all know the rules, if not one another's names.

Much of the informal play Tyrec and his friends engage in takes place
outdoors, at times and in places mainly of their own choosing. The boys
often play games they have devised themselves, complete with rules and
systems of enforcement. Thus, the organization of Tyrec's daily life provides him with opportunities to develop skills in peer mediation, conflict
management, personal responsibility and strategizing. The following
excerpts from field notes give a sense of this ongoing acquisition of social
competencies, which involves a game between Tyrec and a group of
friends, Shawn, Ken, Reggie, and Clayton:

The game was sort of like volleyball but much more complex. The players are
organized in a rough circle. They volley the ball to one another. Each player must
watch carefully to make sure that the person who volleyed the ball to them
jumped before hitting the ball. If you hit the ball but did not jump then you are
out. If you can cause a person to go out then you "gain a life."

They often dispute whether or not the person jumped:

"Naw, man, that ain't [it]. You did just like this." (Shawn jumps, but his feet
barely leave the ground.) "That ain't my point." Ken did not protest. He just
said, "Okay, play it over." Play resumes for another two minutes, then they argue
again.

When the disputes evolve into prolonged arguments, the boys typically
resort to some sort of informal conflict resolution. In this instance, they
walk up the block to find a friend to adjudicate:

Shawn suggested that they go ask Reggie. Reggie lives in the next block to Tyrec.
They put down the ball and walked to the end of Reggie's block and they yelled
to [people inside the house] . . . "Yo! Reggie–Reggie." "Come here." "Is Reggie
up there?" Reggie walks down . . . Each person tried to tell his story at the same
time. Reggie hollered, "Wait, one at a time. Ken, you first." Ken gave his version
of the story, then Tyrec gave his, and Shawn went last. It turns out Shawn was
correct. Ken was out. Ken did not protest. He accepted Reggie's ruling. He just
sat on the hood of a parked car and watched. Reggie and Clayton now join in the
fun.

With a new cast of players, the game resumes, interspersed with arguments, for another thirty minutes. Next, they set up a race, running to a
point three blocks away, a public building with a small plot of grass outside. There, they initiate a different game ("Scram Ball"); the boys' play
continues well into the hot summer night.

As they pursue their various activities, Tyrec and his friends frequently show genuine excitement and pleasure or, sometimes, agitation. Unlike middle-class children, working-class and poor children rarely complain of being "bored." We heard Tyrec whine about a variety of things (e.g., being restricted to inside play), but unlike middle-class children, we never heard him complain that he had nothing to do. Despite the lack of organized activities, he has no trouble filling up his schedule. He has ideas, plans, and activities to engage in with his friends. Unlike his middle-class counterparts, Tyrec needs no adult assistance to pursue the great majority of his plans. He doesn't need to pressure his mother to drive him to a friend's house or to organize a sleep-over or to take him to a store.

In sum, in the routines of his daily life, Tyrec learned important life skills not available to Garrett. He and his friends found numerous ways of entertaining themselves, showing creativity and independence. This experience was extremely valuable, but it was also distinctly different from the more bureaucratic experience of organized activities that dominated Garrett's life. Tyrec and his peers did not get training in the enactment of *organizational* rules. Nor, as I show later in the book, did working-class and poor children receive the training observed in middle-class homes in how to pressure an organization to be responsive to a child's individualized needs. In short, the leisure activities involved in concerted cultivation had the potential to offer more payoff in the world of institutions than did the spontaneous play involved in the accomplishment of natural growth.

Tyrec and his friends did not experience their leisure time as *lacking* any important component. In particular, they did not seem to either want or expect adult involvement in their play. Middle-class children, on the other hand, who are accustomed to their parents' and other adults' regular monitoring of their activities, often feel *entitled* to adult attention and intervention in their play. The next chapter helps make this class-related difference clear by looking at how playtime activities are approached in the white poor family of Katie Brindle.

Children's Play Is for Children: Katie Brindle

Katie told me excitedly on the phone, "I'm making a doll house! My Grandmom brought me some boxes and I am making a doll house!" When I got [to the apartment], I asked her about the doll house. She shrugged her shoulders and looked discouraged. She said, "I don't know how to make it."

Katie picks up the box off the Formica counter [in the kitchen] and carries it high in the air over to the living room and plops it down on the rug. She says, "Mom, will you help me?" CiCi says, "Nah." Katie is silent but disappointed.

In middle-class homes, adults treat children's activities seriously. A request for help is not likely to be waved aside. Since parents in these homes often are preoccupied with their children's lives, things that are important to children can easily become major events for their parents as well. This in turn increases the pressure on children to succeed (recall how Mr. Tallinger yells to "encourage" Garrett during a soccer game). Middle-class parents follow up on children's interests, often by enrolling them in organized activities, but also by watching impromptu skits or joining in backyard ball games or playing word games with their children after dinner. Parents usually enjoy this involvement, but they also see it as part of their *obligation* to their children. Parental involvement is a key component of the child-rearing strategy of concerted cultivation. As a result, middle-class children gain a sense of being *entitled* to have adults focus attention on minute details of their lives.

The working-class and poor children we observed, mainly nine- and ten-year-olds, were still young enough to enjoy the attention of their parents. Sometimes they would request adults to pay attention to them or to assist them with their activities. As this chapter shows, adults often (but not always) decline such requests. Generally, children accept these decisions silently, as Katie does with her dollhouse project. They do not pressure adults to cater to their wishes. A significant consequence of working-class and poor parents' view of their children's social lives as not particularly important and their children's acceptance of that perspective is that the children are not trained to see themselves as special and worthy of being catered to in daily life. Children appear to gain a sense of *constraint*, as opposed to entitlement, in their workings with the larger world.

A feeling of constraint is not the only outcome, however. When parents follow the child-rearing strategy of the accomplishment of natural growth, providing close supervision in custodial matters and granting children autonomy in leisure matters, the children appear to take real pleasure in their playtime. The lack of adult attention and involvement in their activities leaves children in working-class and poor homes free to concentrate on pleasing themselves. The children we studied tended to show more creativity, spontaneity, enjoyment, and initiative in their leisure pastimes than we saw among middle-class children at play in organized activities.

The fact that working-class and poor parents pay less attention to their children's playtime activities does *not* mean that these parents don't enjoy seeing their children have fun. But, as we saw with Tyrec Taylor, this pleasure does not necessarily prompt parents to feel that they *ought* to regularly provide their children with such experiences. Nor do working-class and poor parents seem to feel obligated to attend to or follow up on children's displays of creativity. In general, children's leisure activities are treated as pleasant but inconsequential and a separate world from those of adults. Of much greater importance are the many steps involved in getting children through the day: getting them up, showered, fed, dressed, bundled up in winter jackets, and out the door in time for school, and then at the end of the day, making sure that they get home safely, have dinner, complete their homework, and get to bed at a reasonable hour.

These tasks often take more time, are much more labor intensive and create more frustration for poor and working-class families than for their middle-class counterparts. Trying to make ends meet through public assistance requires repeated encounters with cumbersome bureaucracies. No access or only limited access to private transportation means that even routine tasks like grocery shopping may require waiting for buses; keeping appointments with health-care professionals can involve similarly complicated logistics. In addition, in settings where resources are chronically strained, little problems (e.g., broken washing machines, an unexpected delay in a cash reimbursement) can have serious, far-reaching consequences. Both poor and working-class children are aware of the constraints in their lives, but for poor children, the effects of inadequate resources are more immediate and overwhelming.

It is important to remember, though, that even where economic conditions are the same or nearly the same, individuals may respond differently. Moreover, regardless of their economic position, families (and individuals within families) differ in terms of various other limitations (and opportunities) they face. As C. Wright Mills noted, there is an interaction between social structure and biography.[1] The power of Mills's observation is confirmed by the story that unfolds in this chapter. The Brindle family faces problems—including sexual abuse, severe depression, and HIV infection—that are not class specific and that would be challenging for all individuals, regardless of the extent of their economic security. If, however, this family had had even moderate financial resources—if the social service agencies they relied on had been able to provide even the minimum level of support required to meet the family's basic needs—the range of choices open to them would have been greater and the consequences of those choices less potentially catastrophic. Put differently, a family's social structural location gives them a different pool of resources to address similar life problems, but, even within a similar social class location, there are some differences in the ways that people use the resources they have in hand.

THE BRINDLE FAMILY

Katie Brindle is a white nine-year-old who lives in a small three-bedroom apartment with her mother, CiCi, and her eighteen-month-old half brother Melvin (nicknamed "Melmel"). Katie's half sister, Jenna, who is eighteen, lives with the family off and on bringing Rodeo, a six-week-old pit bull puppy with her. The Brindles' apartment is located in a rundown building in an overwhelmingly white working-class neighborhood that is dominated by small houses. About five minutes away on foot from the residences are small stores, including an ice cream store, a twenty-four-hour convenience store, a hardware store, and a gas station. Katie attends Lower Richmond Elementary School, which is only a few blocks from her apartment building.[2] The nearest grocery store, however, is about a twenty-minute bus ride away.

The Brindles' apartment is not well maintained. The living room ceiling leaks; Ms. Brindle must periodically move the furniture to keep it out of the way of dripping water. The toilet runs constantly. The mustard-colored rag rug at the entrance to the unit has prominent dark stains on it. Roaches appear regularly; even during the day, they crawl up the walls. At night, when the bathroom light is turned on, roaches scatter, scurrying across the white tiles. These ever-present pests bother Ms. Brindle; she calls the apartment a "roach motel." The physical disrepair of the Brindles' unit is especially obvious because there are almost no decorations. All of the walls are bare; the kitchen counters are completely cleared off; the living room coffee table is empty. There seems to be no clutter of any kind in the apartment. Ms. Brindle insists that Katie not leave her belongings, such as her backpack or coat, lying around. Immediately upon arriving home, she is expected to put her things in their proper places. Every part of the apartment is always very tidy and clean. The smell of bleach often lingers in the air. The only noticeable decorative touch is in the kitchen. There, a frame of Ms. Brindle's General Education Degree (GED) certificate sits on the counter. She is very proud of having earned her GED. At Christmastime, the apartment takes on a slightly festive look, with a real Christmas tree (that Ms. Brindle scrimped to buy), a string of lights hung in the kitchen, and a decorative foil picture of Santa that covers the door.

Ms. Brindle is a gaunt thirty-seven-year-old who looks worn down. Although she has a history of alcohol and drug use, recently she has been sober and clean. She was briefly married at sixteen; she is single now. Each of her three living children has a different father, none of whom Ms. Brindle married. Her first child, "Penny" (with Jenna's father), was a victim of sudden infant death syndrome; although it has been nearly twenty years since Penny's death, her name often comes up in conversation. Jenna was born when Ms. Brindle was nineteen. Jenna's father has been inconsistently (and only peripherally) involved in his daughter's life. Currently, he lives more than a thousand miles away, in Florida. Katie's father is a man Ms. Brindle had only a brief relationship with. At first, he denied paternity; a blood test confirmed fatherhood. He pays the Department of Human Services child support to help offset the public assistance payment to the family. DHS passes along a small amount of this money to Ms. Brindle. Katie's father refuses to see or visit with his daughter. At times, after Ms. Brindle makes repeated phone calls to his parents' home, he sends gifts. Katie treasures the two videos he sent her as a Christmas present a few years earlier. The year of the study he did not send anything for the holidays or for Katie's birthday. The father of the youngest child, Melmel, is the most visible and active of the three men. He routinely takes his son for visits, often a few times per month. Ms. Brindle is not currently employed. The family survives on public assistance, food stamps, and a medical assistance card. In order to have money to buy the children Christmas presents, particularly a winter coat for Katie, and a doll, Ms. Brindle says she "[let] some bills go" until after the holidays.

Katie is a short, bouncy fourth-grader. Her very straight, thin hair is blonde shading into light brown; it's cut to just above her shoulders. She is solidly built, but, despite her worries, she is not fat; indeed, she is not even pudgy. Remarks about her body are common at home. Her mother, for example, comments ruefully to Jenna that Katie "has a butt that could kill." While Katie and her relatives sit around watching television, there is much talk about hair color, hair length, hairstyles, nails, manicures, outfits, and weight. These are matters that preoccupy Katie (as well as many other young girls). She likes to think of herself as being about fifteen. A picture taken on Christmas Day shows her trying to look alluring and coquettish in a fresh white, long-sleeved blouse; a black, shiny full skirt; white nylons; and canvas flats. Her hair is pulled up in a French twist (an elaborate hairstyle more typically seen on adult women) and she is wearing lipstick.

In some ways, Katie acts as maturely as she tries to look. For instance, when she comes home from school, she fixes herself a snack, such as a bowl of Campbell's tomato soup. Her actions look competent and routine as she opens the can, pours the soup into an aluminum pot, and heats it on the stove. She neither asks for nor receives any adult assistance. Around her peers, however, especially her cousin, Amy, who is about the same age, Katie seems more like the nine-year-old child she really is. Much like other children we observed, outside of the home — away from her mother — she is more energetic, louder, and bossier than she is at home. Every weekend, she and Amy play together for hours on end at their grandmother's house. Katie has a flair for the dramatic and seems to be a "natural" actress. She and Amy have great fun putting on skits of their own devising. Compared to Tyrec Taylor and other boys in the study, gender clearly influences aspects of her play. She is more restricted in movements. Katie plays with neighborhood children in the large parking lot of the Brindles' apartment building. There she rides her bike, plays tag, and visits with other children, but she does not wander several blocks from home in a group of boys as Tyrec and other boys we observed do. Much of her play is more sedentary than the active movements of boys, with a stress on femininity. In the house, she enjoys her Barbies (she has fifteen). With a neighborhood girl, she will have long periods of practicing the development of herself as a beauty object (something that was never observed with the boys in the study). Katie and her friend will practice dressing up the Barbies and playing with each other's hair. Katie also watches television and plays Nintendo. As a result of her own initiative, not her mother's, Katie participates in two organized activities: she sings in a choir that meets after school for an hour, once a week. On some Friday evenings, she takes a van with neighborhood children to a Christian youth program where they sing Christian songs, learn Bible stories, and play games.

Katie has had more than her share of problems, though, and she sometimes volunteers stories of feeling lonely and abandoned. Her mother confided (during the in-depth interview) that Katie had been sexually molested when she was in first grade.[3] Last year, when she was a third-grader, Katie missed quite a bit of school. She was hospitalized in a program in part due to her displays of self-destructive behavior.

Ms. Brindle's family—her mother, Tammy; and adult brothers, John and Ryan; and Amy—live nearby.[4] Ryan and Amy's mother are divorced; Amy lives with her mother during the week and stays with her father and grandmother on weekends. Katie can take the bus by herself to her "Grandmom's" house; it is a ten-minute ride up one street. She visits almost every weekend. Amy is usually there as well because weekends are when she sees her father (Ms. Brindle's brother Ryan). Although Ms. Brindle unabashedly describes her relatives as "dysfunctional," it is her extended family that provides the structure around which she and her children organize their lives. Grandmom baby-sits for Katie on weekends, and both she and Ryan sometimes provide Ms. Brindle and the children with transportation (the Brindles have no car). Katie's best friend is her cousin, Amy, and Ms. Brindle's best friend is her former sister-in-law Mary (once married to John, Ms. Brindle's schizophrenic older brother). Ms. Brindle and Mary talk daily and see each other often during the week. Mary's daughters, who are in their late teens, also come by the Brindles' apartment regularly.

The level of racial integration in Katie's world varies. The stores close to the apartment are staffed and used by whites, almost exclusively. Although there are a few African American families in the apartment building, the neighborhood is overwhelmingly white. The Brindle family benefits from the racial segregation that exists in city housing.[5] Rather than live in a public housing project, where all of the families are poor, owing to segregation, they have access to neighborhoods where nearly all the families are of the same racial group (in this case, white) but occupy different economic positions. Still, key aspects of Katie's life are racially integrated. For example, her classrooms are about one-half Black and one-half white. At recess, she occasionally plays with Black girls. A few of the children she plays with around her apartment complex are Black, and she occasionally lends her bike to them for brief periods of time. She has seen other Black adults in social settings, including an African American man her mother dated.

The lack of economic resources makes almost every aspect of daily life for the Brindles more complicated and stressful than it is for middle-class (or even working-class) families. Putting together a meal can be a challenge. Food stamps are issued every fourteen or nineteen days. The family often runs out of food before it is time to go pick up the next batch of stamps. Getting the stamps is an ordeal, requiring a long bus ride and an even longer wait at the disbursement office. The buses are slow and often late. In the summer, Ms. Brindle walks; it takes her about an hour. She tries to avoid having to bring Melmel on these trips, but he does accompany her on most of her other outings. She carries him to the bus stop and holds him on her lap during the long bus rides.

ROUTINE LABOR AT HOME: CARING FOR CHILDREN

In all of the families we visited, regardless of social class, parents were caregivers. It was parents, not children, who were responsible for making sure there was food in the house, that children were bathed, that they had clean clothes to wear, got dressed in clothes that matched, and went to bed in time to get enough sleep. Parents watched over their children when they were sick, signed them up for school and other activities, and took them to the dentist and the doctor. These routines, present in all families, were taxing for adults, even in middle-class families. Children, while often charming, can be difficult, too. Parents in all social classes struggled with children who dawdled, lost things, rejected food as unacceptable, did not do as they were asked, and, at times, resisted, subverted, and tested the limits of their parents' control.

In the Brindle family, all caregiving falls to Katie's mom. Ms. Brindle is an unusually well-organized person. She believes that papers, toys, clothing, and so on, should be put away neatly in their assigned places. Complete outfits hang on the hangers in Katie's closet. For example, on one hanger, sweatpants, a matching T-shirt, and sweater are grouped together. On other hangers there are similar arrangements of clothing. With each load of laundry, Ms. Brindle regroups and changes the outfits. She also prefers that Katie not leave things to the last moment, especially homework. She thinks it should be done soon after her daughter gets home from school. Katie sometimes resists, "forgetting" to do her schoolwork. Any work that has not been completed before bedtime must be done in the morning, before school, in the living room or dining room as there is no desk in her bedroom. As the field notes below show, this means less sleep and more work for both mother and daughter:

(Katie and CiCi are up before 7 A.M. Mom makes some hot chocolate for Katie.) Katie is on the love seat, sitting lengthwise . . . She is in her pink nightgown and her hair is disheveled. Her blue notebook is in her lap and she is looking at a list of words. Her pencil is in her mouth.

The homework is evidently to make contractions out of a list of spelling words and then to put them in alphabetical order. There are sixteen words . . . Around 7:10, Katie announces, "I've done ten and I have only six more on the list." Her Mom says, "That's a lot."

When Katie gets stuck on a problem, she turns to her mother for help. Unlike in middle-class homes, where parents typically help in stages, offering a series of prompts designed to get their children to figure out the correct answer, Katie's mother issues a straightforward directive. She tells Katie the specific numbers required to match the words she is having trouble with:

Katie . . . hands her mother the list and asks, "What do I do now?" Katie sits with one leg up and underneath her nightgown; the other leg is dangling over the edge of the couch . . . [CiCi] looks at the list and looks puzzled . . . Katie sits quietly and yawns a few times while she is waiting. Her mom is trying to figure it out. Then she hands the paper back to Katie and says, "Make that one ten and then ten eleven and eleven twelve and twelve thirteen." Katie erases the numbers.

For about twenty minutes, Katie works on her word list while her mother periodically reminds her to eat her breakfast and to get ready for school. Katie doesn't ignore her mother. She does as she is told, but at a snail's pace:

Her mom says that she should get a donut. Katie gets a donut and begins to slowly eat it . . . Her mother says, "You need to get dressed." She then asks, "What do you want to wear? You only have a few outfits here. Most are at

Grandma's." She continues, "Do you want to wear your pink sweatsuit?" Katie says, "No, it makes me look fat." Her mother replies, "You aren't fat." Katie doesn't answer.

Katie finishes the list but declares that now she has to copy it over. Ms. Brindle doesn't check over Katie's answers or make any further references to the word list. Since Katie makes no moves toward getting dressed, her mother again calmly reminds her that she needs to get ready for school. Then she tunes in "Good Morning America." Katie is soon watching the TV program rather than copying over her homework. Ms. Brindle doesn't object, as there are no rules in the family regarding TV for children.

Katie continues to yawn steadily. She puts the draft list of words on the rug on the floor and props the notebook up on her knees and slowly begins to write. She is moving lethargically. Her mom says, "I am going to buy a pencil sharpener. I am tired of sharpening a pencil with a knife." . . . Katie looks at the television and then down at her homework. It is slow progress, she seems to be dawdling . . . At 7:44, Katie says, "I'm done." She stretches, arching her body, and yawns. Her mom says, "You need to get dressed." Katie doesn't move. Her mom waits a minute . . . [and then] goes to the closet and pulls out two hangers of clothes . . . With a hanger in each hand, [she] says to Katie, "Do you want to wear this (holding up one hanger) or this (holding up the other hanger)?" Katie says, pointing, "This one."

Katie continues to watch "Good Morning America" intently. After another, more formal command from her mother, she pulls on her clothes, still watching TV. Her mother sits on the couch, smoking a cigarette. It's 8:00. Katie is dressed, but her hair still needs attention. This is Ms. Brindle's job. She brushes Katie's hair, and after a quick, whispered consultation with her daughter, pulls her hair up into a half ponytail, explaining, "She doesn't like her hair up, but I like it up."

It is almost time to go. Katie pulls herself away from the TV, looks around in the dining room area, and then goes to her bedroom for a few seconds. When she returns,

she stands directly in front of her mother (blocking her mother's view of the television) and asks, "Mom, where's my book bag?" Her mother looks frustrated. She furrows her eyebrows, sighs deeply, and raises her voice as she says, "That is the key word, your book bag."

Ms. Brindle joins the search. Standing at the open door to Katie's room, she points in, looking annoyed. Katie smiles, slips by her mother and retrieves her book bag from her room. At last, it is time to bundle up for the fifteen-degree weather outside, and then say farewell:

CiCi zips up [Katie's] coat but doesn't put on the hood. Katie doesn't have any mittens on her hands . . . CiCi stands and goes over to the door and opens it. Katie goes out first. Her mom leans over and kisses her on the lips, and says affectionately, "Good-bye, monster."

This sequence of steps took ninety minutes. It is a labor-intensive routine that Katie and her mother enact every single school day (with minor variations) and most weekends (with some modifications). This particular morning, Melmel stayed asleep, but often Ms. Brindle cares for him at the same time — changing his diaper, getting him dressed, giving him a bottle of milk or "Hi-C" juice and then carrying him around while she supervises Katie. Like other single parents with young children, Ms. Brindle's responsibilities are many and they are nonnegotiable; her children cannot manage without her daily assistance.

POOR FAMILIES: LOVE'S LABORS MULTIPLIED

All parents are faced with multiple, daily child-rearing tasks. But, in poor families, the difficulties involved in executing those tasks are much greater than in middle-class families *and* working-class ones. The additional burden created by poverty is not connected to the competence of individuals (although individuals do vary in their social skills). Rather, it is the result of the uneven distribution of structural resources. Unlike in Western European countries, where all families with dependent children get a monthly stipend, in the United States, financial stability is considered a matter of individual responsibility. Public assistance does not cover the minimum costs of raising children. Moreover, the social resources available to the poor are not simply insufficient; they are also bureaucratic, slow working and stigmatized.

Ms. Brindle is not currently employed, but she has held jobs in the past and seems proud of it (e.g., noting that she had worked at McDonald's, she adds, "I was good at it"). She hopes to return to work once Melmel starts school. In the meantime, the Brindles try to survive on public assistance. Twice a month, Ms. Brindle has to go in person to collect her food stamps and cash stipend. Usually, due to lack of child care, she takes Melmel with her. However, on this day his older sister Jenna watched him. Going to get food stamps is a chore she "hate[s]." The bus ride is long, the disbursement office is bleak, and, on days when food stamps are released, it is crowded with slow-moving lines of tired women (men are vastly outnumbered) towing young children. The lines form outside the building, before the office opens. The day we go, it takes fifteen minutes of inching forward before we even get inside. Once we have edged into the building, we join around seventy-five people who are waiting in another long line in a small, dusty and dirty room. There are no public restrooms; there are no drinking fountains. We wait another thirty minutes. The cashiers move slowly; they look bored and disinterested. At 9:05, we are done but exhausted by the wait.

While standing in line Ms. Brindle says, sounding anxious and a bit desperate, "I am out of everything. Milk, eggs, bread." We go to the grocery store immediately after we get the food stamps. Katie's mother buys four boxes of cereal, a loaf of white bread, a gallon of milk, bologna, American cheese, a dozen eggs, and a cake mix and frosting. It is Katie's birthday that day. The cake mix calls for vegetable oil. This is an unusual and added expense. Ms. Brindle looks stressed while she is staring at the glistening plastic bottles of yellow oil. She sighs deeply and says, "I wish food was free."[6]

We then head back home; the entire expedition having taken approximately two hours.

Under conditions where every dollar for food matters, unexpected losses present serious problems. One afternoon when Ms. Brindle returns to the apartment after getting her food stamps (she had gone by herself), she is upset. She thinks she has been shortchanged:

CiCi sat down at the dining room table. She sighed and took off her coat and put it on the chair next to her. She looked at Jenna and said, "I think they gypped me forty dollars. There were all these people in line shouting to hurry up and I tried to count it, but I couldn't concentrate." CiCi sounded sad.

She started counting each page in the first [food stamp] booklet and then the second booklet. . . . Katie made a noise — a humming noise (it wasn't loud) — while CiCi was counting. CiCi said in an angry tone, "Be quiet. That's what happened in line. I couldn't concentrate. Everyone was yelling." . . . CiCi looked at Jenna and said, "They're not supposed to do that. They gave me all these books with low numbers (dollar amounts). They're not supposed to do that. They're supposed to give me high numbers." Katie did not say anything after her mom yelled at her but remained quietly sitting on the couch.

Jenna, seeking to reassure her mother, says, "Don't worry. You don't have to feed me." Nine-year-old Katie is keenly aware of her family's limited resources. She rejects Jenna's logic, saying, "Well, it's still forty dollars."

Doing laundry, a tedious but straightforward chore in middle class homes, is cumbersome, expensive, and frustrating for Ms. Brindle. She finds it difficult to keep a sufficient supply of quarters available. Banks often refuse to sell rolled coins to noncustomers; she does not have a bank account (using money orders when necessary). The grocery store, which does provide quarters, is a twenty-minute bus ride away. Of much greater significance, however, is the fact that the three washers and two dryers at the apartment complex are routinely out of order:

CiCi says, "I wish I had a car to drive. I'm almost out of clothes." (She looks at her pile of dirty clothes next to the love seat.) I ask, "Is the washing machine broken?" She replies, "When I first went down, I was freakin' out. I went down and the water was coming out of the washers. Today the washers were still full of water. And I went to the ones up [at a nearby complex]. They were locked, so I think they're messed up too. . . . The heat isn't on [in the laundry room]. It's ridiculous . . . that's why the pipes broke. It's forty below and stuff."

For Katie, broken washing machines sometimes mean no school. In rare cases when she is completely out of clean clothes, she has to stay at home until the laundry can be done.

Having to rely on public transportation, particularly with young children, also makes life more difficult. Little things like handing the fare to the bus driver can be challenging if you are juggling a toddler, a diaper bag, and packages. Similarly, once on the bus, even seated it can be tiring to hold or watch over young children on long rides. Buses often are late, sometimes don't come, and always are much slower than traveling by car. Finally, taking public transportation can be hazardous. Mothers and children stand out in the heat in summer, in the cold in winter, and in rainstorms many months of the year. Buses travel along busy streets, so as they wait at bus stops, parents must watch children very closely to make certain that they keep away from oncoming traffic. Melmel likes buses; he seems to relish the sensation of movement. And Ms. Brindle sometimes uses bus rides as an opportunity for one-on-one time with her son. For example, while riding to a municipal court session (to contest her eviction notice), she smiles at Melmel and says warmly, "Melmel, I love you!"[7] A ride in a car is always preferable, if it can be arranged. In Ms. Brindle's case this is difficult because her brother's car is sometimes not running and even when it is, her schedule and his are hard to coordinate. The same is true for her mother's car. In addition, child car seats are required by law, but they are expensive, heavy, and difficult to move from car to car. When Melmel rides in his grandmother's car, which has no car seat, she keeps an eye out for the police. If she sees a police officer, she pushes her grandson down below the level of the car windows, trying to hide him from view. She says she feels "like a criminal." She can't afford to be caught: "The ticket is a thousand dollars!"

Much as with transportation, poor families have few choices about where they live. Thus, Katie's family makes do with roaches in their apartment, a poorly maintained building, snow and ice on the steps, chronically broken appliances, and leaky plumbing. So far, though, they have been "lucky" with their neighbors, meaning that no serious threats have materialized in this apartment building. Ms. Brindle's former sister-in-law and close friend, Mary, was not so fortunate. Drug dealers moved into the complex.

Despite its many problems, the Brindles' apartment at least provides the family with an autonomous, private living space. Midway into the observation period, however, even that was threatened. Ms. Brindle began falling behind in her rent payments. When she first moved into the apartment, she had expected to split the $600 monthly fee with Jenna. Jenna became sick and then was diagnosed as HIV positive. She could not contribute her share of the rent, and her mother could not afford it by herself. The waiting list for public housing is years long. Moving in with Katie's grandmother was a possibility, but only as a last resort. The house is already crowded: Ms. Brindle's brothers John (the schizophrenic) and Ryan live there. The Brindle family would have to live in the basement. In addition, the wood-burning stove and kerosene heaters Ms. Brindle's mother uses to heat her house would aggravate Jenna's allergies. But most important, Jenna and Grandmom do not get along. They have had many years of bitter conflicts, including a low point when Jenna was ten and her grandmother called her a "whore."

Stymied and unsure of what to do next, Ms. Brindle waited, first using up her last month's rent, and then hoping to move any day. But as the days dragged on, her landlord decided to begin eviction proceedings. On a cold day in February, Ms. Brindle, Melmel, and a field-worker go to municipal court. After waiting hours, they are finally called to the bench. During the brief interaction, the court official tells Ms. Brindle that she has thirty days to move out. The next week, however, she receives a "failure to appear" notice from the court. According to court records, Ms. Brindle had not appeared, and thus her landlord had the right to lock her out of the apartment immediately. Trying to contact the court is an exercise in frustration:

CiCi says, "I called that number that they gave me and they kept telling me I had to call back. I got tired of calling back. I asked who was I supposed to talk to. I got tired of calling back. Then I got this notice in the mail and I was mad."

In the meantime, Jenna decides to move to Florida to live with her father, and to avoid the cold northeastern winter. After she gets there, things do not work out as planned. Jenna's father proves to be less helpful than she had expected, other arrangements fall through, her health worsens, and she is briefly hospitalized. Frantic with worry, Ms. Brindle decides to move to Florida when Jenna asks her to come. To get money for a ticket, Ms. Brindle sells her living room and bedroom sets. But, the buyers of the bedroom furniture are late in bringing their payment. The delay is excruciating. Ms. Brindle worries that the deal will fall through, leaving her without the money she needs to finance the trip:

She says, "I need to get the bedroom set sold. It was supposed to be gone but because of the snow they couldn't come get it. They had the money, but who knows if they have the money now? I need the money to get the tickets and I am supposed to go down to pay for the tickets tomorrow. (Her voice is rising with anxiety.) I am waiting for a fifty-dollar check. That will give me enough for the tickets and then anything extra is money to go down there with."

Ms. Brindle is desperate to go to Florida. Having already lost one child, she is distraught beyond words by Jenna's illness. In the fall, when Jenna was first diagnosed, Ms. Brindle attempted suicide. Depressed and overwhelmed, she swallowed a large number of pills with alcohol (in the apartment, with the three children in other rooms). She was rushed to the hospital, had her stomach pumped, and survived. She is determined to take care of Jenna, but the logistics of getting to Florida overwhelm her. She toys with the possibility of leaving Katie behind until the end of the school year. She begins by suggesting that Katie stay with Grandmom until June, but Katie says, "No, I'll go." Later, Katie even more firmly rejects the idea of living with Aunt Mary while her mother is in Florida:

CiCi says, "You could stay here." A minute passes by and CiCi says, "You could stay with Mary."
    Mary who is walking toward the kitchen at this point says, "Eh-eh. If she stayed with me, I would hit her." Mary looks at Katie and says, "Your mom doesn't hit you cuz she's afraid she'll hurt you. But I would hit you so you stop acting like a brat."
    CiCi says under her breath, "That's right." Katie does not say anything.

Aunt Mary volunteers, "I would hit her like my father hit me," and then tells a story of how he beat her so badly she bled, but she altered her behavior thereafter.

Katie says to CiCi, "You did punch me in the face once." CiCi says, "I slapped your face. Don't exaggerate." Katie says, "I went to school with a black eye."

The afternoon wears on; most of the time, everyone is watching soap operas and *Oprah*. With her mother and aunt only a few feet away, Katie begins to hit herself. There is no mistaking that they have heard and seen her, but there is no reaction on their part:

Katie starts hitting her forehead with her fist. She is sitting on the bed and falls backwards as she beats her forehead. She is hitting with her right hand. She continues for about three minutes, which seems to me like a very long time.

Moreover, Melmel begins to mimic her:

Melmel climbs up on the bed between her and myself and imitates Katie. He does this for about a minute. CiCi and Mary watch without saying anything. Katie says to me, "That's why I was in the hospital." I ask, "Why?" She says, "For hurting myself." I ask, "What did they do to you?" She says, "They locked me up." I ask, "And then what did they do?" Katie says, "They taught me about self-esteem and told me not to hurt myself." I looked over once and CiCi and Mary were watching Oprah.

Clearly, Katie does not want to stay behind, either with her grandmother or her aunt. Knowing her daughter's flair for being dramatic, Ms. Brindle may think that Katie is deliberately exaggerating her feelings and thus ignores her. Perhaps, though, she simply cannot allow herself to acknowledge her youngest daughter's feelings, regardless of their validity. Ms. Brindle has a history of depression, and she seems to be haunted by the death of her first child. She feels she *must* go to Florida to help Jenna. Leaving Katie in someone else's care would simplify several aspects of the move. (When the move finally happened, Ms. Brindle took both Melmel and Katie with her.)

All of the families in the study — all families everywhere — face problems. Differences arise in terms of the specific kinds and amounts of difficulties, the ways in which individuals' temperaments shape their responses to the challenges they face, and the structural resources available to families. The Brindles had more numerous and deeper psychological problems than other poor families we visited. Many of the other challenges they faced, though, were common among poor families and arose from the same basic dilemma: insufficient resources for getting children through the day and meeting their needs. The sorts of difficulties we observed Ms. Brindle trying to cope with — going to get food stamps, finding working laundry machines, dealing with landlords and problematic neighbors, and sorting out errors on the part of powerful bureaucracies — are all *routine* problems for families below the poverty level.

These everyday sorts of dilemmas fit the definition of social structural problems: they are created by the way the social structural system is organized. Mixed into these social structural problems are the difficulties that arise from the individual biographies of family members. Thus, in observing real families as they move through their days, what we see are the outcomes of an ongoing *interaction* between structure and biography. Within the sample of working-class and poor families, the structural problems were the most oppressive ingredient in the structure-biography mixture. Insufficient resources shaped where families lived, what jobs parents held (or didn't hold), how individuals traveled from place to place, and how much and what kind of care parents could provide for young children.

In this context, it is not surprising to find that children's leisure activities are given a lower priority. As the next section shows, however, it is not simply the press of everyday life that prompts poor (and working-class) parents to remain relatively uninvolved in their children's play and not inclined to follow up on children's budding interests in music, art, drama, or sports by enrolling them in organized activities. The sense of an *obligation to cultivate* their children that is so apparent among middle-class parents is uncommon among their poor and working-class counterparts. Likewise, the sense of being *entitled* to adult attention that is so prevalent among middle-class children is absent in their poor and working-class peers.

LEAVING CHILD'S PLAY TO CHILDREN

Middle-class parents often are busy, even at home. They certainly do not always stop to watch every time one or more of their children is engaged in some sort of performance, be it playing the piano, putting on a skit, or doing a dance. Still, these parents appeared to feel an obligation to cultivate their children's talents. Often, they would meet that obligation by watching, evaluating, and encouraging their children's at-home performances.[8] At times, parents would also voluntarily participate in children's activities, playing board and word games with them, engaging in backyard sports and helping with projects.

Working-class and poor parents also sometimes join their children in play. For example, in the white working-class Yanelli family (see Chapter 11), Billy, the focal child, and his father would sit outside on the sidewalk in front of their house and play cards while Mr. Yanelli smoked a cigarette. In Katie's family, too, adults sometimes participate. Ms. Brindle periodically agrees to watch Katie and her cousin, Amy, perform little skits. Katie's mother also occasionally plays Monopoly with her.

Although in all the families we studied, adults seemed willing to take time occasionally to observe a child's activity or to join a child in a game, adults in working-class and poor families make relatively few interventions in children's leisure activities, especially compared to the level of involvement we observed in middle-class homes. Most working-class and poor parents did not consider children's activities as consequential or, more specifically, as something that *ought to* involve adult time or energy. In their view, children's activities are something they do with one another, not with adults. Therefore, there was a separation between adults' and children's worlds. When working-class and poor children ask for adult participation, their requests may be seen as unnecessary and possibly annoying as well:

Amy says out of the blue, "Katie is good at dying. She is good at dying and crying." Katie turns and tells us, "Shoot me." . . . Without affect or enthusiasm, Gmom (Grandmom) makes a play gun out of her fingers and aims at Katie's chest and says (in a monotone), "Bang." . . . Katie has backed up . . . [She] begins a slow, dramatic performance of dying, clutching her heart with both hands, then stretching both hands and arms completely outward [and then] leaning back and falling onto the day bed. She slowly slides off the day bed and onto the floor, and — as a final touch — lets her head drop and rest against her left shoulder. She lies still.

Amy is hopping up and down with excitement . . . I smile and say, "Great." Grandmom says nothing; she looks bored. Katie scrambles up and says, "Shoot me again." This time I shoot her with my right hand. She repeats the performance. Grandmom is [not paying attention to Katie at all but is] watching TV.

By the third time Katie asks to be shot, Grandmom looks quite annoyed, but she does not say anything. There is no fourth request because, in a move typical of young children playing informally, Katie and Amy suddenly shift gears. They retreat to the kitchen to plot a Christmas skit and then come out to the living room to perform. In middle-class homes, parents routinely praise their children's displays of creativity. At Grandmom's house, the skit is assiduously ignored by the adults:

Amy says to us, "I'm Santa and you (to Katie) are a spoiled brat." Amy puts on her hat and Katie puts on her hat, and Amy says, "Watch us! Watch us! I'm a Santa and you are a child. First you're a spoiled brat and then you aren't."

I am watching them, but no one else is watching. Grandmom is watching TV. (She's looking straight ahead; Amy's father is there, but he ignores the girls' performance; Uncle John is also present, sitting on the couch, seemingly oblivious to everything around him.)[9]

When the girls escalate their demands for attention, Grandmom complies, but with a notable lack of enthusiasm:

Katie pretends to be a child coming to Santa. Amy [Santa] sits in the chair and receives her . . . Grandmom is not paying attention but is watching "Roseanne" [on TV]. Amy — indignant — reaches over and turns off the television as she says, "Grandmom! You aren't watching!" Grandmom doesn't say anything but focuses her attention on Amy for a little bit.[10] Katie is standing next to her cousin. Katie makes little hops up and down. Amy repeats the drama: (holding up a bright red, furry Christmas stocking) she says, "This elf has a stocking with rocks in it because he has been given coal." (She takes the rocks out and pours them from hand to hand.) Amy and Katie abruptly leave and go into [the next] room and huddle together. Grandmom does not seem at all interested in the skit.

The girls come back to the living room. In a louder, stage projection, voice they announce, "This is the first part." Wearing Christmas stockings on their heads, they perform a short skit where Katie explains that she is "an orphan. (pause) My parents are deceased." The orphan comes, beseechingly, to see Santa (Amy). Just as the skit is beginning to gather momentum, Amy's father comes into the room.

[Ryan] does not look up to see what the girls are doing. Instead, he pulls out an older upright vacuum cleaner. He plugs it in and . . . begins to vacuum up the tinsel, which is underneath the girls' feet and underneath the tree. Without looking up, he vacuums steadily . . . Amy is forced to move up the stairs to get out of the way of her father. She and Katie do not acknowledge this interruption.

Turning to the audience (which at this point consists only of me), Amy announces firmly, "That is the end of part one." I smile and say, "Good job!" The girls regroup, plot out part two, come into the living room, and present that installment. Again, their grandmother offers the girls only the slightest acknowledgment, and Ryan continues to completely ignore his niece and daughter.

The vacuuming has gotten noisier; Ryan says, "This don't sound right." Ryan pulls the vacuum back, and in the entryway (exactly where the girls are performing), he lays the vacuum down and exposes the bottom of the machine. Ryan crouches down to look at the machine; Grandmom, ignoring the girls, gets on her knees to inspect.

The girls bow together and retreat to plot the third part. I join the investigation of the vacuum cleaner. The brush is matted with tinsel that has become tightly wound around the roller. Grandmom and I work together to extract the tinsel. Meanwhile, the girls have finished preparing part three. They come back. They stand right next to Grandmom and begin their skit. Since I am now down on the floor, involved with the vacuum cleaner, no one at all watches this phase of the play.

The girls do not pause or ask anyone to watch, but Amy announces in a loud stage voice, "Part Three." This time they do a little dance . . . They hop up and down and swing their legs back and forth and chatter about Santa and his elves and how they are coming for a visit.

Grandmom is looking annoyed. The girls are standing almost on top of her and their legs are close to her; they are singing in loud and enthusiastic voices. She grimaces but doesn't tell them to stop. She focuses more closely on the machine.[11]

Katie's activities are not always ignored. For example, her mother watches, smiling occasionally, as Katie presents an at-home reenactment of the school ceremony in which she received a perfect attendance award for a three-month period in the early fall. Ms. Brindle also approves of Katie's involvement in choir, a one-hour, after-school (no-fee) activity that Katie signed herself up for (and walks to and from school once a week to take part in). As she explains during the in-depth interview, Ms. Brindle thinks Katie's participation in the choir is a good idea for a couple of reasons:

It's just that it gives her something to do and to be with other kids and that makes her feel better, to do that, instead of being home and being bored . . . It makes her happy, you know. It gives her something to do. I have no complaints.

She does more than provide verbal support. Ms. Brindle makes a special trip to the store and spends money that could have been used for many other purposes to purchase a special dark skirt that Katie wore at the choir's holiday performance.[12] What Ms. Brindle doesn't do that is routine for middle-class mothers is view her daughter's interest in singing as a signal to look for other ways to help her develop that interest into a formal talent. Similarly, Ms. Brindle does not discuss Katie's interest in drama or express regret that she cannot afford to cultivate her daughter's talent. Instead, she frames Katie's skills and interests as character traits — singing and acting are part of what makes Katie, Katie. She sees the shows her daughter puts on as "cute" and as a way for Katie "to get attention." She thinks that other people telling Katie that she is doing a good job might give her daughter more confidence, but she does not see developing Katie's incipient talents as part of her role as a mother.

There is no emphasis on providing materials Katie might use at home to further develop her creativity. Moreover, because children in poor neighborhoods have relatively few possessions, creating entertainment from makeshift sources is common. For instance, all of the makeshift costumes Katie and Amy so enjoy playing with remain stashed at Grandmom's; Katie has none at her apartment. While middle-class homes typically have a nearly inexhaustible supply of paper, crayons, markers, stickers, and assorted other craft supplies for children's use, the Brindle house has none, literally. The family does not own a ruler or marking pens. Paper of any kind is in short supply. When Katie fashions snowflakes from clean cardboard she found in a dumpster at the apartment complex, her mother accepts the one Katie has made for her, saying only, "Winter will be over soon." She offers no praise, no comment about Katie's resourcefulness or creativity. Ms. Brindle sees these various creative endeavors as Katie's projects, not hers. Thus, when Katie asks her to help build a dollhouse out of a cardboard box, she refuses, casually and without guilt.

Similarly, Ms. Brindle does not seem to think that Melmel needs any special assistance or toys. She appears to see little difference between Melmel's entertaining himself by pounding on the coffee table, rolling around on the floor, or poking Jenna's puppy versus playing with his "developmentally appropriate" toys, which except for special occasions, remain neatly stacked in a closet.

Certainly, the many burdens in Ms. Brindle's life contribute to her relative inattention to the details of Katie's leisure pursuits. The economic burdens are formidable and are compounded by her daughter's health problems. But, large as those problems are, they probably account only in part for the approach Ms. Brindle takes. Even if she had less on her mind, Katie's mother probably would not substantially change how she views her daughter's talents or alter her response to Katie's bids for adult attention. She tries hard to meet her children's basic needs. She is willing to sell her belongings and move a thousand miles away in order to care for her oldest daughter. She enjoys seeing Katie having fun with her cousin, Amy, and Melmel swaying with the movement of the bus. But nurturing her children's creative development is not something she sees as her responsibility. In general, she believes that children's play is for children.

DISCUSSION

In our observations, simple life tasks were harder to accomplish for families that had the most limited economic resources, so poor mothers had more economic strain in their lives than did working-class mothers. In both social classes, children were keenly aware of their family's limited economic resources. Katie worried when it appeared that her mother had been shorted food stamps; she was cautious about asking for food at her Grandmom's house, even though she was hungry. In the Brindle family, it was routine for the refrigerator to be empty once or twice a month. Although both poor and working-class families faced formidable economic constraints, poor families were more overwhelmed. Among the poor families, some families, such as the Brindles, had many more life difficulties than did other poor families. Similarly, children such as Katie Brindle, with her history of sexual abuse, had faced many more life difficulties than had other children.[13] Thus, within broad social class categories, there is variation in the biographies of individuals.

When I began this study, I expected to find marked differences in child-rearing strategies between poor and working-class families. This was not the case. As with Tyrec Taylor, Katie Brindle's life is dominated by informal play, both with children she joins outdoors, in the parking lot of her apartment building, and with her cousin, Amy, at their Grandmom's house. In both working-class and poor families, parents seemed preoccupied by the amount of work involved in caring for children and by the effects of inadequate economic resources. In a somewhat different vein, the pleasures and obligations of rich and deep kinship ties also demanded adults' attention. These factors combined to make parents keenly aware of constraints, and also to set constraints in children's lives. Nevertheless, within those boundaries, children were allowed a great deal of latitude (especially in comparison to middle-class children). Parents appeared to believe that children would thrive naturally, without the benefit of special toys or lessons. These things might make children happy, but they were not, in these parents' view, critical for children's well-being. As a result, there was a separation between children's and adults' spheres.

There were advantages to this cultural logic of child rearing. For parents, there was less labor and a more leisurely pace than in middle-class homes. Children's activities did not control their parents' time. Weekday evenings and weekends were not spent rushing to and from children's events. Nor did parents have to spend scarce resources on enrolling children in activities. Children benefited too. They appeared to be more relaxed as well as more vibrant. They were not as tired. They did not seem staid or bored. When they were playing, they were fully engaged in the process; it seemed to be truly fun to them. In addition, since they were usually in control of their own play, children could shift to a new game when they felt like it — which was often. Children also were spared school-like experiences at home, with their parents relentlessly pushing their educational development, a pattern that we next see with Alexander Williams.

PART II

Language Use

WORDS ARE PART AND PARCEL of the human experience. Yet there are important variations in the social patterns of speech. Some researchers, notably Shirley Brice Heath, have found that parents differ in whether they treat young children (who cannot yet talk) as potential conversation partners. Some mothers interact with their infants as if they were engaged in a conversation: "There, there, doesn't that feel better now?" Pause. "Are you ready for your nap?" Pause. The young children are not capable of answering at this point in their lives, but as they become able to, they will come to view themselves as conversation partners for adults. In other families, however, Heath found that parents talked about children but did not behave as if infants and young children are viable conversation partners. Heath argues that these different strategies of sociolinguistic style have important implications for children's schooling.[1]

In this section, I show that the children in the families being studied were also taught to use language differently. Some families — notably the Black middle-class (albeit wealthy) family of Alexander Williams — use language as an end in and of itself. They enjoy words for their own sake, ascribing an intrinsic pleasure to them. They discuss alternate meanings of words. The parents use language as the key mechanism of discipline. This approach often leads to extensive negotiation, bargaining, and whining in the course of daily family life. But it also leads Alexander to acquire a large vocabulary and to be adroit at verbal interaction. For other families, and notably Harold McAllister's Black poor family, language is used in a more functional fashion. Family members are able to communicate their preferences very clearly, as when Harold firmly rejects the idea of a peach-colored towel when shopping with his father, but they use many fewer words to do so. Rather than extensive negotiation, these parents use directives and, when necessary, threats of physical punishment. One consequence of this is that the children we observed rarely, if ever, talked back to adults. Whining, which was pervasive in middle-class homes, was rare in working-class and poor ones. Still, since linguistic interaction often builds vocabulary and other important reading skills, there was an unequal educational benefit for children from the different approaches to language in the home. Working-class and poor children also gained less experience in negotiating with adults, skills that might be useful in institutional encounters in their future.

CHAPTER 6

Developing a Child: Alexander Williams

As we enter Park Lane, [Ms. Williams] says quietly to Alex, "Alexander, you should be thinking of questions you might want to ask the doctor. You can ask him anything you want. Don't be shy. You can ask anything." Alex thinks for a minute, then says: "I have some bumps under my arms from my deodorant." (Mom:) "Really? You mean from your new deodorant?" Alex: "Yes." [Ms. Williams:] "Well, you should ask the doctor."

In a quiet street in a largely Black, middle-class neighborhood in a major northeastern city stand large, old, stone houses with expansive porches and sweeping lawns. Alexander Williams lives in one such six-bedroom home. He is the only child of a middle-class African American couple. His parents, Christina Nile and Terry Williams, met when they were students at a small, predominantly white, religious college in the South. They had been married ten years before Alexander was born. Alexander's mother uses her maiden name, Christina Nile, at work, but she goes by Mrs. Williams at church. A tall woman with honey-colored skin, freckles, and long, black wavy hair, Ms. Williams is positive, bubbly, and energetic. She has a master's degree in liberal arts from an elite college and is a high-level manager in a major corporation. She has a corner office with a view, a personal secretary, and job responsibilities that include overseeing offices across the nation. She finds it hard to leave her office by six, since "that is when the West Coast is just getting warmed up." She knows she works fewer hours than she would if she didn't have Alexander. Although she tries to limit her travel to long days, she has an overnight trip at least once a month.

Alexander's father, Terry Williams, is a tall, thin man, who stands very straight and has a serious demeanor. During the week, he is usually dressed in a formal dark suit, with a crisply ironed white shirt and a conservative tie. During family car trips, or while waiting for Alexander's events to begin, he is often absorbed by the newspaper, but he will occasionally join in the conversation and make wry jokes. He often calls Alex "Handsome" and ruffles his son's hair affectionately. Mr. Williams earned his J.D. degree from a well-regarded private university. A trial lawyer in a small firm, Mr. Williams works long hours handling (primarily) medical malpractice cases. Preparing these cases keeps him busy from five in the morning until midnight for two weeks each month. The other two weeks, he works until around 6 P.M.

The family, as Mr. Williams says, does not lack "creature comforts." Together, Mr. and Ms. Williams earn more than $200,000 annually. They rarely discuss money with their son; we never heard either parent say something was "too expensive." Their large, comfortable home is worth $150,000 in 1995; they drive a new beige Lexus; they have computers and portable phones; their son attends a private school. The Williamses' home is immaculately kept and expensively furnished. In the formal dining room, a long wooden table and tall, straight-backed chairs rest on a thick Oriental rug. A matching buffet stands nearby. The formal living room is always neat though rarely used, except for piano practice. The family spends most of its time in the large kitchen. They also sometimes sit in an upstairs family room decorated in a "country" theme. There are blue-and-white checked wingback chairs and a love seat, wreaths, wooden cats, an armoire-style entertainment center, and paintings with African and African American themes. The room also has a television. Occasionally Mr. Williams watches a basketball game; sometimes, the family watches *The Cosby Show* or *Star Trek* together.

Alexander is a tall, thin boy — a smaller edition of his father — with a winsome smile and a charming manner. He is active and inquisitive. One Saturday afternoon, for example, while the adults talk, he twirls around the kitchen. He keeps his hands on his stomach and pushes out the shirt of his soccer uniform as he circles. On another occasion, after his mother drops him off at the house and continues on to park the car, Alex hops off the steps and jumps up in the air, trying to see through the windows of the house. He is also verbally playful, initiating jokes and bantering with his parents. His mother, who stresses the importance of children being "exposed" to various experiences, is pleased with Alexander's approach to life:

I would have to say that Alexander is a joy. He's a gift to me. He's [a] very energetic, very curious, loving, caring person, that, um . . . is outgoing and who, uh,
really loves to be with people and who loves to explore and loves to read and . . .
just do a lot of fun things.

Alex is enrolled in after-school care on the school grounds of his private school, located near his mother's work.[1] His mother, often accompanied by his father, picks him up at six in the evening. Alex is popular at
school, a boy who "gets along with everybody." He initiates play with
other children freely and easily. He is also busy in and outside of school.
There are weekday evenings, especially near the end of the school year,
when he does not get home until 9 P.M. In a typical week, Alexander
attends a piano lesson, university choir practice, Sunday school, church
choir, and baseball and soccer practice and/or games. He often has
rehearsals linked to school plays and to concerts. In the winter, he plays
basketball as well as indoor tennis. In the summer, he attends special
sports camps.

CONCERTED CULTIVATION

Alex's parents fully support his involvement in extracurricular activities.
Like other middle-class parents, they make accommodations in their own
schedules to meet their son's needs. The Williamses' child-rearing strategy
embraces the logic of concerted cultivation. They consider Alexander's
many commitments an essential component in his overall development. In
addition to the effects of concerted cultivation on the organization of
daily life, concerted cultivation also shapes the use of language. Indeed,
the extensive use of verbal negotiation is a pattern we observed in all of
the middle-class homes and is a special focus of this chapter. It is an
important part of middle-class parents' efforts to foster their children's talents and skills. In Alexander's home, as well as the homes of other middle-
class children, there is a steady stream of speech, interrupted by periods of
silence (as opposed to the pattern in working-class and poor homes, in
which periods of silence are punctuated by speech). Talking fosters the
development of children's knowledge and opinions. Middle-class children
learn to articulate their own views as when, for example, in the opening to
the chapter Ms. Williams encourages Alexander to prepare a question in
advance for the doctor. Reasoning is also the mainstay of discipline and
guidance in middle-class families. Finally, an emphasis on the use of reasoning in the home creates broad-spectrum benefits. Parent-child dia-
logues can boost children's vocabulary, preview or deepen knowledge of

subjects taught in school, and familiarize children with the patterns of verbal interaction that characterize the classroom and other dealings with adults in organizational settings.[2]

The benefits of this aspect of concerted cultivation go beyond academic enrichment, however. Schools expect children to know how to reason with one another; doctors prefer informed patients who take responsibility for their health.[3] Middle-class children, because they assume a position of mutuality or equality vis-à-vis adults, frequently pass judgment on the adults around them. Most of the middle-class parents we observed, including the Williamses, met such judgments with wry humor rather than anger. In general, the children of middle-class parents have a sense that they are special, that their opinions matter, and that adults should, as a matter of routine, adjust situations to meet children's wishes. Thus, one of the benefits of middle-class status appears to be the transmission of exceptional verbal skills that enable children to make special requests of adults in positions of power. This chapter provides examples of Alexander using his repertoire of reasoning skills with adults (his parents and his physician) to gain a customized advantage.[4] These same skills, however, also can make family life exhausting, as children of all ages repeatedly seek to reason with their parents. The very same skills parents encourage in their children can and do lead children to challenge, and even reject, parental authority.

Throughout all their daily negotiations, Ms. Williams is alert for teachable moments. For example, as I show below, although distracted, she still manages to squeeze in a short math lesson while looking for her husband's car. As a result, Alexander is learning to be adept with language. This ability to use language instrumentally, that is, to use vocabulary along with reasoning and negotiating skills to achieve specific ends, is an important class-based advantage. Middle-class children, including Alexander, practice their nascent language skills to "customize" certain situations, and in so doing receive benefits.

DEVELOPING ALEXANDER

Daily life in the Williams family owes much of its pace and rhythm to Alexander's schedule. Neither Alexander nor his parents consider his involvement in many different activities to be a problem. Mr. and Ms. Williams see their son's activities as a means of fostering his talents and skills. Alexander sees them as opportunities for fun and as ways to stave off boredom. He requests to be enrolled in certain activities and he initiates having friends come to the house to visit. Despite their number and variety, Alexander's commitments do not consume *all* of his free time. Still, as this section makes clear, his life is defined by a series of deadlines and schedules interwoven with a series of activities organized and controlled by adults, rather than by children.

Organization of Daily Life

Alexander has many activities, both during the week and on weekends. Saturday morning, for example, starts early, with Alexander's private piano lesson, a twenty-minute drive from the house.

[It's an] eight-fifteen class. But for me, it was a trade off. I am very adamant about Saturday morning TV. I don't know what it contributes. So . . . in my mind, it was . . . um . . . either stay at home and fight on a Saturday morning (laughs) or go do something constructive . . . Eight-fifteen gave us a way to get our day started and get some things done . . . Now Saturday mornings are pretty booked up. You know, the piano lesson, and then straight to choir for a couple of hours. So, he has a very full schedule.

Ms. Williams's vehement opposition to television is based on her view of what Alexander needs to grow and thrive. She objects to the passivity of television and to the fact that "most of the programs that come on Saturday morning really don't contribute anything to your intellect." She feels it is her obligation to help get her son out of the house to cultivate his talents.

Sometimes Alexander complains that "my mother signs me up for everything!" Generally, however, he likes his activities. He says that they make him feel "special" and that without them, life would be "boring." His sense of time is so thoroughly entwined with his activities that he feels disoriented when his schedule is not full. This sense of unease is clear in the following excerpt from a field note taken as the family is returning home from a back-to-school night. The following day Ms. Williams has to take a work-related day trip (a two-hour train ride each way) and will not be home until late at night. Alexander is grumpy because he does not have anything planned for the next day. He wants to have a friend over, but his mother rebuffs him. Whining, he wonders out loud what he will do. His mother, speaking tersely, says:

"You have piano and guitar. You'll have some free time. (pause) I think you'll survive for one night." Alexander does not respond but seems mad. It is quiet for the rest of the trip home.

Both of Alexander's parents believe his activities are important for his development. They view the benefits as wide ranging. In discussing Alexander's piano lessons, Mr. Williams notes that as a result of learning through the Suzuki method,[5] Alexander is already able to read music. He sees music training as beneficial:

I don't know baroque from classical — but he does. How can that not be a benefit in later life? I'm convinced that this rich experience will make him a better person, a better citizen, a better husband, a better father — certainly a better student.

Ms. Williams sees music as building her son's "confidence" and his "poise." In interviews and in conversation, she often stresses the notion of "exposure," making it clear that she sees it as her responsibility to broaden Alexander's worldview, like Louise and Don Tallinger seek to broaden Garrett's worldview. Ms. Williams considers childhood activities a learning ground for important life skills:

Sports provide great opportunities to learn how to be competitive. Learn how to accept defeat. Learn how to accept winning, in a gracious way. Also it gives him the opportunity to learn leadership skills and how to be a team player. Those . . . sports really provide a lot of really great opportunities.

Alexander's activities change regularly; as new seasons commence, some activities wind down and others start up. Since the schedules of sports practices and games are issued no sooner than the start of the new season, advance planning is rarely possible. The sheer number of activities means that inevitably some events will overlap. Some activities, though short-lived, are extremely time consuming. Alexander's school play, for example, requires attendance at three nights of rehearsals the week before the opening. Finally, time constraints also sometimes require that Alexander opt out of activities because his parents cannot adjust their work schedules sufficiently. For instance, Mr. Williams explained that Alex was a good enough soccer player to qualify for the traveling team, but they could not let him sign up because Mr. Williams could not leave work early enough to get Alexander to the out-of-town games.

Participation in organized sports provides middle-class children with more than an outlet for their energy or an opportunity to develop physical skills. Many of the soccer teams in the area where Alex lives, although comprised of third- and fourth-graders, are ability ranked. There are "A" teams, "B" teams, and all-star teams. Children's athletic skills are routinely and publicly assessed on two levels — their performance during any given game, and their presence on a particular team.

Like other middle-class children in the study, Alexander does not seem uncomfortable with the idea of public performance — whether it be playing soccer or playing Mozart. In fact, he seems to enjoy performing. According to a field note, after his solo at a musical production in front of more than two hundred people, he appeared "contained, pleased, aware of the attention he's receiving."

Social Connections

Both Mr. and Ms. Williams consider themselves to be very connected to their extended families. Ms. Williams is the daughter of a minister and a homemaker. She grew up in a medium-sized city in the South. All eight children in the family graduated from college. Ms. Williams says she feels close to her family, even though she lives far from them. She talks on the phone daily with her mother and visits her parents three to four times per year. On two of those visits, she takes Alexander with her to see his grandparents. Mr. Williams is the eldest of nine children; he grew up in a small town in the South. His mother, who worked as a domestic and later as a cook, is retired. His father and his stepfather (neither of whom is still living) had grammar school education and worked as laborers. Mr. Williams talks on the phone with his mother once a week and sees her twice a year. He sends her about $500 per month, and he also helps pay for the college education of one of his nieces.

Because Alexander has no cousins for hundreds of miles, interactions with cousins are not a normal part of his leisure time. Nor does he often play with children from his neighborhood. The occupants of the huge homes on his street are mainly couples without children. Most of Alexander's playmates are drawn from his classroom or from the organized leisure activities in which he participates. Since the great majority of his school activities, church life, soccer games, choir, piano, baseball games, and other commitments are organized by the age (and sometimes gender) of the participants, Alexander tends to interact almost exclusively with children his own age, usually boys.

Impact on Family Life

Alex's many activities keep his already-busy parents even busier. His mother typically moves through these demands in a gracious and sociable fashion. Mr. Williams, on the other hand, sometimes complains about the time consumed by his son's events. He usually brings a newspaper to read while he waits for a school performance to begin, reads in the backseat of the car (with Alexander in the front seat) on the way to events, and sometimes sorts his work mail during soccer practice. This divergence between the spouses, with mothers seeming more invested in children's activities than fathers, is typical of all of the parents we observed. Mothers are also generally more active than fathers in ancillary events such as the "parents group" for Alexander's church youth choir group, which draws only mothers.

Mr. Williams's long hours at work frequently leave him tired on the weekends. Rushing from scheduled event to scheduled event seems to weary him. One Sunday, as the family is hurrying from church to baseball to a school play, he reflects on the irony of all this coming and going on what is supposed to be a day off: "Leisurely Sunday afternoon schedule, huh?"

Besides sometimes being exhausting, Alexander's activities also create tension between his parents over the division of labor in the family. Each commented on this in separate interviews. Mr. Williams feels that he shares equally (a fifty–fifty split) in labor related to caring for Alexander. His wife reports sixty–forty for physical labor and eighty-five–fifteen for mental labor. Mr. Williams does not believe Alexander's activities have had any consequences for his wife's career. She disagrees. Ms. Williams says she consciously chose to make her son her "priority." Although adamant about the rewards she reaps from this decision, she reports, reluctantly, that her choice has required her to "make sacrifices" in her career. In addition, Mr. and Ms. Williams disagree, at times, about how much the family social space should be dominated by Alexander's preferences. For example, one July afternoon, the family sets out on a round of errands. They need to get Alexander's hair cut, put gas in the car, go to the grocery store for weekly shopping, and pick up Chinese food for dinner. Alexander has a tape (entitled "Trout Fishing in America") with songs he enjoys. In one, "Boiled Okra and Spinach," the singer reports he'd rather eat "boogers." Alex sings along with the tape; Alex, his mother, and the field-worker all laugh as they listen to the lyrics. Mr. Williams does not join in the laughter, although at one point he does contribute to a discussion about the name of a song. Later, when he states clearly that he is tired of the tape and wants it turned off, his wife resists, advising him that it "grows on you." He retreats into reading and says nothing more.

Mr. and Ms. Williams also disagree periodically about Alexander's schedule. In his exit interview, Mr. Williams expressed discomfort with the fact that Alexander belonged to two choirs. He seemed to be concerned that being in two choirs might compromise his son's developing masculinity. Eventually, Alexander did drop out of one choir (and immediately enrolled in Friday night basketball). In general, Mr. Williams seems more tired and worn down than Ms. Williams. Compared to his wife, he seems to draw less pleasure from all aspects of Alexander's events. Still, both are enthusiastic about their son's exposure to a wide array of activities. Mr. and Ms. Williams are aware that they allocate a sizable portion of time to Alexander's activities. What they stress, however, is the time they *hold back*. They comment on the activities the family has chosen *not* to take on (such as traveling soccer). Indeed, Alexander's activities do involve fewer travel demands than those of other middle-class children in the study. Garrett Tallinger, for instance, routinely was driven ninety minutes (in each direction) for soccer games.

TALK, TALK, TALK: THE IMPORTANCE OF LANGUAGE USE IN MIDDLE-CLASS FAMILIES

As a family, the Williamses freely share laughter, language, and affection. Although we heard the parents speak sharply to Alexander, we never heard them yell at him nor saw them use physical punishment. Instead, we observed them repeatedly, systematically, and determinedly use verbal negotiation to guide Alex through the challenges in his life. As Basil Bernstein has noted, rather than using authority based on position (e.g., that of being a parent) middle-class parents prefer negotiating interactions with their children in a more personalistic fashion.[6] They use reasoning to bring about a desired action, and they often explain *why* they are asking children to do something.

More generally, the Williamses often appear to be engaged in conversations with Alexander that promote his reasoning and negotiating skills. An excerpt from field notes (describing a conversation between Alexander and his mother during a car ride home after summer camp) captures the kind of pointed questions Ms. Williams frequently asks her son.

As she drives, she asks Alex, "So, how was your day?" Alex: "Okay. We had hot dogs today, but they were burned! They were all black!" Christina: "Oh, great. You shouldn't have eaten any." Alex: "They weren't all black, only half were. The rest were regular." Christina: "Oh, okay. What was that game you were playing this morning? Alex: "It was [called] 'Whatcha doin?'" Christina: "How do you play?"

In this exchange, Ms. Williams is doing more than eliciting information from Alex. She is also giving him the opportunity to develop and practice verbal skills, including how to summarize, highlight important details, clarify, and amplify information.

Such expressions of interest in children's activities often lead to negotiations over small, home-based matters. For instance, during the same car ride, Alexander's mother tries to adjust the family dinner menu to suit her son's preferences. Not all middle-class mothers are as attentive to their children's needs as Ms. Williams is, and no mother is *always* interested in negotiating. But a general pattern of reasoning and accommodating is common. Similarly, although children in working-class and poor homes rarely volunteer food preferences or seek to determine what the entire family will eat for dinner, middle-class children do so frequently.

Sometimes, a form of democratic parenting seems to dominate the Williamses' home. For example, Mr. Williams was "outvoted," two to one, regarding the family's participation in the study. On another occasion, Mr. Williams suggests they take a vote regarding the most efficient route through a traffic jam. But, especially in matters of health and safety, Mr. and Ms. Williams tend to substitute directives in place of discussion or reasoning. On these occasions, they tell Alex what kind of action they expect him to take, as this field note illustrates:

Christina served Alex and put salad on everyone's plate. She and Alex debated over the green beans. Alex: "Mom, I do not want any of those. They are nasty!" Christina, in a sharp and annoyed tone: "I am not going to give you much, Alexander, but you are going to eat them." Terry was fixing his own plate. He did not look at them. Alex replied in a whiny voice, "Well, just give me four. They are nasty." Christina did not reply. She placed six string beans on his plate.

For Mr. Williams, actions related to playing sports competently seem to carry the same weight as health and safety. Thus, at a winter basketball game, he shouts to Alexander repeatedly:

"Alexander stick to your man." "Put your hands up, Alex!" "Shoot the ball! Just don't stand there!" "Alex, get open!" Alexander is a mediocre ball player. He looked at his father as he yelled/talked at him. He appeared to become more nervous and uncoordinated. Alex scored four points and blocked two shots. The final score was 34–8.[7]

While driving another boy home after the game, Mr. Williams delivers a lecture:

He periodically glanced in the rearview mirror as he spoke. "Denny, you and Alexander have to start taking more shots. I don't know how many times that you guys got the ball down to the basket, just to give the ball away. It was as if all of you were scared to shoot."

Alex jumps into the conversation and attempts to assert his own view. His father is dismissive:

Alex interrupted boastfully, "I made two baskets." Terry replied, "And you could have had a lot more if you would have shot the ball every time that you were open." Alex looked disappointed. He sat all the way back in his seat. Terry continued, "Back in my day, we had the opposite problem: All of the guys wanted to be the superstars and you could not stop them from shooting the ball. You guys are scared to shoot the ball."

In marked contrast to working-class and poor parents, however, even when the Williamses issue directives, they often include explanations for their orders. Here, Ms. Williams is reminding her son to pay attention to his teacher:

I want you to play close attention to Mrs. Scott when you are developing your film. Those chemicals are very dangerous. Don't play around in the classroom. You could get that stuff in someone's eye. And if you swallow it, you could die.

Alex chooses to ignore the directive in favor of instructing his misinformed mother:

Alex corrects her, "Mrs. Scott told us that we wouldn't die if we swallowed it. But we would get very sick and would have to get our stomach pumped." Christina does not follow the argument any further. She simply reiterates that he should be careful.

Possibly because the issue is safety, Ms. Williams does not encourage Alex to elaborate here, as she would be likely to do if the topic were less charged. Instead, she restates her directive and thus underscores her expectation that Alex will do as she asks.

On another occasion, when the Williamses' views conflict, each volunteers a reason for the (opposing) directive:

Terry looked toward Alex and asked, while smiling, "How are you going to beat up Fritz if you don't eat your vegetables?" Alex shook his head as he picked up a string bean with his fork, "I am not going to fight him!" Terry, smirking: "Are you going to let him bully you like he does the other kids?" Alex, alternating stares between his father and his plate: "I'll fight him if I have no other choice, but I'll tell one of the teachers so he can get suspended."

Christina, looking at Alex and smiling: "That's right, baby. You do not have to fight. There are better ways to resolve conflict. Go and tell the teacher if anyone is harassing you."

Terry looked at Alex and said firmly, "There are going to be times when you are not going to be able to run, and you are going to have to fight. You are going to have to take a stand and defend yourself."

Overall, the Williamses and other middle-class parents use language frequently, pleasurably, and instrumentally. Their children do likewise. For example, one January evening, Alexander is stumped by a home-work assignment to write five riddles. He sits at the dinner table in the kitchen with his mother and a field-worker. Mr. Williams is at the sink, washing the dinner dishes. He has his back to the group at the dinner table. Without turning around, he says to Alex, "Why don't you go upstairs to the third floor and get one of those books and see if there is a riddle in there?"

Alex [says] smiling, "Yeah. That's a good idea! I'll go upstairs and copy one from out of the book." Terry turns around with a dish in hand, "That was a joke — not a valid suggestion. That is not an option." He smiled as he turned back around to the sink. Christina says, looking at Alex: "There is a word for that you know, plagiarism." Terry says (not turning around), "Someone can sue you for plagia-rizing. Did you know that?" Alex: "That's only if it is copyrighted." They all begin talking at once.[8]

Here we see Alex cheerfully (though gently) goading his father by pre-tending to misunderstand the verbal instruction to consult a book for help. Mr. Williams dutifully rises to the bait. Ms. Williams reshapes this moment of lightheartedness by introducing a new word into Alexander's vocabulary. Mr. Williams goes one step further by connecting the new word to a legal consequence. Alex upstages them both. He demonstrates that he is already familiar with the general idea of plagiarism and that he understands the concept of copyright, as well.

Williams family members also often casually interweave scientific terms or medical terms into their daily conversations. When a field-worker accompanying Alex to the soccer field comments on the boy's deep cough, Alex nonchalantly remarks, "I'm allergic to grass," and then adds, "Yeah. And leaf mold," thereby using a specialized term. The parents also see it to be important to develop their son's nascent political awareness. The African American Baptist church they attend each Sunday includes ser-mons on social and political issues such as the national debt, welfare poli-cies, and poverty programs. They also discuss political issues at home with him over the dinner table, including events in the national news, such as destructive fires set in African American churches in the South.

Finally, we observed Alex and his parents, as well as other middle-class families, using reasoning and negotiation to achieve specific ends. For example, rather than order or direct children, middle-class parents would offer children "choices" for decisions. But then, these parents would unobtrusively guide their children toward the choice that they thought was preferable. In choosing fast food or in choosing a book for a summer reading list, for example, Ms. Williams would ask Alexander what he wanted, but then would suggest one or two options as the most appropriate. Often, when Alexander felt he was making his own decisions, he was in fact following his mother's suggestions.

Overall, a commitment to a strategy of concerted cultivation is sometimes physically and emotionally exhausting for parents, yet this does not seem to lessen the appeal of this approach to child rearing among the middle class. Making a deliberate and conscious effort to raise their son in a way they believe will allow him to maximize his potential as a human being is a top priority for Mr. and Ms. Williams. In this, they are like all the other middle-class parents in our study, including Garrett Tallinger's parents. As Black middle-class parents, however, they see themselves as having an additional, equally important obligation to prepare Alexander for the range of experiences he is likely to encounter growing up as a Black male in American society. We turn now to that aspect of their parenting.

THE ROLE OF RACE

Both Mr. and Ms. Williams are very concerned about the impact of race on Alexander. They monitor his experiences closely. Their actions are very similar to those of other African American middle-class parents in the study.[9] Mr. Williams explains how he and his wife orient their son:

What we try and do with Alexander is teach him that race unfortunately is the most important aspect of our national life. I mean, people look at other people and they see a color first. But that isn't going to define who he is . . . He will succeed, despite racism. And I think he lives his life that way. I mean, he is amazingly, refreshingly an individual. Uh, and he continues to be able to draw people to him . . . He just — he makes friends easily, and I'm happy for him.

Mr. and Ms. Williams are adamant, however, that race not be "an excuse" for failing to succeed in life:

We discuss how race impacts on my life as an attorney, and we discuss how race will impact on his life. The one teaching that he takes away from this is that he is never to use discrimination as an excuse for not doing his best.

Ms. Williams comments that racial issues help shape her decisions about Alex's activities. She monitors the racial composition of each activity before she enrolls her son:

We have been very careful not to put him in situations where he is the only Black child. We've been very careful about that. Not only is that not fair, but we've also been careful to make sure he mixed with a group . . . let's say of white kids whose parents . . . uh, I, never thought I'd be using this — but my dad used to say — are cultured. You know. They've been introduced to many different types of people and can accept that there are differences in people in a positive manner.

Note that Ms. Williams's concerns reflect two distinct goals. She does not want Alexander to be the only Black child in any given activity. In this regard, she seems quite successful. Across all the activities we observed — piano, soccer, guitar, choir, baseball, basketball, and the school play — Alexander was one of the few Black children, but he was never the only Black child. At school, his grade level is about 10 percent Black. His friends include both Black and white children. The Baptist church the family attends has an all-Black, middle-class membership. Ms. Williams's success in achieving her second goal, that the whites with whom her son interacts be "cultured," is more difficult to assess. This does not diminish its importance to her, however. During an interview, she related a story about a painful incident that had taken place several years earlier.

Alexander had attended the birthday party of a child the Williamses did not know well. The invitation was linked to his baby-sitter, Rose. From time to time, Alex would accompany Rose when she baby-sat for other families. A young boy in one of these families took a shine to Alex:

The kid was really attached to Alex . . . Alexander was invited to, I guess it must have been his second or third birthday party . . . we went, and, um . . . the uh, grandparent was there. . . . [During the party,] the grandparent kept saying, um, "That kid is pretty dark." (laughing) [He asked,] "Who is that kid?" Well, I didn't have to say anything because Rose took care of it. (laughing)

This event reinforced Ms. Williams's conviction that she "needed to be very careful" about monitoring the activities Alexander took part in:

We've never been, uh, parents who drop off their kid anywhere. We've always gone with him, and even now we go in . . . to school in the morning and check . . . You know, not every day but, you know, just go and check and see what's going on.

The Williamses are generally happy with their son's school experiences, but they objected to the racial balance at the beginning of the school year.[10] Mr. Williams reports:

For some reason, this year Alexander was the only Black kid in his class —
which was — which was very bad planning, because there were two fifth grades
and there were . . . five (laughs lightly) Black kids in the other fifth-grade classroom, one in this classroom. Utterly ridiculous. Something that I raised holy
hell about.

The Williamses are well positioned to take prompt action on Alex's
behalf because they are well informed. They may be pleased with the
school's emphasis on cultural diversity, but they continue to keep a
watchful eye on both the curriculum and their son's overall school experience. This monitoring is similar to what Ms. Williams's mother and
father did when she was a child. The elementary school in the mid-sized
town in the South where she grew up was all Black. Her parents' worries
centered on academic standards:

They came quite often. They were always there . . . They were very concerned
that we were not getting what we needed to get, in terms of education. We had
excellent teachers. I just remember that.

In ninth grade, when Ms. Williams entered an integrated school, her
parents' concerns shifted and escalated:

Then, when the schools were integrated, that was a bigger concern. They, they
had to come and check to make sure that, that we weren't being knifed or, you
know, hair pulled, you know, which happened quite a bit, you know. A lot of
mean things happened.

By contrast, in Alexander's life, overt racial incidents are unusual, as his
mother acknowledges:

Those situations have been few and far between. I mean I can count them on my
fingers. I remember . . . when Alexander was in first grade . . . first or second
grade . . . there was a little white kid at school who said to Alexander and
another little Black kid, "All you guys could be is garbage men when you grow
up." (She laughs.) . . . And Alexander's standing there saying, "Well, I don't
understand that 'cause my Dad's a lawyer." (laughter) So, it didn't even faze him
what the kid was really saying.

Despite Mr. and Ms. Williams's shared sensitivity to the importance of
racial issues, they do not always agree about the best way or proper time
to teach their son about cultural diversity. Mr. Williams seems mildly
frustrated by what he views as his wife's "protective" approach. He
prefers to talk about race overtly. He strives to "alert" his son, but he
does so in a more "superficial" way than he would like. Mr. and Ms.
Williams also appear to have different ideas about the possibility for

improvement and social change in race relations. Ms. Williams is the more hopeful of the two.

Ms. Williams seems less willing than others to "read" race into a situation.[11] As the incident described below shows, she handles a potentially humiliating experience in a small, family-owned hardware store calmly and with no visible signs of distress and in a different fashion than the field-worker, a young African American man, would have:

(The store is crowded; about a dozen people wait in line.) . . . Christina was stooped over the counter. Her checkbook was on the counter top and she had a pen in hand before the [older woman] clerk stopped her. "We no longer accept checks. Do you have a credit card?" There were people behind us in line and others steadily coming through the door. (I thought Christina was going to "go off." I certainly would have.)

Christina remained calm. . . . She looked the woman in the eye and spoke in a casual voice, "Yes, I do, but last time that I was here, I paid with a check." The woman also spoke casually, "Well, since it is holiday season, we are trying to limit the amount of checks that we accept."

The clearing of throats could be heard behind us. Christina did not pay any attention to it. "Mom," (Alex, shaking his head) "you can't. You promised that you would not use your credit card." Christina had put her checkbook away and was now digging in her wallet, retrieving a credit card. Alex: "Let's get Dad's." Christina looked at Alex, then smiled. She put her card back in the holder. Speaking to the salesperson, she said, "Can you hold the sled for me?" . . . When we approached the door, the woman behind the counter asked, "You'll be right back?" Christina pointed in the direction of the car as she said, "I'm just going to the car and get my husband's credit card." Christina smiled as she left. . . . (I was upset with Christina. This woman was patronizing her.)

Exiting, Ms. Williams and the field-worker discuss the possibility of racism without ever explicitly using the term:

We walked out of the store. I asked Christina, "What did you think that was about? Why didn't she take the check?" Christina, while looking across the street to where Terry was once parked, said nonchalantly, "I don't think it was like that. . . . I can understand why she did not want to accept a check. I have a friend [who told me that] someone had written fifteen thousand dollars' worth of bad money orders." Alex: "How much? Fifteen hundred dollars?" Christina, looking around for Terry, said, "Fifteen thousand. Ten times more than fifteen hundred."[12] (During this conversation, Mr. Williams pulls up in front of the store. Alex gets one of his father's credit cards and he, his mother, and the field-worker go back into the store and finish the transaction.)[13]

As the field-worker's comments make clear, others likely would have perceived the clerk's actions as a racially based insult.[14] Ms. Williams did not. Equally important, she offered an alternative explanation that distracted her son. Thus, Alex seemed to process the events in the hardware store as nothing more than a temporary delay in the purchase of the sled he wanted. As the next section shows, Ms. Williams brings the same careful attention to other aspects of her son's life as she devotes to the dynamics of race. Mr. Williams, too, takes an active, though less sustained, role in "developing Alexander."

EMERGING SIGNS OF ENTITLEMENT

In interactions with professionals, the Williamses, like some other middle-class parents in the study, seem relaxed and communicative. They want Alex to feel this way too, so they teach him how to be an informed, assertive client. On one hot summer afternoon, Ms. Williams uses a doctor visit as an opportunity for this kind of instruction. During the drive to the doctor's office, the field-worker listens as Ms. Williams prepares Alexander to be assertive during his regular checkup:

> As we enter Park Lane, [Christina] says quietly to Alex, "Alexander, you should be thinking of questions you might want to ask the doctor. You can ask him anything you want. Don't be shy. You can ask anything." Alex thinks for a minute, then says, "I have some bumps under my arms from my deodorant." Christina: "Really? You mean from your new deodorant?" Alex: "Yes." Christina: "Well, you should ask the doctor."

Alex's mother is teaching him that he has the right to speak up (e.g., "don't be shy"; "you can ask anything"). Most important, she is role modeling the idea that he should prepare for an encounter with a person in a position of authority by gathering his thoughts ahead of time. During the office visit, both mother and son have the opportunity to activate the class resources that were evident during the conversation in the car.

The doctor, a jovial white man in his late thirties or early forties, enters the examination room and announces that he will begin by going through "the routine questions." When he notes that Alexander is in the ninety-fifth percentile in height, Alex interrupts him.

ALEX: I'm in the what?

DOCTOR: It means that you're taller than more than ninety-five out of a hundred young men when they're, uh, ten years old.

ALEX: I'm not ten.

DOCTOR: Well, they graphed you at ten. You're — nine years and ten months. They — they usually take the closest year to get that graph.

The act of interrupting a person of authority is a display of entitlement. It is also indicative of middle-class child-rearing priorities: the incivility of interrupting a speaker is overlooked in favor of encouraging children's sense of their individual importance and of affirming their right to air their own thoughts and ideas to adults. The casualness with which Alexander corrects the doctor ("I'm not ten") is a further indication of this child's easy assumption of his rights. A final signal, in the form of a clear directive Alex issues to the doctor, comes later, after he has listened to the doctor provide instructions over the phone for the emergency treatment of a child just admitted with an eye wound. "Stay away from my eyelids!" Alex commands, only half jesting.

The value of a feeling of ease when interacting with a professional is underscored when the discussion shifts to Alexander's diet. Ms. Williams readily admits that they do not always follow nutritional guidelines:

DOCTOR: Do you get your fruits and vegetables too?

ALEX: Yeah.

CHRISTINA (high-pitched): Ooooo. . . .

DOCTOR: I see we have a second opinion. (laughter)

ALEX (voice rising): You give me bananas and all in my lunch every day. And I had cabbage for dinner last night.

DOCTOR: Do you get at least one or two fruits, one or two vegetables every day?

ALEX: Yeah.

DOCTOR: Marginally?

CHRISTINA: Ninety-eight percent of the time he eats pretty well.

DOCTOR: OK, I can live with that.

This honesty is a form of capital because it gives the doctor accurate (rather than vague, incomplete, or incorrect) information.[15] Class resources are again activated when Ms. Williams reveals that she "gave up" on a medication. The doctor pleasantly but clearly suggests that she should continue the medication longer. In steering Ms. Williams in a different direction, the doctor acknowledges her relative power by framing his answer as if he is "arguing for it," rather than plainly directing her to execute a medically necessary action. She, in turn, accepts his explanation of the drug's benefits and indicates a willingness to keep her son on the medication for the full recommended period.

Like his mother, Alex also engages in a pattern of conversational give and take with the doctor. And, like his mother, Alexander strives to customize his time with the doctor. When he offers his prepared-in-advance question about the bumps in his armpits, he gets the physician's undivided attention and an implicit acknowledgment that this condition is a valid subject and worthy of consideration in the exam:

DOCTOR: Well, now the most important question. Do you have any questions you want to ask me before I do your physical?

ALEX: Um . . . only one. I've been getting some bumps on my arms, right around here [indicates underarm].

DOCTOR: Underneath?

ALEX: Yeah.

DOCTOR: Okay, I'll have to take a look at those when I come in closer to do the checkup. And I'll see what they are and what I can do. Do they hurt or itch?

ALEX: No, they're just there.

DOCTOR: Okay, I'll take a look at those bumps for you.

At the end of the office visit, when the doctor turns to Alex's mother to ask, "Any questions or worries on your part?" Ms. Williams replies, "No . . . he seems to be coming along very nicely."[16] This statement succinctly captures her view of her son as a project that is progressing well. The exchange also underscores the relative equality of status between Ms. Williams and the doctor — the tone implies a conversation between peers (with the child as a legitimate participant), rather than a communication from a person in authority to persons in a subordinate position.

Throughout this office visit, Alex makes repeated use of his many language skills. And, in remembering to raise the question he prepared in advance, he gains the doctor's full attention and focuses it on an issue of his choosing. In so doing, he successfully shifts the balance of power away from the adults and toward himself. The transition goes smoothly. Alex is used to being treated with respect. He is seen as special and as a person worthy of adult attention and interest. These are key characteristics of the strategy of concerted cultivation. Alex is not "showing off" during his checkup. He is behaving much as he does with his parents — he reasons, negotiates, and jokes with equal ease. As the next section explains, there are certain disadvantages (at least for parents) attached to teaching children how to customize a situation. Middle-class children sometimes use their skills to customize their parents' disciplinary tactics.

DISCIPLINE THROUGH LANGUAGE

Middle-class children, we found, often use their verbal skills to argue with their parents. Rather than following parents' directives silently, as children in the working-class and poor homes generally do, middle-class children tend to bargain, using reasoning to secure small advantages. For instance, after a baseball game, the Williams family heads directly to a school performance in which Alex has a solo part. As they travel in the car, the family discusses foods that actors are cautioned against eating before a performance. Alex agrees to wait to eat his sandwich until after the play. When his mother tells him to stop snacking on potato chips, he secures an agreement to be permitted to eat a little more:

Alex gets out a bag of potato chips. Mr. Williams says, "Bet you can't eat just one." Alex takes a bite of one, then begins to twist-tie the bag closed, but changes his mind and opens the bag again. He eats about five more, then comments, "You're right. I can't eat only one." Ms. Williams says, "Okay, Alexander. That's enough. Put them away." Alex: "Just one more?" Ms. Williams: "Okay, one more." He eats one more chip, then closes the bag.

Alex frequently attempts to systematically refute his parents when he disagrees with something they say. Sometimes, he has the last word:

Alexander commented, looking out the window at a somewhat poor city neighborhood, that it used to be safer in the old days. His mother made a joke about the dangers of dinosaurs. Alexander, annoyed, said that dinosaurs and humans didn't live at the same time and pressed the point that it used to be safer. His mother made ambivalent sounds, and so Alex pressed the point more, insisting, "It was too safer in the old days, before they invented guns!" His mother conceded the point.

Middle-class children employ various tactics when they resist doing what their parents ask of them. Alexander's way of complying with a request his mother makes after he has finished opening his birthday presents in front of his friends is one example:

He opens the last present. He goes across the room and stands next to his mother. His mother prompts him, "What do you say?" Alex hollers to everyone in a very loud voice, "Thank you!" A tone of alienation and boredom (as in, "My-mother-is-making-me-do-this") is slightly detectable in his voice.

Occasionally, Alexander thwarts his parents by simply absenting himself:

His mother wraps both arms around his neck and chest and whispers in his ear, "Tell everyone thanks for coming to your birthday party." She releases him. But even though children and parents are starting to leave, Alexander goes upstairs.

A [Black] mother whispers in her son's ear and, with her hand physically resting on his shoulder, she steers him over to Ms. Williams. He says, looking her in the eye, in a flat but serious voice, "Thank you." The mother, behind him, is saying, "Thank you," too. Ms. Williams says, "Why, thank you for coming." She says, "Let me get Alexander." She goes into the hall and yells up the stairs in a loud voice, "ALEXANDER!" He does not arrive. She yells again, "ALEXANDER! COME SAY GOOD-BYE. PEOPLE ARE LEAVING." Still no Alexander coming down the stairs. She yells again, "ALEXANDER!" In the meantime, two sets of parents have left.

The birthday party involved six boys (two Black, one Asian, and three white) and one girl (white) playing video games during the afternoon at an arcade, a pizza dinner, and now cake, ice cream, and presents back at the house. It has run late. Parents have been hanging around waiting for it to be over, and after the last present is opened, it is rapidly coming to a close. In ninety seconds, six of the seven children leave with their parents. Alexander remains upstairs during many of the good-byes. Even so, when his mother yells to him, she is raising her voice only so that her son can hear her, not because she is exasperated or angry. Indeed, although we observed all of the other middle-class parents yell at their children in frustration from time to time, we did not observe similar outbursts in the Williams family. Nor did we ever hear either parent threaten to hit Alex. Rather, they relied exclusively on language as their mechanism of behavioral control.

In addition, issues that would have been sources of difficulty or discipline in other homes did not cause problems among the Williamses. In working-class and poor homes, for instance, the loss of a library book was treated as a major problem. At the end of the school year, Alexander lost a library book. Late at night (after returning home from a trip to the bookstore), Ms. Williams, the field-worker, and Alexander looked for the missing book. Alexander spent much of the search time turning around in circles and even sometimes jumping on his mother's back. Ms. Williams, saying, "I guess I'm buying that book," gave up the search after about five minutes. She did not scold Alexander. Similarly, signs of disrespect for adults that were cause for chastisement in other families often evoked laughter from Alexander's parents. The Williamses were fully committed to a strategy of concerted cultivation. They seemed delighted with Alexander's overall development and they were unperturbed when he periodically used the skills they taught him to challenge their authority. For them, the benefits of "developing" Alexander outweighed the costs. Across middle-class families generally, the balance between the advantages and disadvantages of an emphasis on language use can be precarious. In the next section, we look at some of the potential drawbacks.

COSTS AND BENEFITS

In a society in which children must attend school, and in which those schools privilege vocabulary, knowledge, and reasoning, middle-class children such as Alexander Williams accrue benefits, even forms of "capital" from the language training they receive in the course of daily life. When Ms. Williams directs her son's attention to a magazine article, for instance, he learns — and then shares — new information.

On the way to the basketball game, Christina pulled a copy of *Time* out of the seat pocket. She skimmed through the magazine and ended up on an article that theorized about the extinction of dinosaurs. She exclaimed, "Alexander — look! An article on dinosaurs. You [could] do your report on this." She passed him the article, and he began to read it. About ten minutes passed and Alex handed the article back. He initiated a conversation about how old the Earth was. He then began to talk about the fact that some dinosaurs are now believed to have been mammals.

Embedded in this kind of casual information gathering and sharing is an important additional dividend. As part of such exchanges, children discover that their own opinions are valued by others, that their ideas are considered interesting and important. Adults tend to listen with care to children as they share information.

Middle-class children also receive grammar instruction in out-of-school hours:

Christina asked him, "What did your teacher say about practice? You know you have not been practicing that much." Alex: "I know. He told me to practice all of this week. I sounded terrible. Me and Tom had practice together during our homework period." Christina then corrected Alex as she drove. She was not scolding him, but she was firm: "*Tom and I*, Alexander." Alex then repeated what she said, "Tom and I had practice together during our homework period."

The ability to marshal evidence to support a position is an important part of the repertoire of skills middle-class parents teach their children. As the son of a lawyer, Alexander is expected, particularly in conversations with his father, to supply evidence for his opinions, even on trivial matters, as during this ride home after church:

Alex and Terry were deeply engaged in a discussion about which of the X-Men (hulking, green-faced comic book characters) was the most powerful. Terry urged Alex to defend his position as he suggested one X-Man was more powerful than the other. Terry often asked, "What do you mean? What episode did that happen in? Where did you read that at?" The importance of structuring an argument and referring to written material is stressed. Alex [takes out and reads from] his *Secrets of the Marvel X-Men* book to prove to his Dad that Wolverine's claws were the only part of his body made of a "titanium alloy."

As he reads aloud from the book, Alexander's parents listen. Like conscientious classroom teachers, they note and comment on an error in pronunciation:

Christina said, "Go to the beginning and read it over again. I think you mispronounced a word." Alex reread it and again mispronounced the word. Christina: "That word is pronounced lead [as in leader]." Terry: "That is a trick word. You have to look at the context to see how the word is pronounced."

On another occasion, one in which the stakes again are very low, Mr. Williams nevertheless pushes Alex to defend his opinions. Noting an inconsistency in his son's stated preferences among types of cars, Mr. Williams wants Alex to supply an explanation for the change:

Terry: "That's not what you said before. Last time, you said the Miata, the Mercedes, and the Bugatti. Which one is it?"[17] Alex (his voice rising): "I didn't say that. Those three have always been my favorites." Christina (soothingly): "Don't worry about it, baby. You can change your mind if you want to. It is your prerogative." . . . Alex, glancing at his Dad, says jovially, "This is America. It's my prerogative to change my mind if I want to."

The sort of verbal jousting between middle-class children and adults recorded in this field note is not unusual. Alexander and other children of his age and class we observed seem similarly comfortable offering information and advice to adults. For instance, a field-worker reported an incident in which Alex coaxed her to try roller-blading: "If you can ice skate, you can roller-blade," Alex confidently assured this adult. And, again like other middle-class children, Alex sometimes gives his parents orders, albeit playfully. Mr. Williams recounted one such episode on an evening when he, Ms. Williams, and a field-worker were attending a school performance. After watching a musical in which Alexander sang from beginning to end, Mr. Williams (who dismisses musicals as a "ridiculous" form of entertainment) remarks that it felt as if the seasons had changed while the play was being performed. Laughing, he tells the field-worker that during the previous night's performance, he had attempted to "sneak out," but Alexander happened to be in the hallway and redirected him. As the group is leaving the building, Mr. Williams points out the spot near a rear door where his son had caught him.

Mr. Williams (chuckling): This is where I came out when I was trying to sneak out and Alexander saw me and said (pointing), "Get back in there."

Mr. Williams reports that he did indeed return to the auditorium for the remainder of the performance.

In this instance, Mr. Williams is clearly amused by his son's actions. Sometimes, however, middle-class parents' emphasis on language use and reasoning results in behavior that is less acceptable. For example, when parents do not comply with rules but instruct their children to do so, the children openly point out the inconsistency. When Ms. Williams, Alex, and a field-worker are doing errands one afternoon, they walk off the sidewalk onto the dirt as they enter the store from the parking lot. Returning to the car, Alexander argues with his mother when she tries to rein him in:

Alex jumped over the flowers to get to the car. His mother and I took the steps. Ms. Williams said, "Alex, don't do that." He said, "Why not? We walked over the dirt on the way in." She said, somewhat weakly, "Yes, but you jumped over the flowers. That is different."

In addition, concerted cultivation can lead to role confusion, particularly over the amount of power that children have in the family. Within short periods of time, for example, there are radical shifts in the status that Alexander's parents accord him. At times Alexander is treated similarly to how adults are treated: his opinions are solicited, he is given a "vote" in family decisions, and he even gives his parents orders. In other moments, however, he is treated as if he is a very young child, as in this example while the family is waiting to enter the church service:

Alexander was leaning on his father. Terry gave Alex a hug. Alex hugged his father tightly. Terry [then] cloaked Alex in his jacket. He made a humming sound as they hugged. Christina [then] asked in . . . a "motherese" tone: "Where's Alexander?" Christina poked Alex who was still under his father's jacket. (She asked) "Where's my baby? Where's Alexander?" Christina . . . exclaimed, "There he is! I see my baby." Alexander laughed as his mother poked him. As a prayer became audible through the sanctuary door, Alex was freed from his play of his parents.[18]

Alexander clearly enjoys this playful moment. In other instances Alexander as well as other middle-class children resist their parents' efforts to treat them as children. Instead, drawing on their verbal skills, they assert that they should be accorded special privileges and, when rebuffed, badger their parents to comply with their requests.[19]

SUMMING UP

The verbal world middle-class children inhabit offers formidable advantages and some significant costs. Compared to the children in the working-class and poor homes we observed, Alexander is better prepared to participate effectively in social interactions, particularly those involving adults. The Williamses' approach to child rearing gives their son a larger vocabulary (e.g., *prerogative* and *plagiarism*); it gives him the tools he needs for customizing situations in and outside the home to maximize his own advantage; it exposes him to broader knowledge about topics of interest to him (e.g., dinosaurs and photography chemicals); it helps him learn to defend an argument with evidence (e.g., why his chosen X-Man was the most powerful); and it provides him with a larger set of skills for defending his individual preferences (e.g., eating one more potato chip).

But concerted cultivation takes time — a great deal of time. Both of Alex's parents tailored their leisure hours to conform to their son's various commitments. The Williamses also devoted their time and attention to talking with Alex. They taught him new words, scoured magazines for articles that might be of interest to him, elicited his opinions, challenged him to support his assertions, and pointed out inconsistencies in his intellectual positions. For his part, Alex — seemingly willingly — gave up most of his free time in order to participate in adult-organized activities.

Alexander was an apt pupil, able to absorb all that his parents taught him. The benefits of his social class position were not, however, limited to the impact of his parents' actions. Alexander himself expanded his opportunities by beginning to implement what he was learning about his position in the social world. Specifically, he seemed to have internalized the idea that it is legitimate and reasonable for others to adjust their actions to suit his preferences; this belief provided the basis for his attempts to customize social interactions, including those involving adults.

The fact that Alexander is a young African American male also shaped various aspects of his life in important ways. He belonged to an all-Black church, and he had regular opportunities to form friendships with other Black children. His parents carefully scrutinized his social environment, always seeking, as Ms. Williams said, to keep him in the company of individuals who were also "cultured."

Although Mr. and Ms. Williams disagreed on elements of how training in race relations should be implemented, they both recognized that their racial and ethnic identity profoundly shaped their and their son's everyday experiences. They were well aware of the potential for Alexander to be exposed to racial injustice, and they went to great lengths to try to protect their son from racial insults and other forms of discrimination. Nevertheless, race did not appear to shape the dominant cultural logic of child rearing in Alexander's family or in other families in the study. All of the middle-class families engaged in extensive reasoning with their children, asking questions, probing assertions, and listening to answers.

This kind of training developed in Alexander and other middle-class children a sense of entitlement. They felt they had a right to weigh in with an opinion, to make special requests, to pass judgment on others, and to offer advice to adults. They expected to receive attention and to be taken very seriously. It is important to recognize that these advantages and entitlements are historically specific. In colonial America, for example, children's actions were highly restricted; thus, the strategies associated with concerted cultivation would have conferred no social class advantage. They are highly effective strategies in the United States today precisely because our society places a premium on assertive, individualized actions executed by persons who command skills in reasoning and negotiation.

Language as a Conduit for Social Life: Harold McAllister

I ask Harold, "How is your [fifth-grade] teacher?" Harold hotly says, "She's mean and she lies." Ms. McAllister is washing dishes, listening quietly. She asks, "What was the name of that man teacher?" Harold says, "Mr. Lindsay?" She says, "No, the other one." He says, "Mr. Terrene." Ms. McAllister smiles and says, "Yeah, I liked him."

Off a busy street, a few blocks from a small business area, lies the Lower Richmond public housing project. Since the road to the housing project dead-ends, and most who live or visit there do not own cars, there is little traffic. Few people wander accidentally through. All the residents are African American, and so is much of the surrounding area (the project edges a large swath of the city that consists exclusively of Black neighborhoods). A white working-class neighborhood is within walking distance, however. The housing project is considered a dangerous area; local businesses, including the pizza parlor, refuse to make deliveries there.

The McAllister family lives in a part of the project consisting of rows of two- and three-story brick units. The brown, blocklike units on their side contain five two-story apartments. Because the apartments have only one small window per room, they are dark on the inside. Sometimes residents keep lights on during the day. Outside, each has its own small yard enclosed by a concrete-and-wood fence. A large deciduous tree stands in front of the McAllisters' unit; its leaves provide welcome shade during the hot summer. Wide concrete sidewalks cut through the spaces between the buildings; at night large floodlights shine down from the corners of each unit. The ground is bare in many places and often is littered with paper, wrappers, and glass.

Residents often sit together outside in lawn chairs or on front stoops, drinking beer, talking, and watching children play. Windows are left open usually during summer, allowing breezes to waft through the units and providing vantage points from which residents can survey the neighborhood.

The first floor of the McAllisters' two-story apartment contains an open living area and a kitchen. The living room is simply furnished, with two turquoise couches, one easy chair, and a wooden stand with a large, open Bible on top. There is a table in the kitchen and, not far from that, a washing machine (there is no dryer). Roaches are a constant problem, despite efforts to beat them back with pesticides. Thus, food is not usually left out. The refrigerator is broken. Ms. McAllister has complained to the manager and although she has been promised a new one, it doesn't arrive during the three weeks we are visiting. Ms. McAllister makes do by storing some food next door in her friend Latifa's refrigerator and some in coolers packed with ice.

Upstairs, there are four bedrooms. Two can hold a double bed, and two a single bed. There is a bed and a dresser in each room; the closets, to save money when they were built, do not have doors. The walls are bare. One bedroom has a window air conditioner in the window; the apartment is quite warm on hot summer days. There is one bathroom. Three televisions are in the house, including one in Ms. McAllister's bedroom. Most of the time at least one set is on. Unlike Alexander Williams' mother, Ms. McAllister does not restrict television watching. Indeed, she finds television useful. As she says, "It will be on all night long because I keep my TV on all night long. That's how I go to sleep." Although the McAllisters once had a phone, for much of Harold's fourth-grade year they haven't had one due to budget constraints. Ms. McAllister receives messages from the school at her sister Lavina's house, and her neighbor Latifa also takes messages.

THE FAMILY

The McAllister household is headed by Ms. Jane McAllister, a tall, lively thirty-three-year-old woman with a highly developed sense of humor and a booming voice. During our visits, she usually was clad in cutoffs and a T-shirt dating from her days as a high school athlete. She receives public assistance but hopes to work again. Ms. McAllister has four children.

Harold (age ten) and his sister Alexis (nine) live with her full time. Their older brother, Lenny (seventeen), and sister Lori (sixteen) live primarily with Ms. McAllister's mother, who lives a few minutes away by bus. Lenny and Lori come by the McAllister apartment regularly during the week and often stay overnight, especially on weekends.

Ms. McAllister is a devoted aunt. She provides a home for her nephews, Runako (eleven) and Guion (nine). The boys' mother, Ms. McAllister's sister, Dara, recently lost her home and is now staying in the housing project with her friend Charmaine. Knowing that the boys do not like their mother's friend and do not feel welcome in her apartment, Ms. McAllister has invited her nephews to stay with her. They often come four or more days per week, eating meals, taking showers, and sharing a bed with Harold. Their presence puts a strain on the already tight food budget.

Another guest is Ms. McAllister's twin sister, Jill, a cocaine addict. She does not have a key, but occasionally enters the apartment by slipping in through a window. She sleeps on the couch. Jill has two daughters, Halima (three), and Monique (ten months). The previous year, when Harold was in third grade, Jill and her children lived with the McAllisters. Subsequently, Jill was accused of child neglect and the girls were removed from her care. Jane and Jill's sister Lavina (who lives in a small apartment about fifteen minutes away by bus) took in Halima and Monique. Lavina has a serious medical disability, but, with help from her live-in boyfriend, she is able to manage caring for Jill's children. Ms. McAllister regularly visits her sister Lavina and her nieces. Jill, however, is able to see the children only under supervision and she does not visit them often (she missed Halima's third birthday party, for example).

In addition to Ms. McAllister, the children, and Jill, the McAllister household includes Keith, Ms. McAllister's common-law husband. Keith is a long-distance truck driver who is often gone for days at a time. He returns home between trips. He plays basketball with the children, especially Harold, but he does not assume the role of a parent. Finally, there is Hank, Harold and Alexis's father. Hank visits regularly even though he and Harold's mother are no longer romantically involved (they never married). At fifty-seven, he is much older than Ms. McAllister (he has daughters older than she is). Hank is a mechanic. He drops by the apartment after work, lies down, and goes to sleep. Ms. McAllister laughingly explains: "Hank will lie on the bed. I'll be coming and going, and he'll be laying down."

Some weekends Harold takes the bus across town to visit Hank in the house he shares with his mother and two brothers. These overnight stays usually are not formally planned in advance; Harold "just shows up."[1] Alexis does not accompany Harold on these trips. Sometimes, though, Hank's daughters (Alexis's half-sisters) come over and take her out. Hank contributes to the household periodically, for example, by buying pizza on Friday nights. He sometimes gives Ms. McAllister money for the children, especially for clothing. He expresses pride in his son's accomplishments and attends key events in Harold's life (e.g., fifth-grade graduation). He does not usually manage Harold's day-to-day care or discipline him.

Table 3 lists the individuals who live in and/or regularly visit the McAllister apartment. Usually, there are five to seven people staying overnight in the house and, when both Jill and Keith are there, as many as nine.[2] The children sleep in different beds on different nights. Sometimes they ask for help finding room:

RUNAKO: Hey, Jane. I can't get in. Harold's spread across the bed.

JANE: Move Harold's butt over. He's sleeping on the short way. Just push him over some.

Unlike in middle-class homes, there is not a clear sense of private space in the McAllister's apartment.

The family lives under formidable economic constraints. Ms. McAllister receives Aid to Families with Dependent Children for Harold and Alexis, and she has a medical card for doctor visits.[3] Although she uses food stamps, food is often in short supply. The children always ask permission before they eat something; we never observed them helping themselves to food. When put out, food usually disappears rapidly, as there are many mouths to feed. For example, one afternoon, an entire large box of saltine crackers and some jam is devoured in thirty minutes as Harold and Alexis, Runako and Guion, a neighbor's three-year-old grandson, myself, and Ms. McAllister snack and talk.

On special occasions food may be plentiful. At a birthday party for Jill's daughter Halima, hot dogs, buns, mustard, Kool-Aid, and Cheese-Its were in abundance. More often, however, there is not quite enough to go around. One Friday night, for instance, the two pizzas in the oven must be divided among Ms. McAllister, Harold, Alexis, Lori, Hank, and Jill. When Harold asks for a second piece of pizza, he is redirected to drink soda. Another night, each child has one meatball, canned yams, and canned spinach for dinner. There is not enough for second helpings.

TABLE 3. OVERVIEW OF MCALLISTER FAMILY

Person	Age	Relationship to Child	Residence
Jane	33	Mother	McAllister home
Lenny	16	Older brother	Grandmother's, but often stayed at McAllister home
Lori	14	Older sister	Grandmother's, but often stayed at McAllister home
Harold	10	Target child	McAllister home
Alexis	8	Younger sister	McAllister home
Dara (mother of Runako and Giuon)	30's	Aunt of Harold / sister to Jane	Stays with a friend in same housing project
Runako	11	Cousin	McAllister home, sometimes stayed with his mom
Guion	9	Cousin	McAllister home, sometimes stayed with his mom
Jill (mother of Halima and Monique, taken away by DHS)	33	Aunt of Harold / twin sister to Jane	McAllister home until kicked out
Hank	56	Father	Lives across town (with his mother and brother), but hangs out at McAllister home
Keith	30's	Common-law-husband of Jane	McAllister home, but is often gone driving a truck long distance

Money is in equally short supply. The family forgoes some things — like dental care, stylish clothing, and hair treatments — and shares others, like transportation costs.[4] Ms. McAllister's sister Dara loans her bus pass to the family for outings and sometimes friends supply car rides. Among the children, the desire for money, and the access it brings to material objects, is palpable. They clamor for money one morning when Lenny comes by and holds out some dollar bills before their eyes. Their longing is clear, too, when they make wishes. In response to, "What would you do if you had a million dollars?" Alexis said:

Oh, boy! I'd buy my brother, my sister, my uncle, my aunt, my nieces, and my nephews, and my grandpop, and my grandmom, and my mom, and my dad, and my friends, not my friends, but mostly my best friend — I'd buy them all clothes . . . and sneakers. . . . And I'd buy some food, and I'd buy my mom some food, and I'd get my brothers and my sisters gifts for their birthdays.

Harold and Alexis, however, do not press their mother or father to buy them things:

We stop outside [a clothing store] and Hank carefully [looks] at clothes and at the prices . . . Harold looks too . . . Harold seems withdrawn, almost wary. He leaves it up to his father to take the lead. The entire time of the trip, I never heard him say, "Can I have xx" or "Can I have yy?" We went past candy, videotapes, books, magazines, sports shirts, sports bags, and he never spoke up.

As this field note suggests, Harold's restraint was disconcerting after so many observations of working-class and middle-class children who routinely ask their parents to purchase items for them.

But Harold does not live a life of total deprivation. Ms. McAllister is committed to meeting her children's basic needs, and, whenever possible, supplying them with "extras." For example, the field-workers noted occasions when she gave the children money to buy a soda or a bag of chips at a store near the housing project. Ms. McAllister sees herself as a very capable mother. Like Alexander Williams's mother, she wants her children to be successful and happy. She strives to provide a strong, positive influence in their lives (unlike the drug-addicted mothers in the project), but she views her role as a parent very differently from the way Ms. Williams views hers. In the McAllister family, as in other poor and working-class families, a parent's key responsibility lies in providing important physical care for children, offering clothing and shelter, teaching the difference between right and wrong, and providing comfort. In all of this, language plays an important, practical role. Unlike Ms. Williams, Ms. McAllister does not continuously attempt to enrich Harold's vocabulary, cultivate his verbal (or physical) talents, cajole him, or attempt to persuade him to act in particular ways. When Harold complains, as in the opening of the chapter, that his teacher "lies," his mother listens quietly and reminds him of a teacher she did like, but unlike Ms. Williams she does not have her son elaborate. Ms. McAllister often issues short, clear directives and she expects prompt, respectful compliance. Harold rarely challenges any directive issued by an adult, nor does he try to reason or negotiate with either of his parents. The strong, clear boundaries Ms. McAllister draws between adults and children do not, however, lead her to tightly control Harold's activities. He and the other children are free to play, watch TV, and spend time with their nearby friends without specifically consulting her. In contrast to middle-class children's worlds, where children's activities often supplant kinship time, extended family networks play a very important role among the McAllisters.

These differences in parenting, especially language use, affect the children's lives both outside and inside the home. The *emerging sense of entitlement* that is apparent when Alexander Williams visits the doctor, for example, is shaped by his ability to use language to control how the doctor perceives him. Alex is at ease with adults (so much so that he casually interrupts the doctor); he visits the doctor often enough to be familiar with the routines; and since he is used to being questioned and having his answers attended to, he supplies information fluidly. It is different when Harold goes to a clinic for a physical for Bible camp. Mistrust of doctors and other professionals and lack of familiarity with the practices and terminology of health-care professionals combine to tongue-tie his mother and constrain him. Harold has neither the language nor conversational skills that Alexander takes for granted. He is unfamiliar with questioning and probing, and he has no experience making special demands of persons in authority. The result is an *emerging sense of constraint*. The positive aspects of Harold's upbringing — the ease he displays with his peers, his resourcefulness in creating games and organizing his own time, his respectful attitude toward adults, his deep connection to family members — are rendered nearly invisible in the "real world" of social institutions. Educators, health-care professionals, employers, and others accept (and help to reproduce) an ideology that values, among other things, reasoning and negotiating skills, large vocabularies, facility in speaking and working with strangers, and time management — the very attributes children like Alexander Williams develop in their daily lives. By looking closely at parts of Harold's life, especially the role of language, this chapter uncovers ways in which these institutional preferences evolve into institutionalized inequality, as differences come to be defined as deficits.

LETTING HAROLD BE "PLAIN OLD HAROLD": THE ACCOMPLISHMENT OF NATURAL GROWTH

Harold McAllister, the target child, is a fourth-grader at Lower Richmond elementary school. With his large shoulders and stocky build, he has the look of a budding football player. This is how Alexis describes her older brother:

Harold is plain old Harold. He never changes. He does the same thing over and over and over again. He listens to the radio. He plays basketball. He listens to the radio. He watches TV. He goes to sleep. He watches TV. He listens to the radio, he watches TV, he plays basketball. And he's just plain old Harold. He don't do nothing that's fun.

In Harold's view, doing the "same thing over and over" *is* fun. He loves sports and would happily play basketball (which he is particularly fond of) or football for most of any given day. He follows professional sports closely. Most afternoons, he is either watching television or, more likely, outside playing ball. The number of children available to play with varies, but for Harold, unlike for Alexander Williams, there is always *someone* to play with. There are forty children of elementary school age residing in the rows of apartments surrounding the McAllister's apartment. With so many children nearby, Harold could choose to play only with others his own age. In fact, though, he spends time with both older and younger children, and with his cousins (who are close to his age).

Family Ties

Unlike Alexander Williams or Garrett Tallinger, Harold has ready access to his extended family. His cousins, Runako and Guion, practically live at his house, and his aunts are close by. But family ties are more than a matter of convenience. The connections linking Harold to his cousins and aunts, to his grandmother, to his father, and to his father's relatives are fundamentally important to him — they form the context of his life. On any given day, he is likely to share a bed with Runako and a basketball with his cousin Guion. He runs errands for his aunts, and he takes the bus by himself to visit his grandmother and his father's relatives.

   Harold celebrates special occasions such as his birthday with his relatives. Among the McAllisters, the parties are not, as in middle-class families, based on friends from school or from extracurricular activities. Extended family members pool their resources and energies, celebrating birthdays with enthusiasm. There is cake and special food; presents, however, are not often part of the occasion. Similarly, at Christmas there is a tree and special food, but no presents. At these and other family events, older children voluntarily play with and take care of their younger siblings and cousins while adults mingle and talk among themselves.

Organization of Daily Life

Organized activities, the backbone of Alexander Williams and Garrett Tallinger's leisure time, are nonexistent in Harold's life.[5] He structures his time much to his own liking. He enjoys tossing a football around with his friends and relatives; he also organizes basketball games, playing off the bare, rusty hoop that hangs from a telephone pole on a side street in the housing project. One obstacle to enjoying sports is a shortage of equipment. Hunting for balls is routine part of Harold's leisure time. For example, one very hot and humid June day, Harold, his cousin Guion, and a field-worker wandered around the housing project for about an hour, searching for a basketball. Later that afternoon, after spending some time listening to music and looking at baseball cards, Harold joined Guion and other children in a water fight that Guion instigated. It was a lively game, filled with laughter, and with efforts to get the adults next door wet (against their wishes).

Harold's daily activities keep him busy, but unlike Alexander Williams and Garrett Tallinger, he almost never seems exhausted by his regime. The lack of adult-organized activities leaves him free to create his own amusements and to set his own pace in pursuing them. He hones his skills at sports, and he is resourceful in finding equipment and playmates. He is adept at dealing with children much younger and much older than he is. But Harold does not acquire the adult-legitimated skills that provide an emerging sense of entitlement, nor does he develop a familiarity with the work-related routines that middle-class children acquire by participating in a roster of organized activities.

When Harold plays outside, his demeanor is very different from the way he behaves inside the apartment. Inside, he is quiet, almost sedate. He rarely talks loudly, doesn't hop around, makes only a few, brief comments, and is not argumentative. Outside, especially when he is engaged in sports, the respectful, often subdued attitude he shows around adults gives way to a much more animated and assertive self. (This shift is clear during a basketball game described later in this chapter.) Sometimes, if he is agitated or angry, Harold will stutter. His mother explains:

He's been in speech class now for like three years, but he just don't take his time. If he would take his time and talk — but if he's laughing or crying, you've got to wait until he calms down in order to hear him.

Harold is more likely to be laughing than crying. The McAllisters are a strikingly playful group; there is frequent laughter and joking. Even when we were getting the study under way, humor was evident. The field-worker asked Harold what time he got up on Saturday mornings. When Harold said 7:00 A.M., the field-worker replied that she would come a bit earlier, then, perhaps around 6:30. Runako's immediate observation, "Dang, they worse than the Jehovah Witnesses!" prompted appreciative laughter among all present. Harold's mother is especially droll. She often delivers her funniest remarks deadpan (i.e., without affect). For example, at the reunion picnic, there are about two hundred people present when I show up. Ms. McAllister alerts one of the field-workers who is already there:

JANE (speaking to the field-worker): Annette is here.

FIELD-WORKER (looking around): Where?

JANE: She the only white person here and you can't find her? (laughter)

The Role of Race

Just how rarely white people are seen in the project is clear when I spend the night and accompany Ms. McAllister at around 10 P.M. as she walks over to an apartment to return Dara's TransPass. En route, Ms. McAllister stops to chat with a couple of friends who are sitting in an old white truck, drinking. Ms. McAllister introduces me, "This is my friend Annette. She's writing a book about my son." Later, she explains the reason for that introduction:

JANE: When they see a white person walking around with somebody Black, they think you on drugs. (Shared laughter.)

JANE: I'm serious. They like, "Yo" [want to buy?]

FIELD-WORKER: When I walk around during the day, they think I'm from DHS [Department of Human Services].

JANE: I'm tellin' you.[6]

Harold's world is only slightly less Black outside the project. The degree of racial segregation in the surrounding urban area is considered "hyper," as it is in many cities in the United States.[7] In the business district a few minutes from Harold's apartment, the shopkeepers are a mixed group. At Maria's Convenience Store, where Harold goes on errands for adults (and, sometimes, to buy treats for himself), the staff includes whites, Asians, and some African Americans. A white working-class residential neighborhood is within walking distance of the housing project, but Harold does not go there to play. On Halloween Ms. McAllister reports that she and a friend take their children across the racial divide "for the candy." They go to the same houses every year and "the people know us." Occasionally there are problems, including people who turn off their lights when they see Black children approaching. Ms. McAllister tempers her disgust at such behavior, noting simply that "the parents were acting stupid."

At school, the racial balance shifts. As noted earlier, Lower Richmond, which is part of a large urban district, is racially integrated: about one-half of the students are white, as are most of the teachers. Most of the administrative staff, such as the yard duty teacher and the cafeteria ladies, are white. Some of the teachers' aides are Black and most of the bus drivers are Black. Harold's third-grade teacher was an African American woman; this year, his teacher is a white male.

Ms. McAllister tells the African American field-worker interviewing her at the start of the study that she does not know of any Black or white children at Harold's school who have been treated unfairly because of their race. Although clearly aware of people who "act stupid," Ms. McAllister, unlike Mr. and Ms. Williams, does not express concern about the impact of race on her children's lives. Instead she stresses the importance of proper care for children in general and is especially critical of adults who "do nothin' for their kids."

GUIDING NATURAL GROWTH

Ms. McAllister, like Ms. Williams, strongly believes that parents should provide good care for their children. Unlike Ms. Williams, she defines that care in terms of natural growth. That is, she stresses the importance of parents providing food, shelter, clothing, and good supervision. Ms. McAllister is a block captain for her section of the housing project. Among other things, during the summer, she controls the "sprinkler cap" for a nearby fire plug that project residents may use on hot summer days. With the cap on, the fire hydrant releases a spray of water that is safe for the children to play in. She criticizes the way other parents in the housing project handle this and other child-related activities:

They have five fire plugs over there. They are rowdy over there. They had three of them on yesterday full blast . . . These people don't do nothin' for their kids. They'll [the kids] leave at nine o'clock [in the morning] and come back at four and not tell their parents where they went. (Shakes head, disgusted.)

Although Ms. McAllister does not actively intervene in her children's daily lives, she does meet what she identifies as her parental obligations. Thus, even though it requires taking the bus, she attends parent-teacher conferences. Similarly, although she is not personally comfortable around health-care professionals, she takes Harold to the doctor for a physical so that he can attend Bible camp. On very limited funds, she manages to buy sufficient food for her nephews as well for her own children. She makes dinner. She arranges for Harold's father to take him shopping when he needs new clothes for camp. Sometimes, she simply "hangs out" with the children, watching them play basketball and joking with them.

Ms. McAllister also emphasizes that she does special things with her children: "In the summer, I'll take them on a picnic on the blanket." And,

We always go [to the zoo] on Valentine's Day cuz that's when the kids get in free. We go like four or five times a year, summertime, too. I like goin' down there in the evening time on Wednesday where you've got less kids and it's nice.

Another demonstration of Ms. McAllister's commitment to good care for children involves a difficult decision she had to make. After prolonged difficulty with her twin sister, Jill (before the study began), whose cocaine addiction interfered with her taking proper care of Halima and Monique, Ms. McAllister called the Department of Human Services (DHS) and reported her sister's neglect. She explains:

FIELD-WORKER: Who called DHS?

JANE: I did. I got tired of it. Halima was having an asthma attack and she don't come back for four hours. I got tired of it. I called DHS six or seven times that day. I got tired of my kids watching them. Lenny and Lori and Harold and Alexis and Guion and Runako. They should have their own (hesitates) should have their own childhood. She'd go off and leave them.

The children's physical safety is also of importance to Ms. McAllister. For example, at Halloween, she took the children trick or treating and she restricted them to eating only packaged candy; they were not allowed to eat "candy corn, . . . cookies, oranges, and apples." Also, as is noted later in the chapter, she instructs the younger children to steer clear of adults in the housing project who "have problems" and scolds teenaged Lori for spending time with the "wrong kind" of people. She extends a similarly protective stance toward the field-workers. She remarks to me casually:

I told the drug dealer, "That [field-worker] is doing a study of my son. I want you to not mess with him or I'm going to come down."[8]

Ms. McAllister is proud of her high school diploma, and she conveys to
the children her expectation that they will pass each grade. Alexis reports:

She says if you didn't pass you'll be on punishment for the whole summer. And
my eyes go wide opened, like this (demonstrates). I'd be scared when I give her
my report card. And she says — 'cause I didn't see it yet — and she said, "You
didn't pass." And I was scared. I said, "Let me see!" And I looked at my report
card, and I said, "I passed."

Alexis also emphasizes her mother's qualities:

My family is not nasty. Because my mom, I mean, this guy that threw a bottle in
the street and it was rolling and the car almost got a flat tire. So my mom told me
to push the glass over on the curb. And he said — the guy said, "Look at her, she's
cleaning up. She's cleaning up the glass." Cuz my mom is clean like that.

Similarly, Harold appears proud that his mother has the key to the sprinkler cap for the fire hydrant. Overall, Ms. McAllister is seen by family
members and neighbors as a capable mother and a good citizen.

THE LANGUAGE OF DAILY LIFE:
KEEPING THINGS SHORT AND SIMPLE

Life in the McAllister household, as in the other poor and working-class
families we observed, does not revolve around extended verbal discussions. The amount of talking in these homes varies, but overall, it is considerably less than in the middle-class homes.[9] Sentences tend to be shorter,
words simpler, and negotiations infrequent, and word play of the kind we
observed with the Tallingers and Williamses is almost nonexistent.[10] This
does not mean that poor and working-class families consider conversation
unimportant. McAllister family members talk about relatives and friends,
tell jokes, and make comments about what is on television — but they do so
intermittently. Short remarks punctuate comfortable silences. Sometimes
speech is bypassed altogether in favor of body language — nods, smiles, and
eye contact. Ms. McAllister typically is brief and direct in her own
remarks, and she does not try to draw her children out or seek their opinions. In most settings, the children are free to speak, but they are not usually specifically encouraged to do so. The overall effect is that language
serves as a practical conduit of daily life, not as a tool for cultivating reasoning skills or a resource to plumb for ways to express feelings or ideas.[11]

   Around the house, the children frequently discuss money among
themselves. They look at newspaper ads and comment on the prices of
various things. They talk about who gave them money (for example, as

when a neighbor gave Runako five dollars for escorting her to the bank's ATM). The serious financial hardships the McAllisters contend with make *all* family members sensitive to the exact price of items, as well as where to find a bargain:

Jane hands Harold and Alexis each a bag of caramel corn, which they open soon afterward. She scolds, "Why you opening those things?" They don't answer. Somehow the price of the caramel corn comes up. Jane says she got them on sale at a gas station up the hill — two bags for a dollar, when usually they cost fifty-nine cents each.[12]

Interspersed with this sort of intermittent talk are adult-issued directives. Children are told to do certain things (e.g., shower, take out the garbage) and not to do others (e.g., curse, talk back). Ms. McAllister uses one-word directives to coordinate the use of the single bathroom. There are almost always at least four children in the apartment and often seven, plus Ms. McAllister and other adults. Ms. McAllister sends the children to wash up by pointing to a child, saying, "Bathroom," and handing him or her a washcloth. Wordlessly, the designated child gets up and goes to the bathroom to take a shower.

Children usually do what adults ask of them. We did not observe whining or protests, even when adults assign time-consuming tasks, such as the hour-long process of hair-braiding, which Lori is told to do for the four-year-old daughter of Aunt Dara's friend Charmaine:

Someone tells Lori, "Go do [Tyneshia's] hair for camp." Without saying anything, Lori gets up and goes inside and takes the little girl with her. They head for the couch near the television; Lori sits on the couch and the girl sits on the floor. [Tyneshia] sits quietly for about an hour, with her head tilted, while Lori carefully does a multitude of braids.

Lori's silent obedience is typical. Generally, children perform requests without comment. For example, at dinner one night, after Harold complains he doesn't like spinach, his mother directs him to finish it anyway:

Mom yells (loudly) at him to eat: "EAT! FINISH THE SPINACH!" (No response. Harold is at the table, dawdling.) Guion and Runako and Alexis finish eating and leave. I finish with Harold; he eats his spinach. He leaves all his yams.

Perhaps because of the expectation that children will do as directed, adults do not routinely offer explanations for directives; periodically, though, the rationale is interwoven with the order itself:

Jane and Runako walk slightly in front of me. I'm in between the two, but Runako keeps curving in front of me. Jane scolds him: "Runako! Walk straight!

Don't get in her way!" He laughs and moves over, then says something about how his friends always get on him for walking crooked. Shortly, he moves in front of me again. This time, Jane snaps: "Runako! Cut that out!" He looks startled (his eyebrows shoot up, and he has a guilty-looking smile).

Runako is not consciously disobeying his aunt — he just lets his attention wander. Sometimes, contravening an adult's directive is a more deliberate decision. Harold speaks up when he feels strongly about something. He voices his objections economically but clearly. Discussions that in the Williamses' home might unfold over several minutes or more are raised and resolved very quickly, as the following example shows. Here, Harold, his father, and I are shopping for items Harold needs for Bible camp.

Harold picks up a plain blue [beach towel] in the bottom rack. He holds it up. His dad says, "You want a plain one?" Harold nods. His dad takes the towel and puts it in the basket. His dad then wanders down an aisle . . . He then picks up a peach [towel] set with an off-white, satin appliquéd duck on it and looks at it. He says, "These come [in a set] but they don't have a big towel." (Mr. McAllister seems to think this is a better buy.)

Harold firmly rejects the peach towel set:

Harold takes a step down the aisle and looks at the [towel set] and then firmly shakes his head. "Them girl colors," he says. His dad picks the set up and raises it, suggesting that Harold is wrong and should get it. He looks at it and looks at Harold. His dad seems (nonverbally) to be protesting mildly but is smiling, too. Harold does not seem to think it is funny. He shakes his head again and says decisively, "Girl colors." His dad smiles . . . [but] seems unsure of what to do next. He walks around and looks at what is in the cart and picks up the blue towel again. [He] unfolds the blue towel, and I offer to help him by extending my arm; we unfold it completely. It is about five feet long. Harold shakes his head; he says, "It big."

   Throughout the entire exchange, Harold utters less than ten words. His father says somewhat more, but still far less than Mr. or Ms. Williams would as they sought to elicit Alexander's opinions.
   Although Harold objects to the peach towel set, he doesn't actually argue with his father. He merely reiterates his position. We observed a child in this family actively argue with an adult only once. The subject, food, may have been a deciding factor in both the child's persistence and the adult's forbearance.

As we leave to take the bus to go to Lavina's house for a birthday party for a three-year-old cousin, Ms. McAllister yells out at all of us as we start across the road toward the bus stop: "Ya'll eat at Lavina's, and get filled up at Lavina's, because I ain't cooking when we come back."

Late that night, around 10 P.M., the family has come back and is sitting watching a play-off basketball game on television and getting ready to go to bed. In Jane's room, Alexis is sitting in the middle of the bed with her back against the wall, and Runako is sitting on the edge of the bed with his back against the wall and his legs stretched out. It is hot. The air conditioner isn't on.

Runako, who was not with the group when Ms. McAllister made the announcement, asks for food. Note that he does not correct his aunt when she presumes that he heard her warning to eat at Lavina's. Instead, he asserts he does not like — and therefore never eats — hot dogs:

RUNAKO: Can I have some food?

JANE (surprised and loudly): Some grub? Didn't I tell you to eat all you could at Lavina's house?

RUNAKO: I did but [didn't like what was there].

JANE: There's no grub. I told ya'll . . .

RUNAKO: I ain't going to eat hot dogs!

JANE (angrily): Say what?

RUNAKO: I don't like hot dogs. (Louder, more defensive) I don't eat hot dogs. You can ask my mom. I don't eat hot dogs.

JANE (very loudly and angrily): Your mom should have said something before we fixed all them damn hot dogs. I'm telling you something right now; I ain't going for it, all right?[13]

Runako is briefly distracted by Alexis. Both are sitting on the single bed (along with Ms. McAllister):

RUNAKO (to Alexis): Keep off! I swear to god, you don't give anyone any room.

Ms. McAllister believes she hears Alexis curse.

JANE (swatting her daughter on the legs with the newspaper): I'm going to smack your ass, hear?

ALEXIS: I didn't say that, Mom!

JANE: Don't [pull] it in here. You know right from wrong. Now I'll go upside [hit] your damn head now.

In a rare move, Harold's mother then asks Runako what is troubling him. Since she (along with Harold and I) had taken the bus back, while

Runako had been given a ride back from the birthday party with Alexis and others in a car, she wonders if something might have happened in the car:

JANE: What happened in the car, Runako? What happened at the car? What happened at Lavina's house?

RUNAKO: (mumbling) Nothing.

JANE: Then why the attitude?

RUNAKO: She [Alexis] getting on my nerves.

JANE: Runako, you get on everyone's nerve and nobody talk to you like that. (Short silence; basketball game continues on the TV.)

JANE [to all present]: Didn't I tell you before ya'll left?

ALEXIS: Right.

By the McAllister family's standards, this exchange is unusual on several counts. It is lengthy, it involves a child challenging (although indirectly) an adult, and it captures Harold's mother deliberately soliciting information from one of the children.

When Ms. McAllister uses directives to protect her children and to train them, her manner is curt by middle-class standards. In warning Alexis and Runako to ignore adults in the housing project who are known to have problems, for instance, she is brief and explicit, but not unkind:

JANE: Who Rip? Rip is drunk. I told [you] about Rip. (A bit later) He was drunk before three o'clock today.

ALEXIS: He drive a Jeep. He drove Jerome up here.

RUNAKO: He was what?

ALEXIS: He was cursing at me.

JANE: Let me tell you something about Rip. (Yelling) DON'T PAY HIM NO MIND, OKAY! He's got a problem too.

Neither the relatively limited amount of speech we observed nor Ms. McAllister's tendency to yell or be brusque are indications of strained or stunted emotional connections among family members. If anything, the unspoken emotions between adults and children in the McAllister household often seemed more palpable to us than the connections in families with a great deal of speech, such as the Tallingers. The following example provides a sense of how adeptly — and routinely — the McAllisters communicate without words:

Harold has a paper plate with a hot dog and chips in his left hand and a canned drink of soda in his right. With his right hand, he is trying to open the soda. And all of a sudden, his hand slips and the soda jolts up and out of the can, [spilling] on his hand and the bench. His mother, who is just a few feet away, catches his eye. They both laugh together at his uncoordinated lurch with the soda. It is a friendly, warm laugh, a soft poking fun at him for his contorted move with his hand. His mom then takes the stuff to the grill, and Harold shakes the soda off his hand.

Everyone in the McAllister household appreciates a good joke and Ms. McAllister, especially, seems alert to the potential for humor in any situation. Nevertheless, the boundaries between adults and children are clearly delineated and carefully maintained. A premium is placed on being respectful toward one's elders. Children automatically refer to adults, especially women, using respectful terms such as Miss Latifa or Miss Jane. In addition, Ms. McAllister does not allow the children to curse.[14]

TALKING THE TALK: LANGUAGE USE AMONG PEERS

Unlike the directive-laden interactions that occur between poor (and working-class) adults and children, language use among peers tends to be free flowing. In many situations when children are off by themselves, they banter back and forth; boys, especially, enjoy boasting to one another. On the basketball court, Harold sheds his quiet demeanor. His whole persona — including his language — seems transformed. A talented player, Harold is both surprisingly quick (given his stocky build) and surprisingly aggressive (given his at-home behavior).

Harold called a "double" (double dribble) on Jarrad. Jarrad protests as he throws Harold the ball. (If you make the call, you get the ball.) Jarrad (angrily): "Man, I didn't double — nigga, you blind as shit!" Harold stops bouncing the ball and walks over to Jarrad. Harold (shouting): "You did, man. Just like this." (Harold starts to dribble the ball; he spins, then fakes, then he does an exaggerated double dribble.) "I seen you!" None of the other players were asked for their opinion, nor did they offer it. Harold keeps the ball and checks it back into play. (Usually if there was a dispute over a foul, the play would be played over. This was not the case. Harold took the ball.) A foul was called on Harold, "Walk." (He committed fouls by walking his butt off.) Harold (protesting): "I walk? Nigga, you crazy. See if you get the ball a — I'm a do the play over. I ain't gotta cheat." Harold keeps the ball. No one protests.

Harold and his friends have more autonomy from adults than their middle-class counterparts. Adults often are not present, and when they are, they do not typically intervene in children's interactions. This is clear, for instance, in the field-worker's description of Harold and his (common-law) stepfather, Keith, shooting baskets together one afternoon:

Harold and Keith were very laid back. Neither was adamant about getting rebounds, nor were they particularly interested in displaying their dribbling skills. Harold was sinking a pretty good amount of shots. Keith was not as skilled.

As this casual shooting continues, about ten young men, varying in age from about seven to fifteen, join in.

Once the others arrive (they all seem to arrive at once), the pace of the game changes. It becomes more showboatish and competitive. Although there is not an actual game going on (one in which the score is kept), definite defensive and offensive strategies are executed. For instance, on numerous occasions Harold would tell one of his friends to "Come get some." This functioned as a competitive invitation to . . . [try] to prevent Harold from making a basket. Harold is extremely talented with a basketball.

Harold escalates the competition by presenting a second challenge:

Harold offers the challenge: "Come on out here so I can break your ankles."[15] This challenge was directed to any and all takers, young and old alike. The older man [who had joined the group], to assist Harold in finding a taker, calls out, "Jarrad — go out there and show what you know. Don't let him take your heart." (Notice the cultural text, which implies that one must be tough or macho in order to be socially accepted.) Jarrad retorts (while flagging Harold — that is, moving his arm in a swiping manner — usually understood as a derogatory gesture), "Harold ain't got nothin' for me." He walks over to Harold and posts him up (assumes a defensive position — crouching directly in front of Harold with his arm extended.) His eyes shift from Harold's eyes to the ball.

As the action unfolds, the others on the court, who had been making jump shots with the other ball, gradually stop to watch.

All eyes were on Harold and Jarrad. Harold is getting hyped and is trying to intimidate Jarrad (bouncing the ball vigorously). "You ready for me to break those ankles! Watch this, y'all." (Everyone was already watching.)

Harold proceeds forward to the basket without warning. Jarrad swipes at the ball. Harold teases him, "You ready for me to take it to you, young bol?"[16] . . . Everywhere Jarrad swats, the ball is no longer there. . . . It is obvious that Jarrad is no match for Harold. Keith and the other older man glance at each other and smile. Harold is now about four feet away from the basket. He dribbles the ball between his legs in one bounce and passes [it] around his back, spins around, runs while dribbling for about two steps, and then goes for the lay up. He misses.

Although Harold misses the shot, he still receives various forms of praise or recognition.[17] This is manifested in the form of smiles, high fives, and comments such as an enthusiastic, "Damn — did you see that!" and "Jarrad garbage — that nigga can't play." . . . Harold strutted (boasting), "Yeah, nigga what? Can't nobody get with this! I'm breakin nigga's ankles — young bol' got skills!"

Harold does indeed have skills — in addition to his ability to dribble, pass, and shoot, he is a good strategist; he is resourceful and creative; he is fluent in the language of the game; and he knows how and when to challenge and taunt. Overall, he is poised and confident on the court. His discourse here is elaborated and embellished. But in his interactions with parents and teachers, the language interactions take a different form. In addition, these talents, while very important in this context, are not as readily translated to the world of educators, employers, or health-care professionals as are the talents his middle-class counterparts acquire in their rounds of organized activities. Off the court, and in the presence of adults, Harold returns to being "plain old Harold," less forceful, more respectful, and quieter.

THE LANGUAGE OF DISCIPLINE: DIRECTIVES AND THREATS

The tendency for children in poor and working-class homes to respond promptly and wordlessly to directives from adults holds true whether the order is to take a shower, put out the garbage, braid a child's hair, or eat vegetables. It is also the typical response to verbal discipline, even when accompanied by threats of physical punishment. In the example below, Alexis is scolded by her Aunt Lavina. She offers no rebuttal. In fact, she responds directly only once — with a wordless nod — when her aunt's question seems to demand it of her. Throughout this episode, Alexis is standing near Lavina's kitchen table, her hands resting on the top of a wooden chair. Lavina, who conducts her interrogation and delivers her ultimatums without consulting Alexis's mother, is positioned at the far end of the same table. She is obviously angry; Alexis, ashamed:

LAVINA: Hey, baby. It sounds like you had a bad day at school.

(Runako says something, making fun of Alexis for getting in trouble.)

LAVINA: Shut up, Runako.

LAVINA (turning again to Alexis): What was your problem? Evidently you had a problem; you were dancing around and going all gymnastics or something in class. Huh?

(Alexis does not look up or answer.)

LAVINA: Didn't we have a talk about this before?

(Alexis does not answer.)

LAVINA: You know, Alexis, behavior is very important. If you can't behave in school, in elementary school, how are you going to behave when you get older and, and have a job. Hum?

(Alexis does not answer.)

LAVINA (speaks to Runako and then turns back to Alexis): I've been talking to you for two months. . . . You always give me the same old excuse. Why you acting out?

(The room is silent. Lavina is staring at Alexis. Alexis is staring at the chair.)

LAVINA (repeating herself): I'm really, really getting tired of it. Why you acting out like this?

(Alexis remains silent. Runako goes in and out of the kitchen, adds sugar to the Kool-Aid. . . .)

LAVINA: There's only a few [days] left in the school year. Please don't let me hear, alright?

(Alexis nods.)

LAVINA: I really don't want to have to beat you up on the ass. That's like a last resort.

In a scolding, as in other interactions between adults and children, the adult talks. The child listens. Children do not, as in middle-class families, test the limits of adults by probing, arguing, and questioning adults. One unintended consequence of this approach is that poor and working-class children typically do not develop the same range of verbal skills their middle-class counterparts acquire. They have little opportunity to practice negotiating with adults and little call to learn to summarize and present their own ideas, opinions, and excuses. The habit of not questioning adults also means that children in these homes are less likely to learn new vocabulary.

Physical discipline

When Lavina backs up her directive with a threat to "beat" Alexis, she is using a strategy common among adults in the poor and working-class families we observed. Ms. McAllister takes a similar tack, especially if a child's misbehavior provokes her anger. Even sixteen-year-old Lori is not immune:

Jane is angry. (Jane walks up to Lori and stands directly in front of Lori's face. Jane is mad and loud.) "I better not see you in none of them niggas' car down the hill, or I'm a slide (punch) you right upside your head, and I mean it."

Ms. McAllister, like her sister Lavina, views the administration of physical punishment as helpful and appropriate to any child under her care. She does not hesitate to discipline her nephews when it seems appropriate, as in this instance at the reunion picnic:

Guion is sitting on a bench, crying. Although I am standing right next to him I cannot hear him (because of the music), but I see tears streaming down his cheek. As Jane walks past, she leans over (to) where Runako is sitting and punches Runako with her balled up fist in the chest and yells at him (I can hear that) "Don't beat on Guion!"

Indeed, physical punishment is so commonly administered by the adults in the family that the children hold animated discussions over which adult is the strictest. One night at dinner time, the children are seated at the table and Ms. McAllister is walking around the living room. A discussion that begins focused on a picture of an aunt dressed in bell bottoms and clogs evolves into a comparison of strategies of physical punishment:

Jane says she don't like clogs because Mom-mom used to "beam" her on the forehead and it would leave a mark. Guion asks who is [harsher], Mom-mom or Pop-pop. This leads to an animated discussion of the grandparents' various strategies for beating kids. Guion and Runako and Harold and Alexis all compare notes and argue back and forth. Jane mostly listens. (She never disagrees with children or defends adults.) The kids talk about marks being left on the forehead and other parts of the body.

As this discussion of discipline across generations suggests, physical punishment is a common feature of the children's lives. Ms. McAllister also uses physical confrontation, and threats of physical confrontation, as a mechanism for resolving serious conflicts in her own life. One evening — the night before Harold is to leave for camp — she reaches her limit of tolerance with her twin sister, Jill. Her sister, she discovers, has taken packages of T-shirts that Hank bought for Harold and sold them. Jill also cut the cord to the air conditioner, so the unit no longer functions. Ms. McAllister, who is extremely angry, denounces her sister. Lori, Harold, Alexis, and a field-worker observe the fight from the beginning; Lenny shows up part of the way through it. The field notes capture the mounting tension and barely restrained violence:

(Jane and Jill do some serious yelling downstairs for about ten minutes.):

JANE: You fucking bitch! You steal Harold's clothes, huh?

JILL: Shut up, Jane.

JANE: Nobody but you around here go stealin' from my kids! I'm about to get you upside the fuckin' head!

JILL: I ain't fuckin' stealin' from you! Don't fuckin' accuse me!

JANE: . . . I'm sick of your stupid fuckin' games. I'm gonna get me a stick and you're gonna get out before I fuck you up!

JILL: Nobody puttin' me the fuck out!

In the middle of this, Alexis is hollering from the bathroom that she needs toilet paper. Ms. McAllister leaves, goes to a neighbor's house and borrows a roll. She returns with a large wooden stick.

JANE: I got me a stick now! You fuckin' hear?!

(Jill doesn't answer.)

JANE (yelling): You gettin' the fuck out! . . .

There's a lull as Jane searches [for Harold's missing shirts]. Lori turns to me (I've slowly come downstairs as I heard the yelling from Lori's room; now I stand against the banister wall of the living room). Lori (to me): "Her's no excuse for it." She says this with her head down; she looks so sad, like she might cry. Alexis is standing on the second step of the stairs, saying to me: "They always do this. The only thing is, it makes me scared."[18] She looks sad.

The density of the housing project also permits neighbors to hear the conflict and a small group gathers outside. The conflict escalates when Keith arrives home. He and Jill have a loud (physical) entanglement, but by this time the children and the field-worker have left the apartment and gone to the basketball court. They return a little later and sweep up the glass and move the broken furniture to the street as per an order issued by Ms. McAllister.[19]

This series of events was painful for all involved. Ms. McAllister was embarrassed that the field-worker witnessed the fight. She knew that it had been a frightening experience and wished it could have been avoided.[20] But, as she explains to me a few days later, she felt she had little choice. If she is to provide her children with a "home" and not just a "house," she could not allow her sister to stay.

I ask her, "Is she going to be moving?" She says firmly, "She is going to go." I say, "It is hard on your nerves." She says, "This is a house but it got to be a home."

I say, "Where will she go?" She shakes her head (to indicate she doesn't know). She says, "The kids won't come in here when she is here." She asks me, "Did you ever notice that?" I nod slowly. She says, "I got to make this a home not a house."

EMERGING SIGNS OF CONSTRAINT

The McAllisters, like other poor and working-class families, display caution and at times distrust toward individuals in positions of authority in dominant institutions. This approach contributes to very different interactions between family members and institutional representatives as compared to those experienced by middle-class families.

At a parent-teacher conference, for example, Ms. McAllister (who is a high school graduate) seems subdued. The gregarious and outgoing nature she displays at home is hidden in this setting. She sits hunched over in the chair and she keeps her jacket zipped up. She is very quiet. When the teacher reports that Harold has not been turning in his homework, Ms. McAllister clearly is flabbergasted, but all she says is, "He did it at home." She does not follow up with the teacher or attempt to intervene on Harold's behalf. In her view, it is up to the teachers to manage her son's education. That is their job, not hers. Thus, when the children complain about a teacher, she does not ask for details. Harold's description of his new (fifth-grade) teacher as "mean" prompts his mother to recall another, more likable, teacher — nothing more.

Similarly, when the McAllisters visit a local clinic so that Harold can get a physical for Bible camp, their experiences contrast sharply with the Williamses'. Here, too, the normally boisterous Ms. McAllister is quiet, sometimes to the point of being inaudible. She has trouble answering the doctor's questions. In some cases, she does not know what he means (e.g., she asks, "What's a tetanus shot?"); in others, she is vague:

DOCTOR: Does he eat something each day — either fish, meat, or egg?

JANE (her response low and muffled): Yes.

DOCTOR (attempting to make eye contact but failing as mom stares intently at paper): A yellow vegetable?

JANE (still no eye contact, looking down): Yeah.

DOCTOR: A green vegetable?

JANE (looking at the doctor): Not all the time.[21]

DOCTOR: No. Fruit or juice?

JANE (low voice, little or no eye contact, looks at the doctor's scribbles on the paper he is filling out): Ummh humn.

DOCTOR: Does he drink milk every day?

JANE (ABRUPTLY and in a considerably louder voice): Yeah.

DOCTOR: Cereal, bread, rice, potato, anything like that?

JANE (shakes her head, looks at doctor): Yes, definitely.

Harold, too, is reserved. When the doctor asks, "What grade are you in at school?" he replies in a quiet, low voice, "Fourth." But, when the topic shifts to sports, his voice grows louder. He becomes confident and enthusiastic. When the doctor reacts with surprised disbelief to Harold's announcement that he plays *all* positions in football, Harold is insistent. "All of them," he reiterates, interrupting when the doctor seeks to clarify things by listing positions ("tailback? lineman?").

Nor is Ms. McAllister always passive or subdued during the visit. For example, when the doctor comes into the waiting room and calls their name, she beckons Runako to come along and, only as an afterthought, asks if her nephew may come too. Ms. McAllister also asks that Harold's hearing and weight be checked. Not content to trust the doctor, she sends Runako down the hall to watch Harold being weighed and report the results back to her.

Nevertheless, there was an important difference in the character of the interaction between the McAllisters and their doctor and the Williamses and their doctor. Neither Harold nor his mother seems as comfortable as Alexander, who was used to extensive verbal conversation at home. Unlike either McAllister, Alexander is equally at ease initiating questions as answering them. Harold, who was used to responding to directives at home, answered questions from the doctor but posed none of his own. Unlike Ms. Williams, Ms. McAllister did not train her son to be assertive with authority figures, nor did she prepare him for his encounter with the doctor. Finally, the two families approached the visit with their doctor with different levels of trust. This unequal level of trust, as well as differences in the amount and quality of information divulged, can yield unequal profits to the individuals involved during a historical moment when professionals define appropriate parenting as involving assertiveness and reject passivity as inappropriate.[22]

DISCUSSION

The verbal world of Harold McAllister and other poor and working-class children offers some important advantages as well as costs. Compared to middle-class children we observed, Harold is more respectful toward adults in his family. In this setting, there are clear boundaries between adults and children. Adults feel comfortable issuing directives to children, which children comply with immediately. Some of the directives that adults issue center on obligations of children to others in the family ("don't beat on Guion" or "go do [her] hair for camp").[23] One consequence of this is that Harold, despite occasional tiffs, is much nicer to his sister (and his cousins) than the siblings we observed in middle-class homes. At family gatherings he voluntarily cares for his sixteen-month-old niece. Overall, children and parents spend less time talking; but, as in the choice of the towel for summer camp, the fewer words spoken ("girl colors") do not impede the clear communication of one's wishes. The use of directives and the pattern of silent compliance are not universal in Harold's life. In his interactions with peers, for example, on the basketball "court," Harold's verbal displays are distinctively different from those inside the household, with elaborated and embellished discourse. Nevertheless, there is a striking difference in linguistic interaction between adults and children in poor and working-class families when compared to that observed in the home of Alexander Williams. Ms. McAllister has the benefit of being able to issue directives without having to justify their decisions at every moment. This can make child rearing somewhat less tiring.

Another advantage is that Harold has more autonomy than middle-class children in making important decisions in daily life. As a child, he controls his leisure schedule. His basketball games are impromptu and allow him to develop important skills and talents. He is resourceful. He appears less exhausted than ten-year-old Alexander. In addition, he has important social competencies, including his deftness in negotiating the "code of the street."[24] His mother has stressed these skills in her upbringing, as she impresses upon her children the importance of "not paying no mind" to others, including drunks and drug dealers who hang out in the neighborhoods that Harold and Alexis negotiate.

Still, in the world of schools, health-care facilities, and other institutional settings, these valuable skills do not translate into the same advantages as the reasoning skills emphasized in the home of Alexander

Williams and other middle-class children. Compared to Alexander Williams, Harold does not gain the development of a large vocabulary, an increase of his knowledge of science and politics, a set of tools to customize situations outside the home to maximize his advantage, and instruction in how to defend his argument with evidence. His knowledge of words, which might appear, for example, on future SAT tests is not continually stressed at home. His effort to protect his cousin at school leads to the risk of suspension. His family has very close ties, but, unlike the Tallingers, they do not look each other in the eye when they speak. In future job interview situations, the closeness of Harold's family may not translate into the same value as the family training of other children who sustain direct eye contact. In these areas, the lack of advantage is *not* connected to the intrinsic value of the McAllister family life or the use of directives at home. Indeed, one can argue that raising children who are polite and respectful and do not whine, needle, or badger their parents is a highly laudable child-rearing goal. Deep and abiding ties with kinship groups are also, one might further argue, important.[25] Rather, it is the specific ways that institutions function that ends up conveying advantages to middle-class children. In their standards, these institutions also permit, and even demand, active parent involvement. In this way as well, middle-class children often gain an advantage, as we see with the experience of Stacey Marshall in the next chapter.

PART III

Families and Institutions

CHILDREN DO NOT LIVE THEIR LIVES out within the walls of the home. Instead, they move out into the world. They are required by law to go to school, and school is a powerful presence in their lives. Many children, as I have shown, have organized lives chock full with activities run by adults; other children have a slower-paced life wherein they hang out with cousins, watch television, and play outside. As children move out of the radar screen of the home environment, parents do not differ by social class in their love and concern for them. As the cases in this next section illustrate, working-class and poor mothers often anxiously watched their children's situations, as when in first, second, third, and fourth grade, Wendy Driver was having trouble learning to read. Similarly, Ms. Marshall kept her attention on her daughters' complaints about "Art" the bus driver.

Still, social class seemed to make a difference in how parents, primarily mothers, managed children's complaints about institutions. Middle-class mothers were often very interventionist, assertively intervening in situations. Sometimes parents were successful, and sometimes they were not. But in the process, they directly taught their children how to "not take no for an answer" and to put pressure on persons in positions of power in institutions to accommodate their needs. By contrast, working-class and poor parents tended to expect educators and other professionals to take a leadership role. This deference was not, it turned out, a stance they took up with other key service providers in their lives. Ms. Driver, for example, considered herself "hot tempered" and would fume about the latest antic of their landlord, but in the school situation, she was much more passive. Since the school was designed around a system of concerted cultivation, and teachers expected the parents to take a leadership role in schooling, the deference of parents such as Ms. Driver was problematic in terms of fostering school success.

Still, cultural resources did not automatically lead to profits. Despite assiduous efforts by the white middle-class mother Ms. Handlon to help her daughter Melanie in school, the experience was often difficult at home and of questionable benefit at school. In addition, it is important to look beyond the issue of individual personalities and look more broadly at the relationship of social patterns and social structures. Schools,

despite their claims to be friendly places, have a legal obligation to turn
parents in if they suspect child abuse or neglect. In this role, they are arms
of the state. Working-class and poor parents, as I have shown, were less
likely to use verbal reasoning as a form of discipline. Instead, many were
likely to use physical punishment. As I will show with the case of Little
Billy Yanelli, the use of a belt at home was in clear conflict with the patterns adopted by the school. In addition, the parents' belief in the importance of Little Billy defending himself on the playground also collided
with school rules. As a result, the Yanelli parents felt alternately defiant,
scared, and powerless. They encouraged their son to hit, when they felt it
was necessary, and, when necessary, he would be hit with a belt at home.
But through their lives, there was a lurking concern that they, and other
working-class and poor families shared: "the school" would suddenly
turn them in for child abuse and "come and take my kids away." By
being in synch with the standards of school officials, the cultural logic of
child rearing of concerted cultivation provided important, and largely
invisible, benefits to the middle-class parents and children that the
working-class and poor parents and children did not gain.

Concerted Cultivation in Organizational Spheres: Stacey Marshall

Suddenly, the first day in [gymnastics] class, everything that Stacey did, you know, uh. . . . Even, even though she was doing a skill, it was like, "Turn your feet this way," or . . . , "Do your hands this way." You know, nothing was very, very good or nothing was good, or even then just right. She [Tina, the instructor] had to alter just about everything [Stacey did]. I was somewhat furious . . . The instructor had come to the door, Tina. So I went to her, and I said . . . "Is there a problem?" (Interview with Ms. Marshall)

All families interact with many different institutions. For middle-class mothers, the boundaries between home and institutions are fluid; mothers cross back and forth, mediating their children's lives. When Ms. Marshall, a middle-class African American mother, discovered how unhappy her ten-year-old daughter, Stacey, was after her first gymnastics class in a private program, she did not hesitate to intervene. Almost seamlessly, the daughter's problem became the mother's problem. Ms. Marshall firmly believed that it was her responsibility as a parent to ensure that Stacey's activities provided an opportunity for positive, self-affirming experiences. Like other middle-class mothers we observed, Ms. Marshall acted like a guardian angel, hovering over her children, closely monitoring their everyday lives, ever ready to swoop down to intervene in institutional settings such as classrooms, doctors' offices, or day camps. Sometimes, her actions embarrassed her children; other times, the girls welcomed their mother's efforts.

Middle-class parents' interventions on behalf of their children can produce a twofold advantage. The children's interactions with teachers, health-care professionals, and camp counselors become more personal-ized, more closely tailored to meet their specific needs. Just as important, the children learn to *expect* this individualization, and they begin to acquire a vocabulary and orientation toward institutions that will be useful in the future, when they come to extract advantages on their own behalf. In the Marshall family, the children have many opportunities to learn how to negotiate the world beyond their home, and in their mother they have an unusually strong role model to help them acquire skills for effective interactions with institutions later in their lives. Nor was this pattern unique to the Marshall family. Other middle-class mothers in the study also played this "guardian angel" role. Middle-class parents were, for example, more likely than other parents in the study to request particular teachers for their children (Table C7, Appendix C).[1]

THE MARSHALL FAMILY

Lorrie and Lonny Marshall, parents of twelve-year-old Fern and ten-year-old Stacey (the target child), are in their forties. Each had been married once before they met; neither had had children. Ms. Marshall, who is tall, thin, and attractive, looks several years younger than she actually is. Her brown hair is relaxed and curled under; her skin is light brown. At home, she often dresses in a pressed, button-down shirt, shorts, and sandals. She has a quiet voice. During conversations, when she is trying to remember something, Ms. Marshall will close her eyes and think for several seconds. She is a college graduate and also holds a master's degree in math. The (Black) sorority she pledged in college remains an important part of her life. Employed full time in the computer industry, she telecommutes one day per week. On the other days, she drives fifty miles (round-trip).

Mr. Marshall is also tall and thin. He is the family comedian; his frequent jokes make life at home more lighthearted. For example, five minutes after meeting me, while looking over the list of publications on my vitae, he exclaimed, "Why, we are so proud of you!" Stacey and Fern adore him. Like his wife, Mr. Marshall has a college degree and was very active in his fraternity as an undergraduate. He is employed as a civil servant. He works nights, often six days a week, but he is not required to travel. He leaves for his job at 2:30 A.M. and returns in the early afternoon. Usually, he takes a nap when he comes home; sometimes he sleeps in the evening. Mr. Marshall is a confirmed sports fan; most evenings he watches a game on television. He coaches Fern's basketball team and travels with the players to out-of-state tournaments. He is disappointed that Stacey shows a lack of interest in basketball.

Both Mr. and Ms. Marshall grew up in the South. Ms. Marshall's parents live about four hours away. She sees them "three or four" times per year but talks to them on the phone weekly. She has two sisters; she talks on the phone with them monthly. All three sisters try to get together to visit their parents at the same time. Mr. Marshall's father died twenty years ago. His mother, a former schoolteacher, comes to her son's home to visit twice a year; he travels to see her an additional two or three times per year. None of the grandparents seem to be an especially important part of Fern and Stacey's lives.[2]

The Marshall girls are fifteen months apart in age. Like their parents, both are tall and thin. Fern is an avid basketball player. Stacey prefers gymnastics. The field-worker described Stacey this way:

She has medium brown skin and wears wire-rimmed glasses. Her hair is styled with a small bang, and then the rest is pulled back into a rather tight ponytail. She wears a white T-shirt with a Tasmanian She-Devil cartoon character on it, and white shorts. When she smiles, I notice her dimples.

As Ms. Marshall says, her daughter is a "personable person" who is more like her talkative father than her quiet mother. Stacey is both a talented gymnast and a good dancer. At home, she often hangs out by herself in her bedroom, watching television; but with friends, she can be lively. At the summer camps she attends, she has collections of friends to regularly chatter and giggle with.

At home, Stacey seems less bubbly. She and Fern annoy one another. The two squabble routinely; spats break out all through the day. For example, one afternoon, Stacey answers the phone, using the extension in her bedroom. She yells to Fern that the call is for her. Then, instead of hanging up, Stacey listens in, eavesdropping on her older sister's conversation. Fern strides into Stacey's bedroom, fuming. Wordlessly but angrily, she disconnects the phone from the wall. Stacey leaves the phone unplugged for a bit, but then returns to eavesdropping. These little tense encounters are often repeated. In the car during a ninety-minute drive, Stacey and Fern fuss at each other, at first jovially, but then angrily, including slapping, spitting, and pulling each other's hair. In general, Mr. and Ms. Marshall treat these sorts of interactions between the girls as part of normal sibling rivalry. The parents often make comments designed to defuse the girls' quarrels. They also frequently simply look at each other and sigh over their daughters' behavior or, in the car, separate them into different seats. There are also, however, moments of warmth as when Stacey uses her birthday money to buy her sister chocolates or when she seeks Fern's fashion advice, explaining to the field-worker, "Fern usually knows what looks right."

The girls and their parents (along with two guinea pigs, Scratch and Tiny) live on a quiet, circular street lined with large, recently built, two-story suburban homes with a market value of about $200,000 each. The Marshalls' neighbors include other Black middle-class families as well as white ones. Their beige-colored house has a small lawn and flowers in the front and a large lawn in the back (the girls are pleading with their parents to install a pool). Along with the family's two cars (a Volvo and a large Sable station wagon), the driveway is home to a basketball hoop. Fern often plays ball there with her friends; sometimes Mr. Marshall joins in. Inside the house are four bedrooms, two and one-half baths, a formal living room with a piano and African art decorating the walls, and a "great room" that opens into the dining area and a large kitchen. This family living area, which is light and airy, has a relaxed feel to it, with a television, director's chair, and comfortable tan corduroy couch on which the girls may leave a book or a Walkman. A gymnastics balance beam is resting on the floor; people step over it as they move through the family room area.

Each of the girls has her own bedroom, and in each there is a television and a telephone, along with the girls' collections of CDs, Walkmans, radios, and other electronic toys. In part because of Ms. Marshall's work, there is a computer in the house. Although the Marshalls' income is around $100,000 per year, the family, especially Ms. Marshall, often worries about money. We heard many comments about the cost of things and about the lack of job security in the computer industry. The company Ms. Marshall works for has downsized in recent years. She has kept her position, but she knows people who have not.

The Marshalls' well-to-do, racially integrated, suburban neighborhood is a transitional area. It is near the boundary with the central city and with a large, all-Black middle-class area; on the other side lies a predominantly white residential area. Stacey and Fern attend a local public school that is part of a district known for having good schools; most of the families in the district are white, but about one-quarter are Black, and there is a sprinkling of Asian and Hispanic families. The racial balance of the girls' daily lives (and of their parents' lives, as well) varies across settings. In many interactions, all of the key players are Black. Ms. Marshall explains that the girls had many very close white friends when they were younger, but over the years, racial barriers have become more prominent. For Fern, the turning point came in middle school; for Stacey, the shift is just occurring. Their social lives now exclusively involve other African American girls who live in their immediate neighborhood or just a few minutes away. The beauty parlor where the girls go on many Saturdays is all Black. The church the family attends is all Black. The Marshalls also frequently socialize with a close friend of Mr. Marshall who lives in an all-Black part of the city. There are, however, some important and time-consuming parts of the Marshalls' lives that take place in predominantly white settings, including shopping in retail stores, participating in organized activities, going to summer camps, and taking part in classes in the gifted program at school.

The family is busy. The hectic pace of their lives is similar to that of the Tallinger and Williams families. Gender plays a powerful role in determining the *kinds* of organized activities in which the children participate. But, in middle-class families, the sheer *number* of such activities does not appear to vary by gender. Stacey is active in gymnastics. Fern is active in basketball. Both girls attend Sunday school; Stacey is in the church youth choir, which rehearses on Friday nights and performs every third Sunday. Both girls are "junior ushers" at church. During the school year, Fern takes piano lessons; until quite recently, Stacey also took piano. During the summer, the girls move from one elaborate summer camp to another (e.g., gymnastics camp, basketball camp, and horseback riding camp). It is their mother who coordinates the girls' many different activities.

Like Mr. and Ms. Williams, Mr. and Ms. Marshall prefer to reason with their children rather than to issue directives. Although we occasionally saw the parents exhibit nonverbal frustration, we never heard them yell at the girls or hit them or threaten to hit them. Rather, they seem committed to the idea of helping their children develop as unique, and uniquely talented, individuals. Mr. and Ms. Marshall are reluctant to squelch Stacey's and Fern's thoughts or actions, even when the girls' behavior might strike others as being rude toward adults. The example below describes an episode at the home of close friends, where Ms. Marshall and the field-worker stopped to drop off the girls. The friends' twenty-year-old son, Mark (whose relationship to Stacey and Fern is similar to that of a cousin), is visiting from California and is having a birthday.

Mark asked everyone how church was. The girls gave a less than enthusiastic reply. Tom (Mark's father) said, "Now, how about some ice cream and cake, people?" Lorrie and I were trying to extricate ourselves from the proceedings. [Stacey was] sitting in a chair playing with one of those water toys that squirt a jet of air, and the goal is to get all the rings onto one stick. It seemed that Stacey was in a real hurry to have us out of there, because she said, "Good-bye, Mom."

There is more chatter and more delay as additional attempts are made to encourage Ms. Marshall and the field-worker to stay and join the party:

Then, Stacey said, "Just leave, Mom — I can't take much more of you." Even Fern was a little taken aback by that — she told Stacey to hush up. And Tom looked at her disapprovingly as he went to answer the phone that had just started to ring. Lorrie mounted no defense of her own, just sighed, looked at Mark, and said, "Mark, you wanna take them back with you?" Everyone laughed, and Stacey said, "I'll go to California — can I go to Disneyland?"[3]

If Stacey's mother is embarrassed or dismayed by her daughter's remark, she doesn't show it. Unlike parents in working-class or poor families, who are comfortable issuing directives, neither Mr. nor Ms. Marshall normally discourages either of their daughters from expressing their feelings simply because those feelings might dismay other adults. Moreover, in other settings, Ms. Marshall directly instructs the girls in strategies for interacting with adults. As we see next, she also works to bring about changes in the way other adults interact with Stacey and Fern.

SELECTING AND CUSTOMIZING CHILDREN'S LEISURE ACTIVITIES

Most middle-class parents are committed to involving their children in a steady schedule of organized activities attuned to the children's particular interests. Such activities often last only a matter of weeks; many change with each season. And, in the summer, the number of choices and the amount of time available both rise steeply. Finding out about activities, assessing their suitability, meeting enrollment deadlines, and coordinating transportation is a time-consuming act of labor. In most homes, it is mothers, not fathers, who do this work. This is true even when the mothers are employed full time. Ms. Marshall, for instance, who enrolled her girls in a series of *different* summer camps, did all of the coordinating and scheduling. Fern's and Stacey's camps were located in different parts of the suburbs, and they had different registration dates, forms to fill out, precamp requirements (physicals), specialties, and directors. Although Mr. Marshall will share in the driving if requested, Mr. and Ms. Marshall agree that it is overwhelmingly Ms. Marshall who handles the girls' lives and their activities, as well as any complaints about Fern's or Stacey's institutional experiences.

Ms. Marshall's efforts on behalf of her daughters are not unusual. Most middle-class mothers undertake similar labor with respect to organized activities. The way in which Stacey came to be involved in gymnastics, for example, is typical in that it takes effort by the mother.

When she was starting third grade I couldn't find a Girl Scout troop for her to be in. She had been a Brownie I think four years. Fern was in a Girl Scout troop. Stacey wasn't old enough to be a Girl Scout. So we went to this free night [laughs]. So Stacey . . . I wanted her to do something and it was a void . . . And I didn't want her sittin' in front of the TV.

By making inquiries, she discovered a township program that Stacey really enjoyed and in which she quickly revealed herself to be talented. When the gymnastic instructor suggests that Stacey develop her talents, Ms. Marshall begins looking for a setting for more advanced training. Not content to rely only on the instructor's recommendation, Stacey's mother also taps into her own social network.

And just listening to some of the parents. I started putting my ear to the grape-vine, and I heard a number of parents mention, "Well, if the kid really likes gym-nastics, you send them to Wright's."

While in this instance Ms. Marshal was gathering information on a recre-ational program, in other instances she was looking to solve educational problems (as when Stacey did not qualify for her school's gifted pro-gram). As with middle-class parents in the sample as a whole, Ms. Marshall's "grapevine" is rich with friends and relatives who are educa-tors, psychologists, lawyers, and even doctors (Table C8, Appendix C). As a result, middle-class parents are more likely to have informal access to valuable information and advice from professionals and experts than are working-class and poor parents.

Finding a good program, verifying Stacey's interest, and then enrolling her does not bring Ms. Marshall's responsibilities to an end, however. Unlike in working-class and poor families, where children are granted autonomy to make their own way in organizations, in the Marshall fam-ily, most aspects of the children's lives are subject to their mother's *on-going* scrutiny.

When Ms. Marshall becomes aware of a problem, she moves quickly, drawing on her work and professional skills and experiences. She dis-plays tremendous assertiveness, doggedness, and, in some cases effective-ness, in pressing institutions to recognize her daughters' individualized needs. Stacey's mother's proactive stance reflects her belief that she has a duty to intervene in situations in which she perceives that her daughter's needs are not being met. This perceived responsibility applies across all areas of her children's lives. She is no more (or less) diligent with regard to Stacey and Fern's leisure activities than she is with regard to their experiences in school or church or the doctor's office. This is clear in the way she handles Stacey's transition from her township gymnastics classes to the private classes at Wright's.

Ms. Marshall describes Stacey's first session at the club as rocky:

The girls were not warm. And these were little . . . eight- and nine-year-old kids. You know, they weren't welcoming her the first night. It was kinda like eyeing each other, to see, you know, "Can you do this? Can you do that?"

More important, Ms. Marshall reports that the instructor is brusque, critical, and not friendly toward Stacey. Ms. Marshall cannot hear what is being said, but she can see the interactions through a window. A key problem is that because her previous instructor had not used the professional jargon for gymnastic moves, Stacey does not know these terms. When the class ends and she walks out, she is visibly upset. Her mother's reaction is a common one among middle-class parents: she does not remind her daughter that in life one has to adjust, that she will need to work even harder, or that there is nothing to be done. Instead, Ms. Marshall focuses on Tina, the instructor, as the source of the problem.

We sat in the car for a minute and I said, "Look, Stace," I said. She said, "I-I," and she started crying. I said, "You wait here." The instructor had come to the door, Tina. So I went to her and I said, "Look." I said, "Is there a problem?" She said, "Aww . . . she'll be fine. She just needs to work on certain things." Blah-blah-blah. And I said, "She's really upset. She said you-you-you [were] pretty much correcting just about everything." And [Tina] said, "Well, she's got — she's gotta learn the terminology."

Ms. Marshall acknowledges that Stacey isn't familiar with specialized and technical gymnastics terms. Nonetheless, she continues to defend her daughter.

I do remember, I said to her, I said, "Look, maybe it's not all the student." You know, I just left it like that. That, you know, sometimes teaching, learning and teaching, is a two-way proposition as far as I'm concerned. And sometimes teachers have to learn how to, you know, meet the needs of the kid. Her style, her immediate style was not accommodating to — to Stacey.

Here Ms. Marshall is asserting the legitimacy of an individualized approach to instruction. She frames her opening remark as a question ("Is there a problem?"). Her purpose, however, is to alert the instructor to the negative impact she has had on Stacey ("She's really upset."). Although her criticism is indirect ("Maybe it's not all the student . . ."), Ms. Marshall makes it clear that she expects her daughter to be treated differently in the future. In this case, Stacey does not hear what her mother says, but she knows that her wishes and feelings are being transmitted to the instructor in a way that she could not do herself.

Moreover, in what is a common procedure in the Marshall home, Stacey's mother pursued the problem. The very next morning she called the gymnastics school and spoke with the owner. She asked (having first checked with Stacey) that her daughter be moved to the advanced beginner class. That class, however, was already full. In many organizations, Stacey would have had to stay in the intermediate class. In this case, the owner accommodated the mother and daughter, assigning a second instructor to the advanced beginner class so that Stacey could join that group. So, this series of institutional interactions results in important gains for Stacey Marshall: she gets access to a gymnastics class better suited to her skill and experience level; and she learns by observing her mother's actions that it is reasonable to expect organizations to accommodate the specialized needs of an individual. As the next section shows, as Stacey's classes in the new program progress, so too does her education in the art of interacting effectively with organizations.

TRANSMISSION OF SKILLS

Ms. Marshall is a conscious role model for Stacey, deliberately teaching her daughter strategies for managing organizational matters. Although it is hard to know how much Stacey absorbs her mother's lessons in how to deal effectively with people in positions of power in organizations, or how much she might draw on those lessons in the future, exposure to such learning as a child has the potential to be a tremendous lifelong asset.[4]

It is important to remember, though, that just because strategies of concerted cultivation can produce such assets does not mean that this form of child rearing is "the best." Every method of raising children is historically specific and subject to change. Concerted cultivation is neither "the only" way nor "the right" way to raise children. However, it is the way that contemporary powerful professionals such as child development specialists assert as the most appropriate and helpful approach to child rearing. In large part because of that endorsement, it is the method favored by the middle classes. Ms. Marshall continually "touches base" with Stacey's instructor, not only learning Tina's opinion but also providing the instructor with information about Stacey's assessment of her experience in the class:

I had mentioned to Tina . . . I had asked her at the place, "How's she doing?" She said, "Oh great, great." I said, "Well, she's a little concerned that she hasn't gotten . . . she's getting a little discouraged." And she [Tina] said, "Oh, well, she shouldn't be." She said, "She'll, she'll get it." But according to Stacey, um, Tina must have said to her after one class, um . . . you know, "You — you must be beginning to feel bad, because really, you're the only one who hasn't gotten it." (Ironic laugh)

Similarly, in her conversations with Stacey, Ms. Marshall lets her daughter know what Tina has said and what kind of behavior and comments her instructor should and should not make. She deems "totally unprofessional" Tina's remark about Stacey being "the only one who hasn't gotten it." She also makes it clear that an active response to that remark would be appropriate:

I said, and — and I said to Stacey, I said, "Look, do you want me to say anything? And so, you know I . . . M — my kids know that (short laugh), um, they know that I will call. They know that I will make an appearance. Um . . . but I — I was leaving that decision to her. And she said, "No. Don't do it, because then in class she'll say something to me [like], 'And your Mom said' such and such."

The last straw came soon. Stacey, arriving home from the gym on a day when her father has picked her up, announces, "She [Tina] told me I'm lazy." This leads Ms. Marshall and Stacey to decide that Stacey should decline the invitation she received to be part of the club's elite gymnastics team. In so doing, Ms. Marshall teaches Stacey that she has the right to turn down such an invitation. Moreover, she explicitly coaches her daughter on how to manage this choice. Drawing on her own professional background, Ms. Marshall advises Stacey to prepare an answer in advance to explain to her instructor and classmates why she doesn't intend to go out for the team.

Before Stacey went to the next class, I said, "What are you gonna to say to them, if they ask you why?" And she said, "I'm . . ." " You know," I said, "I think you better sit down and think about it."'Cause," I said, "they might ask you." And sure enough, they did. Um . . . 'cause, and we talked about it. I said, I said, "It might be feasible for you to just say that you just decided that you weren't ready for it." You know. And leave it at that.

The response from the instructor to Stacey's prepared statement serves to further antagonize Ms. Marshall:

I remember Stacey came out that night from class, and she — she got in, crying. She said, "You were right. She did ask me." And I said, "Well, what did you say?" She said, "We told 'em that I just didn't think I was ready for it." And I said, "Well, what did they say?" She said, "Tina just went 'Hmm'" (said in a disdainful, haughty voice). You know, like that. And here I'm thinking to myself, "Well, I don't really think that was appropriate."

Ms. Marshall is angered by Tina's criticisms because she believes they were harmful to Stacey. In addition, though, she feels that the instructor's remarks created more work for *her.*

Stacey is the type of child that needs a lot of warm fuzzies. She's a child that is very quick to think the negative. (Sigh.) And . . . she would come out and she said, "Well, Tina said this." I would say to myself, "Well, she may be stretching it a little." But the reality of it is, something was said. And obviously it wasn't the right thing. In part this is probably selfish too. I [saw it as], "Oh, God. There's more work for me." You know, to boost this kid's morale.

Partly because of these ongoing problems, and partly because Wright's is a long drive from the Marshall family's home, Stacey's mother began looking for a new program. She was engaged in this process when we began our observations of the family. She made numerous telephone calls to various programs in the county, drove to and inspected two different programs, attended two parent meetings of a program that she enrolled Stacey in but then withdrew her from (Ms. Marshall and other parents were outraged that a construction project begun after the session started reduced the size of the floor and, in their opinion, also created a safety hazard), and called the director of one of the programs to complain. The whole time, she worried. The decision regarding gymnastics seemed to weigh more on Ms. Marshall than on any other member of the family. Even as she was working full time, running the household, driving the children around, and negotiating a variety of complex tasks, she continued to examine the possibilities, determined to find the best choice for Stacey in gymnastics.

In many cases, Stacey accompanied her mother as she hunted for the right program. As a result, she learned what criteria to apply when assessing a program, and she developed a specific vocabulary with which to express her opinion. For example, when Stacey, her mother, and the researcher tour a YMCA with a gymnastics program, Stacey joins in a conversation about the length of the runway. Although only ten, she speaks with authority:

Stacey says, "It saves like six feet of where it is now, so it's in closer . . . So that way they can pull out the rest of the floor . . . We're gonna end up having a longer vaulting runway. . . ."

A few days later, meeting with the coach for the program, Stacey is easily able to describe her skill level and she, not her mother, describes her skills. Thus, when the coach and Stacey's mother discuss the appropriate level, Stacey remains an integral part of the adults' discussion. Outside, she is ready to render an opinion:

Once we were inside the car, Lorrie asks Stacey what she thought. Stacey says, "It's good." After a couple of seconds' pause, Stacey said, "If we come on Saturday, then we can see it when they have the whole gym."

Ms. Marshall will make the final decision about where to enroll Stacey, but she clearly values her daughter's opinion. Stacey is encouraged to give her assessment and when she does, it is treated as important, if not definitive.

INTERVENING IN SCHOOL: EARLY AND OFTEN

Unlike working-class and poor parents, who may, for example, stand their ground with the landlord but silently accept the pronouncements of a classroom teacher, Ms. Marshall takes the same quiet yet assertive approach with all representatives of the many institutions and organizations that affect her daughters' lives. For example, the school Stacey and Fern attend has a gifted-and-talented program that draws an elite group of students and provides them with an enriched, challenging curriculum. Ms. Marshall viewed her daughters' inclusion in the program as a clear advantage; thus, when the girls just missed the IQ score cutoff (Stacey's score of 128 was 2 points shy of the 130 needed), their mother took prompt action.[5] Using informal advice from educators in the school, tips from friends in other districts, the family's substantial economic resources, and her own vast supply of determination, Ms. Marshall learned the guidelines for appealing a decision and followed them. She arranged to have her daughters tested privately (to the tune of $200 per child) and was able to get both girls admitted to the program.

Much as getting Stacey enrolled in the private gymnastics class was only the first in a long series of interventions, so too with the gifted-and-talented program. Ms. Marshall remained in close contact with the consultant for the program, overseeing the selection of teachers for her children and complaining when the math teacher did not inform her (per the policy of the gifted program) of a looming "C" in math. In addition, she consistently drew educators' attention to her daughter's slow, careful, and methodical learning style. These habits often resulted in Stacey not finishing all of the work assigned in the time allotted (e.g., she might finish only about half of the math problems on an exam). In formal testing situations, Stacey did not do as well as she might have, were the test not timed. Ms. Marshall did not pressure her daughter to hurry or insist that she learn new strategies for working faster. Instead, this mother sought to make sure that all key personnel were aware of her daughter's special circumstances. Her clear expectation was that once notified of Stacey's learning style, the teachers would adjust what they required her to accomplish.

Ms. Marshall's belief that she has the right and the responsibility to intervene in the classroom is widely shared by middle-class parents, mothers particularly. At Swan, the middle-class, predominately white suburban school where the research assistants and I carried out classroom observations, the teachers noted that parents frequently came barging into school to complain about minor matters. For example, a scheduling conflict that resulted in some third-graders not getting a chance to perform a skit for their peers in the other third-grade classrooms prompted three different mothers to come in to school the very next morning to let the teacher know how disappointed their children were and to inquire into exactly why some children had gotten the opportunity to perform and others had not. More generally, parents of Swan students did not hesitate to criticize teachers' choice of projects, book report assignments, homework levels, or classroom arrangements. Some mothers had a much more aggressive style than did Ms. Marshall. At Swan School, for example, Mr. and Mrs. Kaplan circulated a petition (with limited success) demanding that a song with the lyric "come let us bow and worship Him now" be removed from the multicultural holiday program. The Kaplans then wrote a letter to the superintendent charging it was a "violation of the separation of church and state." (Over the choir teacher's objections, the song was ultimately removed; the district also instituted a review of policy on the matter.) Yet, despite these differences in style, it was nonetheless the same approach: these middle-class families were engaged in a pattern of concerted cultivation with a close monitoring of their children's institutional experiences.

RACE: CONSTANT WORRIES, INTERMITTENT INTERVENTIONS

As a Black mother who grew up in a town with racially segregated swimming pools, Ms. Marshall knows from personal experience that subtle forms of discrimination are always present. When her own children face difficulty in an institutional setting, the possibility that they are experiencing racial insensitivity or discrimination automatically looms:

It always comes up for me. And part of that has to do with the fact that I grew up in the [South]. I know what it is to have experienced um . . . just, discrimination. Um . . . I know that subtle — subtle discrimination still exists. Any time something happens, with my kids, you know, . . . on a sports team or whatever, in the classroom, I have to kinda grapple with . . . is, well, is race an issue? There's a part of me that believes that . . . sometimes it comes into play — in terms of labeling or — or categorizing. You know. Um . . . when Stacey came out [from the gym at Wright's] and she said, "Well, Tina was sayin' these things." I had to turn an ear. I had to wonder, you know, "Why's she sayin' that?"

Trying to decide whether "turning an ear" is sufficient or whether the situation calls for a more active intervention is not easy. Because the *potential* for racial discrimination is always present, isolating race as the key factor in a specific situation can be hard. Ms. Marshall's response to Stacey's experiences at Wright's is a complicated mixture of ambivalence, second guessing, and insecurity:

[I thought] . . . that it's, that it's a racist attitude. And, um . . . that she's [Tina] [is saying things to Stacey] because this is a little Black kid. You know, that . . . she's not gonna do it [become a star performer]. However . . . from what I've seen, newspaper clippings, they had minority kids who had risen to the top there. So it's not an issue of the entire team is white [or that] my kid would never get on it. That's not true. If my kid was good enough, I — I think they would, I — I'm pretty sure that they'd let her on it. You know, primarily because the goal is to win. You know, and if you're black, red, yellow, green, they would put their kid on the team. You know, because they want to win.

When Fern feels excluded from the camaraderie at her basketball camp (where she is the only Black child among about a hundred girls), Ms. Marshall again hesitates, pondering what the best response might be.

Fern came home one day and she was talkin' to Stacey about it. She . . . I said, "How are things?" She said, "Fine," she said, "except for lunch." I said, "Who'd you eat with?" "Myself." (Deep sigh from Ms. Marshall)

Fern sees it as a racial issue:

Fern said, "*You know.*" I said, "Well, did you talk to 'em?" She said, "Yeah, I talked to them." . . . Apparently there was dialogue . . . about who scored in the game . . . and they were doing things, but when it came time for lunch — she ended up at a table by herself . . . The staff [members] are other kids — high school kids, girls on the team . . . So to some extent . . . maybe there's not another adult that's taking the lead to, like, pull Fern into a lunchtime group. I said to her, "Do you want me to say something?" She said, "No." And part of it is because it's just a week. (Fern's camp lasts one week.)

Ms. Marshall had had only one brief telephone chat with the coach before she enrolled Fern and felt that she did not "have a relationship" with him that would provide a framework "to have a dialogue." She considered, but ultimately decided against, speaking to him.[6]

In some cases, though, she does intervene, usually after a period of watchful scrutiny. She described a situation that arose with the girls' school bus driver:

Fern had shared with me last year. She said, "Art's racist. He makes all the Black kids sit on the back of the bus and he only yells at us. . . ." And blah-blah-blah. Again, in that, you know, I'm listening to this and I'm thinking, "Well, is this just a child, you know, being overly sensitive, or — or what?"

Unlike Fern, who by the time she was twelve brought up racial issues in conversations at home almost daily, Stacey rarely interpreted or discussed events as being racially loaded. But she too noted problems with Art:

When Stacey started riding the bus this year, she started saying the same thing. She says, "Art's, Art only picks on us." She says, "He won't even let us open the windows."

Although aware of her daughters' concerns, Ms. Marshall did not immediately launch an intervention or share the girls' observations with school staff. Instead, she kept her eye on the situation.

I never just leave 'em at the bus stop. The bus picks them up at the end of the corner here. I will always stay there in the car, and I began to watch. You know, just kind of look and see where kids are on the bus.

In addition to restricting where the children could sit, the bus driver also inconsistently enforced policies regarding who could ride the bus:

Policies seemed to be upheld differently for the different races. Apparently there was, on one day, a little white boy was bringing a friend home, and didn't have a note (from his parents). The boy was allowed to ride the bus. A few days later, a little Black girl was riding home with a friend and she was not permitted on the bus.

Near the end of the school year, there was a discussion in Fern's social studies class and other children — including white students — echoed her opinion of Art, who said, "Yeah, Art does this." The white children's validation helped Ms. Marshall overcome her hesitancy about complaining. She called the district's administrative offices and spoke to the director of transportation services who told her, "You know, we don't, we don't stand for that."

Ms. Marshall not only had an idea about the nature of the problem, but she also had in mind the proper organizational solution.

His approach was a bit different than what I told him I thought he should have taken. He said, "Well," he said, "If you were calling earlier, we could have put a camera on the bus." I said, "I'm not asking you to put a camera on the bus; I'm asking you to let this man know that the children perceive something and that parents, at least one parent, is aware of something that he said." He went into the fact that our school district subcontracts the busing service. . . . (This meant that, legally, the district could not speak directly to the driver.) I said, "Well, next thing you do is call the supervisor." (emphasis added)

In the fall, Ms. Marshall plans to call the transportation administrator before school starts to find out who will be driving the school bus. In the meantime, she seems distressed and somewhat at a loss as to what to say when Stacey and Fern express concerns about Art, stressing only that they have to "judge a person as a person" as they make their way in the world.

A CRUCIAL DIMENSION OF CONCERTED CULTIVATION: OVERSEEING INSTITUTIONS

In the theoretical language of Pierre Bourdieu, both Black and white middle-class parents, and mothers in particular, routinely scanned the horizon for opportunities to activate their cultural capital and social capital on behalf of their children.[7] By shrewdly framing their interventions in ways that institutions such as schools and public and private recreational programs found compatible with their organizational processes, parents could gain important advantages for their children. These benefits go beyond specific short-term goals, such as securing a place in the classroom of "the best" fourth-grade teacher or getting into "the best" gymnastics program. By teaching their daughters and sons how to get organizations to meet their individualized needs, white and Black middle-class mothers pass along skills that have the potential to be extremely valuable to their children in adulthood. These are class-based advantages. As later chapters will show, the institutional relationships forged by working-class and poor families differ in important ways from those of middle-class parents, *Black and white.*

Among middle-class families, race played a role, not in terms of whether or how parents intervened in their children's organizational lives, but rather, in the kinds of issues that they kept their eyes on and in the number of potential problems parents and children faced. Middle-class Black parents — whose children tend to spend a large part of their daily lives in predominantly white environments — were attuned to issues of racial exclusion and insensitivity on the part of other children as well as adults. Ms. Marshall and other African American parents were also alert to the possibility that whites might have low expectations for their children, be it in gymnastics or math. This vigilance meant that Black middle-class parents, mothers especially, undertook more labor than did their white middle-class counterparts, as they worried about the racial balance and the insensitivity of other children, and framed appropriate responses to their own children's reactions. From time to time, children and parents both encountered difficult and painful situations, such as the one the Marshall girls faced when they rode the school bus. Acknowledging the legitimacy of their children's observations while still trying to preserve hope for a racially integrated society where people are treated equally was an ongoing challenge for Ms. Marshall and other Black middle-class mothers.

There could be important benefits — or profits — for children when their mothers engaged in concerted cultivation by overseeing, criticizing, and intervening in their institutional lives. Stacey was in the gifted program when she otherwise would not have qualified, she was able to participate in an advanced beginner gymnastics class with additional staffing due to her mother's interventions, and she was in the area's best gymnastic and horseback riding camps thanks to her mother's research. Occasionally Stacey did not appreciate her mother's efforts, but for the most part she appreciated having her mother smooth the way. For the most part, Ms. Marshall's interventions did seem to make things easier for her daughter. This kind of positive connection between intervention and outcome was not always the case in other families, however. The next chapter, which describes the battles over homework that the Handlon family endured, shows the more difficult side of middle-class parents' commitment to intervening in their children's institutional lives.

CHAPTER 9

Concerted Cultivation Gone Awry: Melanie Handlon

"I just figure, if kids didn't have homework, life would be easy." (Ms. Handlon)

In the middle class, children's activities outside of the home often penetrate deeply into the heart of family life and in so doing create opportunities for conflict. For the Handlons, it is homework that poses the most consistent threat to household harmony. Homework conflicts occur, or are mentioned, during virtually every visit field-workers make to the Handlon home. Ms. Handlon's observation that "life would be easy" if it weren't for homework sums up the enormous impact the issue has on this family.

Like the Tallingers, Marshalls, and Williamses, the Handlons have important forms of social, economic, and cultural capital. They are well positioned to intervene in their children's institutional lives. Some of the strategies Mr. and Ms. Handlon pursue are familiar components of concerted cultivation. For example, much like Ms. Marshall, Ms. Handlon tries to ensure the academic success of her daughter, Melanie, by tailoring Melanie's classroom experiences. Unlike Ms. Marshall, though, Ms. Handlon makes only intermittent contact with school staff and is only partly successful in achieving the accommodations she seeks. What is most striking about the Handlons' approach to child rearing is the emphasis they put on activating their resources *inside* the home. Ms. Handlon makes sustained, intense efforts in the area of homework. She expends large quantities of time and energy each weekday afternoon, trying to help Melanie complete her assignments. Ironically, this strategy yields few positive results. It pits mother against daughter, emotionally exhausting both, yet seems to yield few institutional profits.

THE HANDLON FAMILY

June Handlon, a thin, middle-aged woman with wavy red hair, has a relaxed way about her. Her husband, Harold, is a tall, friendly man with a boyish grin. Although he is an enthusiastic golfer, Mr. Handlon nevertheless is about fifty pounds overweight. He has an M.A. in credit and financial management and works as a credit manager in a major corporation. Ms. Handlon completed two years of junior college and is employed as a secretary by the Sylvan Presbyterian Church. She works thirty hours per week.

The Handlons have three children: Harry, an eighth-grader; Tommy, a sixth-grader at the nearby middle school; and Melanie, the focal child, a fourth-grader at the neighborhood elementary school. Harry is tall and thin, with longish brown hair that is mostly hidden under a nearly ever-present baseball cap (worn backward); he loves country music, street hockey, and, most of all, auto racing. Tommy, by contrast, prefers theater and plays to sports. Melanie resembles neither of her brothers. Field notes from the first visit to the Handlon home describe Melanie this way:

Melanie answers the door with a shy smile. She is young and maybe 4' 4" tall. Her hair is long and blond. . . . She has a thin white plastic headband on her head, which pulls her hair back from her face. Her face is pudgy; she has chubby cheeks, which make her eyes seem very small and squinted. She wears a purple turtleneck and matching purple knit pants. The clothes fit her tightly and reveal that she has a young potbelly.

At school, Melanie is more often tentative than assertive. Although she is not especially popular, neither is she a social isolate. She misses school frequently for minor illnesses such as sore throat, sore foot, or cold (but in an interview, Melanie confesses to a field-worker that sometimes she feigns illness deliberately to avoid having to go to school). One teacher worries about her being in the "shadow" of her older brothers. Certainly at meals, where both her brothers jabber nonstop, she has little opportunity to talk.

Still, at times, she can be outgoing and engagingly uninhibited. For example, one day at school she learns how to sing the song "Happy Birthday" in Spanish. That afternoon, pleased with her new accomplishment, Melanie sings the song over and over and over. She sings in the car and while doing her homework. She sings at dinner. In fact, she sings all through the evening. The lack of an appreciative audience for her newest skill does not seem to diminish Melanie's enthusiasm. She also enjoys playful interactions with her father, including pitching a paper airplane at his belly. Thus, while accurately described as shy, Melanie can and does change her behavior as she moves from context to context.

In the Handlon family, most household tasks, as well as scheduling and coordinating family members' activities and providing transportation to and from events and appointments are Ms. Handlon's responsibility. Despite the regularity of Mr. Handlon's work routine (he leaves the house each weekday at 7:30 A.M. and returns home at 6:00 P.M.), he does very little child-related labor. Instead, he handles such matters as videotaping the church pageant and putting up the family's Christmas tree lights.

THE HANDLONS' WORLD

The Handlons, and Melanie in particular, live in a white world. Among the sixty or so children in the two fourth grades at Melanie's elementary school, only five are nonwhite. Similarly, both Melanie's Girl Scout troop and her family's church congregation are overwhelmingly white. The Handlons' nearly all white social world is coupled with a physical environment that is, if anything, even less integrated. The family's four-bedroom home (a two-story, red brick house built in the late 1940s and worth about $245,000) is located in a homogenous suburban neighborhood.

With a family income of between $85,000 and $95,000 per year, the Handlons are solidly middle class and appear to take many elements of middle-class status for granted. They own an array of electronics (TVs, stereo, VCR, electronic keyboard) and each adult has a car. All three children participate in at least some activities organized by adults. The cost of these activities is dismissed as "minimal" and inconsequential. There is no indication that the Handlons feel the need to "pinch pennies." They live in cluttered comfort. On our first visit, Ms. Handlon remarks apologetically and with some embarrassment that "housework isn't my strong suit." Indeed, the dining room table is piled with all sorts of items — coupons, socks, used cups, a laundry basket of clean but unfolded clothes, and piles of papers. In the kitchen, dirty dishes sometimes pile up in the sink and are left unheeded on the table. In the living room, several half-opened boxes of Christmas ornaments rest on the couch for over a week while the Christmas tree is being decorated. This level of untidiness is not common among middle-class families, but it does not appear to cause trouble for the Handlons.

Unlike most middle-class families, the Handlons have many relatives who live close by. Melanie's parents describe themselves as feeling emotionally close to these members of their extended family. They report seeing their relatives about once a week and note that they also spend major holidays with them, including Thanksgiving, at which time they had twenty people at the house. The Handlons' interactions with kin are much more frequent than is typical among the middle class, but they do not approach the kinds of connections that are common among working-class and poor families. Among these groups, as previous chapters have shown, informal play and visits with cousins are not restricted to once a week or special occasions. Instead, they dominate everyday family life.

COMPETING VALUES: THE IMPORTANCE OF ORGANIZED ACTIVITIES AND UNSTRUCTURED TIME

Compared to other middle-class children, Melanie does not have a "heavy" schedule of organized activities. She is by no means idle outside of school, however. During December, she juggles several regularly scheduled commitments with assorted holiday events. Every Sunday includes an early church service, Sunday school, and youth choir practice. Mondays she has a piano lesson; Thursdays she goes to Girl Scouts. In addition to these standing events, Melanie also takes part in a special Girl Scouts "cookies for the homeless" holiday event on a Monday night and a school holiday musical performance on a Tuesday night. In between her two orthodontist appointments and five special rehearsals for the Christmas pageant at her church, she manages to Christmas shop.

Melanie does not complain about her schedule, nor do her parents seem to consider her activities overly taxing. In fact, Ms. Handlon perceives all three of her children as spending less time in organized activities than other children in the neighborhood. Both Mr. and Ms. Handlon believe that children should have free, unstructured time. Mr. Handlon explicitly criticizes the tendency of parents to "overschedule" children. Nevertheless, both Handlons hope Melanie will take on another commitment — they want her to join a swim team in the spring. When tryouts took place the previous year, Melanie had declined to participate. Her parents continue to bring the topic up from time to time, including around Christmastime. Mr. and Ms. Handlon's belief that Melanie's involvement in swimming would be an objectively good thing for her apparently trumps their resistance to the "overscheduling" of children. It can be a difficult trade-off. Middle-class parents (especially mothers) worry that if their children do not enroll in organized activities, they will have no one to play with after school and/or during spring and summer breaks. This kind of concern is clearly present with the Handlons. In addition to their desire to see Melanie enroll in swimming, they would like her to give softball a try. One winter evening, as the family is sitting around watching television, Melanie's mother mentions softball three times. Although on each occasion she frames the decision to play softball as Melanie's, Ms. Handlon urges the activity upon her daughter and explicitly mentions her concern that Melanie not be "left out." Eventually, Melanie says, "Okay, I'll play," and the subject is dropped.

One striking though unintended result of Mr. and Ms. Handlon's tendency to actively encourage Melanie to take activities she does not seek out herself is the speed and frequency with which she will complain, "Mom, I'm bored!" Ironically, although we observed this same pattern of self-proclaimed boredom among other seemingly very busy middle-class children in the study, we did not find it among the comparatively "underscheduled" working-class and poor children.

CULTIVATING ACADEMIC SUCCESS: INTERVENING AT SCHOOL

Like other middle-class mothers, Ms. Handlon plays an active role in monitoring, criticizing, and intervening in Melanie's schooling. She tries to work closely with Melanie's teachers. At the beginning of the school year, for example, she brings Melanie, who is sick, to school for a brief visit so that her daughter can meet her teacher. Once Melanie is feeling better, Ms. Handlon inquires about the work missed, queries the teacher about items she did not understand, and works to facilitate her daughter's transition into fourth grade.

She kind of felt lost because kids had already gone over a lot of the things and Melanie didn't understand what was going on. So I went in, basically, every morning and talked with the teacher and asked questions.[1]

Melanie's minor illnesses persist and so too do her mother's interventions. Hoping to keep Melanie from falling behind, Ms. Handlon requests that the teacher send home spelling lists in advance. She photocopies each new list when it arrives and then cuts it up to make flashcards, gluing each word to an index card. She brings the cards along when she and Melanie go out on errands; as they drive around in the car, they practice spelling the words. Melanie consistently ranks at the bottom of her class academically. The Handlons have hired a private tutor for Melanie, but Ms. Handlon worries that her daughter is "intimidated" and that school is a "negative" experience for her. She believes that Melanie lacks self-

confidence and that "she needs something that [gives] her a positive feeling." She makes these opinions very clear to Melanie's teacher during a
conference. In a parent-teacher conference with Ms. Nettles, Ms. Handlon
makes a pointed comment that Melanie's social study teacher has placed
too much emphasis on the negative in grading a test:

With the social studies test that she brought home with the big N (Needs
Improvement — this is the lowest grade possible) on the top of the paper. I looked
at it and I counted all the ones she got right. I said, "Melanie, compared to the
last social studies test, you got like eighteen right on this one." I said, "That's a
lot more than you got right on the last test so you have improved." Now, looking
at the paper she couldn't see that. It was just a negative, an N . . . So, I'm trying
to get her to start recognizing her positives.

Ms. Handlon's comments during the parent-teacher conference demonstrate her belief that she is *entitled* to point out what she sees as the
teacher's failings with respect to the conduct of Melanie's education. This
is a perspective widely shared by middle-class parents, including the
many mothers with whom Ms. Handlon interacts when she brings
Melanie to and from school or other events. Ms. Handlon's role as the
local Girl Scout leader also provides her with informal opportunities to
exchange information about routine and unusual happenings at the elementary school.[2] Ms. Handlon knows that many mothers have complaints of one kind or another and that many are engaged in specialized
pursuits for their children.

Being embedded in a social network of middle-class mothers shapes
Ms. Handlon's sense of her rights and her responsibilities with regard to
Melanie's education.[3] She and the other mothers seem comfortable passing judgment on all aspects of their children's schooling, critiquing everything from teachers' pedagogical style to the content of their classroom
bulletin boards.

Mr. Ickes (Melanie's fourth-grade social studies teacher). I had a negative opinion
[about him] from parents. They don't like his teaching methods. They don't like
his gruffness. People didn't like Ms. Hortense (Melanie's third-grade teacher) a
lot because she was very old-school and had not changed or adapted her teaching. Her classroom was very boring. There was nothing bright or exciting. Her
bulletin boards were not exciting and not conducive to exciting kids about education. At the beginning of the year, I wasn't one [of the parents who disliked Ms.
Hortense] but Melanie would get a lot right on the paper, and the only thing
acknowledged was what was wrong.

Ms. Handlon's network also provides her with information about
what steps other parents are taking as they try to resolve school-related

problems, such as how to ensure that homework gets done correctly and on time. Her conversations with other mothers help her develop strategies for interacting with educators.

[Some of us mothers] were talking about the conferences that are coming up, and what points are going to be brought up, and what we are going to talk about. And the biggest concern I hear from parents is the amount of homework. It's every night. It's on weekends. It's constant.

Despite her belief that Melanie's teacher assigns too much homework, and her awareness that other parents are concerned about this issue, Ms. Handlon does not raise the topic of homework directly with any of the educators or administrators at the school. Instead, as the rest of this chapter describes, she tries to help Melanie herself, going over her daughter's schoolwork with her at home, each afternoon.

CULTIVATING ACADEMIC SUCCESS: INTERVENING AT HOME

In separate interviews, Mr. and Ms. Handlon each define homework as a major problem within the family. Ms. Handlon is frank and succinct: "Our biggest conflict is homework," she tells the interviewer. Mr. Handlon focuses on the volume of homework the children face. He estimates that Melanie does "two to three hours [of homework] every night." He describes the family routine this way:

That's all we do with them at night is homework. They come home from school, get a snack, and they'll start working on homework. And they're still working on homework, and they're still working on it when I get home. It's entirely too much homework. I don't think I did that much homework in college.

Ms. Handlon voices similar concerns during her interview, and she returns to the topic informally with a field-worker one afternoon as they sit in the family minivan, waiting to pick up Melanie after school,

[Melanie] worked on her homework [Sunday] for four hours with her father. From three until seven. I can't believe that the teachers assign so much on the weekends. Don't they have a life?

Neither Mr. nor Ms. Handlon seems to believe that *all* homework is bad and both appear to accept the view widely held among middle-class parents that children must do homework in order to succeed academically. What the Handlons object to is the quantity of work, the amount of their *children's* time spent doing school assignments, the amount of *their* time given over to their children's homework, and the useless nature of much of the work. These elements, alone and in combination, result in a further problem, namely the constant presence of tension and conflict in the home. Homework sets off painful, protracted battles. Ms. Handlon and Melanie appear to have different ideas about how much help with school-work Ms. Handlon should provide, in what areas, and in what ways.

Melanie contends that her homework often is too difficult for her to complete, even with help. Her mother seems to believe that Melanie needs to concentrate more. Especially in math, Ms. Handlon tries to help by taking Melanie step by step through each problem. Thus, even when the questions are not mentally challenging for Melanie, homework can be very time consuming for both mother and daughter. For assignments in which comprehension is also an issue, much more than time is at stake: a general sense of failure and frustration on both sides are regular hallmarks of these mother-daughter homework sessions.

Not surprisingly, neither Melanie nor her mother looks forward to doing homework. Melanie's first line of defense is to take the offense, as the following excerpt from a field note shows. Climbing into the family's minivan after school, Melanie immediately mentions—and simultane-ously downplays—the fact that she has homework:

MS. HANDLON (in a cheery voice): How are you?

MELANIE: Okay. (pause) I only have math homework today.

MS. HANDLON: How many problems?

MELANIE: Ten. Well, maybe twenty.

MS. HANDLON: That's not too bad. Only math?

MELANIE: Yeah.

Her mother is not ready to drop the topic, however. Probing, she inquires about other subjects. Reluctantly, Melanie discloses the rest of her home-work load. She is hesitant but truthful:

MS. HANDLON: You don't have any social studies?

MELANIE: Well, maybe a little.

MS. HANDLON: What about spelling?

MELANIE: Oh, yeah. I have a spelling test tomorrow.

Once home, Melanie takes time to snack and relax before beginning her homework. She asks permission to put on music. Gleefully, she selects "The Nutcracker" and turns the volume up loud on the stereo. With mother and daughter sitting together at the dining room table, the homework session begins.

MELANIE: What do I do?

Melanie's mother reads the directions out loud and goes over the first problem with Melanie.

MS. HANDLON: See? You carry this remainder and put it in this box.

MELANIE: Oh.

As they move to the second problem, Ms. Handlon continues to help Melanie in a very hands-on fashion.

MS. HANDLON: Okay, what do we do here? How many times will seven go into fifty-two? Well, what's five times seven?

MELANIE: Thirty-five.

MS. HANDLON: Right. So, that's too small. So, what's seven times six? What's seven times seven?

MELANIE: Forty-two. Forty-nine.

MS. HANDLON: Right. So, where do you put that? And what's the remainder? You have to borrow. Right. And then put the remainder in the next box. And how do you do this problem?

On another problem, Melanie resists her mother's effort to make the task seem easier:

MS. HANDLON: This is an easy problem.

MELANIE: These are hard.

MS. HANDLON: It's five! You know your fives.

MELANIE: I know my ones, my fives, and my tens.

MS. HANDLON: So, count by fives. (Melanie counts.)

MS. HANDLON: Right. So what's the answer? (Melanie gives an answer.)

MS. HANDLON: Right. And where do you put that? (Melanie writes it down. Ms. Handlon takes the pencil and erases Melanie's entry.)

MS. HANDLON: Not there. (Melanie tries again.)

MS. HANDLON: Right. And where's the remainder? (Melanie says an answer.)

MS. HANDLON: No. What's the remainder? (Melanie gives another answer.)

MS. HANDLON: Right, and put that there. And then carry that to the next problem. Good.

Melanie and her mother proceed in this fashion for about fifteen minutes. Then the interaction starts to break down. From Melanie's perspective, the problems are hard and she thinks she can't do them. She wants to stop. Her interest flags and her answers are increasingly far off base. Ms. Handlon reacts quickly.

MELANIE: This is hard.

MS. HANDLON: Melanie, I think you're making this harder than it is. How did you do it in school?

MELANIE: We used cubes.

MS. HANDLON: How did you figure out the problems?

MELANIE: We worked as a group.

MS. HANDLON: Who was in your group?

MELANIE: Emily was. But we all worked together.

MS. HANDLON (suggesting a new strategy): Would it help if you used pennies?

When Melanie nods, her mother searches briefly in drawers and in her purse. She comes up with several stacks of pennies, which she puts on the table. Melanie starts lining the pennies up in two adjacent, horizontal lines. She stands up to do this and moves a little to the side of the table. Ms. Handlon comes over, stands next to her and asks, "What are you doing?" Without giving Melanie a chance to explain, Ms. Handlon moves the pennies out of the rows Melanie has organized. Melanie protests:

MELANIE: No! This is how we did it.

MS. HANDLON: Okay, show me how you did it. (Melanie lines up forty-two pennies in two adjacent, horizontal rows. She then takes the pennies and puts them in groups of four. Her mother again intervenes.)

MS. HANDLON: Melanie, explain to me what you are doing. (Melanie continues to move the pennies but says nothing. Then she stops moving the coins.)

MS. HANDLON: And?

MELANIE: And I count the groups.

MS. HANDLON: But you're supposed to divide by seven.

MELANIE: OOHH . . .

MS. HANDLON: That's why I didn't understand what you were doing. (Melanie reorganizes the coins, putting the pennies in groups of seven. She solves the next two problems. When she tries to tackle a problem that requires dividing twenty-seven by six, her mother again becomes heavily involved. Ms. Handlon starts putting the pennies into groups of six for Melanie.)

MS. HANDLON: What's six times one?

MELANIE: Six.

MS. HANDLON (putting six more pennies down): What's six times two?

MELANIE: Twelve.

MS. HANDLON (putting six more pennies down): What's six times three?

MELANIE (counting the pennies): Eighteen.

MS. HANDLON (putting six more pennies down): What six times four?

MELANIE (again counting the pennies): Twenty-four.

MS. HANDLON: Right. So, what's the answer?

MELANIE: Twenty-four.

MS. HANDLON: No, that's what you get when you multiply the numbers. That's not the answer.

MELANIE: Four.

MS. HANDLON: Right. And what's the remainder?

MELANIE: Three.

MS. HANDLON: Right.

As they slowly move from problem to problem, the tension between Melanie and her mother builds. Melanie becomes more and more agitated. Her face turns red, and although she is not crying, she appears to be on the verge of tears. More than forty-five minutes have elapsed since they began the math homework. Ms. Handlon suggests that they take a break and "put some ornaments on the Christmas tree." Melanie doesn't want a "break"; she wants to replace the homework session with cookie baking. Her mother repeats the suggestion of a break and Melanie repeats her desire to make cookies. Ms. Handlon resolves the stalemate by continuing to put down piles of pennies for Melanie and asking her leading questions to get the answers. After about five minutes, Melanie's mood seems to brighten a little. Ms. Handlon gets up for less than a minute, and Melanie continues working. The last two problems Melanie does on her own.

MS. HANDLON: See, you can do it. You just have to try.

MELANIE: This is hard.

The tensions and conflicts that arise as Ms. Handlon and Melanie try to work together to complete her homework assignments are exhausting and distressing. Moreover, because Melanie's mother accepts the principle that Melanie *must* do her homework and also perceives that some assignments, especially math, require assistance, the homework battles are repeated nearly every afternoon.[4] Ms. Handlon believes that in some cases she and Melanie struggle over problems that are caused by the teachers.

Some of the teachers are just not doing a good job. They can't explain things. I think some of them are setting the kids up for failure. Sometimes the kids will bring home questions and assignments and the teacher will write it in such a way that there are really two ways of reading into it. So, if I can't understand it, how can they expect the kids to?

According to Ms. Handlon, Melanie is unnecessarily burdened by her teachers' inability to supply adequate instructions for the assignments they send home. Not surprisingly, the teachers trace the causes of Melanie's ongoing academic difficulties to quite a different source.

THE PERILS OF PARENTAL INVOLVEMENT IN SCHOOLING

In the fall grading period, when Melanie receives the lowest grade possible in both math and social studies, her classroom teacher, Ms. Nettles, seems nearly as frustrated with this outcome as Ms. Handlon is. Ms. Nettles is consistently friendly and cheerful during her interactions with Melanie's mother. She cooperates willingly with Ms. Handlon's request for spelling lists, preparing five weeks of lists in advance and sending them home with Melanie. She seems untroubled that the lists might give Melanie an advantage over her classmates; neither does she complain of the extra work it takes for her to produce the lists for Ms. Handlon. Ms. Nettles is similarly accommodating in her response to Ms. Handlon's request that she supply Melanie's private tutor with sample math problems. In addition, when Melanie's illnesses cause her to miss days of school, Ms. Nettles makes up packets of materials to be worked on at home.

Given the efforts of Ms. Nettles and other teachers at school and Ms. Handlon's efforts at home, why does Melanie continue to flounder? The classroom and resource teachers firmly reject Ms. Handlon's contention that her daughter has too much homework and that Melanie's confidence is fatally undermined by the educators' tendency to emphasize her mistakes and shortcomings instead of praising her progress. Ms. Nettles estimates that the work she assigns the children to do at home can be completed in thirty to forty-five minutes. Garrett Tallinger, who is in Melanie's class, routinely finishes the homework (without his parents' help) in less than this amount of time. Neither do the teachers see any indication that Melanie is "intimidated" or "overwhelmed" by her day-to-day classroom experiences. Ms. Nettles agrees that Melanie "struggles" and that she may have a learning disability, but she rejects Ms. Handlon's view that Melanie is miserable in the classroom:

The whole bit about her not having success in school . . . If you're not here to observe how she is — but I am. And [Melanie] seems content. She seems fine. It's almost like, "I don't know what you're talking about."

Melanie's teachers think her school experience could be much improved if, among other things, Ms. Handlon would comply more consistently with the universalistic, bureaucratic rules of school. Ms. Nettles, in particular, is annoyed by the fact that Melanie habitually arrives late to class. With unusual directness, she complains about this to Ms. Handlon during the parent-teacher conference:

She comes in very late. She usually is the last one here. I mean, I don't even mark her absent any more . . . But some kids are here as early as ten minutes to nine, so if she's coming at ten after they've already had a twenty-minute head start. So, maybe just getting [Melanie here and] started a little bit earlier would be helpful.

Similarly, Ms. Nettles is dismayed by Ms. Handlon's failure to follow up with the paperwork necessary to get Melanie tested for learning disabilities. She reveals her frustration in a comment to the researcher after the parent-teacher conference has concluded:

I mean, I really pushed and stressed to [Ms. Handlon] to have [Melanie] tested because I think she does have a lot of learning problems. And we must have had those forms home to her like a month ago, and the last time I asked they still weren't back.

The elementary school has an on-site reading specialist; she works with Melanie three times a week. It shocks Ms. Nettles that Ms. Handlon has never met this resource teacher.

Most people who have their child seeing a reading specialist will make it a point to set up conferences. I mean, Nita is doing as many conferences because she meets with many different grade levels — and it's like that never occurred to her. I mean, [Melanie's] been seeing her for two years. Don't you think you'd want some feedback?

Ms. Nettles is certain that Ms. Handlon knows Melanie sees the reading specialist each week; when Melanie's absences mount up, her mother explicitly inquires about the reading material her daughter needs to review. In Ms. Nettles's opinion, it is Melanie's mother's *duty* to arrange a meeting with the reading specialist. Moreover, she feels that it is Ms. Handlon, not the resource teacher, who should be responsible for taking the initiative to request such a meeting.

In addition to failing to meet the teachers' expectations in some areas, Ms. Handlon is not always successful in her efforts to forge a closer connection between family and school because the educators view her actions as misguided or pointless. For instance, Ms. Nettles dismisses as simply "odd" Ms. Handlon's special trip to school with Melanie for a brief visit on the first day so that her daughter could meet her new teacher. The teacher also questions the legitimacy of the illnesses that prompt Melanie's many absences.

Ms. Nettles describes Melanie's mother as "defensive" and preoccupied with things like whether or not past and present teachers have been sufficiently supportive of Melanie's self-esteem. These concerns, the teacher feels, prevent Ms. Handlon from paying attention to other, arguably more important, issues (such as having Melanie tested for learning disabilities). After the parent-teacher conference, Ms. Nettles remarks to the researcher, "I don't think she was really listening." Most of Melanie's problems, Ms. Nettles suggests, may be traced to Ms. Handlon's overprotective parenting style:

Mom has consistently been putting things off and making excuses for Melanie since day one. I mean, Melanie was sick over thirty days last year. I think it's a big step for her to be here. But, I think her mom is like, in denial. Melanie is having a very good year. Melanie is very happy, and I think a lot of Melanie's problem is her mother.

Finally, Melanie's teachers are not aware of either the amount or the frequency of Ms. Handlon's efforts to help her daughter do her homework. They have no knowledge of the dramas that unfold in the Handlons' dining room as Melanie and her mother tackle her assignments day after day.[5]

WHY ACTIVATING CAPITAL DOES NOT ALWAYS
YIELD PROFITS

The Handlons, a family with a solid middle-class position, engaged in concerted cultivation. Mr. Handlon had a master's degree and had a managerial position; his wife had attended junior college. All of the children participated in many organized activities. To be sure, there were moments when Ms. Handlon issued directives, especially when frustrated while helping with Melanie with homework. But, although parent-child interactions are not elaborated in this chapter, for most of them, both parents engaged in the kind of reasoning and negotiation that was carried out in Alexander Williams's home.[6] Similar to Ms. Marshall, Ms. Handlon was well informed about school dynamics. Ms. Handlon believed that she had the right to intervene in her daughter's experiences outside the home and, as we have seen, had many criticisms over school practices. Nonetheless, despite these resources, Ms. Handlon was unable to gain clear advantages for Melanie in the areas that were of greatest concern to her, namely, grading and homework. She did, however, succeed in customizing specific elements of Melanie's educational experience: Ms. Nettles agreed to supply the spelling lists, to prepare materials for Melanie's tutor to use, and to send home packets of exercises covering the curriculum Melanie missed during her frequent illness-related absences from school. But the benefits that she gained for her daughter were fewer than one might expect. [7]

As Pierre Bourdieu points out, the complex nature of social life means that multitudes of subtle skills are drawn on in the transmission of social class privilege. Accordingly, there are important variations in the effectiveness of parents' efforts to activate cultural capital. Factors such as the shrewdness of the intervention, the degree to which the parent frames the complaint in a fashion that compels a response from the person in power, and the nature of the child's difficulties each play a role. In the realm of education, there are at least three important reasons why the activation of cultural capital may fail. First, educators sometimes are not aware of middle-class mothers' strenuous efforts to comply with school policies. They cannot be expected to grant privileges in return for actions they know nothing about. The children, however, are not only aware of their parents' efforts but often feel oppressed by them. Despite being well-intentioned, parents' interventions can create acute discomfort in their children and may decrease rather than stimulate students' motivation to work hard in school. Thus, any advantages that *might* result in instances where educators do recognize parents' capital can be negated by the children themselves. Second, educators frequently adopt a relatively rigid definition of what constitutes helpful behavior; parents' actions that fall outside those bounds are ignored or discredited. Thus, parents who repeatedly fail to sign and promptly return to school the forms teachers send home, for example, are considered seriously remiss, regardless of their social class standing. Third, even with similar levels of class resources, some parents may be able to activate the resources more effectively than others. Although Stacey's and Melanie's mothers were equally devoted to their daughters, Ms. Marshall seemed to be able to make more headway than Ms. Handlon.

Ms. Handlon was not alone in trying to be helpful with her children's schooling but not realizing the advantages she had hoped for. Working-class and poor parents often had that experience, as I show in the following chapters, beginning with the experience of Wendy Driver.

CHAPTER 10

Letting Educators Lead the Way: Wendy Driver

I don't want to jump into anything and find out that it's the wrong thing. (Ms. Driver)

This is Wendy's work. She spelled "driver" wrong. . . . If it was me, if our roles were reversed [and I were her parent], I'd be beating [the teacher] on the head. (Mr. Tier, Wendy's fourth-grade teacher, speaking to her mother during a parent-teacher conference)

Across all social classes, parents pay close attention to their children's education. Working-class and poor parents are no less eager than middle-class parents to see their children succeed in school. They take a different approach to helping them reach that goal, however. As Wendy Driver's mother indicates in the quote above, working-class and poor parents often fear doing "the wrong thing" in school-related matters. They tend to be much more respectful of educators' professional expertise than are their middle-class counterparts. Thus, working-class and poor parents typically are deferential rather than demanding toward school personnel; they seek guidance from educators rather than giving advice to them; and they try to maintain a separation between school and home rather than foster an interconnectedness. Ironically, as Wendy's fourth-grade teacher's comment suggests, educators often are not happy with this approach. They want parents of their working-class and poor students to be more assertive. Put differently, they wish these parents would engage in forms of concerted cultivation.

The pattern of parental deference to educators is not the result of idiosyncratic differences in parents' personalities. The same parents we observed silently accepting different teachers' (sometimes contradictory) assessments of their children were firmly vocal with their cable companies, landlords, and local merchants. Working-class and poor parents are capable of being demanding with other adults. Rather, they do not define this approach as appropriate when dealing with school or medical professionals, perhaps in part because they lack the requisite vocabulary to effectively challenge such individuals. Moreover, these parents view education as the job of educators and thus they expect teachers and school staff to be the ones primarily responsible for seeing that their children learn all that they should.

Finally, there are underlying elements of resistance to the deference working-class and poor parents exhibit toward educators. Mothers who nod in silent agreement during a parent-teacher conference may at home, and within earshot of their children, denounce the educator as unfair, untrustworthy, or mean. Particularly in the area of discipline, working-class and poor parents are likely to regard the school's approach as inappropriate. Many encourage their children — in direct violation of school rules — to hit peers who harass them, specifically including the advice to take their retaliatory actions "when the teacher isn't looking." This undercurrent of resistance is also tinged with hostility. Working-class and poor parents resent the power vested in school personnel to act on behalf of students they identify as abused in their home environments. As Wendy Driver's mother explains, the fear these parents have that "they" might "come and take your kids away" is real. Complying with educators' requests, even when they are seen as ridiculous by parents, reduces parents' risk of intervention by state officials. Still, because parents' child-rearing strategies are at odds with the approach of concerted cultivation stressed by "the school," parents such as Wendy Drivers' parents are openly criticized by educators for not taking more of a leadership role in their children's schooling.

THE DRIVER FAMILY

Wendy Driver, the focal child, is a friendly and cheerful ten-year-old,[1] who is in the fourth grade at Lower Richmond School. She lives in a rented two-story brick house with her older brother, Willie; her baby stepsister, Valerie; her mother, Debbie; Mack Fallon, Debbie's boyfriend (and Valerie's father); and two cats, Sweetie and Monster.

Wendy is very thin, with pale skin and big eyes. She often wears colored headbands that pull her long blond hair back from her face. She gives spontaneous hugs to her relatives and other adults, including the field-workers, when they arrive and exit. She often kisses two-month-old

Valerie on the head and sometimes (when her mother is out of the room) wakes the baby up to play with her. In an interview, Wendy describes herself this way:

I'm nice. I'm not cocky, I'm not greedy, and I don't spend that much money on one thing. Like, if I have the money, I'll take my mom and [Mack] out to dinner . . . I like to play Barbies [and] play cards with my cousins. I like to ride my bike and go roller-skating. I like math.

Small pleasures bring an enthusiastic response as on one spring evening when Wendy, seeing a bolt of lightning, jumps up and down excitedly and says, "Let's go outside! Let's go outside!" She is thrilled to watch bolts of lightning from the safety of the front porch.

At school, Wendy is sometimes an assertive leader. During recess and lunch, she and her girlfriends (all white) run around, chase boys, and play various games. One day, we watch as she organizes an attack on the boys' restroom. She orders two girls to approach the lavatory from the near side ("I told you guys to go! Go around . . . ") and bang on the door; meanwhile, she and another girl begin advancing from the other side, crouching down, half-hidden, giggling. Wendy seems similarly uninhibited about expressing her many opinions, including this estimation of Ms. Olean, her dance teacher:

This year I'm dancin' with my cousin Nicole. She goes to dancin', too. And sometimes Ms. Olean can be a real brat. She always hollers at people. Like yesterday me and my cousin Nicole were dancin' and we messed up a little . . . and she's like, "POINT THE TOES! POINT THE TOES!" And she's like, "DO IT!" She's a real brat.

Wendy's parents separated when she was a preschooler; they divorced two years later. Mr. Driver died suddenly during the fall that Wendy started second grade. Her mother began dating Mr. Fallon toward the end of that school year, and about twelve months later, they decided to live together.[2] Wendy's relationship with her mother's boyfriend is amiable. For example, when she reports, after a camping trip, "Mack, I went horseback riding on my trip," Mr. Fallon replies teasingly, "Horseback riding? Are you sure it was a horse and not a donkey?" Still, Wendy continues to miss her dad; at night, she sleeps with a doll that he gave her several years earlier.

Like Wendy, twelve-year-old Willie is an animated, talkative child. He enjoys visiting his cousins, riding his bike, watching television, and going fishing and hunting. Although he describes Mr. Fallon as "nice to us," and notes that Mr. Fallon "drives us places," Willie, like Wendy, misses his father. He and his mother's boyfriend often clash. Mr. Fallon criticizes Willie's ideas, his slowness, and other aspects of his daily behavior. Still, there are pleasurable moments, as when Mr. Fallon and Willie wrestle intently (and quietly, except for grunts) on the living room floor while the rest of the family watches appreciatively.

Willie often plays away from the house (joining cousins and friends), but when he is at home, he seems content to spend time with Wendy. During the summer, while Ms. Driver and Mr. Fallon are at work, Wendy and Willie watch television on and off all day, sprawled out together on the floor in the living room. The two make their own lunch, and they follow house rules about not answering the door unless someone is expected and not answering the telephone except when their mother calls (using an agreed-upon signal). On breaks from watching television, they play games together. When they play Monopoly, Willie, without being asked, reads the cards for his sister, knowing that she has trouble doing so herself. Wendy sometimes does Willie's laundry for him (in addition to doing her own). They seem fond of one another. They argue infrequently and only mildly, particularly compared to middle-class siblings such as the Tallinger brothers and the Marshall sisters. For instance, Wendy comments one afternoon that Willie's girlfriend "dumped" him. Another day, she calls down the stairs to tell Willie that he left his bedroom light on, and then when he asks her to turn it off for him, refuses (requiring Willie to go upstairs and do it himself).

Wendy and Willie's mother, Ms. Driver, is a tall, handsome woman with big bones. She is thirty-two years old. With her short blond hair, clear skin, and lack of makeup, she has healthy, almost tomboyish, looks. She has several tattoos, including a heart with an arrow on one ankle. She often wears acid-washed jeans, with sweatshirts or T-shirts, and sneakers. Ms. Driver has worked as a secretary for fourteen years, beginning immediately after she graduated from high school. She earns between $15,000 and $25,000 per year, working full time; her responsibilities include answering the phone and doing computer work. She says she "hates" her job. If she could afford it — which she can't — she would quit.

After Ms. Driver and Wendy and Willie's father divorced, she and the children moved in with her parents and remained there for five years (until Ms. Driver and Mr. Fallon pooled resources to rent their own house). Since Mr. Driver did not pay child support,[3] and Ms. Driver also needed to pay her parents a share of the rent, she met her expenses by taking a weekend job as a waitress in addition to her other job. When she became pregnant, however, she had to quit that job, and except for occasional shifts, she has not resumed it. In her leisure time, Ms. Driver enjoys watching television, especially talk shows and soap operas. She makes an effort to schedule Valerie's naps to coincide with the timing of her favorite programs.

Mr. Fallon is twenty-six years old. Like Ms. Driver, he is tall, broad shouldered, and tattooed. He has a rapidly receding hairline and a booming voice. A high school graduate, he is employed full time as a "houseman" in a home for disabled people, where, for example, he strips and rewaxes the floors. He wears a uniform — brown pants and a matching shirt — to work. He has held his position (which is unionized) for eight years and earns $20,000 per year. He works every other weekend and many holidays.

Ms. Driver and Mr. Fallon's incomes do not fully cover the family's expenses. Money is a constant topic of conversation: the high cost of items, the need to budget or undertake other money-management strategies, and the lack of funds available are subjects that come up during every field visit, often many times in a few hours. Ms. Driver sighs deeply when Wendy comes home announcing an upcoming school trip. She views these outings, which require a two-dollar contribution on the part of each student, as a major expenditure. The fact that the family has too much money to qualify for assistance but too little to meet their needs is an irony that frustrates Wendy's mother.

It really gets me upset when I go out there and I look for different organizations to help me out with money for the kids, or money for — it's like they turn to me and say, "You make too much money." It's like, "How could I make too much money?" Cause it's like, I'm just barely making it.

Family finances often have a "zero-sum" nature. For example, when Wendy was in third grade, her mother hired a tutor for her. In order to meet that new expense, $20 per week, Ms. Driver had to walk to work; she no longer had enough money to pay for the bus. When Mr. Fallon's car breaks down, they delay repairs. School clothes, Christmas presents, and major household items all are purchased on layaway plans. Neither Ms. Driver nor Mr. Fallon has a checking account; they pay bills with money orders. The three extended families in the Drivers' lives (Ms. Driver's parents, the family of her ex-husband, and Mr. Fallon's family) also struggle economically. Ms. Driver's father juggled two jobs his whole working life. Still, compared to poor families like the McAllisters or the Carrolls, the Drivers have advantages. Food is in ample supply and the children may ask for items when they go to the store. Also, Wendy and Willie are each allowed to request (and usually receive) one expensive item for Christmas (such as a $100 jacket). Ms. Driver squirrels money away for extended family gatherings; Wendy's Holy Communion festivities, which included a buffet lunch for the entire extended family, cost $1,500.

THE DRIVERS' WORLD

Just a few days before the field observations began, Wendy and her family moved into a small, three-bedroom house a few doors down from their previous residence. In this almost wholly white, urban, working-class neighborhood, the narrow streets are lined with houses just like the Drivers'. The rows of residences are squeezed so close to one another that they seem like one continuous building. Many of the houses have front porches that come right to the edge of the sidewalk; the porches are small, with only enough room for two chairs. There is no grass. Many residents, including the Drivers, decorate their houses for holidays such as Valentine's Day, Easter, and Halloween.[4] Children about Wendy and Willie's ages live right up the street, as do many of the Drivers' cousins. The girls walk to school together and play together after school and on weekends.

Although the Drivers' home has three bedrooms and is considerably larger than the homes of many other working-class families, the entire downstairs, which consists of a living room area, a playroom for the baby, and a kitchen, would fit *inside* the family room in the middle-class Marshalls' house. The rent is $650 per month. The interior of the house is immaculately kept. Wendy and Willie are reminded to put their backpacks upstairs in their bedrooms as soon as they come home from school, they are permitted to have only one glass in the living room, and they each do chores to help keep the house neat and clean. The family often spends time together in the living room watching television. It is cozy: there is room for two adults to sit on the love seat and for the children (and field-worker) to sit on the floor. Pictures of the family adorn the walls.

The amount of racial diversity in Wendy's life varies. In her public elementary school, the student body is about one-half Black, and some of the teachers and key school personnel are African American. During free playtime at recess and lunch, however, Wendy plays and socializes with other white girls almost exclusively. Similarly, although there are huge neighborhoods filled with African American poor families not far (about a ten-minute car ride) from Wendy's home, most of her social interactions involve only whites. All of her relatives are white, all of her immediate neighbors are white, all of the children in her dance class and religious study group are white, almost all of the local shopkeepers and their customers are white, and even the shopping mall she visits is frequented mainly by whites. Ms. Driver reports that her ex-husband was "prejudiced" and "hated Blacks"; she has tried to raise the children to be more open-minded than their father.

VALUING THE FAMILY: THE IMPORTANCE OF KINSHIP

It would be hard to overstate the importance of family to the Drivers. The Driver children's lives are also deeply interwoven with those of their extended family. They each have cousins their own age and sex. Wendy's two best friends are her cousins Rosie and Rebecca, who live a few doors away. She sees her maternal grandparents, who also live within walking distance, every day and enjoys these visits. She is obviously fond of her relatives. On Easter Sunday morning, for instance, she telephones her grandmother and sings "You Are My Sunshine" to her. Her grandfather often picks Wendy up after school. As Ms. Driver explains, both grandparents and great-grandparents provide after-school care for the children:

My son goes to my mother's house with his grandfather and his great-grandmother, and Wendy goes to her great-grandmother who lives two doors up from my parents' house and she stays there until I get home from work . . . She sees them every day.

Wendy's mother notes, "Me and mom call each other at least every other day, if not more. Just to see how I'm feeling or what she's been up to." When Ms. Driver's mother turned fifty, she surprised her by hiring a stripper; when she turned sixty, Ms. Driver threw her a party that included a professional singer. In addition to the frequent contact she has with her parents, Ms. Driver sees her siblings (all male) regularly. She also talks to and spends time with a cousin whom she describes as "like a sister."

Along with Ms. Driver's extended family, Wendy and Willie's paternal relatives are mentioned frequently and visited regularly. Their father's brothers ("the uncles"), sister, and parents attend Wendy's and Willie's birthday parties and are invited to all other major family events. Finally, Mr. Fallon's family is a newly emerging part of the Drivers' daily lives. Mr. Fallon has no contact with his father, but he talks to his mother daily. She visits often and is willing to baby-sit her new grandchildren as needed. Mr. Fallon is also in regular contact with his sisters. One, Sara, lives around the corner; she and her children come by the house frequently. His other sister lives in South Carolina; Mr. Fallon sends her coupons from the newspaper each week.

Daily conversation in the Driver home is peppered with references to relatives, upcoming kin events, past events involving relatives, and episodes in the lives of various members of the extended family.[5] Wendy's First Holy Communion party (which took place when she was in second grade) comes up repeatedly. Family members are also likely to bring up the topic of an upcoming family event: Wendy is eagerly anticipating her role as a junior bridesmaid in her paternal aunt's wedding party. She is very excited by the prospect of wearing a very short, straight, hot-pink, off-the-shoulder silk dress and having her hair and nails done for the event. Another common topic of conversation is Valerie's baptism, which will occur during the summer. Ms. Driver and Mr. Fallon plan to invite about a hundred relatives to celebrate the christening at a catered gathering to be held in a nearby hall.

Unlike in the Tallinger family, where no one seemed concerned that Garrett planned to skip his cousin's graduation party, family events are of the utmost importance to the Drivers. This has its downside. With so many relatives planning so many parties and gatherings, scheduling conflicts are inevitable. So, too, are "hurt feelings," as Mr. Fallon explains during a discussion over breakfast one morning before school:

"There's a wedding and a First Communion that day. My cousin has a wedding, and then my brother's kid is making the First Communion . . . and we're going to the Communion — there'll be some feelings hurt." Debbie adds, "Yeah, but it's between a brother and a cousin, so. . . ." (She trailed off, implying that the field-worker would automatically understand which is the more important engagement.)

Given the number of relatives in the extended Driver and Fallon families and the frequency with which they interact, it isn't surprising that misunderstandings and miscommunications arise from time to time. One problem Ms. Driver and Mr. Fallon contend with is the influence Wendy and Willie's deceased father's brothers ("the uncles") have on the children, especially Willie. These men, as well as Ms. Driver's own brothers, are unimpressive role models, as Mr. Fallon makes clear, yelling at Willie one Saturday morning: "You want to be like your uncles? Jobless? You want to be like your uncles?" Willie's mother worries about "the uncles," too. Watching a television talk show about "skinheads," she comments:

"This is what I have to look forward to. Willie's thirteen now. I'll have to start worrying whether he'll be in a gang." I say, "Are you worried he'll join a gang?" Debbie responds, "Well, he is a follower. He's a good kid, but he's a follower. His uncles are a bad influence on him. Like at the wedding, his youngest uncle, Uncle Petey, told him he could have a beer."

ORGANIZATION OF DAILY LIFE

Because Ms. Driver does not know how to drive, she relies on Mr. Fallon for transportation to accomplish family-related chores. Wendy and Willie usually accompany their mother on these outings. Thus, the family spends time together as a unit as Mr. Fallon drives them to the store to shop for groceries, to K-mart to buy school clothes (on layaway), to the mall (to window shop), and, in bad weather, to the homes of local family members to visit. When Mr. Fallon works the weekend shift, the rhythm of family life is radically altered. Ms. Driver and the children are able to walk to local stores, however, as well as to Wendy's dance lessons and religious instruction.

In general, the ebb and flow of the children's lives is left to them to control. Like Katie Brindle and Harold McAllister, Wendy and Willie Driver spend time hanging out with their cousins and neighborhood friends, watching television, playing games, helping with household chores, and accompanying the adults on errands. As in these other families, there are clear and decisive boundaries between adults and children. When the adults want to talk, for example, they simply tell Wendy and Willie to go out of the room; the children, without protest, get up and go. Lastly, there are significant gender differences in what the two children are allowed to do. Ms. Driver restricts her daughter's freedom:

Willie can go out. He goes to friends' houses, and he goes to places by himself. Whereas she is outside that door — and if I call her, she has to be [able to] hear me. If not, forget it. I won't even let her walk to the store, a block and a half away. I will not let her walk a block and a half by herself.[6]

Similarly, only Wendy is required to participate in organized activities.[7] Compared to children in the other working-class and poor families we observed, she is unusually busy. Each week, she has a dance lesson, a Catholic class in religious instruction (CCD), and school choir practice. Unlike her middle-class counterparts, however, Wendy does not take part in these activities in order to cultivate her talents, develop her social skills, or enlarge her circle of friends. When asked what she thinks Wendy is getting from her involvement in dance class, Ms. Driver says simply:

Grace. And I guess just remembering her dances. She has no one else to depend on but herself to memorize them, and she memorizes them.

Similarly, when asked about the CCD instruction, Wendy's mother does not, as Alex Williams's mother would, emphasize the intellectual stimulation the classes provide. She sends Wendy to CCD because she wants to make sure that her daughter is able to be a godmother and "has a religion." She elaborates this point, saying:

This way she'll have all her sacraments. Even though I can't afford a Catholic school, at least she's getting her religion. She's getting it this way.

Compared to the detailed answers and the animated tone we heard as middle-class parents like the Tallingers and Williamses discussed what they saw as the benefits of organized activities, Ms. Driver's response is brief. She is more animated, though, as she reveals her hope that getting Wendy involved in extracurricular activities will keep her daughter "off the streets." When Ms. Driver was a girl she wanted to "spend [time] with my friends and hang around on the corner with everybody else," but her parents were "strict":

My parents didn't believe in that . . . My brothers could, but I couldn't . . . So I had no choice. Either I stayed in or I did activities. So I chose the activities to keep myself busy and occupied, and it gave me a social life.

Although as a child Ms. Driver had thought the classes her parents made her take were "a waste of time," Wendy is more positive. She likes her dance lessons ("I like to dance. It's fun . . . You get to learn all this new stuff"), enjoys choir, and dismisses CCD as "boring." She does not complain to her mother or Mr. Fallon about any of her activities, however. Her extracurricular commitments are not especially important to her; they do not dominate her life or the lives of her family members. The adults typically do not bring up Wendy's classes at all; she mentions them periodically, but she does not dwell on them. Instead, her activities take a "backseat" to other topics of conversation (usually past and future family events).

DIRECTIVES: USING LANGUAGE AS A PRACTICAL TOOL

Similar to the adults in the McAllister family, both Ms. Driver and Mr. Fallon are quite directive, even authoritarian, in their child-rearing techniques. They tell the children what to do. Unlike children in middle-class families, Wendy and Willie rarely, if ever, argue with adults.

Wendy asks her mother, "Can I put the sticker on? Please?" Ms. Driver says, "We aren't going to do that." Wendy is silent.

Debbie, sitting in the kitchen with Mack, tells Willie, "Go in the living room." Willie goes in without comment or protest. He watches TV.

Mr. Fallon, particularly when he is tired or exasperated, is likely to yell his directives. In some instances, Willie might "push it," but usually, after a single protest, he falls silent:[8]

Willie asks if he could hold Valerie, who was in her chair. Debbie says, "No." Willie says (in a whiny voice), "Why not? When am I going to be able to hold her?" Debbie retorts, "When you have your own baby." Willie is silent.

Willie also sometimes needles the adults, but his approach is very different from that of Alexander Williams, for example. Willie is not trying to reason with his mother or Mr. Fallon or show them why they are wrong. Instead, he modifies his request to give it a slightly different form:

Willie wants to go out. Mack says, "No." The phone rings and Willie rushes to answer it. Just before Willie answers it, Mack repeats, "You can't go out." Willie says "Hello?" and then "Just a sec," and puts his hand over the receiver. He says, "Mack?" and Mack's temper starts to rise. He demands loudly, "What did I say? What did I say?" Willie says, "Wait." Mack responds in a lower tone of voice, questioning, "What?" Willie asks, "Can he come over and stay on the porch?" Mack seems to explode with anger, "*What did I say? I said NO VISITORS! You can't go out.*"

Overall, Ms. Driver and Mr. Fallon use language as a tool, a practical necessity rather than an intrinsically interesting dimension of life. Neither adult is likely to urge the children to expound on a topic. In contrast to middle-class parents like Mr. and Ms. Williams, who frequently made a conscious effort to encourage Alexander's language development, the adults in Wendy and Willie's lives do not follow up when the children happen to mention some new piece of information. When, for example, Wendy asks her family members (one by one) if they know what a mortal sin is, her mother says, "Tell us what it is. You're the one who went to CCD." Wendy provides the answer, and both her mother and Mr. Fallon look at her as she speaks, but neither acknowledges her answer. They wait her out and then return to watching television.

INTERVENTIONS IN INSTITUTIONS

Wendy's mother does not nurture her daughter's language development like Alexander Williams's mother does her son's. She does not attempt to draw Wendy out or follow up on new information, such as the meaning of mortal sin. But, just like Ms. Williams, Ms. Driver cares very much about her child, and, just like Ms. Handlon, she wants to help her daughter succeed. Ms. Driver keeps a close and careful eye on Wendy's schooling. Unlike Melanie's mother, she is not forgetful with paperwork. She immediately signs and returns each form Wendy brings home from school and reminds her to turn the papers in to her teacher.

Debbie reminds Wendy, "Don't forget to take those papers to school tomorrow." To me, she explains, "They're testing her again. So I had to sign papers to give my permission." When I ask when the testing will happen, she says, "I don't know when, but they'll call us in there to go over the results and they'll give us a written report of the results."

Wendy is "being tested" as part of an ongoing effort to determine why she has difficulties with spelling, reading, and related language-based activities. Her mother welcomes these official efforts, but she did not request them. Unlike the middle-class mothers we observed, who asked teachers for detailed information about every aspect of their children's classroom performance and relentlessly pursued information and assessments outside of school as well, Ms. Driver seems content with only a vague notion of her daughter's learning disabilities. This attitude contrasts starkly with that of Stacey Marshall's mother, for example. In discussing Stacey's classroom experiences with field-workers, Ms. Marshall routinely described her daughter's academic strengths and weaknesses in detail. Ms. Driver never mentions that Wendy is doing grade-level work in math but is reading at a level a full three years below her grade. Her description is vague:

She's having problems . . . They had a special teacher come in and see if they could find out what the problem is. She has a reading problem, but they haven't put their finger on it yet, so she's been through all kinds of special teachers and testing and everything. She goes to Special Ed, I think it's two classes a day . . . I'm not one hundred percent sure — for her reading. It's very difficult for her to read what's on paper. But then — she can remember things. But not everything. It's like she has a puzzle up there. And we've tried, well, they've tried a lot of things. They just haven't put their finger on it yet.

Wendy's teachers uniformly praise her mother as "supportive" and describe her as "very loving," but they are disappointed in Ms. Driver's failure to take a more active, interventionist role in Wendy's education, especially given the formidable nature of her daughter's learning problems. From Ms. Driver's perspective, however, being actively supportive means doing whatever the teachers tell her to do.

Whatever they would suggest, I would do. They suggested she go to the eye doctor, so I did that. And they checked her and said there was nothing wrong there.

Similarly, she monitors Wendy's homework and supports her efforts to read.

We listen to her read. We help her with her homework. So she has more attention here in a smaller household than it was when I lived with my parents. So, we're trying to help her out more, which I think is helping. And with the two [special education] classes a day at the school, instead of one like last year, she's learning a lot from that. So, we're just hoping it takes time and that she'll just snap out of it.

But Ms. Driver clearly does not have an *independent* understanding of the nature or degree of Wendy's limitations, perhaps because she is unfamiliar with the kind of terms the educators use to describe her daughter's needs (e.g., a limited "sight vocabulary," underdeveloped "language arts skills"). Perhaps, too, her confidence in the school staff makes it easier for her to leave "the details" to them: "Ms. Morton, she's great. She's worked with us for different testing and stuff." Ms. Driver depends on the school staff's expertise to assess the situation and then share the information with her.

I think they just want to keep it in the school till now. And when they get to a point where they can't figure out what it is, and then I guess they'll send me somewhere else . . .

Wendy's mother is not alarmed, because "the school" has told her not to worry about Wendy's grades:

Her report card—as long as it's not spelling and reading—spelling and reading are like F's. And they keep telling me not to worry, because she's in the Special Ed class. But besides that, she does good. I have no behavior problems with her at all.

Ms. Driver wants the best possible outcome for her daughter and she does not know how to achieve that goal without relying heavily on Wendy's teachers.

I wouldn't even know where to start going. On the radio there was something for children having problems reading and this and that, call. And I suggested it to a couple different people, and they were like, wait a second, it's only to get you there and you'll end up paying an arm and a leg. So I said to my mom, "No, I'm going to wait until the first report card and go up and talk to them up there."

Ms. Driver might have placed somewhat less faith in Wendy's teachers' expertise had she known more about the bureaucratic rules educators in Lower Richmond School's large urban district must contend with as they try to identify and resolve children's learning difficulties. One teacher, speaking informally, notes that "[the district administrators] don't want people written up." To assign a student to a special education class full time, teachers are required to file two separate plans of intervention (each requiring a meeting with the principal, counselor, and mother), which each must be tried for 60 days *before* testing is permitted. The entire school year is only 180 days; thus, a *minimum* of two-thirds of the year would elapse before the end of the referral stage. As a practical reality, testing *and* placement in an appropriate classroom could not occur within the same school year, even in the extremely unlikely event that the process were to be initiated on the first day of school. The paperwork for Wendy was begun in the spring of third grade, but her "case" fell through the cracks; the referral had to be reinitiated in fourth grade. The only special help Wendy receives as a fourth-grader is access to the reading resource teacher. Had she attended an elementary school in a smaller suburban district like the one Garrett Tallinger went to, or a private school like the one Alexander Williams was enrolled in, where the educational resources were much more extensive and better funded and the bureaucratic machinery less imposing, Wendy might have received more effective attention, sooner.

Lower Richmond educators, however, tend not to stress these kinds of institutional differences as important factors in Wendy's persistent reading problems. Instead, they often emphasize the critical role of parents. During the parent-teacher conference, Mr. Tier, Wendy's fourth-grade teacher, expresses his outrage that she has made it to fourth grade without knowing how to read. He urges Ms. Driver to be more demanding with him and other school personnel, telling Ms. Driver in a parent-teacher conference: "If our roles were reversed — I'd be beating me on the head."

Here, Mr. Tier suggests that Ms. Driver should take a concerted cultivation approach to her daughter's education. She should aggressively monitor, criticize, and even badger educators rather than simply *following* the professionals' advice. He shifts much of the responsibility for Wendy's current predicament away from these expert decision makers and on to her mother, implying that had Ms. Driver taken this approach from the start, Wendy's reading deficiency would never have been "allowed" to persist.

When Ms. Driver asks Mr. Tier to specify what she should do to help

Wendy, he stresses the role of parents as leaders in developing their children's language skills.

I would just try to get Wendy to get an interest in reading. Go to the library, find out the types of things she's interested in, read to her, just get her — find out her interests and try to capitalize on them. And just see how far you could get. Because I think Wendy could learn how to read.

The school's reading resource teacher, Mr. Johnson, echoes the view that, given the proper encouragement *outside of school,* Wendy "could learn how to read." He adds tutoring to the list of parent-sponsored interventions.

The first thing I would do is seek some outside help. And the outside help would be — I might put her in something like a tutorial program. There is something at the Salvation Army. They have the same thing at the YMCA . . . [I'd] try to read a story and see if they can pick out any of the words, to try to develop a sight vocabulary.

Despite their agreement that Wendy *could* learn to read, and that parental input would be essential in her developing this skill, Mr. Tier and Mr. Johnson do not agree on the underlying cause of Wendy's problems nor on what the most effective institutional response might be. Mr. Johnson is struck by the fact that Wendy performs at grade level in math. He believes she has a reading "phobia," possibly compounded by other learning difficulties. In his view, it is emotional issues (a "social emotional overlay") that are the problem. Mr. Johnson's plan for intervention for fifth grade is to repeat the basic steps involved in reading readiness (a process normally initiated in kindergarten and continued in first grade) to "try to improve her sight vocabulary and some of her language arts skills."

Mr. Tier and Ms. Green (Wendy's third-grade teacher) see Wendy's reading problems differently. Rather than diagnosing Wendy as suffering from a "phobia," they think she may have neurological problems. In contrast to Mr. Johnson, Mr. Tier feels Wendy should be placed in special education classes full time. Mr. Tier also believes that she should repeat fourth grade. Each of Wendy's classroom teachers, beginning in second grade, identified her as a student with learning problems and each feels that he or she tried to get additional help for her. But, as Mr. Tier puts it, somehow Wendy "slipped through the cracks":

Wendy, I think, slipped through the cracks . . . I firmly believe that if Wendy was a little Black girl that she would already have been in a special education type of situation. A kid in fourth grade who can't read a first-grade reader, something is dreadfully wrong here . . . And Wendy is so cute and so sweet. She has a smile for everybody, and I think somehow or other, I think they did her a terrible disservice by just letting her go forward.

Ms. Driver is somewhat aware that the school may not have fully met its responsibilities in Wendy's case. For instance, after the parent-teacher conference in the spring, she realizes that the teachers disagree over whether Wendy should repeat fourth grade.

I went to talk to Mr. Johnson after I saw [Mr. Tier]. He said she's doing fine and she doesn't need to stay back. He said the same thing — that she can't stay back 'cause she's in Special Ed. He said that she's only failing [in] reading and spelling but she's doing fine in math and social studies, so he can't fail her. But the other teacher (she does not use Mr. Tier's name) said she has to stay back. They said the opposite things.

When asked for her own "gut feeling" about whether Wendy should be promoted to fifth grade, Ms. Driver says, "I think she should stay back." Nevertheless, she seems prepared to accept whatever "the school" decides is best for Wendy. Unlike Ms. Marshall, she does not place numerous calls to educators, follow up to find out what happened at the most recent meeting, or express her opinion about what should happen next. Faced with contradictory information, Wendy's mother seems both bewildered and intimidated by the possibility that any intervention on her part might end up introducing more errors and delays in the process of getting the best education for Wendy.[9]

Ms. Driver's seeming willingness to comply with educators' decisions, even when they contradict her own "gut feelings," is not a sign that she lacks interest in Wendy's education. The Lower Richmond teachers readily acknowledge her as a "loving," "supportive," and "concerned" parent. The field-workers observe her keep a close watch every day for over two weeks, on the lookout for "the paper" Wendy was to bring home from the school regarding testing, which failed to arrive. She did not call the school to ask for it, however, but preferred to wait it out.

Neither does Ms. Driver's approach reflect a meek or timid personality. She refers to herself as "hotheaded," and it is clear that she can be assertive. With service providers like her cable company, and with her landlord, she shows no hesitancy in making whatever demands are necessary to achieve the results she wants. When the cable company's service representative does not show up as promised, she calls the company repeatedly and eventually asks to talk to a supervisor. When the hot water heater in their rental house begins leaking, she calls the landlord. When he instructs her to turn off the heater and wait until he can arrange to get the problem corrected, she refuses. Pointing out that she is home alone with a baby and two other young children, she insists that he come promptly and take care of the problem.

Having discovered that her landlord is not a competent plumber, on a different occasion, Ms. Driver decides to take things into her own hands:

I ask about the faucet. Debbie seems outraged. She gets up from the kitchen table and walks to the sink and turns the faucet on to full. "I don't have any pressure! Look at this! This is full." The water is flowing at a steady rate but not rushing down; it looks to be at roughly half pressure. She says, "I am going to call a plumber and have him fix it and then very nicely deduct it from my rent."

This kind of assertiveness is almost wholly absent from Ms. Driver's interactions with educators. The one exception involves Willie rather than Wendy. During a spring concert at the school, Willie, one of only a handful of white children in a crowd of Black children, is overcome by the heat. He grows dizzy and sits down in the middle of the performance. None of the teachers makes a move to help him. Ms. Driver, sitting in the audience, gets up and struggles slowly through the crowded auditorium to reach him. She is furious. Still, although she recounts the story (with obvious anger) many times to extended family members, she does not mention it to any of the teachers or anyone else at the school. Overall, unlike middle-class parents, Ms. Driver keeps her opinions about the school to herself.

Thus, in looking for the source of Ms. Driver's deference toward educators, the answers don't seem to lie in her having either a shy personality or underdeveloped mothering skills. To understand why Wendy's mother is accepting where Stacey Marshall's or Melanie Handlon's mothers would be aggressive, it is more useful to focus on social class position, both in terms of how class shapes worldviews and how class affects economic and educational resources. Ms. Driver understands her role in her daughter's education as involving a different set of responsibilities from those perceived by middle-class mothers. She responds to contacts from the school — such as invitations to the two annual parent-teacher conferences — but she does not initiate them. She views Wendy's school life as a separate realm and one in which she, as a parent, is only an infrequent visitor. She does not, like Ms. Marshall, challenge the school's authority in her daughter's placement. She does not, like Ms. Handlon, consult with other parents about day-to-day experiences in the classroom. Nor does she call Wendy's teachers or come to school to discuss homework assignments. Ms. Driver expects that the teachers will teach and her daughter will learn and that, under normal circumstances, neither requires any additional help from her as a parent. If problems arise, she presumes that Wendy will tell her; or, if the issue is serious, the school will contact her.

One result of this way of looking at parent-school interaction is that for Wendy, school is indeed her own world. Unlike Melanie Handlon, for instance, Wendy does not reexperience her classroom failures at home. In fact, because her mother does not initiate contacts with the school, Wendy has the opportunity to manage certain aspects of her education on her own. If she chooses not to mention a problem to her mother, it is unlikely Ms. Driver will hear about it from other sources. Indeed, in the spring of fourth grade Wendy has a run-in with Mr. Johnson, her reading resource teacher ("cause he kept hollering at me. He kept hollering at other kids and got me scared"). She simply stops going to his special education reading class for two weeks. She tells no one. [10] Ms. Driver, however, does not know about this episode until much later (when Mr. Johnson tells her). She remains unaware of an important school-related issue because her key informant about the educational process is Wendy, not school personnel, or even other parents. School is Wendy's world.

The educational and economic resources associated with Ms. Driver's class position also affect the approach she takes with teachers and other school staff. Ms. Driver's high school education and low-level clerical job do not equip her with the same amount of information, or even the same access to sources of information as those Ms. Marshall gained from her graduate school degree and managerial position. Ms. Marshall is fluent in the jargon educators use (e.g., Mr. Johnson's reference to "social emotional overlay"), and she knows that her daughter's school must allow her as a parent to have Stacey tested independently to determine her eligibility for the gifted program. Ms. Driver, on the other hand, is reluctant to sidestep or even supplement school programs. She worries that paying a private company to boost her daughter's reading skills will just cost her money and not produce results. She does not have Ms. Marshall's grasp of educational terminology, either. In fact, Ms. Driver seems to have significant trouble following the intricacies of the debate among the Lower Richmond staff about the nature of Wendy's learning difficulties (she complains that she "couldn't understand" the periodic reports the school sent her regarding Wendy's educational progress).

That Ms. Driver has real difficulty understanding the terms professionals routinely employ is clear from the following episode at the dentist's office. The children's dentist, Dr. Marks, comes into the room to discuss with Ms. Driver the results of the six-month checkups she has just completed for Wendy and Willie.

Dr. Marks says that Willie has two cavities "on his permanent teeth" and she tells Debbie, "He needs to brush, especially in the back teeth." Wendy has "tooth decay. Let me show you on the X ray." Dr. Marks lights the X-ray viewing table. She points. "See here and here?" Debbie glances at the X ray and nods. "The decay is on her temporary teeth, but you are between a rock and a hard spot because leaving them in will cause potential damage to her permanent teeth." Debbie interjects, "So you want to pull them?" Dr. Marks says, "Yes," adding, "They are loose. We can do them on the same appointment." Debbie does not seem anxious or upset at this news of cavities.

Ms. Driver makes another appointment for Wendy and Willie and then steps into the waiting room to face her questioning children:

Debbie tells Willie, "You have two cavities that have to be filled." She tells Wendy, "You have to have two teeth pulled." Wendy asks, "Do I have cavities?" Debbie says, "No." Wendy, excited, says, "Goody!" and then announces triumphantly to Willie, "You have two cavities and I don't."[11]

Ms. Driver does not equate the term "tooth decay" with "cavity." Over the next ten days, there are many conversations in the Driver household about the teeth Wendy will have pulled. Wendy is disappointed to discover that she can't leave her teeth that are pulled under her pillow for the tooth fairy. In addition, various explanations are offered for why Wendy's teeth must come out. Mr. Fallon says she needs more room in her mouth. After the visit, Wendy was given her two teeth to take home. Both had large black marks on them. To our knowledge, no one in the family ever understood that Wendy's teeth had cavities.

Incompletely or incorrectly understanding the terminology professionals favor was a common problem among parents in the working-class and poor families we observed. It is one of many elements that contribute to these parents' tendency to defer to, or at least silently accept, the pronouncements of professionals such as teachers and health-care providers. In addition to being uncomfortable with the terms school officials and classroom teachers used, most working-class and poor parents believed it was inappropriate for them to intervene in their children's day-to-day classroom experiences. They expected teachers to shoulder the responsibility of educating children, and they presumed that if there were problems, the school would contact them, not vice versa. Still, the deference these parents exhibit in their dealings with school representatives often includes an underlying element of hostility and resistance.

DEFERENCE: HOSTILITY IN DISGUISE?

One area in which working-class and poor parents frequently disagree with educators involves discipline, especially the advisability of physical punishment (this issue is examined in more detail in the next chapter). The emphasis schools place on verbally negotiating problems strikes many of these parents as misguided, at best. Wendy's mother is no exception. In fall of the fifth grade, when Wendy is troubled by a male classmate, Ms. Driver (and Mr. Fallon) advises her to take matters into her own hands:

When I ask what Wendy's new teacher is like, Debbie says, "She seems nice." Mack says, "There is a boy pulling her hair; he sits behind her." Debbie repeats, "Yeah, there is a boy who keeps pulling on her hair." Debbie says, "I said, punch him." Mack elaborates, "Yeah. Hit him when the teacher isn't looking. That will take care of it."[12]

There are deeper reasons for working-class and poor parents to mistrust the judgment of classroom teachers and school staff but not to openly challenge them. The school, as an institution, is an official representative of the state. In practical terms, that means that if school officials have any reason to suspect that a student is in any kind of danger at home, they can take steps to have that child temporarily removed from his or her family. This gives school representatives an enormous power over parents, an imbalance that, reasonably, they both deeply resent and greatly fear.

One night, after our regular visits had finished, Ms. Driver tells me that they took Wendy to the hospital because her wrist was sore.[13] Ms. Driver had not thought this soreness was anything to worry about, but she felt compelled to have Wendy examined by a doctor.

Every time the school sends something home, I am worried if I don't do something about it that they'll report it and DHS [Department of Human Services] will come and take my kids away. So, even though I knew it was nothing, I took her to the hospital to have them tell me it was nothing. Mack amends, "To tell you it was a strain."

Ms. Driver explains:

They send you this big card, and even though I'm her mother, I feel that the school — if you don't do something — that they will report you. And they'll come and take your kids away.

The hospital visit was covered by Ms. Driver's insurance, but it was expensive and inconvenient:

It cost four hundred and ten dollars. I came home at five, and — (Mack interrupts) "We had to go get my Mom." Debbie, explaining, says, "We had to go get his mom to watch Valerie," and then continues, "We took her up and waited and waited and waited." Mack recalls, "I said, 'If it isn't broken, then I am going to break it myself.'" Debbie repeats, "It cost four hundred and ten dollars to tell me what I already knew."

To make matters worse, "the school," vested with an overbearing authority, often seems as likely to get things wrong as right. In Ms. Driver's experience, school nurses not only exaggerate nonexistent problems but fail to recognize real emergencies. When Willie, for example, was in a collision at school, the nurse said "not to worry" and that she thought he would need "some butterfly stitches." But Willie had a huge gash over his eye that required twenty-eight stitches. For Ms. Driver, the conclusion is obvious: school nurses are not to be trusted. They fuss too much over minor matters and do not accurately convey the severity of major matters. In lumping into a single unit nurses in two different schools, ministering to children of different ages and sexes, Wendy's mother demonstrates a common tendency among working-class and poor parents to merge authority figures into one indiscriminate group. Thus, classroom teachers, resource teachers, librarians, and principals are usually all referred to as "the school."

Ms. Driver resents having to take Wendy to the hospital for what she believes is a ridiculous complaint. It is, however, her only sure way to stave off possibly arbitrary and capricious but nevertheless very real threats of coercion from professionals in a position of power. The inconvenience and expense of the hospital trip is small compared to the huge risk that "they" might come and "take your kids away." Other working-class and poor parents voiced similar anxieties and shared the same feeling of distrust with school officials.

DISCUSSION

Daily life for Wendy Driver (and her brother) followed much the same pattern we observed with Tyrec Taylor, Katie Brindle, and Harold

McAllister. The Driver children had vast amounts of leisure time that they spent hanging out with cousins, watching television, helping with household chores, and visiting grandparents. There were firm directives that shaped their actions but also much room for autonomous decision making. The overall cultural logic of child rearing in the family seemed to be the accomplishment of natural growth. The only significant deviation was that Wendy's mother had enrolled her in three organized activities. But this seemed less an effort on her mother's part to expose Wendy to a range of life experiences than a means of protecting her from the street. Although Wendy enjoyed two of the three activities, these did not dominate her leisure time or alter the rhythm of her family life.

Wendy's school situation was extreme in some respects, since even at Lower Richmond, where test scores are routinely in the bottom quartile nationally, most children have learned to read by third grade. In other respects, however, her situation was not unusual. Ms. Driver, like other working-class and poor parents, believed she was doing all she could to help her daughter succeed in school. Wendy's teachers, however, defined the meaning of parental support differently. The educators advocated a version of concerted cultivation. They longed for an idealized world wherein parents were energetic and took a leadership role in monitoring their children's schooling but always stopped considerably short of the kind of intervention the Kaplans undertook when they objected to the music teacher's choice of songs for the school holiday program. Teachers like Mr. Tier and others did not want parents to be deferential and reactive. They sought an approach that was a contradictory blend in which parents were actively involved and consciously responsible for guiding their children's school experience but were still polite, compliant, and supportive of educators' programs. It would be only in situations where differences of opinion arose that parents would immediately defer to the wisdom of educators.

Although the Lower Richmond staff did not acknowledge (and may have been unaware of) the role of social class in shaping their ideal vision of how parents should interact with the school, their wishes amounted to a mandate for concerted cultivation. Mr. Tier's expectation that Ms. Driver "beat him on the head" and take a more aggressive role in guiding Wendy's education presupposed a set of educational and social skills not typically possessed by working-class mothers with high school educations. To match Ms. Marshall's actions, for example, Wendy's mother would have had to engage in extensive discussions about the *substantive* nature of her daughter's educational problems. This in turn would have required a familiarity and facility with terminology such as "auditory reception," "language arts skills," and "decoding skills," jargon far more specialized and complex than the term "tooth decay," whose true meaning apparently had escaped Ms. Driver. And, even had she strengthened and expanded her vocabulary, she still would have needed confidence in her ability to reconcile the conflicting views of Wendy's teachers. In a situation with many uncertainties, confronted by experts who did not agree about the best course of action, Ms. Driver would have needed a bedrock faith in herself as the person best able to determine the right course of action for Wendy. She would have needed to set aside any worries about making mistakes and have been willing to define her intervention as being as valuable, and possibly more valuable, than what would have happened had Wendy's education been left to the school staff only.

In other situations, such as with the cable company and her landlord, Ms. Driver displayed exactly this sense of certainty. She identified certain actions on the part of others as unacceptable and persisted as long as necessary to achieve her goals. She *demanded* responses from these providers. But, intimidated by the professional expertise and authority of school personnel, she did not make similar demands with educators. She did not, for example, pressure the school to review Wendy's situation more rapidly (in third grade) or push to have her daughter placed in full-time special education (in fourth grade) or insist that Wendy not be promoted (at the end of fourth grade). Instead, she worried, waited, and wondered what "the school" would do next.

CHAPTER 11

Beating with a Belt, Fearing "the School": Little Billy Yanelli

The therapist that day . . . he says well you realize that me being a therapist and working for the state or whatever that if I find out you're beating your child that I have to report that.

Now I go through different phases with Billy. I want to be the kind of parent that never hits my kid and everything but Billy gets so out of control that maybe he does need it once in a while. (Ms. Yanelli)

When the founders of the country were raised, children were routinely disciplined by physical force. By the end of the twentieth century and beginning of the twenty-first, dominant child-rearing ideology suggests the importance of reasoning with children and giving children "appropriate choices." Compared with earlier historical times, authoritarian child-rearing methods, particularly disciplining children through corporal punishment, have fallen out of favor.

Yet compliance with professional standards varies systematically rather than randomly. Parents who use belts are at risk for being considered abusive much more than parents who engage in verbal abuse of children (i.e., a mother who tells a child "I don't want to be your mother anymore"). Schools, as arms of the state, selectively enforce child-rearing standards. This has important consequences for the comfort, trust, and experience of family members in these institutions.

In a white working-class neighborhood with narrow streets and narrow houses, "Little Billy" Yanelli lives with his mother and father (who are unmarried). They reside in a small two-bedroom brick house in the city. The front door is just a few steps from the curb and opens immediately into a small living room. The living room is dominated by a huge television with an extra-large screen that takes up most of the wall; the television is always on. With a sofa, recliner, love seat, and coffee table, space is at a premium. There is not really room for two people to walk through the room at the same time. The house (two bedrooms, one bathroom, one small living room, dining room, kitchen, and a finished basement) has a small yard where Mr. Yanelli, known to family members as "Big Billy," grows tomatoes in the summer. The living room, as well as the entire house, is always immaculately kept. When field-workers comment on the orderliness, Ms. Yanelli replies: "Well this house is so small that if there's one coat on a chair or a pair of shoes, it's a mess." Little Billy's parents recently bought the house and renovated it. Mr. Yanelli did all of the work himself on nights and weekends.

Linda Yanelli is thirty-six but looks younger, in part because at home she often is dressed in denim cutoffs and a cotton T-shirt; she has bare feet and her brown hair is pulled back into a ponytail. Ms. Yanelli cleans houses in the suburbs (off the books) for $12 an hour. Her job is tiring. In teams of four, she and her co-workers move from house to house in her bosses' car; she does not get a regularly scheduled lunch break. On Thursdays, for example, she doesn't get home until after 6:00 P.M. because her team cleans nine houses in one day. As a result of his job as a house painter, Mr. Yanelli, a thin, quiet, man in his late thirties, is often dressed in paint-splattered pants and shirts.[1] Someone who has been working since he was fourteen, he dislikes his work intensely, particularly since he switched to a new job with a boss he sees as demanding and greedy. He is up and out at work early in the morning and is often home by 4:30 P.M. He enjoys his son, however, and takes an active role in driving him to his baseball games, assisting the coach, and chastising Billy to swing at the ball. (He will yell, "Swing!" Shaking his head ruefully, he says, "He is afraid of the ball.") Mr. Yanelli also plays cards with Little Billy. As he passes through the house, Mr. Yanelli will affectionately ruffle the top of Billy's head, calling him "Muke," a favorite nickname. In accord with the traditional gender division of labor, however, he is not involved at all in Billy's child care or schooling: "it is her department." Ms. Yanelli also has a twenty-one-year-old son, Manny, from a previous marriage who works and lives at home (although he spends quite a bit of time at his girlfriend's house). When he is working, everyone gets along fine; when he is not working there can be tension between Mr. Yanelli and Manny.

Both of the Yanelli parents dropped out of high school. Neither of the adults has health insurance; the cost of getting sick is a constant cause of worry.[2] When they are really sick, they go to the hospital emergency room, which can cost hundreds of dollars, and then pay off the bill, bit by bit. Money is always tight, although much less so than years ago when Ms. Yanelli was on welfare. Today, she is very proud of the fact that they have a credit card. They do not, however, have a checking account; all bills are paid with money orders. Both enjoy "playing the numbers" and regularly place small bets, as well as bets on the local football team. Occasionally they will "hit" a number; a $250 hit paid for their new dining room furniture.

Both Mr. and Ms. Yanelli came from families in which their parents were struggling economically. Ms. Yanelli's family, for example, moved frequently. Her parents divorced when she was very young, and her mother (Billy's grandmother) married again when Ms. Yanelli was two. Her stepfather, whom she calls "Dad," worked in factory jobs but never learned to read or write. Her biological father died when she was thirteen, allegedly of a suicide in the city prison. Ms. Yanelli is dubious:

He always kept in contact. He always came to see us. He was always a good father. When he was thirty-three years old he hung himself in prison. And there was a lot of debate about — did the policeman do it? There was a lot of stuff with the police at the time. But he would never kill himself. He wasn't that kind of man. He just bought a boat the day before.

Ms. Yanelli is a worrier. In a life-defining event, the three-year old daughter of one of her good friends died of a brain tumor. For years, Ms. Yanelli restricted Little Billy's movements even when he was with his father (e.g., forbidding them to go fishing at a local river) for fear that something might happen. She feels that her fear of losing him led her to be indulgent. She wonders if this is the source of his behavior problems at school.

I'm having so many problems with him right now. I don't know if he's hyperactive. I mean, I've gone through years of trying to find out what's wrong with him. We're good to him. I thought at one point maybe that's what it is; we're too good to him. He's got like a mean streak in him. The more you do for him, the more you love him — he's just got this little mean streak in him and I can't explain it. But . . . we love him to death. He's interested in everything. He's always willing to go, willing to do anything. He's a fun kid. He loves sports. . . . He plays baseball. He wants to play hockey. See, I'm the kind of mother that — I feel like I'm the one that's wrong.

Ten-year-old Little Billy is short and pudgy and often wears long T-shirts that hang down over his pants. Still, with his closely cropped blond hair and a stud earring in his right earlobe he also has a stylish air to him. School is difficult, as he expressed when asked what he liked about his teacher, Mr. Tier:

Nothing. Well, I like that he lets you have extra recess. We always go on walks . . . He's a fun teacher. We learn songs that he makes up, like "The Map Rap." You can learn a lot from having fun. We have a lot of animals in our classroom. Uh, we have nine fish in a humongous tank, three hamsters . . . (Mr. Tier) used big words . . . he used words like "technically," "obstacle." He would use giant words sometimes.

But he also had objections:

Well, when he gets mad . . . he'll pull somebody by the hair or their ear or hit them in the head with his fingers but it hurts. And when he does that we all go, "OW."

When asked how Mr. Tier would describe him, he reported:

That I'm intelligent. I'm not just saying that, because I heard him say it. He would say I'm always getting my homework done. And that I'm a really nice boy and he would say that I keep my grades up.

But he also knew of his reputation:

He would say — a lot of people think I'm trouble. He would describe me as trouble, like that . . . He would say — he thinks I have problems at home.

He was aware of the tension between his parents and "the school," noting that his mother "hates" the principal.

   Billy Yanelli's home is in an all-white neighborhood, but the street demarcating the beginning of an all-Black neighborhood is only a few blocks away. His school, Lower Richmond, is racially integrated among the students and staff. For example, his third-grade teacher, Ms. Green, was African American, as was the school counselor, Ms. Franklin, but his fourth-grade teacher, Mr. Tier, and the principal are white. At home, he mostly plays with white children (including white girls), although occasionally a Black boy from his classroom who lives only a few minutes away by foot will walk over to Billy's house to see if he wants to play. His father had a best friend from childhood, Mitch, who is Black. Mitch is over several times per week. The stores his family frequents are overwhelmingly white; so is his baseball league.

   Similar to Tyrec Taylor, Katie Brindle, and other working-class and poor children, Billy's daily life is primarily built around playing with neighborhood children, of whom there are quite a few. In the summer his one organized sport, baseball, makes the family feel that they are extremely busy, with practices in the evenings and a game on the weekend. He enjoys it.

I like that I'm catching. I like when I get up to bat because I feel like, sometimes I feel nervous, like if there's a really fast pitcher . . . I'm afraid I'm gonna strike out. But then, boom, boom, boom, I'm hitting one in the outfield.

Mostly, however, Little Billy plays with children in the neighborhood in the street, watches television (including Saturday afternoon cooking shows), or rides along while his mother does errands. Like Tyrec Taylor, Billy has much more unstructured free time than did Garrett Tallinger and Alexander Williams. In addition, Billy's parents are very close to their relatives; Little Billy's uncle usually drops by every day and Ms. Yanelli talks to her mom daily.

My brothers calls me every single day, "What are you doin'?" "Nothin'," "See you later . . . " My family talks every day. My other brother will call as soon as he thinks I'm available just to say what are you doin' and how did you make out at the school this morning? My whole family has total contact every day.

With family, "There's always somebody there for them and somebody who cares about them no matter what kind of life they have. That's important."

Still, the Yanellis are not close to all of their relatives. Mr. Yanelli was working a job with his younger brother, Charlie, and he suddenly saw his other brother, Ray, a drug addict, pushing a cart like an old man. Mr. Yanelli gave five dollars to Charlie to hand over to their brother Ray, but he did not go over himself to visit.

At school, Little Billy usually gets B's but is considered to be a behavior problem. His mother calls him the class clown. He often is in trouble at school, for example, for throwing rocks, pulling chairs out from underneath other students as they go to sit down, getting in fights with other children, and various other forms of "acting out." Mr. Tier described him as follows:

He's a goofball. I'm sorry, but he is . . . You know what a goofball is like. He crosses his eyes. He sticks his tongue out and he makes weird sounds.

Mr. Tier was also troubled by Billy's difficulty getting along with his peers. The school counselor, Ms. Franklin, agreed:

Billy's a bright child;, he's got good potential. [But] his mouth gets him into trouble. He says things to other children that set them off a lot of times. He'll talk about kids' mothers . . . He knows how to make other children angry and react . . . I really do feel a lot of his behaviors are inappropriate for a child his age . . . [they are more appropriate] for a much younger child . . . six, seven years old.

Because of his behavioral difficulties at school, the teachers have strongly recommended that Billy see the school counselor on a weekly basis. They have also recommended counseling for the family, which the father considers outrageous. His mother believes it likely that she will ultimately have to acquiesce as she did for the school counseling for Billy, saying, "I feel pushed, I really do." The school counselor, Ms. Franklin, was aware of her reluctance:

The mom has had some real resistance to his being involved in group therapy . . . It's taken a lot of work on our part to get her to permit him to be in these situations. I think she has the idea, as many parents have, that therapy means you're saying your child is crazy. That's not what we were saying.

There were many ways that Ms. Yanelli complied with school standards. For example, it was important to Little Billy's parents that he do well academically. His mother monitored his homework to make sure that it was done. When buying clothes for the fall, she was careful to comply with school guidelines. The mother attended all parent-teacher conferences and even, at times, contacted the school when concerned about a problem. At times, however, the parents were defiant of school regulations. Little Billy's parents, for example, encouraged him to defend himself on the playground in direct opposition to school rules. During fourth grade, tired of hearing that Little Billy was being pummeled by another white boy in his classroom, Mr. Yanelli and his uncle taught him how to fight and instructed him to go to school the next day to "get the job done." When Little Billy was suspended, the parents remained pleased by Little Billy's hitting, although his actions were in direct violation of school rules. Ms. Franklin, the school counselor at Lower Richmond, to whom Ms. Yanelli reported this story, was infuriated, as she recounted:

I felt he was being given the wrong message . . . that this was acceptable behavior. And I said that to her. That's really giving him the wrong message . . . I tried to explain that even though I could appreciate the fact that she wanted him to stand up for himself, that this kind of behavior — fighting — is against school rules. There are people here, if he is having a problem, who will help him. By the same token, Billy has to take responsibility for how he triggers aggressive behaviors in other children.

Ms. Franklin, while noting that Ms. Yanelli "was not unique in her attitude" felt that to "give a child permission to fight" gives him "carte blanche . . . anytime any minor thing happens." The counselor also objected to the traditional division of labor, wherein Mr. Yanelli was not involved in child care for Billy (a very common pattern in earlier decades). She found the family to be deficient in this arena as well: "I certainly don't think that it [his father's lack of involvement] helps Billy at all. First of all, I think parents need to work together in terms of raising children. I think again it gives Billy the wrong message."

These differences in parents' relationships to school — in other words, in the degree of continuity or distance between the culture of child rearing at home and the standards encoded in the school — appeared to surface regularly in family life. As with Wendy Driver's parents, working-class parents such as the Yanellis experienced a sense of distance and distrust, of exclusion and risk, with schools. While both appeared relaxed, chatty, and friendly with other service providers, including the person from whom Ms. Yanelli got her money orders and lottery tickets on Saturday morning, restaurant personnel, and receptionists, they both appeared to be distrustful of the school. Indeed, Ms. Yanelli "hated it" and often felt bullied.

I found a note in his school bag this morning and it said, I'm going to kill you because you didn't give me what I wanted and, uh, you're dead and mother-f-er and your mother is this and your father is that and your grandmom is this. So, I started shaking. I couldn't even wait until 9:00. I just said, oh, my God, I don't believe this. Now, Billy is always getting in trouble for doing things but when it comes to the other kids doing it to him, it's a different story. And I was all ready to go over there prepared for the counselor and to say, yea, I'm tryin' because I am and I got so upset I went over there and said, like, what about these other kids and what they do and they said the reason they do what they do to Billy is because Billy makes them do it. So they had an answer for everything.

Compared to Ms. Marshall, or even Ms. Handlon, who felt relatively effectual in school interactions, Ms. Yanelli found herself completely powerless and frustrated:

INTERVIEWER: So how did you feel about that answer?

MS. YANELLI: I hate the school. I hate it. I tried to get him into Catholic. I have a girlfriend who has a little boy who has the same problems and she put him in Catholic School and his whole life turned around. But, Big Bill isn't Catholic and they said they didn't have any room for him so it's like, every day of my life I'm struggling to get this kid straightened out. It's my life. It's every day. I'm at work and I'm thinking, what's going on? Uh, what can I do tomorrow to make things better? It's just a constant thing.

Ms. Yanelli keenly felt her lower social status, as she expressed after a parent-teacher conference with Mr. Tier, Billy's fourth-grade teacher:

I wanted to ask why he pulls Billy's hair. Why does he pick up Billy's book and throw it across the classroom and say, "You're too slow." . . . I didn't get to talk about the things that I wanted to talk about . . . I'm not very professional. I can't use the words I want to use. Just because they are professional doesn't (voice drops) mean that they are so smart.[3]

Mr. Yanelli shared her frustration, expressing the view that "they" would not give Billy a fair shake since they had decided he was a problematic student. Had the Yanellis reared Billy according to the logic of concerted cultivation, they may still have had problems with him at home and at school. But the strategies they used created more distance, distrust, and difficulty in their relationship with educators than occurred in the case of Ms. Marshall, for example, or other middle-class families. Ms. Yanelli did not feel that she had the "words" to "talk about" what *she* wanted to cover in conferences. Instead, she felt powerless and constrained.

WORRYING ABOUT BEING TURNED IN

This general feeling of unease with the school would, at times, explode into a crisis when the physical discipline practiced at home made them vulnerable for intervention by the school. In family life, the Yanellis gave directives: "Billy don't do that" or "Billy cut it out." They often did not provide reasons. Even when they did provide reasons, they were much briefer than in the Tallinger family. Parents did not, for example, draw out Billy and encourage him to think through the implications for himself. Instead, the parents stated the explanation in a brief fashion (if they provided one at all). Moreover, Ms. Yanelli (who did virtually all of the disciplining) found it helpful to pick up a belt when Billy was exasperating her. This fundamental strategy for child rearing — directives and physical punishment — was not in keeping with the standards promoted by professionals. For example, on this Wednesday in early May, Ms. Yanelli quarreled with her son over his homework. He was working (with the television on) in a slow-paced fashion at 8:00 P.M., although he had started much earlier.

MOM: Billy, please finish that homework. It's 8:00 almost. I'm going to shut the
    TV off. What number are you on? What time did you start your homework?

BILLY: 5:00.

MOM: If you started at 5:00 you should be done at 6:00.

MOM: Billy answer me. Tell me where you're at. (She sounded upset.)

A bit later, Little Billy finished his homework and began a game of Scrabble with his mother and the researcher. This became the source of a new conflict:

MOM: It'll be time for your shower when you're finished.

BILLY: We're playing Scrabble.

MOM: You're getting a shower. Then you can play Scrabble. (Mom's voice was loud and she sounded angry.)

Billy finishes his homework and his mother, the field-worker, and Billy begin a game of Scrabble. Before the game is done, Ms. Yanelli tells Billy it is time for his shower. He ignores. After repeatedly telling Billy to get in the shower his mother got out a belt.

MOM: Billy shower. I don't care if [you] cry, scream.

BILLY: We're not done [with the Scrabble game].

MOM: You're done. Finish your homework earlier.

(Billy stays seated.)

MOM: Come on! Tomorrow you've got a big day. (Billy didn't move.)

Mom went in the other room and got a brown leather belt. She hit Billy twice on the leg . . . Billy was sitting between Big Billy and [the researcher]. Big Billy and [his friend] Tom watched. She said, "Get up right now. Tomorrow I can't get you up in the morning. Get up right now." Billy got up and ran up the steps.

In all of these extended interactions there were elements of reasoning, in the sense that Ms. Yanelli explained why she demanded various behaviors from Billy. Nevertheless, the fundamental process emphasized a series of directives (i.e., "Billy shower," "you're done"). Most important, when the mother felt her son was not sufficiently responsive, she found the force of physical discipline to be a valuable resource. Although Mr. Yanelli was an observer, rather than participant, in these interactions he was supportive of the approach. Indeed, from time to time, if Billy was dragging his feet on a task, his father would comment to no one in particular, "He needs to be beat!" In an interview, Ms. Yanelli indicated that her use of a belt varied enormously; she estimated that over the previous two weeks, she had used it once a week. While we were visiting, it would come up from time to time depending on how the day was going, but we observed her hit with a belt or threaten to hit with a belt at least once a week.[4] In some working-class families, the lines were clearer. It is also important to stress that some working-class families in the study did not use hitting or belts. Thus, there was important variation within the class. But this form of discipline was not observed in middle-class families.[5]

To return to the ideas discussed in Chapter 2, the school selectively validated certain cultural practices as legitimate. Other practices, such as hitting children, while virtually universal in other historical periods, were deemed unacceptable. Adherence to the practices of the accomplishment of natural growth, rather than concerted cultivation, had important consequences when the families interacted with the school. The Yanelli family keenly felt the school to be a threatening force. In other words, their failure to use elaborate reasoning (a cultural practice) was transformed into a lack of resources when they confronted school authorities. They felt worried, powerless, and scared.

For example, Little Billy's mother was worried that the school might turn her in to the state. Because of behavior problems at school, the educators stridently insisted that the school therapist who regularly visited the school see Little Billy. Once Billy's mother met with the school counselor, however, he warned her, as noted at the beginning of the chapter, that he was legally required to turn her in to government officials if he found that she was engaging in child abuse. Ms. Yanelli felt rightfully threatened, since she felt that, as noted above, "Billy gets so out of control that maybe he does need it once in a while."

I said to the therapist, you know, we'll be in [the grocery store] once in a while and Billy will slide down the aisle on his stomach and I'll take him by the hair and I'll pull him down the aisle. Is that child abuse? . . . So, am I going to have people over here saying I abuse my child if Billy sits in a class with him and says my mom pulled my hair? . . . I don't know. I guess I'll just have to take it as it comes. But there are times when I chase him up the stairs with a belt in my hand. I do.

This clash, between the parents' ideas of what Billy needs and the school standards for child rearing, created small crises in the home. One day in May, for example, I stopped by for a visit (after the formal observations were over) to find Ms. Yanelli deeply upset. She had been disciplining him, and Billy had raised his arm to block the impact of his mother's belt, ending up with three very distinct red marks on his forearm from where it had landed. His mother was frantic that "he had to go school that way." She was agitated, pacing around the kitchen smoking a cigarette, trying to figure out what to do.[6]

In short, Ms. Yanelli's failure to use reasoning and her adoption of a belt made her vulnerable, since she moved in a "field" (the school) that privileged reasoning. If she had lived a century earlier, the use of a belt would not have been so problematic. Today, however, it carries a potentially catastrophic risk: that her son could show the teacher his marks on his arm, she could be arrested for child abuse, and her son could be put in foster care temporarily or permanently. Regardless of the likelihood of this sequence occurring, Ms. Yanelli was worried about the actions of the school.

Thus, different family backgrounds engender different levels of benefit in educational fields. In this instance, the cost to working-class families for their lack of capital takes the form of an ongoing feeling of the threat of a looming catastrophe. This gap in the connections between working-class and poor families and schools is important. It undermines their feeling of trust or comfort at school, a feeling that other researchers have argued is pivotal in the formation of effective and productive family-school relationships.[7]

TAKING STOCK

Middle-class parents (including wealthier members of the middle class) such as the Marshalls, Williamses, and Tallingers often exuded confidence in their interactions with school officials. They did not appear to hold similar fears of the school. The idea that authorities would "come and take my kids away" was never expressed in any observation of or interview with middle-class parents in the way it repeatedly appeared among working-class and poor families. For example, after returning from an out-of-state soccer tournament for Garrett, Ms. Tallinger recounted that she and some other parents had left the children in a hotel room with a video and a cellular phone and gone out to dinner at a restaurant about a block away. She told me in a light tone with a smile on her face, "Don't turn us in!" Overall, the demeanor of Garrett's mother was vastly different from that of Little Billy's mother. She was joking about the matter rather than treating it gravely. More to the point, middle-class parents never gave any indication that they worried about what the school could do to them. They did not appear to see themselves in the vulnerable position that gave rise to so much fear and worry on the part of Little Billy's parents. Thus, their use of reasoning as a child-rearing strategy had an invisible benefit: it put them in sync with patterns of dominant cultural repertoires. This facilitated their ease with school officials.

In sum, these standards are developed by professionals and encoded in schools. In other words, social workers, psychologists, medical doctors, and other professionals have issued standards for proper child rearing and caution about what constitutes incorrect child rearing.[8] Teachers and administrators in schools have adopted these standards. Moreover, the schools, for better or worse, are an arm of the state, and are therefore legally required to report children they believe to be abused or neglected. Since school attendance is compulsory for young children, families cannot avoid the school or, indirectly, the eyes of state officials. In this context, the middle-class families — with their greater likelihood of adopting professionals' standards — appear to enjoy largely invisible benefits not available to working-class and poor families.

The Power and Limits
of Social Class

At the end of fifth grade, the children looked forward with trepidation and excitement to their transition to being with "big kids" in the local middle school. Lower Richmond and Swan schools each separately marked this life transition with a graduation ceremony, held on hot, sunny days in June. At Lower Richmond, there was tremendous enthusiasm for the ceremony, particularly on the part of the children and their families. Many parents arrived at school carrying bouquets of flowers and clusters of circular, shiny silver balloons emblazoned with phrases such as "CONGRATULATIONS GRADUATE!" Mothers, especially African American mothers, were in starched, immaculate, pale-colored suits and outfits of the style often worn to weddings, church, and special events. The girls, including Wendy Driver and Tara Carroll, wore frilly dresses. A number of girls wore prom dresses. Billy Yanelli was in a formal jacket, slacks, white shirt, and tie. Harold McAllister was less formal but no less carefully prepared in an assiduously ironed, print dress shirt, slacks, and dress shoes. The school provided yellow carnation wrist corsages for the girls and boutonnieres for the boys. In the "cafetorium," parents, grandmothers, young children, and older siblings sat on children's chairs, reading the list of graduates, chatting, and laughing together. To the strains of a scratchy "Pomp and Circumstance," the children entered in a formal march: from opposing sides of the auditorium, two children, each at the same moment, began a promenade (step, pause, step, pause). Some of the boys, including Harold McAllister, had a pained expression on their faces when beginning the processional. When Harold heard family members hooting, he flashed a grin, and then adopted a look of studied casualness.

Jane, Lori, and Alexis laugh when they see Harold enter the room, and say "Yo, Harold! Go!" Someone whistles lowly. Someone else says, "Lookin good, Har." Harold grins at his family, and as he walks, makes an attempt to appear cool and casual, as if all this fuss doesn't mean so much to him.

Many of the children looked elated, smiling broadly at their families as they made their formal entrance. During the ceremony, some Lower Richmond parents erupted with joy when their children received special recognition; they yelled out "All Right!" or "Yes!" or the child's name. Some parents stood up to applaud their children.

Even on this very happy occasion, however, feelings of distrust toward the school sometimes surfaced. A number of parents disapprovingly discussed how a few children had been banned from the ceremony for behavior problems. Billy Yanelli's father and mother were sitting proudly in the audience (both having taken off from work). Although Mr. Yanelli told me, "I like this school" (particularly compared to the one that Billy was about to attend), his discomfort was apparent.

Big Billy Yanelli made a number of . . . derogatory . . . comments throughout the ceremony, either to himself or for the benefit of [Ms. Yanelli], who sat next to him — mostly ignoring him. Once, when a male teacher climbed the steps to the stage, Big Billy said: "He's so stupid. What a goof." At the beginning of the ceremony, as the principal adjusted the microphone and prepared to speak, Big Billy pretended to mimic her: "Okay, everyone is suspended."

The celebration at Swan had a somewhat different feel. Many Swan children, including Garrett Tallinger and Melanie Handlon, smiled and seemed pleased, but they were not bursting with excitement. Those Swan parents who were dressed more than casually simply had on their work outfits (i.e., suits, skirts and jackets — a "professional" rather than dressy kind of look). Swan boys looked neat but also casual: a number wore polo shirts, some wore button-down shirts, and only a few had on ties. Girls wore what looked like nice Sunday dresses — not very frilly but pretty and neat. Educators gave out awards for accomplishments ranging from perfect attendance to special achievement in math. Swan parents conveyed mild and polite pride when their children were recognized; they clapped politely but briefly, took pictures, and stayed in their chairs.

The future also was portrayed differently at Swan:

Swan seemed much more hopeful and Lower Richmond more aware of danger and trouble kids might face in their lives. Swan songs were about how bright the future was, how many new doors would open for the kids, how exciting it all was. The first two songs sung at Lower Richmond had to do with confronting despair, jealousy, pain, and trouble, with waking up the next day ready to try again, with renewal for struggle, with how many kids were hurting in the world. One of the male teachers also gave an admonition to the kids to "keep their hands in their pockets next year" in middle school when someone taunted them. The emphasis appeared to be on a certain kind of behavior (restraint, "good citizenship," avoiding fights, being respectful) rather than on academic achievement, as it was at Swan.

Of course, the parents themselves differed in how much education they had. For example, the Yanellis both went only through tenth grade. They hoped that their son Little Billy would go to a state college, but they were unsure. The middle-class families had little doubt that their children would attend college. Middle-class children, including Stacey Marshall, often chattered about which college they might want to go to when they were older. The Tallingers visited the campuses of Ivy League universities when they were in the area for soccer tournaments. Alexander Williams's parents were helping one of his cousins pay for her education at an elite private university. Thus, for these middle-class children, it was a matter of *which* college they would attend. In these contrasting visions of the future, the fifth-grade graduation was a different milestone.

THE POWER OF SOCIAL CLASS

In the United States, people disagree about the importance of social class in daily life. Many Americans believe that this country is fundamentally *open*. They assume the society is best understood as a collection of individuals. They believe that people who demonstrate hard work, effort, and talent are likely to achieve upward mobility. Put differently, many Americans believe in the American Dream. In this view, children should have roughly equal life chances. The extent to which life chances vary can be traced to differences in aspirations, talent, and hard work on the part of individuals. This perspective rejects the notion that parents' social location systematically shapes children's life experiences and outcomes. Instead, outcomes are seen as resting more in the hands of individuals.

In a distinctly different but still related vein, some social scientists acknowledge that there are systemic forms of inequality, including, for example, differences in parents' educational levels, occupational prestige, and income, as well as in their child-rearing practices. These scholars, however, see such differences within society as a matter of *gradation*. To explain unequal life outcomes, they see it as helpful to look at, for example, differences in mothers' years of education or the range of incomes by households in a particular city. These different threads are interwoven in an intricate and often baffling pattern. Scholars who take this perspective on inequality typically focus on the ways specific patterns are related (e.g., the number of years of mothers' schooling and the size of children's vocabularies, or the number of years of mothers' education and parental involvement in schooling). Implicitly and explicitly, social scientists who share this perspective do not accept the position that there are identifiable, categorical differences in groups. They do not believe that the differences that do exist across society cohere into patterns recognizable as social classes.

In this book, I have challenged both views. Rather than seeing society as a collection of individuals, I stressed the importance of individuals' social structural location in shaping their daily lives. Following a well-established European tradition, I rejected analyses that see differences in American families as best interpreted as a matter of fine gradations. Instead, I see as more valuable a *categorical* analysis, wherein families are grouped into social categories such as poor, working class, and middle class. I argued that these categories are helpful in understanding the behavior of family members, not simply in one particular aspect but across a number of spheres. Family practices cohere by social class. Social scientists who accept this perspective may disagree about the number and type of categories and whether there should be, for example, an upper-middle-class category as well as a lower-middle-class one. Still, they agree that the observed differences in how people act can be meaningfully and fruitfully grouped into categories, without violating the complexity of daily life. My own view is that seeing selected aspects of family life as differentiated by social class is simply a better way to understand the reality of American family life. I also believe that social location at birth can be very important in shaping the routines of daily life, even when family members are not particularly conscious of the existence of social classes.

Thus, I have stressed how social class dynamics are woven into the texture and rhythm of children and parents' daily lives. Class position influences critical aspects of family life: time use, language use, and kin ties. Working-class and middle-class mothers may express beliefs that reflect a similar notion of "intensive mothering," but their behavior is quite different.[1] For that reason, I have described sets of paired beliefs and actions as a "cultural logic" of child rearing. When children and parents move outside the home into the world of social institutions, they find that these cultural practices are not given equal value. There are signs that middle-class children benefit, in ways that are invisible to them and to their parents, from the degree of similarity between the cultural repertoires in the home and those standards adopted by institutions. In the next section, I acknowledge areas of family life that did not appear to be heavily influenced by social class. Then I turn to highlighting the ways that social class membership matters and to discussing why these differences exist and what can be done to lessen or eliminate them.

THE LIMITS OF SOCIAL CLASS

Among the families we observed, some aspects of daily life did not vary systematically by social class. There were episodes of laughter, emotional connection, and happiness as well as quiet comfort in every family.[2] Harold McAllister and his mother laughed together as he almost dropped his hot dog but then, in an awkward grab, caught it. After a baseball game, Mr. Williams rubbed Alexander's head affectionately and called him "handsome." Ms. Handlon gave her daughter a big squeeze around her shoulders after the Christmas Eve pageant, and Melanie beamed. One summer afternoon, Mr. Yanelli and Billy played cards together, sitting cross-legged on the sidewalk. These moments of connection seemed deeply meaningful to both children and parents in all social classes, even as they take different shape by social class, in terms of language, activity, and character.

All the families we observed also had rituals: favorite meals they often ate, television programs they watched, toys or games that were very important, family outings they looked forward to, and other common experiences. The content of their rituals varied (especially by social class); what did not vary was that the children enjoyed these experiences and they provided a sense of membership in a family. Also, in all social classes, a substantial part of the children's days was spent in repetitive rituals: getting up, making the bed, taking a shower, getting dressed, brushing hair and teeth, eating breakfast, finding school books and papers, and waiting for adults to get ready. These moments were interspersed with hours, days, and weeks of household work, tedious demands, mundane tasks, and tension. This was true for all families, regardless of social class. Nor were any families immune to life tragedies: across all social classes there were premature deaths due to car accidents or suicides.

Across all social classes children and parents had different temperaments: some were shy and quiet; some were outgoing and talkative. Some had a sense of humor and some did not. The degree of organization and order- liness in daily life also did not vary systematically by social class. Some houses were clean and some were a disaster. Some of the messiest ones were middle-class homes in which the entryway was a paragon of order but the living spaces, particularly the upstairs, were in a tumble. Despite the formidable differences among the families detailed in the previous chapters, in each home, after a few visits, the research assistants and I found that the surroundings felt normal, comfortable, and safe. Put dif- ferently, they all felt like home.

CONCERTED CULTIVATION AND THE ACCOMPLISHMENT OF NATURAL GROWTH

Despite these important areas of shared practices, social class made a sig- nificant difference in the routines of children's daily lives. The white and Black middle-class parents engaged in practices of *concerted cultivation*. In these families, parents actively fostered and assessed their children's talents, opinions, and skills. They scheduled their children for activities. They reasoned with them. They hovered over them and outside the home they did not hesitate to intervene on the children's behalf. They made a deliberate and sustained effort to stimulate children's development and to cultivate their cognitive and social skills. The working-class and poor parents viewed children's development as unfolding spontaneously, as long as they were provided with comfort, food, shelter, and other basic support. I have called this cultural logic of child rearing the *accomplish- ment of natural growth*. As with concerted cultivation, this commitment, too, required ongoing effort; sustaining children's natural growth despite formidable life challenges is properly viewed as accomplishment. Parents who relied on natural growth generally organized their children's lives so they spent time in and around home, in informal play with peers, sib- lings, and cousins. As a result, the children had more autonomy regard- ing leisure time and more opportunities for child-initiated play. They also were more responsible for their lives outside the home. Unlike in middle-class families, adult-organized activities were uncommon. Instead of the relentless focus on reasoning and negotiation that took place in middle-class families, there was less speech (including less whining and badgering) in working-class and poor homes. Boundaries between adults and children were clearly marked; parents generally used language not as an aim in itself but more as a conduit for social life. Directives were common. In their institutional encounters, working-class and poor parents turned over responsibility to professionals; when parents did try to intervene, they felt that they were less capable and less efficacious than they would have liked. While working-class and poor children differed in important ways, particularly in the stability of their lives, surprisingly there was not a major difference between them in their cultural logic of child rearing. Instead, in this study the cultural divide appeared to be between the middle class and everyone else.

Across all social classes, child-rearing practices often appeared to be natural. Like breathing, child rearing usually seemed automatic and unconscious. Parents were scarcely aware that they were orienting their children in specific ways.[3] For example, the Handlon and the Tallinger children had cousins their own ages who lived within a twenty-minute drive. They saw their cousins, however, only on special occasions, not several times per week as did children in the Driver and McAllister families. While firmly committed to the strategy of concerted cultivation, Mr. and Ms. Williams did not seem especially conscious of their approach. Although both parents mentioned the pleasure they experienced from knowing that Alexander was curious, they did not appear to link that trait to their own extensive use of reasoning with him. Nor did they analyze their failure to use directives. The fact that most of Alexander's time was spent with other children his own age, rather than with his cousins (in part because they lived so far away), also was not a subject of reflection or discussion. Parts of their lives, of course, did reflect conscious choices and deliberate actions, including Ms. Williams's vehement objections to television and both parents' commitment to furthering Alexander's musical talents. The scarcity of time was also a subject of discussion. Even here, however, the focus was on the details of life (e.g., missing a baseball game to take part in a school play) rather than on the overall approach to child rearing.

Similarly, in families using the accomplishment of natural growth, there was tremendous economic constraint and almost constant talk about money. But there was a "taken for granted" character to daily life that presumed a focus on natural growth rather than concerted cultivation. Ms. McAllister stressed her strengths as a mother. As she fed, clothed, and cared for her children, took them on picnics, and watched out for them, she compared her actions favorably to the behavior of mothers living nearby, including those who took drugs. She did not compare herself to the Ms. Tallingers or Ms. Williamses of the world.

THE INTERSECTION OF RACE AND CLASS

In *Race Matters,* Professor Cornell West reports his frustration in trying to hail a cab to get to a photo shoot for the cover of his latest book. As he waited and waited, ten taxis without passengers passed him by, stopping (often within his vision) instead to pick up people whose skin color was not black. Furious, he gave up, took the subway, and was late for the appointment.[4] Professor West and other middle-class African Americans report feeling enraged over this inability to signal their class position in social interactions with strangers. In these situations, race trumps social class.[5]

The middle-class Black fathers in this study told similar tales. One father reported white women clutching their purses and looking terrified as he walked briskly one evening to use the cash machine in an upscale shopping district. Also, as I have shown, the mothers and fathers of middle-class African American children kept a keen eye out for signs of racial problems. Their worries were confirmed, as when a first-grade boy told Alexander Williams (son of a lawyer) that he could only be a garbage man when he grew up, or when Fern Marshall, the only Black girl in a camp of a hundred white girls, had fun during the morning basketball activities but at lunchtime found it more difficult (than if she had been white) to blend into the groups of girls chattering away. Although they moved heavily within white worlds, parents sought to avoid having their children be the only Black child at an event. In addition, parents sought to have their children develop a positive self-image that specifically included their racial identity. Thus, for example, they attended all-Black middle-class Baptist churches every Sunday.

Given this evidence, it would be a mistake to suggest that race did not matter in children's lives. It did. Nevertheless, the role of race was less powerful than I had expected. In terms of the areas this book has focused on — how children spend their time, the way parents use language and discipline in the home, the nature of the families' social connections, and the strategies used for intervening in institutions — white and Black parents engaged in very similar, often identical, practices with their children.[6] As the children age, the relative importance of race in their daily lives is likely to increase.[7] Most African Americans do not date or marry outside their own racial and ethnic groups. Housing markets are heavily segregated for Black homeowners, regardless of their income.[8] African Americans also are likely to encounter racism in their interpersonal contact with whites, particularly in employment settings. In fourth grade, however, in very central ways, race mattered less in children's daily lives than did their social class.[9] Black and white middle-class children were given enormous amounts of individualized attention, with their parents organizing their own time around their children's leisure activities. This prioritizing profoundly affected parents' leisure time. In these situations, race made little to no difference. Mr. Williams, after a week of working until midnight preparing for a trial, spent Sunday driving Alexander to baseball practice, home for a quick shower and change, and then off to a school play. Mr. Tallinger flew across the country on a red-eye, had a short nap, went to work, and then was out late at a soccer practice on a chilly spring evening, yearning for the event to be over so that he could get home and sleep.

Similarly, it was the middle-class children, Black and white, who squabbled and fought with their siblings and talked back to their parents. These behaviors were simply not tolerated in working-class and poor families, Black or white.[10] Still, the biggest differences in the cultural logic of child rearing in the day-to-day behavior of children in this study were between middle-class children on the one hand (including wealthy members of the middle class) and working-class and poor children on the other. As a middle-class Black boy, Alexander Williams had much more in common with *white* middle-class Garrett Tallinger than he did with less-privileged Black boys, such as Tyrec Taylor or Harold McAllister.

HOW DOES IT MATTER?

Both concerted cultivation and the accomplishment of natural growth offer intrinsic benefits (and burdens) for parents and their children. Nevertheless, these practices are accorded different social values by important social institutions. There are signs that some family cultural practices, notably those associated with concerted cultivation, give children advantages that other cultural practices do not.

In terms of the rhythms of daily life, both concerted cultivation and the accomplishment of natural growth have advantages and disadvantages. Middle-class children learn to develop and value an individualized sense of self. Middle-class children are allowed to participate in a variety of coveted activities: gymnastics, soccer, summer camps, and so on. These activities improve their skills and teach them, as Mr. Tallinger noted, to be better athletes than their parents were at comparable ages. They learn to handle moments of humiliation on the field as well as moments of glory. Middle-class children learn, as Mr. Williams noted, the difference between baroque and classical music. They learn to perform. They learn to present themselves. But this cultivation has a cost. Family schedules are disrupted. Dinner hours are very hard to arrange. Siblings such as Spencer and Sam Tallinger spend dreary hours waiting at athletic fields and riding in the car going from one event to another. Family life, despite quiet interludes, is frequently frenetic. Parents, especially mothers, must reconcile conflicting priorities, juggling events whose deadlines are much tighter than the deadlines connected to serving meals or getting children ready for bed. The domination of children's activities can take a toll on families. At times, everyone in the middle-class families — including ten-year-old children — seemed exhausted. Thus, there are formidable costs, as well as benefits to this child-rearing approach.

Working-class and poor children also had advantages, as well as costs, from the cultural logic of child rearing they experienced. Working-class and poor children learned to entertain themselves. They played outside, creating their own games, as Tyrec Taylor did with his friends. They did not complain of being bored. Working-class and poor children also appeared to have boundless energy. They did not have the exhaustion that we saw in middle-class children the same age. Some working-class and poor children longed to be in organized activities — Katie Brindle wanted to take ballet and Harold McAllister wanted to play football. When finances, a lack of transportation, and limited availability of programs conspired to prevent or limit their participation, they were disappointed. Many were also deeply aware of the economic constraints and the limited consumption permitted by their family's budget. Living spaces were small, and often there was not much privacy. The television was almost always on and, like many middle-class children growing up in the 1950s, working-class and poor children watched unrestricted amounts of television. As a result, family members spent more time together in shared space than occurred in middle-class homes. Indeed, family ties were very strong, particularly among siblings. Working-class and poor children also developed very close ties with their cousins and other extended family members.

Within the home, these two approaches to child rearing each have identifiable strengths and weaknesses. When we turn to examining institutional dynamics outside the home, however, the unequal benefits of middle-class children's lives compared to working-class and poor children's lives become clearer. In crucial ways, middle-class family members appeared reasonably comfortable and entitled, while working-class and poor family members appeared uncomfortable and constrained. For example, neither Harold nor his mother seemed as comfortable as Alexander and his mother had been as they interacted with their physician. Alexander was used to extensive conversation at home; with the doctor, he was at ease initiating questions. Harold, who was used to responding to directives at home, primarily answered questions from the doctor, rather than posing his own. Unlike Ms. Williams, Ms. McAllister did not see the enthusiastic efforts of her daughter Alexis to share information about her birthmark as appropriate behavior. Ms. Williams not only permitted Alexander to hop up and down on the stool to express his enthusiasm; she explicitly trained him to be assertive and well prepared for his encounter with the doctor. Harold was reserved. He did not show an emerging sense of entitlement, as Alexander and other middle-class children did. Absorbing his mother's apparent need to conceal the truth about the range of foods in his diet, Harold appeared cautious, displaying an emerging sense of constraint.

This pattern occurred in school interactions, as well. Some working-class and poor parents had warm and friendly relations with educators. Overall, however, working-class and poor parents in this study had much more distance or separation from the school than did middle-class mothers. At home, Ms. McAllister could be quite assertive, but at school she was subdued. The parent-teacher conference yielded Ms. McAllister few insights into her son's educational experience.[11]

Other working-class and poor parents also appeared baffled, intimidated, and subdued in parent-teacher conferences. Ms. Driver, frantically worried because Wendy, a fourth-grader, was not yet able to read, resisted intervening, saying, "I don't want to jump into anything and find it is the wrong thing." When working-class and poor parents did try to intervene in their children's educational experiences, they often felt ineffectual. Billy Yanelli's mother appeared relaxed and chatty when she interacted with service personnel, such as the person who sold her lottery tickets on Saturday morning. With "the school," however, she was very apprehensive. She distrusted school personnel. She felt bullied and powerless.

There were also moments in which parents encouraged children to outwardly comply with school officials but, at the same time, urged them to resist school authority. Although well aware of school rules prohibiting fighting, the Yanellis directly trained their son to "beat up" a boy who was bothering him. Similarly, when Wendy Driver complained about a boy who pestered her and pulled her ponytail, and the teacher did not respond, her mother advised her to "punch him." Ms. Driver's boyfriend added, "Hit him when the teacher isn't looking." [12]

The unequal level of trust, as well as differences in the amount and quality of information divulged, can yield unequal *profits* during a historical period such as ours, when professionals applaud assertiveness and reject passivity as an inappropriate parenting strategy.[13] Middle-class children and parents often (but not always) accrued advantages or profits from their efforts. Alexander Williams succeeded in having the doctor take his medical concerns seriously. The Marshall children ended up in the gifted program, even though they did not qualify.

Overall, the routine rituals of family life are not equally legitimized in the broader society. Parents' efforts to reason with children (even two-year-olds) are seen as more educationally valuable than parents' use of directives. Spending time playing soccer or baseball is deemed by professionals as more valuable than time spent watching television. Moreover, differences in the cultural logic of child rearing are attached to unequal currency in the broader society. The middle-class strategy of concerted cultivation appears to have greater promise of being capitalized into social profits than does the strategy of the accomplishment of natural growth found in working-class and poor homes. Alexander Williams's vocabulary grew at home, in the evenings, as he bantered with his parents about plagiarism and copyright as well as about the X-Men. Harold McAllister, Billy Yanelli, and Wendy Driver learned how to manage their own time, play without the direction of adults, and occupy themselves for long periods of time without being bored. Although these are important life skills, they do not have the same payoff on standardized achievement tests as the experiences of Alexander Williams.

These potential benefits for middle-class children, and costs for working-class and poor children, are necessarily speculative, since at the end of the study, the children were still in elementary school. Still, there are important signs of hidden advantages being sown at early ages. The middle-class children have extensive experience with adults in their lives with whom they have a relatively contained, bureaucratically regulated, and somewhat superficial relationship. As children spend eight weeks playing soccer, baseball, basketball, and other activities, they meet and interact with adults acting as coaches, assistant coaches, car pool drivers, and so on. This contact with relative strangers, although of a different quality than contact with cousins, aunts, and uncles, provides work-related skills. For instance, as Garrett shakes the hand of a stranger and looks him or her in the eye, he is being groomed, in an effortless fashion, for job interviews he will have as an adult (employment experts stress the importance of good eye contact). In the McAllister home, family members have great affection and warmth toward one another, but they do not generally look each other in the eye when they speak; this training is likely to be a liability in job interviews. In settings as varied as health care and gymnastics, middle-class children learn at a young age to be assertive and demanding. They expect, as did Stacey Marshall, for institutions to be responsive to *them* and to accommodate their individual needs. By contrast, when Wendy Driver is told to hit the boy who is pestering her (when the teacher isn't looking) or Billy Yanelli is told to physically defend himself, despite school rules, they are not learning how to make bureaucratic institutions work to their advantage. Instead, they are being given lessons in frustration and powerlessness.

WHY? THE SEARCH FOR EXPLANATIONS[14]

As I discuss shortly, some commentators today decry the "overscheduled" lives of children; they long for the days when most children had unstructured lives, filled with informal play. But this is a romanticized view of the family in the past. Although there have always been important social class differences in childhood, for much of U.S. history, children played an important economic role in family life. For example, in colonial America, a boy of six or seven was expected to move out of his parents' home to live with a skilled craftsman as an apprentice. As the country gradually industrialized, children's small, "nimble fingers" were useful in factory work.[15] Children also were economic assets on family farms. According to a 1920 study in North Dakota children helped herd cattle and dig holes for fence posts. They also had daily responsibilities, as this description of a nine-year-old boy's chores shows: "Built the fires in the morning, swept the floor of a two-room house, and brought in fuel and water; in addition, before he made a two-mile trip to school, he helped feed stock (five horses and twelve cows) and chopped wood; in the evening he did the chores and washed dishes."[16] Children, especially working-class and poor children, also helped with the informal paid labor their mothers did, such as laundry and "sewing, embroidering, flower making, and tag tying"; most older siblings looked after younger siblings, as well. Children did have some time for unstructured leisure, but it was limited.

Viviana Zelizer shows that through the end of the nineteenth century and into the early decades of the twentieth century, these practices were accompanied by beliefs supporting the importance of children working hard. If anything, the concern was that without specific training in "useful work," children might grow up to be "paupers and thieves."[17] In children's books and magazines, in which stories stressed "the virtues of work, duty, and discipline," Zelizer notes, "The standard villain . . . was an idle child."[18] The period after 1920 saw a dramatic decline in children's economic contributions, however, as child labor laws were put into place and a new vision of the "economically useless but sentimentally priceless child" took hold.[19]

Thus, although a definitive account of historical changes in children's leisure practices remains to be written, it appears that it was for only a relatively brief historical period that children were granted long stretches of leisure time with unstructured play. In the period after World War II, white and Black children were permitted to play for hours on end with other neighborhood children, after school, during evenings, and on weekends. Other than going to church, the few organized activities children participated in (e.g., music lessons or Scouts) began at a later age than is typical today. The "institutionalization of children's leisure" and the rise of concerted cultivation more generally are recent developments.[20] Today's parents are not transmitting practices they learned in their families of origin. Parents of the eighty-eight children in our study were born in the 1950s and 1960s. *None* reported having had a very active schedule of organized activities as a child. Rather, the middle-class parents in this study and, possibly throughout the country, appear to have been raised according to the logic of the accomplishment of natural growth.

In attempting to understand this historical shift, particularly the institutionalization of children's leisure and the emphasis on "intensive mothering," commentators often point to the impact of modern life, especially the impact of increasing "rationalization."[21] This view, termed the "McDonaldization of society" by George Ritzer, finds an increasing standardization of daily life, with an emphasis on efficiency, predictability, control, and calculability.[22] Ritzer notes that these principles from the world of fast food have been adapted to other parts of social life, including Kidsports Fun and Fitness Club, Kinder Care, Kampgrounds of America, Toys 'R' Us, and other stores.[23] Family life, too, is becoming increasingly rationalized, being

> invaded by not only public schools, the courts, social service workers,
> gardeners, housekeepers, day-care providers, lawyers, doctors, televisions,
> frozen dinners, pizza delivery, manufactured clothing, and disposable
> diapers, but also, and more critically, by the *ideology* behind such insti-

tutions, persons, and products. They bring with them . . . the logic of . . .
impersonal, competitive, contractual, commodified, efficient, profit-
maximizing, self-interested relations.[24]

Busy affluent parents can hire chauffeurs to take children to their organized activities, hire educators at "Learning Centers" in shopping malls to
help children do homework and improve in school, and hire personal
shoppers to help buy and wrap holiday gifts. The services available for
birthday parties (e.g., a special room at McDonald's, an overnight at a
science museum, or a professional party coordinator) are signs of the
increasing rationalization of family life.

The rationalization of children's leisure is evident in the proliferation
of organized activities with a predictable schedule, delivering a particular
quantity of experience within a specific time period, under the control of
adults. That children's time use has shifted from unstructured play to
organized activities does not mean that families no longer have fun during their leisure hours. Many find the time spent together during soccer
and baseball games, for example, to be very enjoyable. The point is that
areas of family life are growing more systematic, predictable, and regulated than they have been in the recent past. Forces that have converged
to bring about this change include increasing concerns about the safety of
children who play unsupervised on local streets, rises in employment
(resulting in adults being at home less), and a decline in the availability of
neighborhood playmates due to a dropping birth rate and the effects of
suburbanization, especially the increased size of homes and decreased
density of housing.[25]

Greater emphasis on the use of reasoning in the home, particularly as
a form of discipline, as well as interventions in institutions, can also be
seen as a form of rationalization, particularly the well-documented trend
of "scientific motherhood." Still, any analysis of the rise of concerted cultivation must also, I believe, grapple with the changing position of the
United States in the world economy, and the accompanying decline in
highly paid manufacturing jobs and increase in less desirable service-sec-
tor jobs. This restructuring makes it very likely that when today's children are adults, their standard of living will be lower than that of their
parents. It means that there will be fewer "good jobs" and more "bad
jobs," and that the competition for them will be intense. Moreover, since
children must be successful in school to gain access to desirable positions,
many middle-class parents are anxious to make sure their children perform well academically. Institutional gatekeepers, such as college admissions officers, applaud extracurricular activities. Thus, many parents see

children's activities as more than interesting and enjoyable pastimes. They also provide potential advantages for children in the sorting process.

All of these factors may contribute to the rise of a new standard of child rearing in the middle class. As Hays shows, this new standard is legitimated in a variety of ways.[26] Professionals actively support advancement of children's creative and leisure talents, cognitive growth, and school performance through the active involvement of their parents as cultivators. The older logic of child rearing, the accomplishment of natural growth, receives less institutional support. If this analysis is correct, if there has been a shift in the cultural repertoires of child rearing, and if that change has been legitimated, why is there a class difference in child-rearing strategies? Why doesn't everyone raise their children the same way?

THE ROLE OF RESOURCES

Parents' economic resources helped create the class differences in child rearing discussed in this book. Children's activities were expensive. A $25 enrollment fee, which middle-class parents dismissed as "insignificant," "modest," or "negligible," was a formidable expense for all poor families and many in the working class. The enrollment fee was just the tip of the iceberg. Many activities also required special clothing. Stacey Marshall needed gymnastic leotards as well as a training warm-up suit. She had special bags to carry her equipment to and from the gym, and a balance beam at home. Participating in tournaments required paying special fees. Children's hectic schedules increased the number of meals eaten out, as the families raced from one event to the next. Tournaments out of the local area resulted in special fees as well as hotel bills and restaurant bills. There were special end-of-season events, banquets, and gifts for the coaches. There were assorted hidden costs, such as car maintenance and gas. In 1994, the Tallingers estimated the cost (including all of the factors listed above, except car repair) of Garrett's activities at $4,000 annually; nor was that figure unusual.[27] Thus, in addition to disposable income for the cost of lessons and activities, families usually needed other advantages, such as reliable private transportation and flexibility in work schedules to be able to get children to events. These resources were disproportionately concentrated in middle-class families.

Differences in educational resources are important as well. Middle-class parents' superior levels of education gave them larger vocabularies and more knowledge. More education facilitated concerted cultivation, particularly with respect to interventions in institutions outside the home. As I have shown, poor and working-class parents had difficulty understanding key terms bantered about by professionals, such as "tetanus shot" or "cavity." Middle-class parents' educational backgrounds also gave them the confidence to criticize educational professionals and intervene in school matters. For working-class and poor parents, educators were social superiors. For middle-class parents, they were equals or subordinates. In addition, research indicates that middle-class parents tend to be more sensitive to shifts in child-rearing standards than do working-class parents, probably because middle-class parents tend to be more attuned to the advice of professionals.[28]

Others have shown that parents' occupations and working conditions, particularly the complexity of their work, influence important aspects of their child-rearing beliefs.[29] In this study, there were not only suggestions that parents' work mattered, but also signs that the experience of adulthood itself influenced how individuals conceived of childhood. Middle-class parents, spared severe economic struggles, often were preoccupied with the pleasures and difficulties of their work lives.[30] They tended to view childhood as an opportunity for play, but also as a chance to develop talents and skills that could be valuable in the self-actualization processes that take place in adulthood. Mr. Tallinger, for example, saw implications for the world of work in his assessment of the value of sports for Garrett, noting that playing soccer taught his son to be "hard nosed" and "competitive." Ms. Williams, similarly, mentioned the value of Alexander learning to work with others on a team. Middle-class parents were very aware of the "declining fortunes" of the middle class and of the country as a whole at the close of the twentieth century. They worried about their own economic futures and those of their children.[31] This uncertainty made them feel it was important that children be developed in a variety of ways in order to enhance their future possibilities.

The experiences and concerns that shaped the views of the working-class and poor parents had little in common with those of the middle-class parents. For working-class families, it was the deadening quality of work and the press of economic shortages that defined their experience of adulthood and influenced their vision of childhood. For poor families, it was dependence on public assistance and severe economic shortages that most affected their views about adulthood and childhood. Working-class and poor families had many more worries about basic issues: how to endure food shortages, get children to doctors despite a lack of reliable transportation, purchase clothing, and manage other life necessities.

Thinking back over their childhoods, these adults acknowledged periods of hardship but also recalled times without the kinds of worries that troubled them at present. Many appeared to want their own youngsters to spend their time being happy and relaxed. There would be plenty of time for their children to face the burdens of life when they reached adulthood. In summary, then, parents' conceptions of adulthood and childhood appeared to be closely connected to their lived experiences. The factors influencing parents' child-rearing strategies thus seem to go beyond the role of education per se to encompass these adults' occupational and economic experiences as well.

In fact, it was the interweaving of life experiences and resources, including parents' economic resources, occupational conditions, and educational backgrounds, that seemed to be most important in leading middle-class parents to engage in concerted cultivation and working-class and poor families to engage in the accomplishment of natural growth. Still, the structural location of families did not *determine* their child-rearing practices. The agency of actors and the indeterminacy of social life are inevitable. It is important to keep in mind this "relative autonomy" of individuals in the enactment of social structural position and biographical outcomes.[32]

Aside from economic and social resources, there are other factors that might influence child-rearing practices by social class. Indeed, one might imagine two different scenarios: if the resources of the poor and working-class families were transformed overnight so that they equaled those of the middle-class families, would their cultural logic of child rearing shift as well? Or are there cultural attitudes and beliefs that are somewhat independent of economic and social resources that are influencing parents' practices here? Unfortunately, the size and scope of this study do not permit a clear answer to this question. On the one hand, some poor and working-class parents reported that they wanted their children to have more organized activities, expressed a belief in the importance of listening to children, and felt it was important for them as parents to play an active role in their children's schooling. In these families, the parents' practices appeared to be directly limited by their resources. On the other hand, in other families, parents did not view children's participation in activities as particularly important. Ms. Taylor, for example, "prayed" that Tyrec would not want to play football again; she did not see his involvement in the sport as helping him in any special way.

Other parents were even more dubious. For example, during the parent interviews, the research assistants and I described the real-life schedules of two children (using data from the twelve families we were observing). One schedule was similar to that of Alexander Williams: restricted television, required reading, and many organized activities, including piano lessons (for analytical purposes, the child was described as disliking his piano lessons and not being permitted to quit, neither of which was true for Alexander). Some working-class and poor parents found this scenario unappealing.[33] One white, poor mother complained:

I think he, I think, uh, I think he wants more. I think he doesn't enjoy doing what he's doing half of the time (light laughter). I think his parents are too strict. And he's not a child (laughter).

In addition, even parents who remarked that this kind of schedule would pay off "job-wise" when the child was an adult, still expressed serious reservations, as these comments (each from different interviews) show:

"I think he is a sad kid."

"He must be dead-dog tired."

"Unless you're planning on him being Liberace as far as piano . . . I think it is a waste of money . . . I think he is cutting himself kind of short. He's not being involved with anything as far as friends."

Thus, the belief systems of working-class and poor parents were mixed: some longed for a schedule of organized activities for their children; others did not. Still, there were a few indications that if parents' economic and social resources were to change, their cultural practices would shift as well. A number of middle-class children in the study had parents who were upwardly mobile. The parents were middle class, but the children's grandparents were poor or working class. In some cases, these grandparents objected to the child-rearing practices associated with concerted cultivation. They were bewildered by their grandchildren's hectic schedules of organized activities, outraged that the parents would reason with the children instead of giving them clear directives, and awed by the intensive involvement of mothers in the children's schooling. The small number of cases limits generalizing, but the evidence does suggest that it is economic and social resources that are key in shaping child-rearing practices; as parents' own social class position shifts, so do their cultural beliefs and practices in child rearing. Untangling the effects of material and cultural resources on parents and children's choices is beyond the scope of this study. These two forces are inextricably interwoven in daily life.

WHAT IS TO BE DONE?

In his thoughtful book *The Price of Citizenship,* historian Michael Katz shows that in recent years Americans' conception of welfare has grown excessively narrow.[34] A preoccupation with public assistance to the poor has led Americans to overlook two other important forms of social distribution: social insurance programs and taxation policies. Yet in size and scope, social insurance programs, particularly Social Security and Medicare, dwarf the cost of payments to poor families. Moreover, these programs have been effective in reducing the percentage of poor among the elderly. It is very likely that the state could take similar steps to reduce inequality among American families. State intervention would probably be the most direct and effective way to reduce the kinds of social inequality described in this book. For example, a child allowance, similar to what Sweden and other Western European nations provide, would likely be very effective in eliminating child poverty and reducing the gap in economic and social resources.[35] As David Karen points out, increasing the "safety net" for poor and working-class families would be helpful:

> Anything that can be done to provide a safety net for the poor (and working class) will increase the resources of . . . children and therefore make it possible for them to engage in some of the activities that they're currently excluded from. This exclusion takes place not only because they don't have the money to participate but also because parental time is so limited. If parental time (say, thanks to fewer hours at work) were more available, there might be more access to participation. Under this rubric, I'd put things like universal health care, state-supported daycare, (and) a guaranteed minimum income. [36]

In addition, an increase in federal and state recreation monies would be useful since, in interviews I conducted with directors of recreation programs in the regions surrounding Swan and Lower Richmond schools, it was clear that as the township became more affluent, more elaborate recreational programs were available. Vouchers for extracurricular activities *and* transportation to activities (e.g., music lessons, art lessons, sports programs, and specialized summer camps) are another possibility. A problem is that neighborhoods are often relatively homogenous by social class. Consolidating neighborhoods so that working-class and poor children become part of more affluent neighborhoods would be likely to increase access to desirable facilities. What is far less likely, however, is the existence of the political will to support this redistribution of wealth. Instead, Americans, as is their wont, are likely to remain preoccupied with more individual solutions. Since, however, the problems differ by social class, the solutions do as well. Below, I review some of the possibilities.

Slowing It Down: Policy Implications for Middle-Class Families

The frenetic schedule of some middle-class families is a topic that increasingly bubbles up in media reports. As a result, there is an emerging social movement of professionals and middle-class parents to resist the scheduling of children's lives. Books, including *The Over-Scheduled Child*, insist that children's schedules are out of control:

> It is Tuesday at 6:45 A.M. Belinda, age seven, is still asleep. School doesn't start until 9:00 A.M. and her mother usually lets her sleep until 7:30 A.M. But not on Tuesdays. That's the day Belinda has a 7:30 A.M. piano lesson. From it she goes directly to school, which lasts until three. Then the babysitter drives Belinda to gymnastics for the 4:00–6:30 P.M. class. While Tuesday is the busiest day, the rest of the week is filled up too, with religious school and choir practice, ballet, and (Belinda's favorite) horseback riding. "She's pretty worn out by the end of the day," her mother laments . . . "I'm not really sure it is a good thing [to be so busy]. But I want to give her the advantages I didn't have."[37]

The authors are outraged by this kind of schedule:

> We sense that our family lives are out of whack, but we aren't sure why. We know we are doing too much for our kids, but we don't know where it might be okay to cut back — . . . every time we . . . turn [around] . . . someone else is adding something new to the list of things we are supposed to be doing for our children to make sure they turn out right.[38]

Resistance is spreading. At the collective level, grassroots organizations such as "Family Life First," based in Wayzata, Minnesota, are pressuring coaches and adult leaders of other organized activities to make family time a priority (by, for example, not scheduling events on Sundays or not penalizing children who miss games while on family vacations). Ridgewood, New Jersey, gained national attention when citizens declared a community-wide (voluntary) "Family Night" and arranged for children's organized activities (and homework) to be canceled for the evening. These incipient movements have in common an explicit recognition that children's schedules are absurd, that family life is in thrall to a frenzy of "hyper-scheduling."[39] Decrying the development of children's appointment books, professionals call for children to have more opportunities for unstructured play.[40] At the individual level, parents are encouraged to set strict limits on children's activities. Some parents proudly announce on websites that they require their children to limit themselves to only one activity at a time.

A systematic critique of parents' role in supervising and intervening in institutions has not yet emerged. Indeed, many professionals actively recruit and encourage parental involvement in schooling. Doubts about the value of extensive reasoning with children, on the other hand, are mounting. Problems stemming from the blurring of boundaries between parents and children are especially well covered by professionals and the media. With titles such as *Parents in Charge: Setting Healthy, Loving Boundaries for You and Your Child* and *I'll Be the Parent, You Be the Child*, professionals are signaling the need for parents to provide directives to children. The books provide cautionary tales of rude, obnoxious, and ungrateful children who refuse to be polite to guests, who feel that they, as children, may decide when they will or will not join the family for dinner, and who are unable to convey appreciation for the gifts they receive. Describing these children as out of control and craving adult intervention, the authors call for parents to "set limits and make decisions." The solution the experts offer calls mainly for individual action: each parent is encouraged to look within her or himself to find the necessary strength to take charge, to give clear directives to children, and to resist the temptation to seek their children's approval.

Ironically, the new agenda for middle-class parents, whether expressed collectively or individually, amounts to a reinstatement of many of the elements of the strategy of the accomplishment of natural growth. For overburdened and exhausted parents, the policy recommendations center on setting limits: reducing the number of children's activities, scheduling family time, making family events a higher priority than children's events, and generally putting the needs of the group ahead of the needs of the individual.

Gaining Compliance with Dominant Standards: Implications for Working-Class and Poor Families

For working-class and poor families, the policy recommendations center on trying to gain advantages for children in institutional settings. Some programs stress the importance of reading to children, bolstering vocabulary, and addressing "summer setback" (a reference to working-class and poor children's tendency to lose academic ground when they are out of school while middle-class children's academic growth spurts ahead).[41]

Here, it is important to bear in mind the ever-changing nature of institutional standards (phonics is "in" one year, whole language the next; computers are promoted and then challenged). Providing children with the resources needed to comply with institutional standards may be helpful, but it leaves unexamined the problematic nature of class-based child-rearing methods themselves. It is possible that policies could be developed to help professionals learn how to be more sensitive to differences in cultural practices and how to "code switch"; they, in turn, might be able to teach children to "code switch" as they move between home and encounters with institutions. One promising development is the success of programs that offer to working-class and poor children the kinds of concerted cultivation middle-class children get at home. Examples include intensive interventions in high schools and in "I Had a Dream" philanthropic ventures through which schools and private tutors take on the roles often carried out by middle-class parents (and the tutors they hire). These programs have improved children's school performance; reduced suspensions, behavior problems, and teen pregnancies; and increased college admittance rates. Many have been shown to double the high school graduation rates of students.[42] Other interventions have produced similarly positive results.[43] In some, for example, high school teachers provide low-income students with tours of college campuses, remind them about key deadlines, and help them fill out college applications. Programs such as these, as well as more traditional programs, such as "Big Brother/Big Sister," have improved school experiences.[44] In sum, policy recommendations for working-class and poor children do not address hectic schedules or the need for greater parental control, as those for middle-class children do. Rather, they focus on gaining institutional advantages for children by encouraging parents to use reasoning to bolster their children's vocabulary and to play a more active role in their children's schooling.

BIOGRAPHY AND SOCIAL STRUCTURE

The birth of a new family member is usually treated as a joyous event. Family members mark the arrival of the newest niece, nephew, daughter, or grandson with celebrations beforehand, such as baby showers, excitement and gifts on the baby's arrival, with visits to the hospital and detailed conversations about who the baby looks like, and formal blessings such as christenings or "dedications" in churches of various denominations. All of these events celebrate the promise offered by this new life.

Each person's life also unfolds in a unique way. Within the same family, brothers and sisters have different temperaments and preferences as well as different genetic configurations. Fern Marshall spent hours and hours each week playing basketball while Stacey was absorbed with gymnastics; Garrett Tallinger was quiet while Spencer was such a chatterbox that, as his father said in mock despair, "You can't shut him up." Melanie Handlon's older brother was tall and thin while she was short and stocky. Moreover, even members of the same family do not have the same child-rearing experience. Family configurations change over time and parents' life circumstances and parenting styles change as well. There are important variations in the choices siblings make and in their life outcomes.

But this unique character of each human life, as well as the distinctive gifts that each individual brings to a family, should not blind us to the way that membership in a broader social group matters in the creation of inequality. Social group membership structures life opportunities. The chances of attaining key and widely sought goals — high scores on standardized tests such as the SAT, graduation from college, professional jobs, and sustained employment — are not equal for all the infants whose births are celebrated by their families. It turns out that the family into which we are born, an event over which we have no control, matters quite a lot. It matters in part because the system of institutions is selective, building on some cultural patterns more than on others. To be sure, there are also significant amounts of upward and downward mobility. There are those in the population who overcome the predicted odds, particularly certain immigrant groups. The social structure of inequality is not all determining. But it exists. This system of social location, largely unacknowledged by most Americans, means that Katie Brindle, Wendy Driver, and Tyrec Taylor have important elements of their lives in common, just as Garrett Tallinger, Alexander Williams, and Stacey Marshall have important aspects of their lives in common. It means that class, in some instances, is more important than race. And it suggests that boys and girls of the same social class, while having important gender-related differences in their lives, also have important commonalities.[45]

Americans tend to resist the notion that they live in a society of social classes. Most people describe themselves as middle class. When asked about social divisions, many readily discuss the power of race, but the idea of social class is not a systematic part of the vocabulary of most Americans.[46] Nor is there a set of widely discussed beliefs, as in earlier decades, of the importance of eliminating poverty or narrowing gaps in social inequality.

Looking at social class differences in the standards of institutions provides a vocabulary for understanding inequality. It highlights the ways in which institutional standards give some people an advantage over others as well as the unequal ways that cultural practices in the home pay off in settings outside the home. Such a focus helps to undercut the middle-class presumption of moral superiority over the poor and the working class. And a vocabulary of social structure and social class is vastly preferable to a moral vocabulary that blames individuals for their life circumstances and saves the harshest criticism for those deemed the "undeserving poor."[47] It is also more accurate than relying only on race categories. The social position of one's family of origin has profound implications for life experiences and life outcomes. But the inequality our system creates and sustains is invisible and thus unrecognized. We would be better off as a country if we could enlarge our truncated vocabulary about the importance of social class. For only then might we begin to acknowledge more systematically the class divisions among us.

Methodology: Enduring Dilemmas in Fieldwork

It is very unusual to study families in a "naturalistic fashion," observing them within their own homes. Many people are deeply curious about the process. Space considerations preclude a detailed description, but in this appendix I describe some of the difficulties and dilemmas that arose during the study.

DRAWING THE SAMPLE

The family observations that form the core of the book were only one aspect of a multidimensional study that also included observations in elementary school classrooms and interviews with a large number of parents. The earliest phase of the project began in 1990, when I interviewed (with the help of an African American woman undergraduate) the parents of thirty-one children from a third-grade classroom in a public school in Lawrenceville (pseudonym), a smaller university community (population 25,000) in the Midwest. The remaining fifty-seven children were drawn from elementary schools located in a large northeastern metropolitan area. I decided to focus on third-graders because I wanted children who were young enough for their parents to still be heavily involved in managing their lives (and thus transmitting social class influences to them) and yet old enough to have some autonomy regarding their free time. I also hoped to catch children before peer-group influences became decisive factors in their lives. Initially, I had hoped to interview children and parents; but I gave up on interviewing children when normally chatty children fell silent in front of a tape recorder.[1]

The decision to include both white and African American children and to define social class categories using a combination of parents' educational levels and occupations grew out of empirical realities I encountered in Lawrenceville. Although I was originally planning to study whites across different social classes, the schools were about half white and half Black. Moreover, there had been a parental boycott by Black parents in recent years to protest insensitivity on the part of the district toward the needs of Black children. In this context, it did not make sense to study the impact of parental involvement on schooling and exclude the Black parents. Table C1, Appendix C, shows the distribution of the total sample (eighty-eight children) by race.

MEASURING SOCIAL CLASS IN A SMALL SAMPLE

Social scientists disagree over the proper way to measure inequality in the real world. Some take a gradational approach: on the basis of the key elements of inequality—especially occupational prestige, education, and income—they rank individuals or families in a relatively seamless hierarchy. Yet occupations differ greatly, particularly in the amount of autonomy workers enjoy, the degree to which some people supervise others, the pay, the cleanliness or dirtiness of the work performed, and the amount of prestige that the job commands. I think of these differences in nongradational terms.

There is also disagreement over how to conceptualize classes (i.e., whether to use a Marxian and Weberian approach).[2] Regardless of approach, however, most current conceptualizations deploy a relatively large number of class categories in order to attain a fine-grained differentiation of economic positions. It was impossible for me to approximate such an approach in this study. Since my purpose was to develop an *intensive,* realistic portrait of family life, I was able to analyze only a small number of families. Indeed, with a small sample, and with a desire to compare children across gender and race lines, adopting the fine-grained differentiation of categories characteristic of neo-Marxist and neo-Weberian studies was untenable and unreasonable.

Initially, I settled on two class categories, guided by the populations represented in the town where I was observing. Since employers or self-employed workers were less common than others in the population as a whole, I decided to concentrate exclusively on parents who were employees rather than employers or self-employed. The question then became how to differentiate within this heterogeneous group. Various criteria have been proposed for this purpose, but authority in the workplace and "credential barriers" are the two most commonly used. The former entails the differentiation of those with supervisory or managerial authority over other workers from those with neither. The latter criterion entails separating occupations with stringent educational requirements from those with less demanding ones. On the basis of these considerations, coupled with a pragmatic assessment of what was realistically feasible, I settled on an approach that differentiated a working class and a middle class, each broadly construed. I planned to assign the families to one of these categories on the basis of discussions with each of the employed adults in which they would provide extensive information about the work they did, the nature of the organization that employed them (if there was one), and their place in it. If a family included two full-time workers with divergent class designations, I would assign the family to the higher category (i.e., "middle class"), irrespective of which family member had the defining job.

This plan was adjusted when I discovered that in Lawrenceville schools a substantial number of children were from households supported by public assistance. To ignore them would have been to restrict the scope of the study in a somewhat arbitrary fashion. As a result, I added a group of poor families not involved in the labor market — families that are traditionally excluded in social class groupings. In the end, I worked with three categories: middle-class families, working-class families, and poor families (see Table C1 for criteria for inclusion).

These social class categories conceal important internal variations. Both the Williams family (Black) and the Tallinger family (white) have very high incomes (i.e., annual incomes of more than $175,000). The differences in income among middle-class families, while real, did not appear to be linked to differences in child-rearing methods among middle-class parents (including the more wealthy ones) in my limited sample. Moreover, no other available data show compelling intraclass divisions. Thus, using one term — middle class — to cover the middle-class families of varying wealth seemed reasonable.

In a somewhat different vein, Table C3 makes it clear that these differences in social class are heavily interwoven with different forms of family structure, a pattern that is also found nationally.[3] Thus, the Black and white middle-class children we observed all reside with both of their biological parents. Although some of the poor children have regular contact with their fathers, none of the Black or white poor children in the intensive observations had their biological fathers at home. The working-class families were in between. This pattern raises questions of whether the pattern of concerted cultivation depends on the presence of a two-parent marriage. The scope of the sample cannot provide a satisfactory answer to this question. Still, indications are that family structure, while it may influence aspects of the cultural logic of child rearing, does not determine it. For example, in the sample of thirty-six middle-class families, there were three single parents. These single-parent families clearly used the cultural logic of concerted cultivation. The parents did complain in interviews, however, that being a single parent hampered their ability to enroll their children into as many organized activities as they wished. National data reveal that children in two-parent homes spend more time in organized activities than do children in single-parent homes. [4]

CHOOSING THE SCHOOLS

In an ideal world, I would have found schools and neighborhoods that were racially integrated *and* integrated by social class. In reality, of course, American children live in settings that tend to be homogenous by race and, to a lesser extent, by social class, and they typically go to schools that are similarly homogenous.[5] In the end, I opted for schools that were racially integrated but were relatively homogenous by social class.[6] After I had identified a group of schools that met my basic criteria, I used informal networks to meet with high-level administrators in the relevant school districts. These administrators selected the final sites from the list of choices I presented, and, on my behalf, they also made the first overtures to the principals involved. Detailed descriptions of Lower Richmond public elementary school and Swan public elementary school (the sources for almost all the children discussed at length in the book), are presented in Chapter 2.

From December 1993 to June 1994, I observed at least twice a week (frequently more often) in a third-grade classroom at Lower Richmond. I began similar observations in a third-grade classroom at Swan in April 1994. A research assistant continued at Swan weekly, observing the now fourth-grade children from September through December. In addition, I went back to each school occasionally when the children were in fourth grade; in fifth grade the research assistants and I attended graduation.

Lower Richmond's third-grade teacher, Ms. Green, generously welcomed me into her classroom and facilitated my integration and that of a Black woman undergraduate student who was assisting me. While in the classroom, I sometimes simply observed, but other times, I helped out with art projects and computer lessons and lent a hand shepherding children from place to place in the school. I brought in food on various occasions, including cookies for the class on Valentine's Day.[7] I got to know the students well; the girls would give me a hug when I got to school. Once I established a warm rapport with the children, the next step was to interview parents.

Based on the classroom teacher's knowledge of the children, I separated them into groups by race and class and selected every "*n*th" name. I wrote the parents a letter (the schools released the children's addresses) explaining that I was writing a book on how children spend their time when they are out of school and, more generally, examining the work it takes parents to get children through the day. I mailed these requests for interviews at the end of the children's third-grade year (Lower Richmond) and in the fall of the children's fourth-grade year (Swan).[8] I then called all of the parents to talk about the project and schedule an interview.

Across the two sites, only one mother refused participation outright (some fathers eventually declined). In addition, two or three parents who had initially agreed to be interviewed were not interviewed because of scheduling difficulties. Overall, however, the response rate for families was more than 90 percent. I still did not have a sample with which I felt comfortable, however. Despite their racially diverse character, the two schools did not include enough middle-class Black and poor white children for the study. I broadened the sample to include third-graders at Swan and also recruited through fliers and informal networks.[9] The bulk of the interviews with parents took place in 1993 and 1994, but some were not completed until 1997. An additional sixty interviews with educators and other adults working with children were also conducted. For example, the third-grade and fourth-grade teachers at the schools were interviewed (including in Lawrenceville), along with other school personnel (i.e., reading specialists, music and art teachers, the school nurse, bus drivers, and yard duty teachers) as well as numerous providers of children's leisure services. Where possible, these interviews were focused on the children in our study. (A chronological overview of the study is presented in Table C9, Appendix C.)

RECRUITING THE FAMILIES

The classroom observations and interviews with parents were crucial in gaining access to families for the observation phase. Ms. Green's third-grade classroom at Lower Richmond yielded seven of the twelve children: Brindle, Taylor, Irwin, Driver, Carroll, Yanelli, and McAllister. The fourth-grade classroom at Swan yielded two more: Tallinger and Handlon. Selecting the families involved a conscious, complicated calculus. The interview phase had helped identify certain kinds of experiences and family traits (especially the number of organized activities, the strength of kinship ties, and the depth of family-school relationships) as broadly characteristic of each social class. I wanted most of the families we observed to be as representative of these traits as possible. We tried to avoid selecting children whose parents were either unusually active in school or unusually quiet in their interactions with teachers. Among the middle-class families, we further limited the pool to only those with two parents in the home. Thus, in most cases, the research assistants and I had only three or four children per category to choose among.[10]

In making the final choices for the observational phase, I wanted to balance the sample by gender, race, and class. I wanted, as well, to look at children who, although from different races and social classes, shared key characteristics. For example, despite different class locations, some children shared church involvement, extended family nearby, or participation in organized activities. Overall, the research team and I tried to "mix and match" the children we chose in order to lessen the chance that differences in the behavior we observed were connected to some unknown variable such as parental involvement in the school.

I also sought "deviant cases." In particular, I very much wanted to include a middle-class child who participated in *no* organized activities. I was unable to find a single such child among the families we interviewed, nor could Swan teachers or parents think of a possible candidate. I was more successful in finding deviant cases in terms of child-rearing strategies and family location, such as families with middle-class characteristics who live in working-class or poor neighborhoods. Two families offered this form of contrast. The Irwins, a deeply religious interracial family (white mother, Black father) whose household income and education levels put them between working class and middle class, lived in a working-class neighborhood. Their child-rearing strategies were dominated by the logic of the accomplishment of natural growth, but we also observed signs of concerted cultivation. The Greeleys were the other deviant case. Ms. Greeley, a white single mother with a live-in African American boyfriend, had been raised in a middle-class family. She developed a drug problem serious enough to cause her to temporarily lose custody of her children. At the time of the study, the Greeleys were living below the poverty level in a white working-class neighborhood. Despite her relatively privileged childhood, most of Ms. Greeley's child-rearing strategies appeared to reflect her current class position: She followed the pattern of the accomplishment of natural growth. These two deviant cases suggest that social class may be more influential than neighborhood, but only a large representative sample could provide a solid basis for untangling these important issues.

Of the list the research assistants and I originally drew up, nine out of twelve families agreed to participate: both white middle-class families, all four of the working-class families, and three of the four poor families.[11] The Black middle-class category was empty. The mothers at Swan school that I approached declined, citing issues of privacy. Although I was reluctant to go outside the pool of children from Swan and Lower Richmond, I didn't have much choice. I turned to a racially diverse private school where an acquaintance's children were enrolled. There, I made contact with the Williams family. By the spring of 1995, I lacked only a white poor boy and a Black middle-class girl. For the boy, I went back to Lower Richmond school area. A social services agency director in the region (whose name I got out of the phone book) referred me to the Greeleys.[12] For the Black middle-class girl category, I tapped into a wide range of informal contacts before I found a willing family who met the criteria I cared most about. The girl, Stacey Marshall, was an appropriate age (ten), but she had already completed fifth grade and was entering sixth grade in the fall (when she would turn eleven). Feeling that it was better to be flexible on the child's grade level than on the family's race and class, I recruited the Marshalls.[13] So, the final sample of families consisted of nine drawn from either Lower Richmond or Swan elementary school and three from other sources. Given the intrusive nature of home-based observations, I was very pleased with the overall response rate of 63 percent (I asked nineteen families to get twelve).

I found the process of recruiting the families very stressful. A number of people doubted that I would be able to do the field observations. They told me that families — especially families picked from schools rather than friends of friends — would never agree to participate. In most cases, my approach to recruitment was to send a letter and then follow up with a phone call. Before making the telephone calls, I would pace the floor anxiously and my heart would pound. Even when I had cleared that first hurdle, I continued to find the first encounters to secure written permission and to schedule the home visits scary. Nevertheless, I tried to appear upbeat, comfortable, and lighthearted in all of my conversations with the families. I stressed that unlike what television shows would have us believe, family life was quite difficult and that taking care of children was challenging. I explained that the research assistants and I were used to yelling and to messy rooms. I emphasized that I wanted to paint a realistic picture of family life, and I told stories of my own experiences growing up and fighting with my siblings.

Of course, no matter how persuasively I made my case, not all families agreed to participate. Some, in turning me down, explained, "We are not the perfect family." Those who did agree often told us (in response to a question we posed in interviews at the end of the study) that they wanted to "help us out" and that the $350 we offered to help offset the inconvenience of the visits made participating more attractive.[14] I believe the money made a decisive difference for most, but not all, of the families. Indeed, two families on public assistance who were asked to be in the study declined. My own assessment is that especially among the working-class and poor families, the children were strong allies. At the interview stage, I believe the fact that the children knew me and seemed to like me was a tremendous help in gaining parents' cooperation.[15] In addition, the parents had an extended period of time to get to know us before we asked them to be in the observational study. The process of recruiting parents for interviews and then conducting the interviews involved multiple contacts, including a call to confirm the night before. The interviews lasted from 90 to 120 minutes, and almost all were conducted in the participating families' homes. As a thank-you we brought along a bakery pie and then mailed a handwritten thank-you note. Since we interviewed parents separately, we repeated the whole process in families where we interviewed the fathers. [16]

It is possible that among the families who agreed to be observed, the mothers were unusually secure in their roles, did not have drug problems, and were generally less concerned about the possibility of being "turned in" to the state for being "bad" or "abusive" parents. Although some of the families (the Brindles especially) had a larger share of life problems than others, they all fell within the range of families we observed across the school sites. Still, with a nonrandom sample, one cannot generalize from these results to the broader population.

THE RESEARCHERS

Although it would have been my preference, it was impossible for me to do all of the fieldwork and interviews. I needed help. The first year, four

students—three white women and one African American woman—
assisted me. With me, these students interviewed parents in the study of
eighty-eight families and conducted observations for more than half of
the families: Brindle, Carroll, Driver, Handlon, Irwin, Tallinger, and
Yanelli. At the end of the school year, when these students departed, I
hired two sociology graduate students, an African American man and a
white woman. During the summer of 1994, they observed the Taylor,
McAllister, and Williams families. The last summer, 1995, four graduate
students helped: an African American woman from the anthropology
department, two white women from the sociology department (including
the one who had worked on the project the previous summer), and a
white man from the psychology department. These research assistants
observed the Greeley and Marshall families and finished the observations
of the Williams family. (See Table C9.)

As is a truism in ethnographic research, our own biographies influenced the research, especially my reasons for beginning the study and
what we saw. At the time of the study, none of us had children. Frankly,
part of my own motivation for undertaking the project was a long-stand-
ing desire to better understand the inner workings of families. As a child,
I had longed to have a "normal" family. My parents' unusual, even eccen-
tric, characters made me attuned to variations in family life.[17] Although
my illusions regarding the existence of a normal family have since faded,
my childhood experiences shaped the current study. In each of their children, my parents nurtured a love of reading, a sense of humor, a streak of
unconventionality, and a pattern of persistence. I could not have persisted
so doggedly with my efforts to recruit families for naturalistic observations without these qualities. The most important childhood legacy, however, was that I felt comfortable in families where there was yelling,
drinking, emotional turmoil, and disciplining by hitting. This comfort
with diverse family interactions turned out to be valuable.

Similarly, for the research assistants, personal history was influential.
For example, the disciplinary practices in the students' childhood homes
seemed to affect what each recorded in his or her field notes as noteworthy.
Some field-workers with middle-class origins were upset by parents' threats
to "beat" children. A field-worker from a working-class family was not
troubled by that, but he was shocked by the disrespect that many middle-
class children used in routine interactions with their parents. A twenty-
minute car ride with a whining middle-class four-year-old left this research
assistant with a headache and a general feeling of disgust ("I wanted to
kick his mother's butt for letting him get away with that whining . . .

Who's the parent?"). Finally, over time, some researchers developed "favorite" families and some families developed "favorite" researchers.

Overall, however, the field notes taken by the different researchers were quite similar. I believe this resulted in part from the fact that some things were "striking" to all members of the team. I was deliberately heavy-handed, however, in my efforts to achieve intellectual integration. There were weekly meetings for the whole group and team meetings every week for everyone who was actively observing a family. I also had extended telephone conversations with the research assistants after many field visits and discussed with them at that time what they should write up in their field notes.

The field-workers found the study unusual and (usually) interesting. Like me, they enjoyed getting to know the families. Being in the field always involved a balancing act, though. We needed to be authentic, but we also needed to remain neutral. Sometimes little strategies helped. For example, when I was with families in which small children were often present (Brindle, Driver, McAllister, and Yanelli), I usually asked to hold the babies. I like to hold babies, but doing so in the field was also a way to help me blend into the setting. Other field-workers enjoyed playing basketball with the children or talking about music. Still, some aspects of the fieldwork necessarily required suppression of the self. I did not, for example, express my outrage over some parents' political views; and I pretended to thoroughly enjoy all of the food I was offered, even things I intensely dislike. The research assistants were similarly self-monitoring.

All of us found the fieldwork emotionally exhausting. One of the graduate students summed up how taxing the observations were:

"I remember having this awful day during which I visited the McAllisters in the morning and the Tallingers in the afternoon; I got a horrible headache, was distraught for days, and was suddenly aware of how ambivalent I felt about class. . . . Every day there are poor people and comfortable people living in the same world, ignoring (or not seeing) each other and having wildly divergent experiences. But we generally don't see this."[18]

THE VISITS

The family observations all took place in 1994 and 1995. We learned to ritualize our entry into (and exit from) families. Often there were several telephone conversations and a face-to-face meeting with the parents before the family agreed. Then we would arrange a time to get together to sign consent forms and schedule home visits. For that meeting, two research assistants and I would go to the family's home. We brought calendars (one for us and one, with refrigerator magnets, for the family) and a bakery cake along with us.

In that first meeting, we would work out mutually acceptable times for the observations (the visits lasted two or three hours) and decide which member of the research team would be in the home at what time. In scheduling the visits, we tried to include a range of time slots so that we could observe a variety of common events, such as before-school preparations and afternoon or evening homework sessions, dinner, Saturday morning activities, church (if applicable), a visit with relatives, a health-care visit, a family party, organized activities, and miscellaneous errands.[19] In addition, we tried to schedule one overnight stay with each family. A typical pattern of visits might start with the field-worker arriving shortly after the child got home from school, hanging out through dinner, and then leaving. Other times, one of us might arrive at 6:30 in the morning to see what was involved in preparing a child for school; or we might meet the child at school to observe the family's afternoon and evening schedule. We often carried tape recorders, especially after family members had gotten used to us.

All of the families considered the request to observe them odd. Mr. Tallinger summed up the majority view. Following up on the field-worker's description of the research project as "unusual," he said:

"Yeah, I know. It's really unusual. The only people weirder than the people agreeing to be watched are the people who want to watch!"

The first few visits were very awkward. No one seemed quite sure what to do (including us). Not surprisingly, families felt the need to socialize with us, particularly during the first few minutes after we arrived. They asked us about our journey and almost always offered us soft drinks. The children, however, usually had something that they were doing or wanted to do. So, we often plopped down on the floor to watch television with them, or went outside to play ball. We also rode along in the car as parents and children went on errands. Family members got used to us. We found that the tension eased, particularly on the third day, and again on the tenth day. The children were young, so it was hard for them to sustain "company manners" for a relatively long period of time. We had the sense that normal family rhythms resumed over the course of our visits. Moreover, the key purpose of the study was to *compare* how different families organized their lives. There was no particular evidence that some families relaxed more than others on a systematic basis by class or race.

The children all seemed to like our visits, but their level of enthusiasm varied by class. Poor and working-class children were genuinely excited to see us. Having adults paying close attention to them at home was out of the ordinary. At the end of any given day of observing, it was common for these children, especially the girls, to plead with us to stay longer. As the Irwin's daughter explained in an exit interview, "It was nice to have somebody different in the house." Little Billy Yanelli said that having the field-workers in his home "felt good" to him. And Harold McAllister, when queried, smiled shyly and replied that he "liked it" when the field-workers were at his house. Middle-class children were more blasé; they were used to having adults pay close attention to them.[20]

For all children, the visits worked best as they became routinized. Overall, repeated visits just to "hang out" with the children worked well, going to their sports activities worked well, and going to church was relatively easy, as was going along on family outings. More unusual events (e.g., doctor visits, overnights) were more difficult because they were more disruptive.

Our experiences with the first families we observed taught us that we needed to develop an exit strategy. Leaving the field is no easier than entering it. We instituted pizza parties as a way of saying thank-you and good-bye. Pizza was a rare treat in the working-class and poor homes and the children looked forward to the party. They seemed to feel genuinely thanked by it. For the middle-class children (whose parents bought pizza so often that one father had memorized the local vendor's telephone number), the party was not a special treat, and they did not seem to feel thanked by it.

Even after the study had formally ended, contact with the families continued. We did a few "mop up" visits, particularly doctor visits or special recitals, for most families. In the first year or two following the end of the project, I stopped in for brief visits with many of the families (most, but not all, encouraged the research assistants and me to come back for a visit "anytime"). I continue to stay in touch with the families (I did not, however, circulate the draft manuscript of this book among the families, although I will give them a copy of the book). Every year since the children were in fourth grade, I have sent them a Christmas card with a five-dollar bill tucked inside. I plan to reinterview the children as young adults.

DILEMMAS

It would be possible to write an entire book on the methodological dilemmas that emerged. I limit the focus here to the issue of differences in the extent to which the families understood the project and the problem of observation versus intervention.

Understanding us. We left it up to the parents to discuss the project with their children. In a play within a play, the concepts of concerted cultivation and the accomplishment of natural growth seemed to guide how the parents informed their children. In middle-class families, the project was presented as part of the children's development, a kind of enrichment activity not so different from taking piano lessons or playing soccer. Middle-class children were allowed, even encouraged, to play a key role in the decision making. In the working-class and poor families, the parents did not solicit their children's opinions; they simply told them that the family would be participating. Sometimes, even that information was not supplied until the day the research assistants and I arrived at the home to set up the schedule for the observations. For example, when we showed up at the McAllisters' house, Harold's mother, who had signed the parental consent forms earlier, without telling her son, explained the study to him this way:

She says, "A man is going to come tomorrow to interview you. You have to be here. Don't dump him!" Harold doesn't ask any questions.

The research assistants and I noted — and worried about the ethical implications of — evidence of a class difference in how much the families understood about the basic mission of the project. Many of the working-class and poor families had a truncated notion of who we were and what we were doing. For example, as I was completing an exit interview with Wendy Driver's mother, I packed up my tape recorder and mentioned that I needed to go because I had to teach. Looking very surprised, she raised her eyebrows, and her voice, as she asked, "You teach? What grade do you teach?" Ms. Driver knew I worked at Temple University and had signed many consent forms, each of which listed me as an "Associate Professor." Nevertheless, Wendy's mother obviously had not formed any clear idea about my job. Middle-class parents, on the other hand, asked very detailed questions. Having been to college themselves, and having read books similar to this one, they asked me about the courses I taught at Temple, and some asked questions about other col-

leges in the area. Thus, despite many discussions of the study with families, many working-class and poor families maintained a limited understanding of the study, a pattern found by other ethnographers.[21]

The question of interventions. Problems surfaced when we were in situations that clashed with our own definitions of proper parenting, definitions which (as I noted above) varied across the team. It is one thing to
believe, intellectually, as many do, that child-rearing practices are historically specific and that it is a mistake to valorize the practices of the middle class. It is quite another thing to be in the same intimate space with
family members when different practices exist. (In some ways, it is comparable to the difference between being aware that automobile accidents
and heart attacks happen all the time and actually being an eyewitness to
one.) Further compounding the problem was the fact that as project
leader I needed to both guide the research assistants and allow them the
necessary autonomy to do what they thought was ethically and morally
right in a given situation. These dilemmas were a constant source of tension in the project. In my view, both then and now, there are no easy
answers. I often felt as if I was "between a rock and a hard place."

I was deeply committed to the idea that the research assistants and I
needed to approach the families with tremendous respect. My view was
that it was their house, and that in raising their children, parents were
doing the best they could. It was unacceptable for me or anyone on my
research team to try to change them. This I took to be a moral issue, the
"rock" that underlay the project.

Two other factors shaped my stance on intervening in family life. I
wanted family members to trust and to feel comfortable around the
research assistants and me. Criticism would not be helpful in building
rapport. If anything, it would threaten it. Equally important, intervening
to alter family dynamics would jeopardize the fundamental purpose of
the study, which was to see how the families acted in their natural routines. Having a field-worker sitting smack in the middle of the living
room was hardly "normal"; I certainly didn't want to add yet more dis-
ruption. All of our efforts needed to be aimed at *minimizing* the influence
of the study on family interaction.

The rule of thumb I followed, and instructed the research assistants to
follow, was to "hang out" and not to intervene unless there was blood or
an imminent threat of serious danger. I added one caveat: no research
assistant was ever to do anything she or he felt really uncomfortable
doing. When they were in the field, the final decision was theirs.

This firm commitment to respect the families and their practices did not make the observations easy. For example, when faced with bitter sibling rivalry, one field-worker wrote that "it was incredibly hard to resist the temptation to intervene and force [the child] back into his seat." It was also sometimes painful to watch the way parents treated their children. In general, such occasions were rare, but in one family, the Brindles, difficult moments were nearly continuous. The family was under tremendous economic and psychological stress. It quickly became clear that I would need to do the home visits rather than have one of the research assistants do them.[22]

There were three occasions, however, in which scheduling conflicts resulted in another field-worker going to Katie Brindle's home. Even in a brief visit (after school, from 1:45 P.M. to 4:20 P.M.), the interactions the researcher observed were emotionally draining: Katie methodically hit herself on the head; her aunt recounted — with approval — an episode from her own childhood in which her father beat her with a belt so badly that she bled. The field-worker summed up her feelings after the visit:

I hate going there. I hate it because I feel like I can never say what I think. For example, when Mary tells me how she should hit Katie, I just nod. I just sit and watch Katie hit her head, Melmel stick his finger in a plug, and CiCi scream at Katie. UUUGHHHH.

Fortunately, these family dynamics we observed among the Brindles were the exception. Indeed, most of the time the family visits were relatively easy, and even with the Brindles there were many relaxed and fun moments. Often we had fun "hanging out" with the kids, playing basketball and wall ball, watching television, driving around in the car, or lying on the floor, talking. In a quirk of fate, we began the observational phase of the study with the Brindle family. All of the families that came after were much easier than they might have seemed had the research assistants and I not been so challenged at first.

FROM DATA TO A BOOK

The intellectual journey was not complete when we finished our visits with the families. In some ways, it had just begun.[23] Because of the intensity of the research experience (as well as changes in my personal life), I followed the active period of field-work with a lull of reflection. Gradually, I began to analyze the data, mainly by reading, rereading, and reading again the field notes from the families (for each family, there was a chronologically arranged file of notes). For the interviews of the parents of the eighty-eight children, I coded the response data and then entered this information into a qualitative software program. [24]For the twelve families, though, I proceeded the old-fashioned way: I read field notes, read the literature, talked to people, and reread the notes. I tried to link the bits and pieces of data to ideas; when the argument took shape, I looked for disconfirming evidence. In writing the book, I first considered organizing the chapters analytically, comparing all of the families with respect to one overarching theme. But ultimately, following the book *The Second Shift* by Arlie Hochschild, I chose to try to bring the families to life by devoting a separate chapter to each.[25] I had begun the study interested in how children spend their time and in the nature of the interactions between families and institutions; those themes flourished in the book. Yet other, unexpected themes also emerged: particularly the role of language, the relative importance of kinship ties, the analogies of concerted cultivation and natural growth, and the limitations of social class in daily life.

Sometimes people ask me to name the most important thing that I learned from the study. I tell them that I discovered that *all* the families, despite their differences, felt safe and normal, after we had spent time together. They all felt like home. In addition, I was struck by how hard parents try, how much effort they put into each day as they pursue their lives; by the pleasures and frustrations the children experience in their daily routines; and by the challenges that all children face in growing up. Garrett Tallinger was resource rich compared to Harold McAllister, and yet Garrett had major disappointments in areas of his life that mattered to him, and Harold had some important life benefits that Garrett lacked, even as his family struggled economically. No child or adult has a smooth path in life: all have some share of pain and disappointment, as well as joy and rewards. Still, some paths are less rocky than others. Class position matters, every step of the way.

Theory: Understanding
the Work of Pierre Bourdieu

Pierre Bourdieu's work provides a context for examining the impact of social class position. His model draws attention to conflict, change, and systemic inequality, and it highlights the fluid nature of the relationship between structure and agency.[1] Bourdieu argues that individuals of different social locations are socialized differently.[2] This socialization provides children, and later adults, with a sense of what is comfortable or what is natural (he terms this *habitus*). These background experiences also shape the amount and forms of resources *(capital)* individuals inherit and draw upon as they confront various institutional arrangements *(fields)* in the social world.[3]

Bourdieu is always attuned to power, especially the domination of powerful groups over scarce resources. He is interested in the power of individuals to *define* what constitutes a highly valued activity, but also to the reasons why particular social practices are valued more highly than others. Indeed, Bourdieu sees a pattern of domination and inequality at the heart of the social structure. His work suggests the importance of studying the strategies individuals use to maintain or improve their social position, as well as their children's position. In any given society, the transmission of privilege is "mis-recognized." Individuals tend to see their society's social arrangements as legitimate. Status, privilege, and similar social rewards allegedly are "earned" by individuals; that is, they are perceived as resulting from intelligence, talent, effort, and other strategically displayed skills. Bourdieu, in showing how cultural capital is acquired and used in daily life, makes clear that individuals' social position is not the result of personal attributes such as effort or intelligence. In particular, he argues that individuals in privileged social locations are advantaged in ways that are not a result of the intrinsic merit of their cultural experiences. Rather, cultural training in the home is awarded unequal value in dominant institutions because of the close compatibility between the standards of child rearing in privileged homes and the (arbitrary) standards proposed by these institutions.

To make this book more readable, I refrained from lading it down with Bourdieu's terminology. Still, the book is a reasonably straightforward, if *partial*, empirical application of Bourdieu's broader theoretical model. For example, in *Distinction: A Social Critique on the Judgment of Taste* as well as other works, Bourdieu clearly intends for habitus to be a set of internalized dispositions that operate in a large number of social spheres.[4] In his discussion of habitus Bourdieu includes the preferences in food, furniture, music, makeup, books, and movies. The focus of *Unequal Childhoods* is much narrower, looking primarily at time use for children's leisure activities, language use in the home, and interventions of adults in children's institutional lives. Still, it is reasonable to assert that the elements discussed in this book, taken together, do constitute a set of dispositions that children learn, or habitus. Concerted cultivation and the accomplishment of natural growth are aspects of the habitus of the families discussed in this book.[5]

Bourdieu also points to nuanced class differences in the interactions between actors and institutions. He notes that people have a wide array of resources, social networks, and cultural training, and that they do not always use all of these resources in all settings. This sensitivity to the complexity and fluidity of social life makes his theory significantly more persuasive than other theories of social inequality, such as a culture of poverty model.[6]

Bourdieu builds his model using a (cumbersome) specialized vocabulary. The central concepts are the three mentioned above: habitus, field, and capital. The notion of habitus stresses the set of dispositions toward culture, society, and one's future that the individual generally learns at home and then takes for granted. Bourdieu suggests that differences in habitus give individuals varying cultural skills, social connections, educational practices, and other cultural resources, which then can be translated into different forms of value (i.e., capital) as individuals move out into the world. It is possible to adopt new habits later in life, but these late-acquired dispositions lack the comfortable (natural) feel associated with those learned in childhood.

The concept of field is crucial. It encompasses some of the same dynamics captured in terms such as *market* or *social institution*. But, as David Swartz points out, Bourdieu also seeks something broader with the idea of field: "Bourdieu . . . sees the image of 'field' as superior to that of 'institution' for two reasons: first, he wants to emphasize the conflictual character of social life where the idea of institution suggests consensus; second, he wants a concept that can cover social worlds where practices are only weakly institutionalized and boundaries are not well established."[7]

Bourdieu argues that in key areas, social space is stratified—some groups will be excluded and others included (and some will exclude themselves). He draws an analogy with a card game: there are fields that provide both the "rules of the game" and the social space wherein variations in capital exist. Bourdieu focuses on the intersection of the cards being dealt and the skill with which players play.[8] He emphasizes that the nature of the game is arbitrary and the slots at the top are limited. He would never suggest, for example, that more parents could improve their children's school success by adopting particular practices. Instead, he would point out that the number of elite slots in society is limited. Thus, any effort to spread an elite practice to all members of the society would result in the practice being devalued and replaced by a different sorting mechanism. In this sense, his model suggests that inequality is a perpetual characteristic of social groups. In any given interaction, however, Bourdieu stresses that the outcome is uncertain. Strategies may not pay off. In addition, he notes that individuals with a similar set of resources may differ in the skill with which they use their capital.

Overall, Bourdieu's work provides a dynamic model of structural inequality; it enables researchers to capture "moments" of cultural and social reproduction. To understand the character of these moments, researchers need to look at the *contexts* in which capital is situated, the efforts by individuals to activate their capital, the skill with which they do so, and the institutional response to the activation of resources. Unfortunately, Bourdieu's empirical work has not paid sufficient attention to the difference between the possession of capital and the activation of capital.[9] Nor has he focused attention on the crucial mediating role of individuals who serve as "gatekeepers" and decision makers in organizations. For example, in this book, in a few instances I have sought to show how parents transmitted different habitus in the home; how this habitus, in specific institutional encounters, functioned as a form of cultural capital; and how (depending on how it was activated) the cultural capital yielded (or didn't yield) an educational profit. Ms. Marshall taught her daughter a set of dispositions in the home, including a disposition to challenge adults in positions of authority. Ms. Marshall drew on this disposition (habitus) and activated her cultural capital when Stacey was turned down from the gifted program. Through a shrewd activation of cultural capital, Ms. Marshall gained profits for her daughter, including access to the gifted program (which as an enriched curriculum might lead to higher test scores as well as more favorable placement in courses in the future). Ms. Marshall was able to obtain these results as a consequence of her disposition and capacity to intervene in institutional settings in which her daughters' daily lives unfolded.

Overall, these moments of interaction between parents and key actors in institutions are the life blood of the stratification process and need to be examined more in the future. Bourdieu does not show empirically how individuals draw on class-based cultural resources in their moments of interaction with institutions. Parents appear to have an uneven ability to customize their interactions with such institutions. Similarly, they have an unequal ability to persuade professionals to comply with their wishes.

In sum, we need to understand the individually insignificant but cumulatively important ways in which parents from the dominant classes actually facilitate their children's progress through key social settings. This book is one effort to do just that.

Supporting Tables

TABLE C1. DISTRIBUTION OF CHILDREN
IN THE STUDY BY SOCIAL CLASS AND RACE

Social Class	White	Black	Total
Middle class[1]	Melanie Handlon Garrett Tallinger (sample total = 18)	Stacey Marshall Alexander Williams (sample total = 18)	(sample total = 36)
Working class[2]	Wendy Driver Billy Yanelli (sample total = 14)	Tyrec Taylor Jessica Irwin[4] (sample total = 12)	(sample total = 26)
Poor[3]	Katie Brindle Karl Greeley (sample total = 12)	Tara Carroll Harold McAllister (sample total = 14)	(sample total = 26)
Total	(sample total = 44)	(sample total = 44)	(sample total = 88)

1. Middle-class children are those who live in households in which at least one parent is employed in a position that either entails substantial managerial authority or that centrally draws upon highly complex, educationally certified (i.e., college-level) skills.

2. Working-class children are those who live in households in which neither parent is employed in a middle-class position and at least one parent is employed in a position with little or no managerial authority and that does not draw on highly complex, educationally certified skills. This category includes lower-level white collar workers.

3. Poor children are those who live in households in which parents receive public assistance and do not participate in the labor force on a regular, continuous basis.

4. Interracial girl: Black father and white mother.

TABLE C2. SOCIAL AND DEMOGRAPHIC
CHARACTERISTICS OF CATCHMENT
AREAS OF SCHOOLS IN THE STUDY

	Lower Richmond	Swan
Total persons	8,170	12,579
Total households	11,122	4,464
Total families	6,794	3,290
Median family income	$37,095	$60,773
Median housing value	$75,289	$160,651
Median rent	$487	$611

Composition by percentages

Race[1]

	Lower Richmond	Swan
White	89.2	92.2
Black	8.1	5.5
Asian/Pacific Islander	1.6	0.9
Hispanic[2]	0.5	1.0
Other	0.5	0.4

Education[3]

	Lower Richmond	Swan
Less than high school	27.6	15.2
High school graduate	33.5	21.7
Some college/Less than B.A.	16.4	19.9
Bachelor's degree	13.5	24.9
Graduate school	9.0	18.3

Unemployment[4]

Male

	Lower Richmond	Swan
Unemployed	7.7	1.9
Not in the labor force	26.1	14.4

Female

	Lower Richmond	Swan
Unemployed	6.1	2.3
Not in the labor force	42.2	54.3

Total

	Lower Richmond	Swan
Unemployed	6.9	2.1
Not in the labor force	34.9	39.1

Housing

	Lower Richmond	Swan
Owner occupied	67.9	84.5
Renter occupied	32.1	15.5
Receiving public assistance[5]	5.9	2.2

SOURCE: Information in this table has been produced from a configuration of 1990 census tracts that approximate the catchment areas of each school.

1. Not all columns total 100% due to rounding error.

2. Includes only white Hispanics. Others who identified as Hispanic were categorized by their racial identity.

3. Includes persons 25 and older.

4. Includes all civilians 16 years old and over. Figures reflect the census bureau's definitions of employment, unemployment, and participation in the labor force.

5. Proportion of households.

TABLE C3. FAMILY STRUCTURE BY SOCIAL CLASS AND RACE

	Two Parents, Original Intact		Blended Families[1]		Single Parent[2]		Grandparent/ Guardian	
	Black	*White*	*Black*	*White*	*Black*	*White*	*Black*	*White*
Middle Class	Alexander Williams Stacey Marshall (sample total = 13)	Melanie Handlon Garrett Tallinger (sample total = 17)	(sample total = 2)	(sample total = 1)	(sample total = 3)	(sample total = 0)	(sample total = 0)	(sample total = 0)
Working Class	Jessica Irwin (Black father/ white mother) Billy Yanelli (white)[3] (black sample total = 6) (white sample total = 6) (biracial sample total = 1)		(sample total = 0)	Wendy Driver[4] (sample total = 1)	Tyrec Taylor (mother)[5] (sample total = 3)	(sample total = 5)	(sample total = 2)	(sample total = 2)
Poor	(sample total = 0)	(sample total = 3)	Harold McAllister[6] (sample total = 1)	Karl Greeley[4] (sample total = 1)	(sample total = 11)	Katie Brindle (mother) (sample total = 8)	Tara Carroll (grandmother)[7] (sample total = 2)	(sample total = 0)

1. Blended families include single-parent and two-parent households in which a parent has remarried or there are other live-in adults who are romantically attached.
2. Primary caretaker is listed in parentheses.
3. Parents are not married; mother has older child from previous relationship.
4. Mother and live-in boyfriend.
5. Parents are separated; saw father regularly.
6. Saw father regularly.
7. Saw mother regularly; had little contact with father.

TABLE C4. AVERAGE NUMBER OF ORGANIZED ACTIVITIES BY SOCIAL CLASS, RACE, AND CHILD'S GENDER[1]

	Middle Class	Working Class	Poor
All Children			
Organized activities	4.9	2.5	1.5
Items with missing data[2]	2.5	3.0	2.0
N	36	26	26
Blacks			
Organized activities	5.2	2.8	1.6
Items with missing data	2.0	3.8	2.9
N	18	12	14
Whites			
Organized activities	4.6	2.3	1.4
Items with missing data	2.9	2.3	0.9
N	18	14	12
Girls			
Organized activities	4.7	2.6	1.5
Items with missing data	1.5	2.3	2.0
N	18	11	15
Boys			
Organized activities	5.1	2.5	1.5
Items with missing data	3.4	3.5	1.9
N	18	15	11

1. Organized activities include Brownies or Cub Scouts, music lessons, team sports (soccer, Little League, etc.), non-team sports (gymnastics, karate, etc.), Tot Tumbling, dance lessons (ballet, tap, etc.), religious classes, choir, art classes, and any activity offered through a recreational center that requires formal enrollment.

2. Not every respondent was asked about all of the activities that were eventually coded (though each was asked if his/her child participated in any activities not explicitly mentioned).

TABLE C5. PARTICIPATION IN ACTIVITIES
OUTSIDE OF SCHOOL: BOYS

	Activities Organized by Adults	Informal Activities
Middle class		
Garrett Tallinger (white)	Soccer team Traveling soccer team Baseball team Basketball team (summer) Swim team Piano Saxophone (through school)	Plays with siblings in yard Watches television Plays computer games Overnights with friends
Alexander Williams (Black)	Soccer team Baseball team Choir Church Choir Sunday school Piano (Suzuki) School plays Guitar (through school)	Restricted television Plays outside occasionally with two other boys Visits friends from school
Working class		
Billy Yanelli (white)	Baseball team	Watches television Visits relatives Rides bike Plays outside in the street Hangs out with neighborhood kids
Tyrec Taylor (Black)	Football team Vacation Bible School Sunday school (off/on)	Watches television Plays outside in the street Rides bike with neighborhood boys Visits relatives Goes to swimming pool
Poor		
Karl Greeley (white)	Goes to swimming pool Walks dog with neighbor	Watches television Plays Nintendo Plays with siblings
Harold McAllister (Black)	Bible study in neighbor's house (occasionally) Bible camp (1 week)	Visits relatives Plays ball with neighbor children Watches television Watches videos

TABLE C6. PARTICIPATION IN ACTIVITIES
OUTSIDE OF SCHOOL: GIRLS

	Activities Organized by Adults	Informal Activities
Middle class		
Melanie Handlon (white)	Girl Scouts Piano Sunday school Church Church pageant Violin (through school) Softball team	Restricted television Plays outside with children in the neighborhood Bakes cookies with mother Swims (not on swim team) Listens to music
Stacey Marshall (Black)	Gymnastics lessons Gymnastic teams Church Sunday school Youth choir	Watches television Plays outside Visits friends from school Rides bike
Working class		
Wendy Driver (white)	Catholic education (CCD) Dance lessons School choir	Watches television Visits relatives Does housework Rides bike Plays outside in the street Hangs out with cousins
Jessica Irwin (Black father/ white mother)	Church Sunday school Saturday art class School band	Restricted television Reads Plays outside with neighborhood children Visits relatives
Poor		
Katie Brindle (white)	School choir Friday evening church group (rarely)	Watches television Visits relatives Plays with Barbies Rides bike Plays with neighborhood children
Tara Carroll (Black)	Church Sunday school	Watches television Visits relatives Plays with dolls Plays Nintendo Plays with neighborhood children

TABLE C7. PROPORTION WHO HAVE
REQUESTED A TEACHER BY SOCIAL CLASS[1]

	Middle Class	Working Class
Requested a Teacher	34.4%	15.8%
N	32	19

1. Based on information provided by each child's primary caregiver. Poor group is excluded because most poor white families had to be recruited from outside the schools being studied. Since we did not have extensive information about these schools, we did not ask the same questions about their school experiences. The study includes 36 middle-class families and 26 working-class families. Lower numbers are reported here as a result of missing data.

TABLE C8. PROPORTION WHO KNOW
PROFESSIONALS BY SOCIAL CLASS[1]

	Middle Class	Working Class	Poor
Teacher	93.5%	47.6%	33.3%
Psychologist	48.4%	19.0%	8.7%
Lawyer	67.7%	35.0%	13.6%
Doctor	70.4%	15.0%	18.2%
N	27–31	20–21	22–24

1. Based on information provided by each child's primary caregiver. The study includes 36 middle-class families, 26 working-class families, and 26 poor families. Lower numbers are reported here as a result of missing data.

TABLE C9. OVERVIEW OF DATA
COLLECTION PROCESS

1989–90	Observation in two third-grade classrooms in Lawrenceville (mid-western town of 25,000); in-depth interviews separately with mothers, fathers, and guardians of 31 children, approximately one-half white and one-half Black; one observation of one white middle-class family one day; interviews with professionals working with children; work done primarily by Lareau with some assistance from an African American graduate student
1992–93	Receive grant from the Spencer Foundation
	Study of third-grade class in an integrated public school in large urban school district "Lower Richmond," which draws mostly white working-class and African American children from a low-income housing project in a northeastern city. Participant observation by Lareau from December to June in Ms. Green's classroom; an undergraduate African-American woman also visits the classroom
	Study of a public school in a small suburban district, "Swan," which draws mostly white middle-class students with some white working-class and some Black (about ten percent are from middle-class African American families). Participant observation in Swan from April to June by Lareau of a third-grade classroom of Ms. DeColli
	One half-time research assistant (RA) for help with library work and general project management (but not fieldwork)
	Spring 1993: decide to hire RAs for fieldwork
1993–94	Hire five RAs (four white women and one Black woman)
	Experienced RA from 1992–93 moves to Midwest but returns for retreats and acts as an advisor and consultant to remaining RAs
	Spend one month training RAs
	One RA visits Swan fourth grade of Ms. Nettles
	Occasional visits to Lower Richmond fourth grades: Mr. Tier, Ms. Bernstein, and Ms. Stanton
	RAs and Lareau carry out in-depth interviews for separate interviews with mothers, fathers, and guardians from Lower Richmond and Swan (equal numbers of white and Black children) of 40 families, mostly from classrooms where there have been observations (one RA quits in December)
	November: choose 12 families for intensive visits
	December/January: complete Carroll, Brindle, and Handlon. Plan to visit 12–14 times for two to three hours per visit and go with the families on outings (i.e., doctor, dentist, church); plan to carry out exit interviews with target child, siblings, mother, and father or guardian

TABLE C9. *(continued)*

1993–94 *(continued)*	January: revise plan to visit 20 times, usually in the space of one month, often daily, as well as interview
	February-May: complete Driver, Irwin, and Yanelli; start Tallinger
	June: RAs scatter (one quits grad school and moves to New York, one moves to LA, and two work on comprehensive exams)
Summer 1994	Hire two new research assistants (one white woman and one African American man)
	Finish Tallinger, start and finish Mcallister and Taylor, and start Williams
Summer 1995	One research assistant returns (white woman; African American man has moved to Boston); hire three additional research assistants (a white woman, a white man, and a Black woman)
	Start and finish Marshall and Greeley; finish Williams
Summer 1996	Read field notes, analyze data
	Transcribe interviews; write papers
Spring and Summer 1997	Present results in several talks
	Receive feedback; begin to revise approach
	Recruit 17 additional families (mostly black middle-class families and white poor families) for interviews, bringing final sample to 88 families
Summer 1998	Continue data analysis, writing papers, and revise
	Begin book
Spring, Summer, Fall 1999	Draft first chapters for the book
	Receive writing grant for fall semester; released from teaching
2000	Complete draft of five chapters; begin review process
2001	Revise draft; cut length by one-half; add five more chapters
	Finish complete copy of book; do second review
2002	Complete revisions

Notes

CHAPTER I: CONCERTED CULTIVATION

1. Choosing words to describe social groups also becomes a source of worry, especially over the possibility of reinforcing negative stereotypes. I found the available terms to describe members of racial and ethnic groups to be problematic in one way or another. The families I visited uniformly described themselves as "Black." Recognizing that some readers have strong views that Black should be capitalized, I have followed that convention, despite the lack of symmetry with the term white. In sum, this book alternates among the terms "Black," "Black American," "African American," and "white," with the understanding that "white" here refers to the subgroup of non-Hispanic whites.

2. Some readers have expressed concern that this phrase, "the accomplishment of natural growth," underemphasizes all the labor that mothers and fathers do to take care of children. They correctly note that working-class and poor parents themselves would be unlikely to use such a term to describe the process of caring for children. These concerns are important. As I stress in the text (especially in the chapter on Katie Brindle, Chapter 5) it does take an enormous amount of work for parents, especially mothers, of all classes to take care of children. But poor and working-class mothers have fewer resources with which to negotiate these demands. Those whose lives the research assistants and I studied approached the task somewhat differently than did middle-class parents. They did not seem to view children's leisure time as their responsibility; nor did they see themselves as responsible for assertively intervening in their children's school experiences. Rather, the working-class and poor parents carried out their chores, drew boundaries and restrictions around their children, and then, within these limits, allowed their children to carry out their lives. It is in this sense that I use the term "the accomplishment of natural growth."

3. I define a child-rearing context to include the routines of daily life, the dis-

positions of daily life, or the "habitus" of daily life. I focus on two contexts: concerted cultivation and the accomplishment of natural growth. In this book, I primarily use the concept of child rearing, but at times I also use the term *socialization*. Many sociologists have vigorously criticized this concept, noting that it suggests (inaccurately) that children are passive rather than active agents and that the relationship between parents and their children is unidirectional rather than reciprocal and dynamic. See, for example, William Corsaro, *Sociology of Childhood;* Barrie Thorne, *Gender Play;* and Glen Elder, "The Life Course as Development Theory." Nonetheless, existing terms can, ideally, be revitalized to offer more sophisticated understandings of social processes. Child rearing and socialization have the virtue of being relatively succinct and less jargon laden than other alternatives. As a result, I use them.

4. For discussions of the role of professionals, see Eliot Freidson, *Professional Powers;* Magali Sarfatti Larson, *The Rise of Professionalism;* and, although quite old, the still valuable collection by Amitai Etzioni, *The Semi-Professionals and Their Organizations.* Of course, professional standards are always contested and are subject to change over time. I do not mean to suggest there are not pockets of resistance and contestation. At the most general level, however, there is virtually uniform support for the idea that parents should talk to children at length, read to children, and take a proactive, assertive role in medical care.

5. Sharon Hays, in her 1996 book *The Cultural Contradictions of Motherhood,* studies the attitudes of middle-class and working-class mothers toward child rearing. She finds a shared commitment to "intensive mothering," although there are some differences among the women in her study in their views of punishment (with middle-class mothers leaning toward reasoning and working-class women toward physical punishment). My study focused much more on behavior than attitudes. If I looked at attitudes, I saw fewer differences; for example, all exhibited the desire to be a good mother and to have their children grow and thrive. The differences I found, however, were significant in how parents *enacted* their visions of what it meant to be a good parent.

6. See Urie Bronfenbrenner's article, "Socialization and Social Class through Time and Space."

7. Katherine Newman, *Declining Fortunes,* as well as Donald Barlett and James B. Steele, *America: What Went Wrong?* See also Michael Hout and Claude Fischer, "A Century of Inequality."

8. Some readers expressed the concern that the contrast to natural would be "unnatural," but this is not the sense in which the term *natural growth* is used here. Rather, the contrast is with words such as cultivated, artificial, artifice, or manufactured. This contrast in the logic of child rearing is a heuristic device that should not be pushed too far since, as sociologists have shown, all social life is constructed in specific social contexts. Indeed, family life has varied dramatically over time. See Philippe Aries, *Centuries of Childhood,* Herbert Gutman, *The Black Family in Slavery and Freedom, 1750–1925,* and Nancy Scheper-Hughes, *Death without Weeping.*

9. Elijah Anderson, *Code of the Street;* see especially Chapter 2.

10. For a more extensive discussion of the work of Pierre Bourdieu see the theoretical appendix; see also David Swartz's excellent book *Culture and Power.*

11. I did not study the full range of families in American society, including elite families of tremendous wealth, nor, at the other end of the spectrum, homeless families. In addition, I have a purposively drawn sample. Thus, I cannot state whether there are other forms of child rearing corresponding to other cultural logics. Still, data from quantitative studies based on nationally representative data support the patterns I observed. For differences by parents' social class position and children's time use, see especially Sandra Hofferth and John Sandberg, "Changes in American Children's Time, 1981–1997." Patterns of language use with children are harder to capture in national surveys, but the work of Melvin Kohn and Carmi Schooler, especially *Work and Personality*, shows differences in parents' child-rearing values. Duane Alwin's studies of parents' desires are generally consistent with the results reported here. See Duane Alwin, "Trends in Parental Socialization Values." For differences in interventions in institutions, there is extensive work showing social class differences in parent involvement in education. See the U. S. Department of Education, *The Condition of Education, 2001*, p.175.

12. In this book, unless otherwise noted, the statistics reported are from 1993 to 1995, which was when the data were collected. Similarly, unless otherwise noted, all monetary amounts are given in (unadjusted) dollars from 1994 to 1995. The figure reported here is from Everett Ladd, *Thinking about America*, pp. 21–22.

13. This quote is from President Bill Clinton's 1993 speech to the Democratic Leadership Council. It is cited in Jennifer Hochschild, *Facing Up to the American Dream*, p. 18.

14. Paul Kingston, *The Classless Society*, p. 2.

15. As I explain in more detail in the methodological appendix, family structure is intertwined with class position in this sample. The Black and white middle-class children that we observed all resided with both of their biological parents. By contrast, although some of the poor children have regular contact with their fathers, none of the Black or white poor children in the intensive observations had their biological fathers at home. The working-class families were in between. This pattern raises questions such as whether, for example, the pattern of concerted cultivation depends on the presence of a two-parent marriage. The scope of the sample precludes a satisfactory answer.

16. As I explain in Appendix A, three of the twelve children came from sources outside of the schools.

17. Arlie Hochschild, *The Second Shift*.

18. My concern here is the vast diversity in views among white Americans as well as Black Americans. The phrase "a white perspective" seems inaccurate. This is not to say that whites don't experience considerable benefits from their race in our stratified society. They do. Whites benefit from racial discrimination in many ways, including their improved ability to secure housing loans and employment as well as relatively higher market values for their homes in racially segregated neighborhoods. There are also well-documented differences in street interaction, including the ability to secure a taxi on a busy street. Thus the question is not the amount of racial discrimination in our society. Instead the question is how much being a member of a dominant group, interested in studying racial

differences in daily life, precludes one from "seeing" or "understanding" important dimensions of the phenomenon. See Douglas Massey and Nancy Denton, *American Apartheid;* Kathleen Neckerman and Joleen Kirschenmann, "Hiring Strategies, Racial Bias, and Inner-City Workers"; and Elijah Anderson, *Streetwise.* Finally, there is an extensive literature on "whiteness" and the benefits that whites gain from their position of privilege. See, among others, Phil Cohen, "Laboring under Whiteness."

19. See Julia Wrigley, "Do Young Children Need Intellectual Stimulation?" and Linda A. Pollock, *Forgotten Children.*

20. As I explain in more detail in Appendix A, some of the families in the study, including the Williamses, were upper–middle class. The project, however, was hampered by its small sample size and my desire to compare different racial and ethnic groups. As a result, the differences between middle-class and upper-middle-class families are not a major focus of the work. Within the scope of the sample of thirty-six middle-class families, however, clear differences did not emerge between the middle class and upper–middle class. As a result, in this book I use only the term *middle class* to encompass both.

CHAPTER 2: SOCIAL STRUCTURE AND DAILY LIFE

1. William Kornblum, *Sociology: The Central Questions*, p. 72.

2. Jepperson defines an institution as "a social order or pattern that has attained a certain state or property . . . . Put another way, institutions are those social patterns that, when chronically reproduced, owe their survival to relatively self-activating social processes." Ronald L. Jepperson, "Institutions, Institutional Effects, and Institutionalism," p. 145.

3. C. Wright Mills, *The Sociological Imagination*, p. 161.

4. Lower Richmond teachers also coordinate their classroom efforts with an after-school tutoring program that takes place at the local housing project, even though it is not a formal school-sponsored activity.

5. Most of the quotes reported in the book are from tape-recorded interviews or tape recordings made during family observations. At times, following traditional ethnographic work, the excerpts are from field notes that the research assistants and I wrote up immediately after the observations. In those instances, we added quotation marks only if we were certain that we could remember the exchange verbatim. As a result, there are excerpts from field notes that recount speech without the use of quotation marks. (I did not carry notebooks or permit others to write notes during field visits; rather we "hung out.") In editing the quotes for readability I removed false starts, "um," "you know," "like," and stuttering when they did not appear to be analytically significant. The signal of a . . . indicates the omission of words (or in a few cases a slight reordering of sentences). Finally, the research assistants and I had different nicknames for the family members that we used in our field notes (e.g., "Mr. Tallinger," "Mr. T." or "Don"). Rather than tamper with the text of field notes, I have allowed this variability to remain.

Brackets are used in the field notes to set off text inserted by me, usually for clarification, such as when a person's name is used in place of a personal pronoun, or as a side comment I added during the writing of the book. Parentheses are used to show the field-worker's side comments, which were inserted at the time the field notes were written.

6. For example, on a spelling test, a third-grader composed a sentence in which he said that he wanted to kill his teacher. This unusual incident generated considerable discussion in the hallways.

7. The average housing value at Swan was around $160,500 in the 1990 census compared to $75,000 in the Lower Richmond area. Compared to many urban areas, housing prices were modest in this geographical region, a pattern that continues to the present.

8. Parent volunteers for organized activities had similar complaints. A father who oversees the local Cub Scout troops is dismayed by the number of parents who "drop [their] kid off and use the time to go do errands."

9. There were differences in important aspects of school life. There was more emphasis on order and control of children's bodies at Lower Richmond than at Swan. In Lower Richmond, for example, lining up children in an orderly way took longer and involved more teacher input than at Swan School. (There were also separate girls' and boys' lines at Lower Richmond, while at Swan there was one, gender integrated, line.) Yard duty teachers yelled more on the playground at Lower Richmond than at Swan school and physical fights were much more frequent at Lower Richmond. These differences in practices, however, should not obscure the important point of the cultural repertoires that teachers sought to enact and envisioned as most appropriate for children. In this regard, as well as in their own personal lives, educators supported the concerted cultivation of children's talents, particularly the development of their reasoning skills.

10. See Jean Anyon, *Ghetto Schooling*, and Jonathon Kozol, *Savage Inequalities*. See also the U. S. Department of Education, *The Condition of Education, 2001*.

11. An exposition of how these beliefs developed, were transmitted, were contested, and changed over time is beyond the scope of this work. Still, it is apparent that professionals' standards are shaped by multiple forces. These include what teachers learned from their professional training (i.e., teacher education programs), from the publications by National Teachers' Organizations, from district in-service trainings and materials, and from informal conversation with teachers and administrators.

12. See especially Shirley Brice Heath, *Ways with Words*.

13. See Joyce Epstein and Mavis G. Sanders, "Connecting Home, School, and Community," as well as Annette Lareau, *Home Advantage*.

14. In this book, all statistics, unless otherwise noted, are targeted to 1993–1995 (usually 1995), which was the time of data collection. William Kornblum, *Sociology: The Central Questions,* p. 159.

15. Childhood poverty has been demonstrated to predict a host of negative life outcomes, including lower levels of health, scores on standardized tests, school grades, and emotional well-being. See Greg J. Duncan and Jeanne Brooks-Gunn, eds., *Consequences of Growing Up Poor*. For a comparative view of poverty rates in the United States and other industrialized countries, see Rainwater and Smeeding, "Doing Poorly."

16. See Greg J. Duncan and Jeanne Brooks-Gunn, eds., *Consequences of Growing Up Poor*. In 1997, 20% of all children were officially poor, but for white children the figure was 16% and for Black children it was 37%; for Black children under the age of six, 40% were poor. Lawrence Mishel, Jared Bernstein, and John Schmitt, *The State of Working America 1998–1999*, p. 281.

17. For example between 1989 and 1997 the wealth of the top fifth of the country grew by 9% while it declined by 6% for the bottom tenth of the population. Mishel et al., *The State of Working America*, p, 264. See also Michael Hout and Claude S. Fischer, "A Century of Inequality."

18. See Dalton Conley, *Being Black, Living in the Red*, and Melvin Oliver and Thomas Shapiro, *Black Wealth/White Wealth*.

19. The high school dropout rate in 1995 was 9% for whites and 12% for Black youth; by the end of the decade it had dropped slightly for white youth and increased slightly for Black youth. See U. S. Department of Education, *The Condition of Education, 2001*, p. 142.

20. In 1995, 28% of young people 25–29 had completed a bachelor's degree; by 2000 it had risen to 33%. There is a significant difference between the proportion of white high school graduates who eventually earn college degrees (31% in 1995, 36% in 2001) and Black high school graduates who eventually earn degrees (18% in 1995, and 21% in 2001). For the adult population as a whole, (ages 25–64) the proportion of college graduates is 24%. See U. S. Department of Education, *Condition of Education 1995*, pp. 245–249, and U. S. Department of Education, *Condition of Education 2001*, pp. 142, 150–151.

21. See Dalton Conley, *Being Black, Living in the Red*, as well as U. S. Department of Education, *The Condition of Education, 2001*.

22. See Derek Bok and William G. Bowen, *The Shape of the River*.

23. See Donald Barlett and James B. Steele, *America: What Went Wrong?* and Arne Kalleberg, Barbara F. Reskin, and Ken Hudson, "Bad Jobs in America."

24. For example, only 51% of children of high school dropouts can recognize the colors red, yellow, blue, and green by name, but the figures for high school graduates is 78%, for parents with some college it is 92%, and for college graduates it is 95%. For knowing all of the letters of the alphabet, the respective figures are 9%, 19%, 29%, and 42%. U. S. Department of Education, *Condition of Education 1995*, p. 182.

25. See U. S. Department of Education, *Condition of Education, 1995* and Entwhistle et al., *Children, Schools, and Inequality*. At the same level of parental education, white students generally receive higher scores than do Black students. See also Christopher Jencks and Meredith Phillips, eds., *The Black-White Test Score Gap*.

26. In 1995, 61% of high school graduates enrolled in college; for children of high school dropouts, the rate was 27%, for children of high school graduates 47%, and for children of college graduates, 88%. U. S. Department of Education, *Condition of Education, 2001*, p. 147.

27. As Paul Kingston has noted (personal communication) the relationship between parents' educational level and occupational level is far from automatic. There is a considerable amount of downward mobility. Also, there is variation among brothers and sisters in the same family. Still, parents' social class position

remains one of the most powerful predictors of children's educational success and life outcomes. See Paul Kingston's book *The Classless Society* for an elaboration of this position as well as Christopher Jencks et al., *Inequality,* and *Who Gets Ahead?*

28. Kingston, therefore, does *not* deny the existence of inequality: "Beyond question, huge inequalities exist and Americans recognize them." Nevertheless, in his book *The Classless Society,* he is particularly adamant in asserting that cultural habits — as manifest in family life or childrearing, for example — are not associated with different economic groups: "My thesis is that groups of people having a common economic position — what are commonly designated as 'classes' — do not significantly share distinct, life-defining experiences" (p. 1).

29. Jan Pakulski and Malcolm Waters, *The Death of Class,* p. 4.

30. For examples within this tradition see Paul Willis, *Learning to Labour,* and Basil Bernstein, *Class, Codes, and Control.*

31. It is true, of course, that people do not generally see themselves as anything but middle class. Nevertheless, I am not asserting that powerful patterns of class-consciousness exist.

32. My debt to Bourdieu is enormous, especially regarding his preoccupation in the transmission of advantage. Although some have critiqued his model of social reproduction for being overly deterministic, a close reading of his theoretical ideas makes clear that Bourdieu sees a great deal of indeterminacy in how life trajectories unfold (see Marlis Buchman's book *The Script of Life* for a particularly lucid description of Bourdieu's model). Still, there is one key way that I have parted company with Bourdieu. As Elliot Weininger has noted in his article "Class and Causation in Bourdieu," Bourdieu has a gradational (rather than categorical) conception of class structure. In addition, Bourdieu is deeply interested in fractions or divisions within a social class, an issue that space (and sample size) does not permit me to develop here.

CHAPTER 3: THE HECTIC PACE OF CONCERTED CULTIVATION

1. Recent national data also suggest that children of highly educated parents have more organized activities and busier schedules. See especially Sandra L. Hofferth and John F. Sandberg, "Changes in American Children's Time, 1981–1997," as well as Elliot Weininger and Annette Lareau, "Children's Participation in Organized Activities and the Gender Dynamic of the 'Time Bind.'" There are also a number of older studies on children's organized leisure activities, including the classic piece by Janet Lever, "Sex Differences in the Complexity of Children's Play"; Elliot Medrich et al., *The Serious Business of Growing Up*; and Gary Alan Fine, *With the Boys.*

2. See David M. Halbfinger, "Our Town," wherein parents report spending almost $6,000 annually on hockey alone.

3. As with many American households, the Tallingers had accumulated debt and had limited savings. For a more detailed discussion of the Tallingers' financial situation (as well as the Yanelli, Driver, and Greeley families), see the dissertation by Patricia Berhau, *Class and the Experiences of Consumers.*

4. See Gai Ingham Berlage's paper, "Are Children's Competitive Team Sports Teaching Corporate Values?" for a study of fathers of children on hockey and

soccer travel teams. Fathers expressed the belief that their son's participation would increase "teamwork" and "self-discipline." Still, the actual impact on their work careers is unclear, and a study of college athletes, James Shulman and William Bowen, *The Game of Life,* challenges some of these assumptions about the long-term effects of athletic participation.

5. See Melvin Kohn and Carmi Schooler, *Work and Personality.*

6. Perhaps in recognition of this reality, Intercounty soccer team organizers require team members to sign a document pledging to make this activity their priority.

7. Mr. Tallinger believes in the value of spanking, however. With Sam in particular, he uses spanking as a threat. For a detailed look at the role of reasoning in concerted cultivation, see Chapter 6.

CHAPTER 4: A CHILD'S PACE

1. Elijah Anderson documents the importance of complying with codes of respect, particularly in children's relations with adults. See his book *Code of the Street.*

2. We did not observe middle-class Black children use such terms; rather they called adults by their first names. We also did not observe poor and working-class white children automatically use honorific terms with adults, which is suggestive of a difference across racial groups in this aspect of family life within working-class and poor families.

3. During their four-year separation, Ms. Taylor and Mr. Taylor reconciled at one point. They lived together again for eighteen months before splitting up a second time.

4. Tyrec's closest friends, the boys we observed him play with daily, all are Black. In an interview, however, his mother reported that he has three good friends who are white.

5. It is unclear the degree to which Tyrec wanted to sign up again. What is salient here is that the mother was "praying" that he would not want to do so. Unlike in the middle-class families, there was no presumption of children being involved in organizations and activities. For a discussion of the crucial role of mothers in screening programs before allowing children to participate in recreational services, see Dennis R. Howard and Robert Madrigal, "Who Makes the Decision: The Parent or the Child?"

CHAPTER 5: CHILDREN'S PLAY IS FOR CHILDREN

1. C. Wright Mills, *The Sociological Imagination.*

2. Although the Brindles have moved frequently in the past (Jenna, who went to school only through tenth grade, attended twenty different schools), they have been in their current neighborhood for more than two years, and Katie has been in the same elementary school for four years.

3. Although the person was never caught, Ms. Brindle suspects a neighbor in the apartment building where they lived previously. The man was the father of one of Katie's playmates.

4. John is schizophrenic and cannot work; Ryan is illiterate but he is employed.

5. Unlike Black families from similar economic circumstances, the Brindles lived in a neighborhood that housed families from varying economic circumstances. Overall, Massey and Denton, *American Apartheid,* have shown poor white families do not experience the same form of hyper-segregation as Black families.

6. For a discussion of poor mothers' efforts to make ends meet as they grocery shop, see Marjorie DeVault, *Feeding the Family,* especially the chapter on "provisioning."

7. She is less direct with Katie, but with her, too, there are special, affectionate rituals. For example, when Katie is away from home (typically, at her grandmother's house) and calls her mother on the telephone, Ms. Brindle says in a warm and loving tone, "I love you," and, "I miss you too." In addition, she and Katie have developed a ritual to make it easier to say good-bye. They count to three together, "Okay, one, two, three," and hang up at the exact same moment. Ms. Brindle explains, "[Katie] doesn't like to hang up and so we count together."

8. Middle-class parents are especially likely to stop what they are doing to watch a child if the child specifically requests that they do so. Although some may ask for a temporary delay before the start of the performance they are supposed to watch, few of these parents simply refuse their children's requests.

9. Katie does draw adult attention when she demonstrates her ability to cry on command: "[Katie] scrunches up her face and begins to make fake sobs; she — in an agitated and very persuasive way — begins to frantically run her hands through her hair; she throws her entire body on the couch and the sobs get louder." This acting stint prompts comments from the adults, but not ones aimed at cultivating Katie's talents: Ryan says, "That is some job — especially the hands and the hair." . . . [His mother remarks,] "Oh yeah, she really does a job there." (Uncle John continues to show no affect of any kind.) See Shirley Brice Heath, *Ways with Words,* for a discussion of viewing adults, rather than children, as appropriate conversation partners.

10. In a setting where the television was virtually always on, and was only casually attended to, this action by Amy appeared to be an effort to gain her grandmom's attention. Grandmom did not appear to define Amy's action as disrespectful.

11. I am surprised that no one is watching. Occasionally, I crane my neck up and around to watch the girls from my spot on the floor.

12. She suggested that Katie use her birthday money to purchase dark shoes to complete the outfit.

13. This family was particularly vulnerable to intervention by state officials as their routine child-rearing practices sometimes violated prevailing standards. As I discuss briefly in Appendix A, the field-workers and I found visits to this family more difficult than the visits to other families.

PART II: LANGUAGE USE

1. Shirley Brice Heath, *Ways with Words.*

CHAPTER 6: DEVELOPING A CHILD

1. As I explain in Appendix A, Alexander did not attend school where the classroom observations for this study were conducted. Instead, an acquaintance consulted the directory for the private school her daughter attends and supplied me with the addresses of the two Black families with children in the fourth grade. I sent the Williams family a letter. After a series of meetings (and my compliance with their request to see a copy of my previous book and my résumé), they agreed to be in the study. Because of this difference in recruitment, we do not have data from classroom observations or parent-teacher conferences for this family.

2. This is not to suggest that parent-child talking is the only pathway to academic success. There is compelling evidence of academic achievement in immigrant populations, for example, where this kind of cultivation of language skills is limited. Still, even here, the social origins of the immigrants appear to matter in children's educational experiences. (See, for example, Alejandro Portes and Dag MacLeod, "Educational Progress of Children of Immigrants.") In addition, some middle-class children have learning disabilities, differ in achievement motivation, and are subject to other mediating factors that impede school success. Thus, extensive reasoning at home does not ensure school success. The argument is that it can provide a key advantage. Research linking family background to differences in reading levels and aptitude test scores also supports this position. See Betty Hart and Todd Risley, *Meaningful Differences*.

3. See Betty Hart and Todd Risley, *Meaningful Differences*, as well as Shirley Brice Heath, *Ways with Words*. See also Jonathan B. Imber, "Doctor No Longer Knows Best."

4. Not all adults, of course, comply with these special requests. Children also vary, in part by temperament, in how gregarious and assertive they are.

5. The Suzuki method is labor intensive. Beginning at age four, children are required to listen to music an average of one hour a day. Both the child and the parents also are expected to practice daily and to attend every scheduled lesson.

6. Basil Bernstein, *Class, Codes, and Control*.

7. Christina commented, "I like the fact that the two coaches are young guys, but they are not coaching them. Look at the other coach, how he's talking to his team from the sideline." Terry, sounding angry, says, "Those guys would not know what strategy was if it smacked them in the face. Look at them — their team is losing and they're sitting on the bench, laughing." By the second half, it was evident that Alex's team was not going to win. The parents, especially Terry, quieted down considerably.

8. The field-worker was astounded by Alex's knowledge. He wrote in the field notes, "I lost it (the thread of the conversation after Alex mentioned copyright). I was impressed that he knew about copyright laws."

9. See also findings reported by Jennifer Hochschild in her book *Facing Up to the American Dream*.

10. By the time this interview took place, the observation period had ended, and Alexander was in fifth grade.

11. For discussions of Black middle-class adults managing racial encounters in public, see especially Joe Feagin and Melvin P. Sikes, *Living with Racism.*

12. Note that although she is clearly distracted, Ms. Williams automatically transforms her interaction with her son into an educative moment, by stressing the difference between $1,500 and $15,000.

13. Ms. Williams never indicated to the field-worker why she did not want to use one of her many credit cards. Her sense of privacy was keen. Many of our visits with the family took place during events that occurred outside the home. While other families in the study often volunteered exactly what they were doing on various weekends, Ms. Williams preferred to say they would "be away" or that a time "was not good." In general, the Williams family did not volunteer information that other families in the study routinely discussed. We sought to be sensitive to family members' preferences, despite the very intrusive nature of the field-work. We did not probe for details of matters only tangentially related to our research interests. As a result, we never determined the source of the problem here.

14. I have frequented the same store and have paid for my purchases with checks. I am white and middle-aged. One of the clerks, an older woman, often would look at my checks suspiciously and ask, "Have you written checks here before?" Neither she nor any other clerk has ever refused one of my checks, however. Nor have I ever seen a sign posted in the store to indicate that checks are not accepted.

15. Not all parents readily provide health-care professionals with accurate information. We observed a pattern of silent resistance or defiance directed toward medical personnel by (mainly) working-class and poor parents.

16. Not all physicians invite the kind of participation from children that this one did, but even when professionals were less open, we saw this mother and others actively seek to monitor and intervene in their children's experiences.

17. At the car show, Alex gave a different selection when he told the field-worker his three favorites. Mr. Williams noticed.

18. The field-worker noted, "This is an affectionate family, not an aggressive affection as in the poor families." He objected, however, to the display: "I was glad to see the unity in the family but . . . it was not developmentally appropriate. They are either on the extreme of too old or too young."

19. Many psychologists also insist that this kind of confusion over parent-child roles is harmful for children. For complaints see Paul Kropp, *I'll Be the Parent, You Be the Child*, and Dana Chidekel, *Parents in Charge.*

CHAPTER 7: LANGUAGE AS A CONDUIT FOR SOCIAL LIFE

1. On Father's Day weekend, for example, Harold took the bus across town by himself and visited. With help from his grandmother, he made his father breakfast.

2. The family also has a German shepherd, Luke, who stays in the front yard, tied to a tree. He does not come in the house. Family members pet and talk to Luke as they come and go. He is the only dog on the block.

3. Since the study was completed, a major welfare reform was passed, changing the terms of public assistance for poor families.

4. Other researchers have described similar sorts of economies among the poor. See Kathy Edin and Laura Lein, *Making Ends Meet,* and Susan Holloway et al., *Through My Own Eyes.*

5. During an interview, his mother reported that Harold wanted to be on a sports team but that she "couldn't find one around here" and was not going to travel "all the way over" (about a forty-five-minute bus ride) to a community that did have a team. We found that there was a football team that was close to the housing project, but Ms. McAllister was not aware of it. It also was costly. In addition to paying registration fees, the players were involved in fund-raisers, and Harold would have had to have bus fare to get back and forth to practices and games.

6. Whites who drive into the housing project often receive prolonged, hostile stares from residents (arriving in a car is itself the sign of outsider status, since few living in public housing can afford a car). This hostility is situationally specific, however. When I attended the big family reunion picnic after the study ended, although I was one of only two white people in a crowd of more than two hundred, no one stared (perhaps because neither white drug users nor Department of Human Service officials would likely attend such an event).

7. Douglas Massey and Nancy Denton, *American Apartheid.*

8. It is striking that she only mentions the Black male field-worker, and did not include the white female field-worker, or me, a middle-age white woman. I concluded that she did not see white women to be at risk for intimidation in the project in the way a young Black male would be.

9. In one of the more carefully done studies of speech, Betty Hart and Todd Risley, *Meaningful Differences,* found (using a sample of forty-two children) that by about the age of three, children of professionals had larger vocabularies and spoke more per hour than the *parents* of similarly aged children on welfare.

10. As I explain below, Harold did engage in elaborated and embellished speech in his interactions with peers.

11. On the issue of language use and social class, see the classic work of Basil Bernstein, especially *Class, Codes, and Control.*

12. Unlike Ms. Williams, Ms. McAllister does not use this as a "teachable moment" for a short math lesson.

13. I found this exchange distressing, partly because Runako did not actually hear the announcement that Ms. McAllister would not be cooking that evening. I also found it difficult to accept the idea of a child going to bed hungry. In keeping with the field work approach, however, I did not say anything or express my concern. Indeed, worried about being seen as judgmental on a highly sensitive topic, I didn't ask Ms. McAllister about the logic behind her reasoning. I presumed, however, that aside from potato chips and orange juice, there wasn't much food in the house or, given the tight economic constraints, what food there was had been reserved for other purposes.

14. Note that in the example presented earlier, when Ms. McAllister yells at Alexis for swearing, she implicitly acknowledges that her daughter may say such words outside the house ("Don't in here.").

15. The field-worker explained the meaning of this term in his field notes: "Breaking someone's ankles is an offensive term used to refer to how low the ball is being dribbled (i.e., at ankle height). At this height, it is very difficult to control and dribble the ball. The term also refers to the speed and swift change of direction that an offensive player uses. This can cause the defensive player to twist his ankles." The field-worker, himself a good basketball player, also described Harold's game as "A lot better than [mine]."

16. This term, often pronounced as "bull," is used as a taunt here, referring to someone with prowess, but as Elijah Anderson notes in *Code of the Street,* it can also mean friend (p. 81). In our observations we did not see Harold engage in a classic form of "the dozens." Janice Hale-Benson, *Black Children.*

17. As the field-worker pointed out in his field notes, this episode demonstrates that often it is more important how one looks or performs in attempting to reach a goal than it is to actually achieve the objective.

18. The field-worker, Caitlin, wrote: "I give her what I hope is an understanding look and reach out to pet her shoulder." The fight was difficult for the field-worker (Caitlin) to witness, especially because the children seemed upset.

19. Ms. McAllister threatened Jill with a stick, but she did not hit her. A few days later, when I visited, Ms. McAllister reported that she would have hit her sister if the field-worker had not been present.

20. Another field-worker arrived early the next morning. His field notes record Ms. McAllister's concern.

JANE: (smiling) I know Caitlin think I'm crazy. (I try to act as if I haven't heard.) Me and my sister had got into it yesterday, and I know Caitlin was scared, but I had to kick [my sister] out. I was tired of her shit. She on drugs. . . . I threw all of [Jill's] shit out of the door and Caitlin was like this [Jane stands stiff and erect, wide-eyed]. I felt bad that she had to see me get like that. (She begins to laugh again.) I know I scared her. (Jane is shaking her head as she smiles.) The kids were out there watchin'. I tried to give them the signal to get her out here. So I tell [them] to pick up the glass and stuff out on the pavement in the front. Caitlin starts pickin' it up, too. I have to tell her, "Not you, Caitlin!"

21. The field-workers have not seen any of the children eat a green or yellow vegetable since the visits began. The dinner including canned spinach and yams came after this checkup.

22. Carol Heimer and Lisa Staffen, *For the Sake of the Children.*

23. It is theoretically possible that concerted cultivation, particularly the emphasis on reasoning, could still cultivate a keen sense of familial obligations. But there are countervailing forces. In concerted cultivation there is a stress on individualized choices and leisure activities, which take people out of the family into wider and more diverse arenas. This reduces the time available for family members to "hang out" together. Schedule conflicts also increase. There also are increasing numbers of conflicts as children, with voices that count in family decision making, often complain about having to sit through family gatherings. They prefer to spend time with their own friends. In the accomplishment of natural growth, children have fewer individualized alternatives.

24. Anderson, *Code of the Street.*

25. There are limits to familial support, as when Ms. McAllister felt she had no choice but to have her drug-addicted sister, Jill, leave. Still, Ms. McAllister's decision was rooted in other family obligations. Notably, her duty as Harold and Alexis' mother "to make it a home not a house" overrode her obligation to her twin sister. In middle-class homes, Black and white, familial obligations were fewer, partially because family members were farther away. But see the next chapter for a discussion of a Black middle-class girl, Stacey Marshall, who has a very acrimonious sibling relationship as well as weak extended ties.

CHAPTER 8: CONCERTED CULTIVATION IN ORGANIZATIONAL SPHERES

1. For similar results on parent involvement in schooling see Elizabeth Useem, "Student Selection into Course Sequences in Mathematics," Annette Lareau, *Home Advantage,* and the U. S. Department of Education, *The Condition of Education, 2001.* But see also John Diamond, "Beyond Social Class."

2. During the summer, the girls went to spend a week visiting their maternal grandparents, but after a few days, they called home, clamoring for their parents to come and get them. They found life with these elderly relatives unduly restrictive.

3. The field-worker was shocked. She noted that Stacey's remark "[was] something that would have gotten a lot of kids slapped in the mouth."

4. It is also possible, of course, that children could learn helplessness and dependence upon their parents to fix life problems for them.

5. As Appendix A explains, Stacey was not a student at Swan and thus was in a different district. While the cutoff for entrance to the gifted program at Swan School is 125 (which Garrett Tallinger missed by a few points), at her school the cutoff was 130.

6. When I asked Ms. Marshall what she would have said to the coach, she explained that she would start by tackling the problem indirectly:

> That I'm concerned, that she's a little uncomfortable at lunchtime. I would probably ask, I'd say, "How are things?" I would start out with, "Is everything okay?" You know, "Do you know my kid Fern? I'm just a little concerned because she said, she's, you know, she's eating alone." Or, "I just, I'd like for this to be a wholesome experience and just wonder. . . ."

7. In the language of Pierre Bourdieu, the Marshall family was reading "the field." (See Appendix B for a discussion of the concept of *field.*)

CHAPTER 9: CONCERTED CULTIVATION GONE AWRY

1. Indeed, Ms. Handlon reported, "The first week I had to walk her to her class. She wouldn't get out of the car unless I did." She said that Melanie was not crying, but "I could tell she was just scared and she asked, 'Will you walk me in?' It was probably about a week and then she was confident enough for me to just drop her at the door so she could go in by herself."

2. When we interviewed Ms. Handlon in the fall, she estimated that in the

previous two weeks she had had eight casual conversations with other mothers about school matters. The conversations were often brief and occurred before or after Melanie's organized activities (e.g., Girl Scouts, meetings, church) or before or after school.

3. Note that these are preexisting networks; Ms. Handlon does not have to build them. She chooses to participate and then draws on the information she learns.

4. Ms. Handlon does not usually help either of the older boys. Harry generally does little homework; his grades suffer. Their mother is dismayed by this, but she feels she needs to let the boys, especially Harry, learn for themselves that they need to do their homework.

5. Since home observations were confidential, we did not tell the teachers what we observed.

6. Negotiations were routine, as this Saturday morning when Tommy decides to make some fresh juice: Mrs. Handlon says that it is fine to use this squeezer.

Tommy says, "Can I use the electric one?" Mrs. Handlon says, "No use this one." Tommy says, "Why can't I use the electric one?" Mrs. Handlon says, "This one is here." Tommy says, "I don't mean to argue but the electric one is already out." Mrs. Handlon says, "Well that must mean somebody used it. All right, you can use it if you rinse it out when you're done."

Mrs. Handlon sounds a little frustrated at the end of this conversation.

7. Note that Ms. Handlon had fewer class resources than did Ms. Marshall. She had considerably less education, and in her job as a secretary she did not exert the same kind of managerial authority. Her husband had more class resources, but he was not active in managing Melanie's schooling. Thus, it is possible that Ms. Handlon's inability to effectively activate class resources could be linked to her own, relatively limited, resources. Also there are families who are rich in class resources but who have parents or children who are impaired, for example, with mental health problems or substance abuse problems. My point here is that class location does not guarantee the transmission of advantages.

CHAPTER 10: LETTING EDUCATORS LEAD THE WAY

1. Wendy was nine when the visits began but turned ten during the course of the study.

2. When we began observing the family, Ms. Driver and Mr. Fallon and the children had been living together for just under a year. They eventually married (Valerie was about two years old at the time).

3. When their father died, Wendy and Willie became eligible for Social Security benefits, which they now receive.

4. See Maria Kefalas, *Working-Class Heroes,* for a discussion of a comparable neighborhood in Chicago.

5. Field-workers noted that during a typical two-hour visit to the Driver family, they would hear more than twenty-five references to kin.

6. Moreover, as we observed in all the families, regardless of social class, much more attention is paid to Wendy's physical appearance than to Willie's. The

adults, and Wendy herself, focus repeatedly on her clothes, hairstyle, shoe size, and overall creation as a present and future object of beauty.

7. Willie expressed an interest in joining a hockey team, but the combined costs of the equipment and the activity fee were prohibitively expensive. Ms. Driver wished that there were programs "where kids could just go and play for nothing."

8. In an exit interview, Ms. Driver complained that Willie had acted differently during the visits, often "pushing it" and "not taking 'no' for an answer." She noted, however, that he seemed to have begun testing the limits in other situations as well.

9. In the end, the teachers recommended that Wendy repeat fourth grade, and the principal approved their decision. On the last day of school, however, Mr. Tier learned that a higher district official would not permit the retention (for reasons not made clear to Mr. Tier). Instead, in fifth grade Wendy went into an intensive special education program at Lower Richmond, in a classroom with only thirteen children. Mr. Tier was mollified because he felt Wendy "would be getting the attention she needs."

10. Mr. Johnson's explanation was different. He said, "We had one little problem. I yelled at her one time and she stopped coming. . . . I had given her an assignment, and she came in and she told me her mother didn't know how to do the assignment." The assignment, for Black history month, was to match names to occupations. Mr. Johnson thought Wendy was making up an excuse for not doing her work: "I mean, it just didn't make sense to me. So I got a little perturbed and I told her, 'You can't tell me, if your mother completed high school [she] couldn't do this.' I mean, you just say that you didn't do it. . . . If you didn't do something, you just didn't do it. I can accept that more so than you telling me that your mother — so that upset her." Her classroom teacher, Mr. Tier (who did not have a good relationship with Mr. Johnson) presumed that Mr. Johnson's schedule had changed and that Wendy would resume at some point.

11. I wrote in my field notes, "I am flabbergasted by this." Still, since the aim of the study was to learn as much as possible about how families interact with institutions, I did not correct her.

12. Several people in Mr. Fallon's family believe in hitting. His sister, Sar, for example, told Wendy one afternoon when she picked her up from school and Wendy complained about another child hurting her, "You've got to learn to fight!"

13. We did not observe this visit. Overall, it was very difficult to go along on medical visits, unless the trips were for appointments made well in advance, such as a wellness checkup or a camp physical.

CHAPTER 11: BEATING WITH A BELT, FEARING THE SCHOOL

1. He worked "off the books" for many years but recently changed jobs, taking a pay cut, so that he could pay taxes and begin to qualify for Social Security benefits.

2. A clerk at the emergency room, however, told Ms. Yanelli about a state

program providing health insurance for children; as a result Billy has a medical card.

3. This parent-teacher conference was in the fall, after I had interviewed Ms. Yanelli but before she was asked to be in the observational study. In this conference, Mr. Tier told her very directly that he thought that Billy had psychological problems. (Mr. Tier, not known for his tactfulness, also expressed frustration about Billy rolling down a muddy hill during a field trip, saying in the conference, "Even kids that were fat and stupid got themselves down the hill.") Ms. Yanelli was very distressed by the conference. Taking my number from the consent form I had given her, she called me at home that evening to discuss it. She thought Billy's report card was excellent. She was bewildered about why Mr. Tier would not discuss the report card in the conference but make claims of Billy having psychological problems. What is striking in this conversation and many others is that despite Ms. Yanelli's clear sense that educators are acting inappropriately, she feels incapable of influencing the situation. Furthermore, she blames herself for her powerlessness. As she said that evening, "I think, 'Why do you let the school do this to you time after time?'"

4. Given the dominant emphasis on reasoning in middle-class settings it is important to point out that reasoning is not without drawbacks. In middle-class families results could be ineffectual, as when parents were trying to reason with a cranky, grumpy, loud five-year-old.

5. Other research has shown that parents of lower levels of education are likely to use physical discipline, particularly with sons. See Ronald L. Simons et al., "Intergenerational Transmission of Harsh Parenting."

6. To our knowledge, no one at Lower Richmond noticed the next day.

7. See Joyce Epstein's work as well as James Coleman's work on this point.

8. See Jacques Donzelot, *The Policing of Families.*

CHAPTER 12: THE POWER AND LIMITS OF SOCIAL CLASS

1. See Sharon Hays, *The Cultural Contradictions of Motherhood.*

2. Some researchers claim that happiness is not particularly connected to age, gender, race, or affluence. See David G. Meyers and Ed Diener, "Who Is Happy?"

3. Middle-class parents were self-aware of how hectic their lives were; they often talked about the lack of time. Some parents also mentioned how their own childhoods had been so different from those of their own children in terms of organized activities. But middle-class parents did not seem to be particularly aware of their emphasis on reasoning and, especially, their interventions in institutions. Nor were they, or working-class and poor parents, particularly aware that radically different approaches to child rearing were being carried out. Instead, parents viewed their approaches to child rearing as natural.

4. Cornell West, *Race Matters.*

5. See Jennifer Hochschild, *Facing Up to the American Dream;* Ellis Cose, *The Rage of a Privileged Class;* Beverly Daniel Tatum, *Why Are the Black Kids Sitting Together in the Cafeteria?;* and Elizabeth Higginbotham, *Too Much to Ask.*

6. In this study there were also, in some contexts, differences in sociolinguistic terms (including special words for white people). For a more general discussion of this issue see Mary Patillo-McCoy, *Black Picket Fences,* and Douglas Massey and Nancy Denton, *American Apartheid.* I also did not study a racially isolated school. See, among others, Eric A. Hanushek et. al., "New Evidence about Brown v. Board of Education."

7. See Ellis Cose, *The Rage of a Privileged Class,* and Mary Waters, *Black Identities.*

8. Douglas Massey and Nancy Denton, *American Apartheid.*

9. This study's findings are compatible with others that have shown children to be aware of race at relatively early ages. Indeed, girls often played in racially segregated groups on the playground. (Boys were likely to be in racially integrated groups.) Thus, this study suggests that racial dynamics certainly exist in children's lives, but they are not (yet) an organizing feature in the same way that social class membership is. For a piece that stresses the salience of race in the lives of preschoolers, see Debra Van Ausdale and Joe R. Feagin, "Using Racial and Ethnic Concepts."

10. A majority of middle-class and working-class parents self-report the use of reasoning in child rearing. Since there is an emphasis in broader cultural repertoires of the importance of using reasoning, it is not surprising that parents of all social classes might report that they use reasoning. Indeed, for many of the working-class and poor parents, physical discipline was a "last resort." Studies do consistently show that more educated mothers, however, are more likely to stress reasoning. See, among others, Cheryl Blueston and Catherine S. Tamis-LeMonda, "Correlates of Parenting Styles in Predominantly Working- and Middle-Class African American Mothers."

11. Of course, some middle-class parents also appeared slightly anxious during parent-teacher meetings. But overall, middle-class parents spoke more, and they asked educators more questions, including more critical and penetrating ones, than did working-class and poor parents.

12. Working-class and poor children often resisted and tested school rules, but they did not seem to be engaged in the same process of seeking an accommodation by educators to their own *individual* preferences that I witnessed among middle-class children. Working-class and poor children tended to react to adults' offers or, at times, plead with educators to repeat previous experiences, such as reading a particular story, watching a movie, or going to the computer room. In these interactions, the boundaries between adults and children were firmer and clearer than those with middle-class children.

13. Carol Heimer and Lisa Staffen, *For the Sake of the Children.*

14. My discussion here is necessarily speculative. Parents of all social classes took for granted key aspects of their child rearing and thus had difficulty articulating the rationale behind their actions.

15. In the South, children between the ages of ten and thirteen comprised one-third of the workers in textile mills between 1870 and 1900. Viviana Zelizer, *Pricing the Priceless Child.* See especially chapter 2.

16. Quoted in Zelizer, *Pricing the Priceless Child,* p. 78.

17. Zelizer, *Pricing the Priceless Child,* p. 67.

18. Zelizer, *Pricing the Priceless Child*, p. 59.

19. Zelizer, *Pricing the Priceless Child*, p. 97.

20. See William Corsaro, *Sociology of Childhood*.

21. As Randall Collins notes, Max Weber assigns multiple meanings to the term *rationalization*. Here I am referring to the meaning that "emerges when Weber compares different types of institutions. Bureaucracy is described as a rational form of administrative organization as opposed to the irrational elements found in patrimonialism . . . . The key [conditions] here seem to be predictability and regularity . . . . There is a strong implication that rationality is based on written rules, and hence on paperwork." Randall Collins, *Max Weber: A Skeleton Key*, pp. 63, 78.

22. Ritzer also discusses the importance of efficiency. See George Ritzer, *The McDonaldization of Society*.

23. Ritzer, *The McDonaldization of Society*, p. 3.

24. Hays, *The Cultural Contradictions of Motherhood*, p. 11.

25. On safety see Mark Warr and Christopher G. Ellison, "Rethinking Social Reactions to Crime," as well as Joel Best, *Threatened Children*. On changes in work-family relationships see Rosanna Hertz and Nancy L. Marshall, *Working Families*, as well as demographic research. On time spent with children, see Suzanne Bianchi, "Maternal Employment and Time with Children." On suburbanization see Kenneth T. Jackson, *Crabgrass Frontier*.

26. Hays, *Cultural Contradictions of Motherhood*.

27. In 2002, enrolling a child in a single sport could cost as much as $5000 per year. The estimates for ice hockey include $100 skates (which usually need to be replaced twice a year), $60 gloves, and annual league fees of up to $2,700. David M. Halbfinger, "Our Town: A Hockey Parent's Life."

28. See the classic article by Urie Bronfenbrenner on this point, "Socialization and Social Class through Time and Space."

29. See the extensive writings by Melvin Kohn on this point, especially his book (with Carmi Schooler) *Work and Personality*.

30. Middle-class families did not live problem-free lives. The point here is that middle-class families have more varied occupational experiences; their superior educational training also gives them access to jobs with more economic returns.

31. Katherine Newman, *Declining Fortunes*, and Donald L. Barlett and James B. Steele, *America: What Went Wrong?*

32. Erik Olin Wright, *Class, Crisis, and the State*, chapter 1.

33. Not all middle-class parents we interviewed approved of this scenario, either. Many thought it was wrong to force a child to take piano lessons that he did not enjoy. Still, unlike working-class and poor parents, many stressed the importance of "exposure."

34. Michael Katz, *The Price of Citizenship*.

35. See Lawrence Mishel et al., *The State of Working America*, p. 289.

36. David Karen, letter to author, 7 June 2002. See Jody Heymann, *The Widening Gap*.

37. Alvin Rosenfeld and Nicole Wise, *The Over-Scheduled Child*, pp. 1–2.

38. Rosenfeld and Wise, *The Over-Scheduled Child*, pp. 1–2.

39. See Maria Newman, "Time Out! (for Overextended Families): A Town Takes a Rare Break from the Frenzy of Hyperscheduling."

40. For example: "Like wild animals raised in captivity who never develop their inborn potential to hunt for themselves, children who are robbed of the opportunity to come up with their own games and entertain themselves at those times in their lives when these capacities are developing may very well become dependent upon others to determine their good times." Dana Chidekel, *Parents in Charge,* pp. 94–95.

41. See work by Doris Entwistle and Karl Alexander on this topic, including Entwistle, Alexander, and Olsen, *Children, Schools, and Inequality.*

42. For details of one program, see a series of articles by Dale Mezzacappa in the *Philadelphia Inquirer,* including, "Ten Years of Learning, Living, Loving." Overall, the program was most successful for students in the regular educational track (as opposed to those in special education) and for young men rather than women.

43. For example, in the Chicago-based "I Had a Dream" program, 72% of the cohort graduated from high school, compared to 35% of the control group. For Paterson, New Jersey, 60% of the 1993 cohort graduated compared to 33% of the control group. These interventions begin in third grade (as opposed to sixth in the Say Yes program). See the "I Had a Dream Foundation" Web site for a summary of in-house statistics as well as research evaluations conducted by independent researchers <http://www.ihad.org> (accessed 12 December 2002).

44. Among others, see Hugh Mehan et al., *Constructing School Success,* and an evaluation by Public/Private Ventures of the Big Brother/Big Sister Program, Joseph Tierney et al., "Making a Difference."

45. As Barrie Thorne has noted in *Gender Play,* the significance of gender varied across context. As she suggests, we observed children self-segregating into gender homogenous groups, as when Harold McAllister, Tyrec Taylor, Wendy Driver, and Jessica Irwin separated into informal, gendered groups in their neighborhoods. But if there was a scarcity of near-age children, then boys, such as Billy Yanelli and Garrett Tallinger, would play with girls; Katie Brindle would play with both boys and girls. In addition, children, particularly Karl Greeley, spent a great deal of time playing with their younger siblings. For an overview of the research on gender role socialization in childhood, see Eleanor Maccoby, *The Two Sexes.*

46. See David Halle's book, *America's Working Man.*

47. Michael B. Katz, *The Undeserving Poor.*

APPENDIX A

1. In retrospect, the decision to forgo interviewing the children was a serious mistake. I did, however, carry out "exit interviews" with children in the observation study.

2. See the work of Erik Olin Wright, especially his essay in the edited collection by John Hall, *Reworking Class,* as well as the work of Robert Erickson and John Goldthorpe, including *The Constant Flux.* Without artificially minimizing the divergences between Goldthorpe and Wright (the foremost of which is

undoubtedly the latter's insistence on retaining a capitalist class within his schema), it can be said that both use similar criteria (skills or credentials and authority) in drawing distinctions between categories of employees. For assistance with this discussion, I am grateful to Elliot Weininger.

3. See Frances Goldscheider and Linda Waite, *New Families, No Families?*

4. See Elliot Weininger and Annette Lareau, "Children's Participation in Organized Activities and the Gender Dynamics of the 'Time Bind.'"

5. Douglas Massey and Nancy Denton, *American Apartheid.*

6. Although I still see this choice as reasonable, it has drawbacks. It is hard to know whether poor or working-class families living in middle-class neighborhoods would adopt the same cultural logic of child rearing had they been living in poor or working-class neighborhoods. This problem is compounded by the small samples necessitated by intensive field research.

7. In addition, I made a donation of $100 to the school. In Lower Richmond the principal directed it to Ms. Green; at Swan it went to the Parent Association.

8. I began with Lower Richmond, but the method I used for selecting and recruiting interviewees was the same at both school sites. The content of the letters sent to parents at the two sites differed somewhat; for Lower Richmond parents, for example, I enclosed a photograph of their child taken (by me) during third grade.

9. Ten white poor families were recruited from welfare offices and other community programs. I paid these participants $25 per interview; none of the other families was paid.

10. We resisted the temptation to ask only those families who we thought, on the basis of the rapport established during the interview phase, would agree to be observed. We stuck by our first priority of recruiting the most representative families.

11. One white working-class and two Black poor families on welfare declined. The mother in the white family explained, "We're not the perfect family." One of the Black families objected to my request to have access to welfare records and declined for that reason. (I dropped the request after that.) The other Black family agreed but then dropped out after only a couple of days. The mother's schedule changed frequently and there were indications of a possible problem with drugs within the family.

12. In some respects the Greeleys were not a typical poor family. They owned a car, for example. Still, they met enough of my basic criteria (e.g., they received various forms of public assistance, including medical coverage) to be included. Although the family lived in the same Lower Richmond neighborhood, they lived across a school boundary line and the son attended a different school.

13. This decision turned out to be problematic, however. A grade level can make a significant difference; Stacey seemed much more preteen than the other children we observed.

14. The payment was a lump sum (in cash), usually at the very end, when the intensive three weeks of field visits had been completed. In addition to offsetting some of the inconvenience to the families, the money was intended to compensate for expenses such as feeding the field-workers dinner. The amount offered meant something different to each family, depending on their income level.

15. A drawback to my having made friends with the children in their classroom was that some working-class and poor parents then assumed that I was affiliated with the school district. I worried this would increase their sense of distrust. In addition to assuring parents that all information was confidential, I made repeated efforts to clarify the fact that I worked at a college and was not in any way associated with the school district.

16. See Annette Lareau, "My Wife Can Tell Me Who I Know" for a discussion of problems in interviewing fathers.

17. My parents' marriage was loving but cantankerous; there was a lot of yelling. There were other quirks, as well. My father worked for many years as a tutor, but there were also years when he did not work. This left my mother, who was a teacher, as the sole source of support for the family of four children. There were other ways that my family was seen as unusual: both my parents were atheists, my mother swore like a sailor, and my father had an unending series of broken-down cars he was always trying to fix.

18. I recorded similar feelings in my journal, noting that ". . . A two-site day is too much; it wears you out and doubles your field notes and makes your head spin with the contrast of [lack of] safety and opulence . . . [but to sustain the comparative character of the study] you need to have a two site (or really three site) day all of the time. . . ."

19. We weren't able to observe each of these events for every child. We observed a doctor or dentist visit for each of the four middle-class children (Tallinger, Williams, Marshall, and Handlon), three of the four working-class children (Driver, Taylor, and Yanelli but not Irwin), and two of the four poor children (Greeley and McAllister but not Carroll or Brindle). Thus, there are healthcare visits for nine of the twelve children. All of these visits were tape-recorded. For parent-teacher conferences, we have nine of the twelve (i.e., everyone except Greeley, Marshall, and Williams). These were also tape-recorded. For the overnights, we have nine of the twelve (all except Carroll, Taylor, and Williams).

20. Alexander Williams was an exception. Despite his upper-middle-class position, he was clearly excited to be part of the study and happy to spend time with the field-workers.

21. See, among others, Guadalupe Valdes, *Con Respeto.*

22. I believed it was my responsibility as principal investigator to take over in any situation that a graduate student identified as prohibitively difficult emotionally.

23. I found the question of intellectual ownership troublesome with regard to writing this book. I had encouraged the research assistants to use the data in their own work, and I had presented papers with some of them in conferences. But since I find writing a book manuscript difficult at best, involving coauthors seemed like an invitation to disaster. I also felt that although the data collection was crucial, it was a *part* of the study, not the whole. I had done the Lawrenceville field-work, written the grant, and organized and run the project. In the end, I settled on a public recognition of the research assistants' role (in the beginning of the book) and private thank-yous to them rather than coauthorship of the book.

24. Folio Views for Windows 4.2, Open Market, Inc.

25. See Arlie Hochschild's *The Second Shift.*

APPENDIX B

1. For an excellent summary and analysis, see David Swartz's book, *Culture and Power*. See also Pierre Bourdieu, "Cultural Reproduction and Social Reproduction," *Outline of the Theory of Practice*, and *Distinction*, as well as Bourdieu and Wacquant, *An Invitation to Reflexive Sociology*. Marlis Buchmann's book, *The Script of Life*, also has a lucid summary of Bourdieu's model (see pp. 31–38).

2. Bourdieu, *Outline of the Theory of Practice*.

3. Rogers Brubaker, "Rethinking Classical Theory"; Craig Calhoun et al., *Bourdieu: Critical Perspectives*.

4. As he writes: The habitus "is a general, transposable disposition which carries out a systematic, universal application — beyond the limits of what has been directly learnt — of the necessity inherent in the learning conditions." Bourdieu, *Distinction*, p. 170. See also pp. 172–73 in *Distinction*.

5. When Bourdieu discusses the habitus, as in *Distinction*, he often focuses on cultural consumption and taste rather than child-rearing strategies per se. He makes clear, however, that he sees disparate elements of a habitus to share a common principle. Thus, for example, choices in food and in child rearing will not be unconnected. In other words, habitus is a principle that connects these preferences in diverse arenas. Additionally, Bourdieu talks about the existence of different habitus by social class. It is not generally the case that each individual's habitus is powerfully unique; instead there is a class habitus, but there are variations within this category. As he writes:

> The singular habitus of members of the same class are united in a relationship of homology, that is, of diversity within homogeneity reflecting the diversity within homogeneity characteristic of their social conditions of production. Each individual system of dispositions is a structural variant of the others, expressing the singularity of its position within the class and its trajectory. 'Personal' style, the particular stamp marking all of the products of the same habitus, whether practices or works, is never more than a deviation in relation to the style of a period or class. (Pierre Bourdieu, *The Logic of Practice*, p. 60)

6. Social scientists and others have tended to focus only on certain elements of Bourdieu's model, especially the idea of cultural capital. Bourdieu's very important concept of *field*, which captures these standards, generally has been neglected. As a result, the "double vision" offered by Bourdieu's model — the simultaneous focus on biography and social structure that is achieved through the study of fields and the practices of individuals — is often absent in empirical work.

7. Swartz, *Culture and Power*, p. 120.

8. Bourdieu, "Marriage Strategies as Strategies of Social Reproduction," and *Outline of the Theory of Practice*.

9. Annette Lareau and Erin McNamara Horvat, "Moments of Social Inclusion and Exclusion."

Bibliography

Alwin, Duane F. 1984. "Trends in Parental Socialization Values." *American Journal of Sociology* 90 (2): 359–82.

Anderson, Elijah. 1990. *Streetwise*. Chicago: University of Chicago Press.

———. 1999. *Code of the Street: Decency, Violence, and the Moral Life of the Inner City*. New York: W. W. Norton.

Anyon, Jean. 1997. *Ghetto Schooling: A Political Economy of Urban Educational Reform*. New York: Teachers College Press.

Arendell, Terry. 2000. "Soccer Moms and the New Care Work." Working paper. Center for Working Families, University of California, Berkeley.

Aries, Philippe. 1962. *Centuries of Childhood: A Social History of the Family*. New York: Basic Books.

Averill, Patricia M., and Thomas G. Power. 1995. "Parental Attitudes and Children's Experiences in Soccer." *International Journal of Behavioral Development* 18 (2): 263–76.

Barlett, Donald L., and James B. Steele. 1992. *America: What Went Wrong?* Kansas City: Andrews and McMeel.

Bellah, Robert N., Richard Madsen, William M. Sullivan, Ann Swidler, and Steven M. Tipton. 1996. *Habits of the Heart*. 2d ed. Berkeley: University of California Press.

Belluck, Pam. 2000. "Parents Try to Reclaim Their Children's Time." In *New York Times* on the Web. http://www.nytimes.com/library/national/061300family-practices.html, accessed 12 December 2002.

Berhau, Patricia. 2000. "Class and the Experiences of Consumers: A Study in the Practices of Acquisition." Ph.D. diss., Temple University.

Berlage, Gai Ingham. 1982. "Are Children's Competitive Team Sports Teaching Corporate Values?" *ARENA Review* 6 (1): 15–21.

Bernstein, Basil. 1971. *Class, Codes, and Control: Theoretical Studies Towards a Sociology of Language.* New York: Schocken.

Best, Joel. 1993. *Threatened Children.* Chicago: University of Chicago Press.

Bianchi, Suzanne M. 2000. "Maternal Employment and Time with Children." *Demography* 37 (4): 401–14.

Bianchi, Suzanne M., and John Robinson. 1997. "What Did You Do Today?" *Journal of Marriage and the Family* 59: 332–44.

Bluestone, Cheryl, and Catherine S. Tamis-LeMonda. 1999. "Correlates of Parenting Styles in Predominantly Working- and Middle-Class African American Mothers." *Journal of Marriage and the Family* 61 (November): 881–93.

Bok, Derek, and William G. Bowen. 1998. *The Shape of the River: Long-Term Consequences of Considering Race in College and University Admissions.* Princeton: Princeton University Press.

Bourdieu, Pierre. 1976. "Marriage Strategies as Strategies of Social Reproduction." Pp. 117–44 in *Family and Society,* edited by R. Forster and O. Ranum. Baltimore: Johns Hopkins University Press.

———. 1977a. "Cultural Reproduction and Social Reproduction." Pp. 487–511 in *Power and Ideology in Education,* edited by J. Karabel and A. H. Halsey. New York: Oxford University Press.

———. 1977b. *Outline of the Theory of Practice.* Cambridge: Cambridge University Press.

———. 1984. *Distinction: A Social Critique of the Judgment of Taste.* Cambridge, Mass.: Harvard University Press.

———. 1990. *The Logic of Practice.* Stanford: Stanford University Press.

Bourdieu, Pierre, and Jean-Claude Passeron. 1990 [1970]. *Reproduction in Education, Society, and Culture.* Trans. Richard Nice. London: Sage.

Bourdieu, Pierre, and Loïc J.D. Wacquant. 1992. *An Invitation to Reflexive Sociology.* Chicago: University of Chicago Press.

Bronfenbrenner, Urie. 1966. "Socialization and Social Class through Time and Space." Pp. 362–77 in *Class, Status, and Power,* edited by R. Bendix and S. M. Lipset. New York: The Free Press.

Brubaker, Rogers. 1985. "Rethinking Classical Theory: The Sociological Vision of Pierre Bourdieu." *Theory and Society* 14(6): 745–75.

Buchmann, Marlis. 1989. *The Script of Life in Modern Society: Entry into Adulthood in a Changing World.* Chicago: University of Chicago Press.

Calhoun, Craig, Edward LiPuma, and Moishe Postone, eds. 1993. *Bourdieu: Critical Perspectives.* Chicago: The University of Chicago Press.

Caplow, Theodore, Howard M. Bahr, Bruce A. Chadwick, Rubin Hill, and Margaret Holmes Williamson. 1982. *Middletown Families: Fifty Years of Change and Continuity.* Toronto: Bantam.

Chidekel, Dana. 2002. *Parents in Charge.* New York: Simon & Schuster.

Cicourel, Aaron, and John Kitsuse. 1963. *The Educational Decision-Makers.* Indianapolis: Bobbs-Merrill.

Cochran, Moncrieff, Mary Larner, David Riley, Lars Gunnarsson, and Charles R. Henderson Jr. 1990. *Extending Families: The Social Networks of Parents and Their Children.* Cambridge: Cambridge University Press.

Cohen, Phil. 1997. "Laboring under Whiteness." Pp. 244–82 in *Displacing*

Whiteness, edited by Ruth Frankenberg. Durham, N.C.: Duke University Press.

Coleman, James S. 1987. "Families and Schools." *Educational Researcher* 16 (6): 32–38.

———. 1988. "Social Capital in the Creation of Human Capital." *American Journal of Sociology* 94 (Supplement 95): S94–S120.

Collins, Randall. 1979. *The Credential Society.* New York: Academic Press.

———. 1986. *Max Weber: A Skeleton Key.* Beverly Hills: Sage.

———. 2000. "Situational Stratification." *Sociological Theory* 18 (1): 17–43.

Conley, Dalton. 1999. *Being Black, Living in the Red: Race, Wealth, and Social Policy in America.* Berkeley, Calif.: University of California Press.

Corsaro, William A. 1997. *The Sociology of Childhood.* Thousand Oaks, Calif.: Pine Forge.

Cose, Ellis. 1993. *The Rage of a Privileged Class.* New York: HarperCollins.

Daley, Kerry J., ed. 2001. *Minding the Time in Family Experience: Emerging Perspectives and Issues. Contemporary Perspectives in Family Research,* edited by Felix M. Berardo, vol. 3. New York: JAI.

Deater-Deckard, Kirby, Kenneth A. Dodge, John E. Bates, and Gregory S. Petit. 1996. "Physical Discipline among African American and European American Mothers: Links to Children's Externalizing Behaviors." *Developmental Psychology* 32 (6): 1065–72.

DeVault, Marjorie L. 1991. *Feeding the Family: The Social Organization of Caring as Gendered Work.* Chicago: University of Chicago Press.

Diamond, John. 2000. "Beyond Social Class: Cultural Resources and Educational Participation among Low-Income Black Parents." *Berkeley Journal of Sociology* 44: 15–54.

Doherty, William 2002. "Frequently Asked Questions." In Family Life 1st. www.familylife1st.org/faq.html, accessed 12 December 2002..

Donzelot, Jacques. 1979. *The Policing of Families.* New York: Pantheon.

Duncan, Greg J., and Jeanne Brooks-Gunn, eds. 1997. *Consequences of Growing Up Poor.* New York: Russell Sage Foundation.

Edin, Kathryn, and Laura Lein. 1997. *Making Ends Meet: How Single Mothers Survive Welfare and Low-Wage Work.* New York: Russell Sage Foundation.

Elder, Glen H., Jr. 1998. "The Life Course as Development Theory." *Child Development* 69 (1): 1–12.

Entwisle, Doris R., Karl L. Alexander, and Linda Steffel Olson. 1997. *Children, Schools, and Inequality.* Boulder: Westview.

Epstein, Joyce L., and Mavis G. Sanders. 2000. "Connecting Home, School, and Community: New Directions for Social Research." Pp. 285–306 in *Handbook of the Sociology of Education,* edited by Maureen T. Hallinan. New York: Kluwer Academic/Plenum.

Erickson, Robert, and John H. Goldthorpe. 1993. *The Constant Flux.* Oxford: Clarendon.

Etzioni, Amitai, ed. 1969. *The Semi-Professions and Their Organizations: Teachers, Nurses, Social Workers.* New York: The Free Press.

Family Life 1st <familylife1st@wayzata.k12.mn.us>. 2002. "History." In Family Life 1st. www.familylife1st.org/history.html, accessed 12 December 2002.

Feagin, Joe, and Melvin P. Sikes. 1994. *Living with Racism: The Black Middle-Class Experience*. Boston: Beacon.

Fine, Gary Alan. 1987. *With the Boys: Little League Baseball and Preadolescent Culture*. Chicago: University of Chicago Press.

Fischer, Claude S. 1982. *To Dwell among Friends: Personal Networks in Town and City*. Chicago: University of Chicago Press.

Freidson, Eliot. 1986. *Professional Powers: A Study of the Institutionalization of Formal Knowledge*. Chicago: University of Chicago Press.

Furstenberg, Frank F., Jr., and Andrew J. Cherlin. 1991. *Divided Families: What Happens to Children When Parents Part*. Cambridge: Harvard University Press.

Furstenberg, Frank F., Jr., Thomas D. Cook, Jacquelynne Eccles, Glen H. Elder Jr., and Arnold Sameroff. 1999. *Managing to Make It: Urban Families and Adolescent Success*. Chicago: University of Chicago Press.

Galinsky, Ellen. 1999. *Ask the Children: What America's Children Really Think about Working Parents*. New York: William Morrow.

Gardner, Howard, and Thomas Hatch. 1989. "Multiple Intelligences Go to School." *Educational Researcher* 18 (8): 4–10.

Garey, Anita Ilta. 1999. *Weaving Work and Motherhood*. Philadelphia: Temple University Press.

Goldenberg, Claude N. 1987. "Low-Income Hispanic Parents' Contributions to Their First-Grade Children's Word-Recognition Skills." *Anthropology & Education Quarterly* 18 (3): 149–79.

Goldscheider, Frances K., and Linda J. Waite. 1991. *New Families, No Families? The Transformation of the American Home*. Berkeley: University of California Press.

Gordon, Linda. 1989. *Heroes of Their Own Lives: The Politics and History of Family Violence*. New York: Penguin.

Grusky, David, and Jesper Sorenson. 1998. "Can Class Analysis Be Salvaged?" *American Journal of Sociology* 103 (5): 1187–234.

Gutman, Herbert G. 1976. *The Black Family in Slavery and Freedom, 1750–1925*. New York: Vintage.

Halbfinger, David M. 2002. "Our Town: A Hockey Parent's Life: Time, Money, and Yes, Frustration." *New York Times,* January 12, page 29.

Hale-Benson, Janice E. 1982. *Black Children: Their Roots, Culture, and Learning Style*. Rev. ed. Baltimore: Johns Hopkins University Press.

Hall, John R., ed. 1997. *Reworking Class*. Ithaca: Cornell University Press.

Halle, David. 1984. *America's Working Man: Work, Home, and Politics Among Blue-Collar Property Owners*. Chicago: University of Chicago Press.

———. 1993. *Inside Culture*. Chicago: University of Chicago Press.

Handel, Gerald. 1988. "Socialization and the Social Self." Pp. 3–10 in *Childhood Socialization,* edited by Gerald Handel. New York: Aldine de Gruyter.

Hanushek, Eric A, John F. Kain, and Steven G. Rivkin. 2002. "New Evidence about Brown v. Board of Education: The Complex Effects of School Racial Composition on Achievement." Working paper 8741. National Bureau of Economic Research. http://www.nber.org/papers/w8741, accessed 12 December 2002.

Hart, Betty, and Todd R. Risley. 1995. *Meaningful Differences in the Everyday Experiences of Young American Children.* Baltimore: Paul H. Brookes.

Hays, Sharon. 1996. *The Cultural Contradictions of Motherhood.* New Haven: Yale University Press.

Heath, Shirley Brice. 1983. *Ways with Words: Language, Life, and Work in Communities and Classrooms.* Cambridge: Cambridge University Press.

Heimer, Carol A., and Lisa R. Staffen. 1998. *For the Sake of the Children.* Chicago: University of Chicago Press.

Hertz, Rosanna, and Nancy L. Marshall, eds. 2001. *Working Families.* Berkeley: University of California Press.

Hess, Robert D., and Gerald Handel. 1974. *Family Worlds.* Chicago: University of Chicago Press.

Heymann, Jody. 2001. *The Widening Gap: Why America's Working Families Are in Jeopardy and What Can Be Done about It.* New York: Basic Books.

Higginbotham, Elizabeth. 2001. *Too Much to Ask.* Chapel Hill: University of North Carolina Press.

Hochschild, Arlie Russell. 1989. *The Second Shift.* New York: Viking.

———. 1997. *The Time Bind: When Work Becomes Home and Home Becomes Work.* New York: Metropolitan Books.

Hochschild, Jennifer L. 1995. *Facing Up to the American Dream: Race, Class, and the Soul of the Nation.* Princeton, N.J.: Princeton University Press.

Hofferth, Sandra L. 1999. "Family Reading to Young Children." Unpublished manuscript. Ann Arbor, Michigan. http://www.ethno.isr.umich.edu/06papers.html, accessed 12 December 2002.

Hofferth, Sandra L., and John Sandberg. 2001. "Changes in American Children's Time, 1981–1997." In *Children at the Millennium: Where Have We Come From, Where Are We Going?* edited by Sandra L. Hofferth and Timothy J. Owens. Vol. 6 of Advances in Life Course Research. Oxford: JAI.

———. 2001. "How American Children Spend Their Time." *Journal of Marriage and the Family* 63 (4): 295–308.

Hoggart, Richard. 1957. *The Uses of Literacy.* Boston: Beacon.

Holloway, Susan D., Bruce Fuller, Marylee F. Rambaud, and Costanza Eggers-Pierola. 1997. *Through My Own Eyes: Single Mothers and the Cultures of Poverty.* Cambridge: Harvard University Press.

Hout, Michael. 1988. "More Universalism, Less Structural Mobility: The American Occupational Structure in the 1980s." *American Journal of Sociology* 93 (3): 1358–400.

Hout, Michael, and Claude S. Fischer. 2002. "A Century of Inequality: Family Income, Wealth, and Consumption, 1900–2000." Paper presented at the Conference on Education, Human Capital, and Social Inequality, Economy, Justice, and Society Program, University of California, Davis, May 3–4

Howard, Dennis R., and Robert Madrigal. 1990. "Who Makes the Decision: The Parent or the Child? The Perceived Influence of Parents and Children on the Purchase of Recreational Services." *Journal of Leisure Research,* 22 (2): 244–58.

"I Have a Dream" Foundation. 2002. www.ihad.org, accessed 12 December 2002.

Imber, Jonathan B. 1991."Doctor No Longer Knows Best." Pp. 298–317 in *America at Century's End,* edited by Alan Wolfe. Berkeley: University of California Press.

Jackson, Kenneth T. 1985. *Crabgrass Frontier: The Suburbanization of the United States.* New York: Oxford University Press.

Jacobs, Jerry A., and Kathleen Gerson. 1998. "Who Are the Overworked Americans?" *Review of Social Economy* 56 (4): 442–59.

———.Forthcoming. *The Time Divide.* Cambridge, Mass.: Harvard University Press.

James, Michael S. 2002. "Fast-Track Kids." *ABCNews.com,* March 15. http://more.abcnews.go.com/sections/us/dailynews/childhood020315.html, accessed 12 December 2002..

Jencks, Christopher, M. Smith, H. Leland, M. J. Bane, D. Cohen, H. Gintis, B. Heyns, and S. Michelson. 1972. *Inequality: A Reassessment of the Effect of Family and Schooling in America.* New York: Basic Books.

Jencks, Christopher, Susan Bartlett, Mary Corcoran, James Cruse, David Eaglesfield, Gregory Jackson, Kent McClelland, Peter Mueser, Michael Olneck, Joseph Schwartz, Sherry Ward, and Jill Williams. 1979. *Who Gets Ahead? The Determinants of Economic Success in America.* New York: Basic Books.

Jencks, Christopher, and Meredith Phillips, eds. 1998. *The Black-White Test Score Gap.* Washington, D.C.: Brookings Institution.

Jepperson, Ronald L. 1991. "Institutions, Institutional Effects, and Institutionalism." Pp. 143–63 in *The New Institutionalism in Organizational Analysis,* edited by Walter W. Powell and Paul J. DiMaggio. Chicago: University of Chicago Press.

Kalleberg, Arne L., Barbara F. Reskin, and Ken Hudson. 2000. "Bad Jobs in America: Standard and Nonstandard Employment Relations and Job Quality in the United States." *American Sociological Review* 65 (2): 256–78.

Karen, David. 2002. Personal communication to the author, June 7.

Katz, Michael B. 1989. *The Undeserving Poor: From the War on Poverty to the War on Welfare.* New York: Pantheon.

———. 2001. *The Price of Citizenship.* New York: Metropolitan Books.

Kefalas, Maria. 2003. *Working-Class Heroes.* Berkeley: University of California Press.

Kingston, Paul W. 2000. *The Classless Society.* Stanford: Stanford University Press.

Kohn, Melvin L. 1977. *Class and Conformity.* 2d ed. Chicago: The University of Chicago Press.

Kohn, Melvin L., and Carmi Schooler, eds. 1983. *Work and Personality: An Inquiry into the Impact of Social Stratification.* Norwood, N.J.: Ablex.

Kohn, Melvin L., and Kazimierz M. Slomczynski. 1990. *Social Structure and Self-Direction: A Comparative Analysis of the United States and Poland.* Cambridge: Basil Blackwell.

Kornblum, William. 1998. *Sociology: The Central Questions.* Belmont, Calif.: International Thomson.

Kozol, Jonathon. 1992. *Savage Inequalities: Children in America's Schools.* New York: HarperCollins.

Kropp, Paul. 2001. *I'll Be the Parent, You Be the Child*. New York: Fisher.

Ladd, Everett. 1993. "Thinking about America." *The Public Perspective* 4 (5): 19–34.

Lamborn, Susie D., et al. 1991. "Patterns of Competence and Adjustment among Adolescents from Authoritative, Authoritarian, Indulgent, and Neglectful Families." *Child Development* 62: 1049–65.

Lamont, Michele. 1992. *Money, Morals, and Manners*. Chicago: University of Chicago Press.

———. 2000. *The Dignity of Working Men: Morality and the Boundaries of Race, Class, and Immigration*. Cambridge: Harvard University Press.

Lamont, Michele, and Annette Lareau. 1988. "Cultural Capital." *Sociological Theory* 6: 153–68.

Lamont, Michelle, and Virag Molnar. 2002. "The Study of Boundaries across the Social Sciences." *Annual Review of Sociology* 28, 167–195.

Lareau, Annette. 2000a. *Home Advantage*. 2d ed. Lanham, Md: Rowman and Littlefield.

———. 2000b. "My Wife Can Tell Me Who I Know: Methodological and Conceptual Problems in Studying Fathers." *Qualitative Sociology* 23 (4): 407–33.

———. 2002. Studying Families: A Realistic Account. Unpublished manuscript, Temple University.

Lareau, Annette, and Erin McNamara Horvat. 1999. "Moments of Social Inclusion and Exclusion: Race, Class and Cultural Capital in Family-School Relationships." *Sociology of Education* 72: 37–53.

Lareau, Annette, and Jeffrey Shultz, eds. 1996. *Journeys through Ethnography: Realistic Accounts of Fieldwork*. Boulder: Westview.

Larson, Magali Sarfatti. 1977. *The Rise of Professionalism: A Sociological Analysis*. Berkeley: University of California Press.

Larson, Reed W., and Suman Verma. 1999. "How Children and Adolescents Spend Time across the World: Work, Play, and Developmental Opportunities." *Psychological Bulletin* 125 (6): 701–36.

Lever, Janet. 1988. "Sex Differences in the Complexity of Children's Games." Pp. 325–44 in *Childhood Socialization*, edited by Gerald Handel. New York: Aldine de Gruyter.

Louv, Richard. 1988. *Childhood's Future*. New York: Doubleday.

Lucas, Samuel Roundfield. 1999. *Tracking Inequality: Stratification and Mobility in American High Schools*. New York: Teachers College Press.

Lynd, Robert S., and Helen Merrell Lynd. 1929. *Middletown*. New York: Harcourt Brace Jovanovich.

———. 1965. *Middletown in Transition: A Study in Cultural Conflicts*. New York: Harcourt Brace Jovanovich.

Maccoby, Eleanor E. 1998. *The Two Sexes: Growing up Apart, Coming Together*. Cambridge: Harvard University Press.

MacLeod, Jay. 1995. *Ain't No Making It: Aspirations and Attainment in a Low-Income Neighborhood*. Boulder, Colo: Westview.

Massey, Douglas, and Nancy Denton. 1993. *American Apartheid*. Cambridge: Harvard University Press.

Mayer, Susan E. 1997. *What Money Can't Buy: Family Income and Children's Life Chances.* Chicago: University of Chicago Press.

McLaughlin, Milbrey W., Merita A. Irby, and Juliet Langman. 1994. *Urban Sanctuaries: Neighborhood Organizations in the Lives and Futures of Inner-City Youth.* San Francisco: Jossey-Bass.

Medrich, Elliot, Judith A. Roizen, Victor Rubin, and Stuart Buckley. 1982. *The Serious Business of Growing Up.* Berkeley: University of California Press.

Mehan, Hugh, Lea Hubbard, Irene Villanueva, and Angela Lintz. 1996. *Constructing School Success: The Consequences of Untracking Low-Achieving Students.* Cambridge: Cambridge University Press.

Menaghan, Elizabeth G. 1991. "Work Experiences and Family Interaction Processes: The Long Reach of the Job?" *Annual Review of Sociology* 17: 419–44.

Meyers, David G., and Ed Diener. 1995. "Who Is Happy?" *Psychological Science* 6 (1): 10–19.

Mezzacappa, Dale. 1997. "Ten Years of Learning, Living, Loving: The 'Say Yes to Education' Program Celebrates Success Stories on Its Anniversary." *Philadelphia Inquirer,* July 28, A1, A28.

Mills, C. Wright. 1959. *The Sociological Imagination.* Oxford: Oxford University Press.

Mishel, Lawrence, Jared Bernstein, and John Schmitt. 1999. *The State of Working America 1998–99.* Ithaca: Cornell University Press.

Morgan, William R., Duane F. Alwin, and Larry J. Griffin. 1979. "Social Origins, Parental Values, and the Transmission of Inequality." *American Journal of Sociology* 85 (1): 156–66.

Neckerman, Kathleen, and Joleen Kirschenmann. 1991. "Hiring Strategies, Racial Bias, and Inner-City Workers." *Social Problems* 38 (November): 433–47.

Newman, Katherine S. 1993. *Declining Fortunes: The Withering of the American Dream.* New York: Basic Books.

Newman, Maria. 2002. "Time Out! (for Overextended Families): A Town Takes a Rare Break from the Frenzy of Hyperscheduling." *New York Times,* March 27.

Oliver, Melvin L., and Thomas M. Shapiro. 1997. *Black Wealth/White Wealth: A New Perspective on Racial Inequality.* New York: Routledge.

Pakulski, Jan, and Malcolm Waters. 1996. *The Death of Class.* London: Sage.

Patillo-McCoy, Mary. 2000. *Black Picket Fences: Privilege and Peril among the Black Middle Class.* Chicago: University of Chicago Press.

Pollock, Linda A. 1983. *Forgotten Children: Parent-Child Relations from 1500 to 1900.* Cambridge: Cambridge University Press.

Portes, Alejandro. 1998. "Social Capital: Its Origins and Applications in Modern Sociology." *Annual Review of Sociology* 24: 1–24.

Portes, Alejandro, and Dag MacLeod. 1996. "Educational Progress of Children of Immigrants: The Roles of Class, Ethnicity, and School Context." *Sociology of Education* 69 (4): 255–75.

Putnam, Robert D. 2000. *Bowling Alone: The Collapse and Revival of American Community.* New York: Simon & Schuster.

Rainwater, Lee, and Timothy M. Smeeding. 1995. "Doing Poorly: The Real Income of American Children in a Comparative Perspective." Available online at http://www.lisproject.org/publications/liswps/127.pdf, accessed 12 December 2002.

Ritzer, George. 2000. *The McDonaldization of Society.* Thousand Oaks, Calif.: Pine Forge.

Robinson, John P., and Geoffrey Godbey. 1997. *Time for Life.* University Park: Pennsylvania State University Press.

Rosenfeld, Alvin, and Nicole Wise. 2000. *The Over-Scheduled Child.* New York: St. Martin's.

Rubin, Lillian B. 1976. *Worlds of Pain: Life in the Working-Class Family.* New York: Basic Books.

———. 1994. *Families on the Faultline.* New York: HarperCollins.

Rubinowitz, Leonard S., and James E. Rosenbaum. 2000. *Crossing the Class and Color Lines: From Public Housing to White Suburbia.* Chicago: University of Chicago Press.

Sandberg, John F., and Sandra L. Hofferth. 2001. "Changes in Children's Time with Parents, U.S. 1981–1997." *Demography* 38 (3): 423–36.

Scheper-Hughes, Nancy. 1992. *Death without Weeping: The Violence of Everyday Life in Brazil.* Berkeley: University of California Press.

Sewell, William H., and Robert M. Hauser. 1980. "The Wisconsin Longitudinal Study of Social and Psychological Factors in Aspirations and Achievements." *Research in Sociology of Education and Socialization* 1: 59–99.

Shehan, Constance L., ed. 1999. *Through the Eyes of the Child: Revisioning Children as Active Agents of Family Life.* Vol. 1 of Contemporary Perspectives on Family Life, edited by Felix M. Berardo. Stamford, Conn.: JAI.

Shen, Fern. 2002. "'Toys? But I'm 10 Now!'." *Washington Post,* February 17. http://washingtonpost.com/ac2/wp-dyn/A19671–2002Feb16, accessed 12 December 2002.

Shorter, Edward. 1977. *The Making of The Modern Family.* New York: Basic Books.

Shulman, James L., and William G. Bowen. 2001. *The Game of Life: College Sports and Educational Values.* Princeton, N.J.: Princeton University Press.

Sibley, David. 1995. "Families and Domestic Routines: Constructing the Boundaries of Childhood." Pp. 123–37 in *Mapping the Subject: Geographies of Cultural Transformation,* edited by Steve and Nigel Thrift Pile. New York: Routledge.

Simons, Ronald L., Les B. Whitbeck, Rand D. Conger, and Wu Chyi-In. 1991. "Intergenerational Transmission of Harsh Parenting." *Developmental Psychology* 27 (1): 159–71.

Skolnick, Arlene. 1991. *Embattled Paradise: The American Family in an Age of Uncertainty.* New York: Basic Books.

Smetana, Judith, and Susan Chuang. 2001. "Middle–Class African American Parents' Conceptions of Parenting in Early Adolescence." *Journal of Research on Adolescence* 11 (2): 177–98.

Smith, Dorothy E. 1987. *The Everyday World as Problematic: A Feminist Sociology.* Boston: Northeastern University Press.

Steinberg, Laurence, Susie D. Lamborn, Sanford M. Dornbusch, and Nancy Darling. 1992. "Impact of Parenting Practices on Adolescent Achievement." *Child Development* 63 (5): 1266–81.

Swartz, David. 1997. *Culture and Power: The Sociology of Pierre Bourdieu.* Chicago: University of Chicago Press.

Tatum, Beverly Daniel. 1997. *Why Are All the Black Kids Sitting Together in the Cafeteria? And Other Conversations about Race.* New York: Basic Books.

Thompson, Shona M. 1999. *Mother's Taxi.* Albany: State University of New York Press.

Thorne, Barrie. 1993. *Gender Play: Girls and Boys in School.* New Brunswick, N.J.: Rutgers University Press.

———. 2001. "Growing Up in Oakland." Presentation at ASA Annual Meeting. Anaheim, Calif., August 2001.

Thornton, Arland. 1992. "The Influence of the Parental Family on the Attitudes and Behavior of Children." Pp. 247–66 in *The Changing American Family: Sociological and Demographic Perspectives,* edited by Scott J. South and Stewart E. Tolnay. Boulder: Westview.

Tierney, Joseph P., Jean Baldwin Grossman, with Nancy L. Resch. 1995. *Making a Difference: An Impact Study of Big Brothers/Big Sisters.* Philadelphia: Public/Private Ventures. http://www.ppv.org/pdffiles/madipdf, accessed 12 December 2002.

U. S. Department of Education. 1995. *The Condition of Education, 1995.* Washington, D.C.: National Center for Educational Statistics.

———. 2001. *The Condition of Education, 2001.* Washington, D.C.: National Center for Educational Statistics.

Useem, Elizabeth L. 1991. "Student Selection into Course Sequences in Mathematics: The Impact of Parental Involvement and School Policies." *Journal of Research on Adolescence* 1 (3): 231–50.

Valdes, Guadalupe. 1996. *Con Respeto: Bridging the Distances between Culturally Diverse Families and Schools.* New York: Teachers College Press.

Van Ausdale, Debra, and Joe Feagin. 1996. "Using Racial and Ethnic Concepts: The Critical Case of Very Young Children." *American Sociological Review* 61 (5): 779–93.

Vanneman, Reeve, and Lynn Weber Cannon. 1987. *The American Perception of Class.* Philadelphia: Temple University Press.

Wacquant, Loïc J. D. 1998. "Negative Social Capital: State Breakdown and Social Destitution in America's Urban Core." *Neth. J. of Housing and the Built Environment* 13 (1): 25–40.

Waksler, Frances. 1991. *Studying the Social Worlds of Children.* Bristol: Falmer.

Walker, Karen. 1995. "'Always There for Me': Friendship Patterns and Expectations among Middle- and Working-Class Men and Women." *Sociological Forum* 10 (2): 273–96.

Waller, Maureen R. Forthcoming. *Fragile Families and Fathers.* Ithaca, N.Y.: Cornell University Press.

Warr, Mark, and Christopher G. Ellison. 2000. "Rethinking Social Reactions to Crime." *American Journal of Sociology* 106 (3): 551–78.

Waters, Mary C. 1999. *Black Identities.* New York: Russell Sage Foundation.

Weininger, Elliot B. 2002. "Class and Causation in Bourdieu." Pp. 49–114 in *Current Perspectives in Social Theory,* vol. 21., edited by Jennifer M. Lehmann. Oxford: Elsevier.

Weininger, Elliot, and Annette Lareau. 2002. "Children's Participation in Organized Activities and the Gender Dynamics of the 'Time Bind'." Paper read at American Sociological Association Annual Meeting, Chicago, Ill., August

Wells, Amy Stuart, and Robert L. Crain. 1997. *Stepping over the Color Line: African American Students in White Suburban Schools.* New Haven: Yale University Press.

West, Cornell. 1993. *Race Matters.* Boston: Beacon.

Willis, Paul E. 1977. *Learning to Labour: How Working Class Kids Get Working Class Jobs.* Farnborough, England: Saxon House.

Wright, Erik Olin. 1978. *Class, Crisis, and the State.* London: New Left Books.

———. 1991. "The Conceptual Status of Class Structure in Class Analysis." Pp. 17–38 in *Bringing Class Back In,* edited by Scott G. McNall, Rhonda F. Levine, and Rick Fantasia. Boulder: Westview.

———. 1997. "Rethinking, Once Again, the Concept of Class Structure." Pp. 41–72 in *Reworking Class,* edited by John R. Hall. Ithaca: Cornell University Press.

Wrigley, Julia. 1989. "Do Young Children Need Intellectual Stimulation? Experts' Advice to Parents, 1900–1985." *History of Education Quarterly* 29 (1): 41–75.

———. 1995. *Other People's Children.* New York: Basic Books.

Zelizer, Viviana A. 1985. *Pricing the Priceless Child: The Changing Social Value of Children.* New York: Basic Books.

Index

Accomplishment of natural growth
benefits of: in children's autonomy and
creativity 67–68, 102–03, 159; compliance without whining or badgering, 147, 153, 208, 238; deeper kinship ties,140, 159; development of
social competences with peers, 67–
68, 81; enjoyment of childlike pleasures, 200, 234; limited demands on
adult labor, 81, 102–3, 139–40,
142, 159; manage own free time,
244, nicer to siblings, 159; no complaints of boredom, 242; social competence, 5; spend more time together
as a family, 242
definition of, 2–3, 31, 238, 289n.2,
290n.8
drawbacks: does not build vocabulary
159–60; does not comply with current standards of health care, 158;
does not develop work-related skills,
67–68, 142, 159; does not increase
knowledge of organizational rules,
81; does not train how to manipulate
institutions to own advantage, 245;
training not valued by institutions
140, 164, 230–32
and fieldwork, 271
parent labor required for, 5, 66, 71, 81,
88–91, 139–40, 144–45
See also Constraint, sense of; Creativity; Economic resources; Institutions;

Kinship; Language use; Time use;
Unstructured activities
integration of, 42–49, 82, 114–16
separation of, 3, 36, 72–76, 82, 142,
159, 215
Anderson, Elijah, 5, 290, 296n.1,
301n.16, n.24
Authority
children correcting adults, 118; 124–
25, 127–32, 169–70
egalitarian aspects of concerted cultivation, 111
respect for adults, 71, 147–51, 159,
207–8, 296n.1, 306n.12
training children for constraint, 134,
157–59
training children for entitlement,
108,124–27
See also Constraint, sense of; Entitlement, sense of; Powerlessness

Boredom
children proclaiming, 186, 207
importance of organized activities in
preventing, 52, 112
lack of expressions of, 81, 142–43, 242
parents' boredom at kids' activities, 47
Bourdieu, Pierre
advantage of his model over a deficit
model, 276, 277
as an analysis of moments of social
reproduction, 277

Compositor: BookMatters
Text: 10/13 Sabon
Display: Sabon
Printer and Binder: Thomson-Shore, Inc.